33626

The Northwest Salmon Crisis
A Documentary History

DEDICATION

For Adam, Anne, and Elizabeth

Cover photo: The run of giant chinook salmon commonly referred to as June hogs was depleted by fishing, then further reduced by the erection of the mainstem Columbia River dams, which hampered the fish's migration. This 85-pound chinook, the largest ever caught at Astoria, was caught in 1925 by Tony Canessa.

The paper used in this publication meets the guidelines for permanence and durability of the Committee on Production Guidelines for Book Longevity of the Counci on Library Resources and the minimum requirements of the American National Standard for Permanence of Paper for Printed Library Materials, ANSI Z39.48-1984.

Library of Congress Cataloging-in-Publication Data
The Northwest salmon crisis : a documentary history / edited by Joseph Cone and Sandy Ridlington.
    p. cm.
    Includes bibliographical references and index.
    ISBN 0-87071-390-6 (cloth : alk. paper)
    1. Pacific salmon—Northwest, Pacific—History—Sources. 2. Fishery conservation—Northwest, Pacific—History—Sources. 3. Pacific salmon—Effect of habitat modification on—Northwest, Pacific—History—Sources. 4. Endangered species—Northwest, Pacific—History—Sources. I. Cone, Joseph. II. Ridlington, Sandy.
SH348.N68 1996
333.93'6—dc20   96-4604
                                                     CIP

The Northwest Salmon Crisis
A Documentary History

Edited by

Joseph Cone and Sandy Ridlington

Contributors

Bill M. Bakke

Michael C. Blumm

F. Lorraine Bodi

Joseph Cone

Douglas W. Dompier

Stanley V. Gregory

Robert Kentta

William L. Lang

James A. Lichatowich

William G. Robbins

Courtland L. Smith

Oregon State University Press
Corvallis, Oregon

PREFACE

SOMETHING EXTREME is happening to salmon in the 1990s. For millions of years Pacific salmon have evolved to populate many hundreds of streams throughout the Northwest. Today more than two hundred of these local populations of salmon are in danger of becoming extinct; more than one hundred other populations have already been driven to extinction during the last hundred years.

This biological crisis has been forced on the attention of residents of the Northwest by efforts to protect the fish under the federal Endangered Species Act. These efforts have sparked a regional controversy over their benefits and costs, which in turn has prompted the *Oregonian* newspaper, the largest in the region, to dub "the future of salmon" as "the central environmental issue of the decade."

This book arose from a desire to help the region's people understand the background of the contemporary crisis. Today's salmon decline did not just happen overnight, but required decades and a combination of adverse factors. Some factors are beyond human control, specifically, recent adverse ocean conditions. But ocean temperature and food supplies have been unfavorable before without bringing so many salmon populations to the brink. We are concerned here with factors within human control because we can, presumably, learn from what we've done and make changes, if we choose. The heart of this book is its collection of documents from the last 140 years. Some of these documents are historical photographs and other graphic images, placed into a context that we think sheds new light on them. But even more important than these visual reference points are the printed documents assembled here. Many of them have been known only to specialists or have long been out of print, but they can now be seen as important mileposts in the sorry journey of the salmon. The documents were chosen by the contributing writers to either reveal a cause of the salmon decline or reflect the concerns of those who saw it coming.

We have provided a brief introduction to each section, and, in conjunction with the contributors, have abbreviated the documents where appropriate. Following each document or set of companion documents, the contributors have provided commentaries that assess their historic significance. All of the contributors are specialists in this history of the salmon, although they come to the task with different perspectives and credentials. Some are university scholars; others are professional biologists and conservationists. Regardless, the writers are at one in their concern to alert their fellow citizens to the past that is prologue to our present controversy. But beyond this purpose, their essays contain, we think, a seeding of ideas that would allow the residents of the Northwest to raise up a different future—a future in which the salmon might be restored to at least some of their former abundance and variety.

In reproducing documents, we have, with few exceptions, adhered to the original spelling and punctuation, however whimsical they may seem to the reader. On the few occasions where the original punctuation might have confused the reader, we have altered it to conform to more traditional punctuation. Textual omissions are indicated by spaced dots.

The development of this book was funded by Oregon Sea Grant, under a grant from the National Sea Grant Office, a division of the National Atmospheric and Oceanic Administration, and by state funds. The book's essayists, on the other hand, come from many backgrounds, public and private, and to them we owe an enormous debt. They bring to the subject of Northwest salmon a passion for this great creature and years of experience describing its plight and alerting the public to its decline. Many of their own publications might appropriately have appeared as documents in this book.

We would like to thank the many private individuals and organizational employees who assisted with photographs and other illustrations. We are also grateful to the staff and editorial board of Oregon State University Press, who, in agreeing to publish this book, implicitly share our view that, in the endless debate surrounding Northwest salmon, it was perhaps time to let primary documents speak for themselves. We would like to offer a special thanks to Jo Alexander, managing editor of OSU Press, who read the manuscript with fresh eyes, asked all the right and difficult questions, and refused to rest until we gave her the answers.

—Joseph Cone and Sandy Ridlington

Contents

V. THE ACCELERATING CRISIS

I. Introduction

THE WORLD OF COLUMBIA RIVER SALMON: NATURE, CULTURE, AND THE GREAT RIVER OF THE WEST

by William G. Robbins

 MORE THAN FIFTY YEARS AGO Peter Noyes, a respected elder in the Colville tribe, related a story about the formation of the Columbia River that he first heard as a small child. According to his account, at some time in the distant past—when Coyote was the really big man on earth and when there was no Columbia River—the Colville country was covered by a big lake. To the west, a long ridge of mountains prevented the waters of the lake from flowing to the ocean. Coyote was wise enough to see that if he could make a passageway through the mountains the salmon would come up from the ocean and provide food for his people. So Coyote used his powers to dig a hole through the mountains that allowed the Columbia River to flow to the ocean as it does today. The salmon were then able to swim up the river and Coyote's people had plenty to eat ever after.[1]

It is proper that this essay begin with the first people to inhabit the Columbia River country, human populations who were the first to make extensive use of the abundant runs of anadromous fish in the Columbia system. Archaeological finds throughout the river's vast drainage, some of them dating as early as 9,000 years ago, indicate protracted and sustained fish harvesting that included a variety of salmonid species. From sites near The Dalles upriver to Kettle Falls, excavations reveal large quantities of salmon bones that have been carbon dated between 7,700 and 9,000 years ago. It is fair to say that from the onset of the Holocene to very recent times the annual salmon runs provided an extremely reliable source of protein for many of the tribal groups living adjacent to the Columbia River. According to the

Previous page: Chinook salmon of this huge girth and length are gravely depleted throughout the Northwest today, but one hundred years ago they established the reputation for quality that built the salmon industry.

2

anthropologist Eugene Hunn, the take of fish during the heyday of commercial exploitation demonstrates that the quantities available to precontact Indians at such strategic fishing stations "far exceeded their needs." At certain places along the great western waterway, geology and the specific timing of individual runs conspired to provide what can arguably be termed the most productive fishery in all of North America.[2]

The physical environment of the Pacific Northwest made all of this possible. The Columbia River system was born of fire and ice: the former characterized by the great volcanic infernos and lava flows of the Miocene Epoch, and the latter by the massive glacial sheets centered in the rugged mountainous country of British Columbia during the Pleistocene (or Ice Age). When the northern hemisphere began to warm during the late Pleistocene, the melting of the great glaciers created a huge inland lake. Over time that tremendous body of water periodically breached the intervening dam of glacial ice and unleashed a series of catastrophic floods through northern Idaho and eastern Washington. When the floods subsided, they left in their wake the familiar contours and landforms that we know today: the famous Grand Coulee and the channeled scablands of eastern Washington; Wallula Gap; the great gorge of the Columbia; and the deep underwater trench known as Astoria Canyon that extends for miles into the Pacific Ocean.[3]

In North America only the Mississippi, the Saint Lawrence, and the Mackenzie rivers surpass the Columbia in volume of water discharged into the ocean. The vast Columbia system drains 259,000 square miles and embraces seven states and the Canadian province of British Columbia. Its source is inconspicuous Columbia Lake, nestled 2,650 feet above sea level between the Selkirks and the Rocky Mountains 80 miles north of the United States border. Its major tributary, the 1,038-mile Snake River, begins at the roof of the continent in Jackson Lake, Wyoming, and after an end run around the Tetons, it flows westerly across southern Idaho's high, arid plains before turning to the north and then west to join the Columbia. Before giant concrete dams controlled the Great River of the West (as it was known to early Euro-Americans), its height fluctuated wildly between late spring and early summer, when melting snow brought the river to flood crest, and the late autumn months, when it subsided. The Scottish naturalist David Douglas, traveling upstream in mid-June 1825, sketched the classic verbal picture of the Columbia in its most turbulent moment:

My ascent was slow, the current at this season being exceedingly powerful, so that I had many excursions on the banks and adjoining hills. The water ran with such rapidity that when the wind blows from a contrary direction it produces a swell like an inland sea; frequently we had to take shelter in the creeks, and although our canoes were considered good, yet we could not see each other except at a short distance, so great was the swell.

In late summer and early fall the river level dropped and exposed such spectacular features as Celilo Falls. The writer Don Holm remarked nearly two decades ago that the Columbia defied easy definition:

> It is more than a waterway filled with fish, exploited by hydro-electric plants, dancing with pleasure and commercial boats and measured out for irrigation. It is, as someone once commented, an expression of a nation's dynamic economic and social movements. . . .
> It is more than just a river.[4]

In its modern geological configuration, the river has served as a natural funnel, providing a water highway through which four varieties of salmon—chinook, coho (silvers), sockeye (bluebacks), and chum (or dog salmon)—and steelhead trout passed upstream to spawning grounds through the vast Columbia drainage. The main river and its primary tributaries and multitude of smaller streams provided a veritable corridor of abundant foodstuffs for native people. Moreover, the annual salmon runs in the main stem were remarkably predictable. According to anthropologist Hunn, the disruption of the runs caused by fluctuating climates, physical disruptions such as landslides, or fish diseases very likely affected only a small segment of the enormous breeding population for any given year. The huge number of salmon harvested during the peak years of the commercial fishery (1880-1940) suggests that the Indian take, while significant for their numbers, did not appreciably deplete salmon populations. Here again the size of the Indian population, which began declining probably as early as 1775—and then precipitously after 1820—plays an important role in determining both the quantity of salmon consumed and the size of the original runs. A recent calculation assumes a native population along the Columbia of about fifty thousand at the onset of the nineteenth century with an annual catch of about 41 million pounds of salmon. The Northwest Power Planning Council, whose responsibilities include mitigating the effects of hydroelectrical development on the anadromous fish, estimates that annual runs in the Columbia in the early nineteenth century ranged from 11 to 16 million salmon.[5]

Unlike the Euro-American commercial fishery that emerged after 1860, the Indian fishery—although characterized by some concentration of fishers along the mid-Columbia—was considerably more dispersed over the thousands of miles of the Columbia system. And while the importance of salmon to the Indian diet undoubtedly varied across that vast landscape, it seems reasonable to assume some degree of dependence on salmon virtually everywhere in the Pacific Northwest. The archaeologist Randall Schalk argues that the cumulative effect of the native population's catch of anadromous salmonids in the region "had to be substantial." He contends that the introduction of the horse to the Columbia Plateau in the early 1700s made it possible for people who lived far from the river to travel there either to fish or to trade with local people. Schalk believes that the stacks of pounded and dried fish that Lewis and Clark reported on the mid-Columbia were of the proper size and weight for transportation by horse to the interior.[6]

Although the salmon runs peaked for only a brief number of days each season (and for each species), the heaviest and most concentrated fishing took place at certain natural obstacles on the Columbia—at Kettle Falls, Priest Rapids, Celilo Falls, and the Long Narrows—and at similar strategic points on tributaries such as Sherar's Falls on the Deschutes and, for spring runs of salmon, at Willamette Falls near present-day Oregon City. In the vicinity of The Dalles, which included spectacular Celilo Falls, the proper mix of topography (which constricted the river) and dry windy climate (which enhanced the drying of fish) combined to forge one of the most productive freshwater fisheries anywhere in the world. Indian people used a variety of techniques, depending on the location and the character of the stream channel, to catch fish: dip nets, two-pronged spears, weirs or traps, seines, and gill nets (some of the latter up to 300 feet long).[7]

The point may seem trite, but it is important to understand that the Columbia River has been a significant force both in geological and human history. To know the Great River is to recognize certain essentials: its sharply differing climatic zones, its markedly contrasting ecosystems, and the distinctively unique cultural groups that have dominated its expansive drainage over the ages. Any inquiry into the question of Columbia River salmon, therefore, *must* consider broader realms of human behavior that bear upon social, economic, and political issues. For at least the last two hundred years, larger global forces have increasingly influenced the course and direction of change in the Columbia River country. This essay will explore the relationship between the natural world of the Columbia River system and the cultural forces that extended their control over the great waterway as the nineteenth century advanced.

The journals of Lewis and Clark provide the first recorded accounts of the prodigious native fishery on the mid-Columbia when the expedition leaders and their crew passed downriver toward the end of their epic transcontinental trek in 1805. From their entrance into the main river at the mouth of the Snake downstream to the Cascades, the captains sketch a dramatic picture of abundance, of a people whose lives were centered on the annual runs of salmon. Traveling upstream from the Yakima River on October 17, Clark observed mat lodges on an island where Indians were drying salmon "on Scaffolds on which they have great numbers." A few miles below the juncture with the Yakima, Clark encountered still another village of three mat lodges and "great quants. of Salmon on scaffolds drying":

> Saw great numbers of Dead Salmon on the Shores and floating in the water, great numbers of Indians on the banks and viewing me and 18 canoes accompanied me from the point. The waters of this river is clear, and a Salmon may be seen at the deabth of 15 or 20 feet. . . . passed three large lodges on the Star. Side near which great number of Salmon was drying on Scaffolds one of those Mat lodges I entered found it crouded with men women and children and near the enterance of those houses I saw maney squars engaged Splitting and drying Salmon.[8]

Five days later at Celilo Falls, Clark reported large quantities of pounded fish neatly preserved in baskets lined with dried salmon skins:

> those 12 baskets of from 90 to 100 w. each (basket) for a Stack. thus preserved those fish may be kept Sound and Sweet Several years, as those people inform me, Great quantities as they inform us are Sold to the whites peoples who visit the mouth of this river as well as the nativs below.

Further downriver at The Dalles, Clark counted 107 scaffolds of dried and pounded fish "which must have contained 10,000 w. of neet fish." And the expedition leaders also learned the value Indians placed on salmon above all other food when the latter refused to trade their fish away. On one occasion the captains purchased eight dogs, "the Indians not verry fond of Selling their good fish, compells us to make use of dogs for food." In their travels on the Columbia below the Wenatchee River, Lewis and Clark encountered more than one hundred native fishing stations. And in one remarkable fall day as they were descending the river, the expedition passed twenty-nine mat lodges where Indians were preparing and drying fish.[9]

The newcomers who came to the Columbia River country in ever increasing numbers in the early nineteenth century brought with them a different cultural vision, a social imagination and core of beliefs— an economic culture, historian Donald Worster called it—a set of values

Columbia Basin Indians traditionally split and dried salmon to preserve it. Edna David (left) and Stella McKinley pose in a salmon-drying shed at Celilo Village, April 1956.

that viewed the natural world as capital, that obliged humankind to use that capital for self-advancement, and a conviction that the social order should promote the accumulation of personal wealth.[10] They looked first to the plentiful furbearing animals of the region, to the rich soils in the valley bottoms, to the magnificent forests, and eventually to the seemingly limitless multitudes of salmon that plied the great Columbia waterway. The newcomers' objective was to turn the natural abundance of the Northwest to advantage in distant markets. Although transportation and processing technology limited the ability of entrepreneurs to capitalize on the salmon runs until the late 1860s, the prospect, the perception that there was great potential in a commercial fishery on the Columbia came with the earliest of the newcomers.

The fur traders who followed Lewis and Clark to the Northwest were the first to suggest that salmon could be turned to account in the marketplace. Alexander Ross, who was on the river in 1811 as a member of John Jacob Astor's Pacific Fur Company, thought Columbia River salmon were "as fine as any in the world, and . . . were a foreign market to present itself, the natives alone might furnish 1,000 tons annually." Fellow Astorian Robert Stuart further embellished the growing lore about the river's potential when he reported "a first rate salmon fishery" at the Long Narrows, where a competent fisher could catch five hundred fish per day during the peak of the run. A few years later when the U.S. House of Representatives inquired into the possibility of establishing settlements in the region, its committee reported that the Columbia was "of the utmost importance" from a commercial perspective, especially "the fisheries on that coast" and "the vast quantities of furs."[11]

But the first effort to commercially exploit the region's abundant salmon populations—as in virtually every entrepreneurial venture in the Columbia River country—must be attributed to the acquisitive abilities and instincts of the Hudson's Bay Company. Only two years after the establishment of its regional outpost at Fort Vancouver, chief factor John McLoughlin asked company officials for permission to trade salted salmon in Spanish California: "If the Business was well-managed we might Salt a thousand Barrels p. Annum in the Columbia. . . . It is certain if the Americans come they will attempt something in this way." In subsequent years McLoughlin continued to press the importance of shipping cargoes of timber and salmon to California and to the Sandwich Islands. At the onset of what has been dubbed the "Oregon Fever" in the early 1840s (the westward trek of white settlers from the Mississippi to the Willamette Valley), the Hudson's Bay Company purchased from native people a sufficient quantity of salted salmon to pack eight hundred barrels of fish for sale in Pacific markets.[12]

The Hudson's Bay Company's chief factor proved to be a prophet of sorts when the American brig *Owyhee* entered the Columbia in 1829, remained for two years trading for salmon, and then departed for Boston with a pack of fifty barrels. But it was another Bostonian, Nathaniel Wyeth, who conceived the most ambitious of the early American efforts to establish a commercial fishery on the Columbia. After an abortive attempt in 1832 when he lost a supply ship at sea, Wyeth and his Columbia River Fishing and Trading Company returned two years later and constructed a trading post on Sauvie Island at the entrance to the Willamette River. When several of his employees sickened and died during the winter (and with the imposing presence of the Hudson's Bay Company nearby), Wyeth ended that second futile effort and sold out to the economically powerful British firm.[13]

Despite Wyeth's failure, other New Englanders persisted in the effort to establish a commercial fishery on the Columbia. Among the

more successful was Captain John Couch of Newburyport, Massachusetts, who sailed out of the Columbia with a cargo of packed fish in
1840 and returned two years later to establish salteries at Willamette
Falls and Pillar Rock. The United States Exploring Expedition under
the command of Lieutenant Charles Wilkes investigated the Columbia River country in the early 1840s and further extolled the region's
extensive fishery. Wilkes reported that the rivers and coast "abound
in salmon of the finest flavor . . . and appear inexhaustible." Of the
many rivers in the Northwest, he thought the Columbia produced
the finest salmon and in the greatest numbers.[14]

The pace of cultural and physical change in the Oregon Country
dramatically quickened with the formal agreement between England
and the United States to extend the boundary westward from the
forty-ninth parallel to the waters of the Pacific. A swelling tide of
Euro-Americans—most of them trekking overland, others coming by
sea to the Willamette and Puget lowlands—quickly overran and pushed
aside an already decimated native population during the 1840s and
1850s. Shortly after the settlement of the boundary issue, the artist
and writer George Catlin, who traveled upriver to The Dalles, witnessed examples of that new spirit afoot in the land:

> The fresh fish for current food and the dried fish for their winter
> consumption, which had been from time immemorial a good
> and certain living for the surrounding tribes, like everything else
> of value belonging to the poor Indian, has attracted the cupidity
> of the "better class," and is now being "turned into money,"
> whilst the ancient and real owners of it may be said to be starv-
> ing to death; dying in sight of what they have lost, and in a
> country where there is actually nothing else to eat.[15]

Imbued with a commercial ethos that viewed the natural world in
terms of its commodity potential, the incoming settler and merchant
population set about imposing familiar flora and fauna on their newly
adopted physical settings. In Richard White's words: "Settlers
husbanded the familiar."[16] Commercial practices and technologies of
the eastern United States were transplanted to the Northwest, including those that were appropriate to take advantage of the region's
magnificent salmon runs.

Although shipments of packed and salted salmon from the Columbia River continued to increase during the 1850s, the salmon
business remained a sideshow to more important commercial undertakings until a series of circumstances and events converged to trigger
open season on the salmon populations of the North Pacific coast.
These included the growth of a sizable market in the working-class
industrial centers of Great Britain and the eastern United States; the

development of efficient technologies for processing and preserving salmon; advancements in ship design and speed of travel; and the extension of a transcontinental railroad down the Columbia River. Andrew Hapgood and the Hume brothers (George, Robert, and William)—state-of-Maine natives like Andrew Pope and Frederick Talbot, who initiated the commercial lumber industry on Puget Sound— brought the first salmon cannery to the Columbia River. Beginning on a raft in the Sacramento River in 1864, Hapgood, Hume, and Company shifted their operation to Eagle Cliff on the north bank of the Columbia in 1866; from that point the salmon cannery industry was off and running. Adapting procedures used for canning lobster, Hapgood and Hume perfected a technique for sealing (and preserving) salmon in airtight cans. [17]

The canning process was especially suited to the inexpensive transport of fish over long distances. The effect of this joining of events and circumstances was the availability in a rapidly expanding market of a relatively cheap and nourishing product, one especially suited (and priced) to working-class tastes. At the front end of the industry—the taking of fish from the river—operators developed and adapted a variety of techniques. Gill nets, made initially of linen webbing, were used extensively from the mouth of the Columbia upriver to Celilo Falls. Stationary fish traps attached to posts driven into the

Horse seining could net dozens of fish at a time.

river bottom were also widely used. According to anthropologist Courtland Smith, more than four hundred fish traps were in use on Northwestern rivers by the late 1920s. Another highly productive method was the use of seines, huge nets that were most effective at low tide, hauled by five to seven teams of horses with crews ranging from twenty to forty workers.[18]

Perhaps the most unusual of all the devices for taking salmon from the Columbia was the fish wheel, an elaborate ferris wheel-like structure powered by the current that scooped fish from the water. First used on the Columbia in 1879, the highly productive wheels (both stationary and mounted on scows) literally pumped salmon from the river; the giant Phelps wheel at The Dalles took 227,000 pounds of salmon from the river from May to July, 1894. And on a single spring day in 1913 the Seufert brothers' wheel no. 5 turned a record catch of

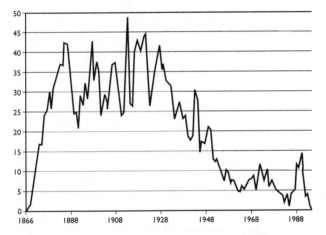

The commercial catch of salmon and steelhead trout on the Columbia River has risen and declined dramatically during the period 1866-1993.
Source: Washington Department of Fish and Wildlife; Oregon Department of Fish and Wildlife.

70,000 pounds. Because competitors thought the owners of fish wheels enjoyed unfair monopoly advantage in the taking of fish, they brought pressure to bear in state legislatures to outlaw the devices. The legislatures of first Oregon (1926) and then Washington (1934) banned the use of fish wheels. Purse seines, an elongated curtain strung behind a boat, were prohibited in 1917.[19]

From beginning to end the Columbia River salmon industry was a tremendously productive operation. The fish-harvesting techniques were extremely efficient, yielding huge quantities of salmon for the numerous canneries located on the Columbia and its lower tributaries, on Puget Sound, and along the myriad coastal streams of the North Pacific. As the authority Anthony Netboy noted, virtually every Oregon coastal stream had canneries:

> By 1874 there were twelve between Astoria and Portland, and by
> 1883 fifty-five on or near the Columbia, packing 630,000 cases of
> 48 one-pound cans valued at $3 million, using only chinook. . . .
> The chinook catch reached a peak of 43 million pounds on the
> Columbia in 1883, coincident with the operation of the maxi-
> mum number of canneries.

Hapgood and Hume dominated cannery production on the lower
Columbia; upriver the Seufert brothers and their big fish wheels controlled the best fishing spots and led all other shippers.[20]

Despite noticeably declining fish runs well before the turn of the
century and an occasional expression of concern about the future, an
aura of unlimited abundance prevailed in most quarters. The remark
of Samuel Clarke during the 1870s very likely expressed the prevailing ethos: "The immense supply of the chinook salmon that forms
the staple of this great commerce is to be had for the taking." While
the salmon catch for all species in the Columbia River reached a high
mark of 46,629,000 pounds in 1911, the take for the more valuable
chinook salmon had already peaked more than twenty-five years earlier. Puget Sound fishers produced an even larger output, one that did
not peak until 1917, and the Alaskan fishery, which got off to a later
start, eventually surpassed both. Columbia River landings show a
steady and appreciable decline after 1925.[21]

In truth, state legislatures did make some overtures toward restricting harvests, but those early efforts proved abortive because
enforcement mechanisms were ineffective. In retrospect, until World
War II, conditions in the salmon cannery business paralleled similar
circumstances in the lumber industry: too many producers, virtually
unlimited access to an abundant resource, and a periodically glutted
market that encouraged waste and kept prices down.[22] But there were
forces at work in the Northwest—in addition to the voracious appetite of the canneries, the increasing number of sports fishers, and the
expanding fleet of ocean trollers—that eventually would place even
greater stress on the steadily diminishing salmon population in the
Columbia system.

The coming of the industrial age to the Pacific Northwest initiated
the slow and then dramatic alteration of the landscape and ecology
of the Columbia River country, including the vast breeding habitat of
its anadromous fishes. The completion of the Northern Pacific Railroad to Portland and Tacoma in 1883 and the simultaneous extension
of hundreds of miles of branch railroads through the rich agricultural
and forested countryside set in motion changes that were detrimental in the long run to the region's still abundant salmon populations.

The introduction of mechanized (and more environmentally intrusive) farming and logging activities further quickened the pace of change. The adaptation of steam power to logging operations (especially in the form of the steam donkey) dramatically speeded up the yarding of logs—and disturbance to riparian environments. Moreover, the steam donkey—and the internal-combustion yarding machines that succeeded it—worked most effectively and economically in settings where clearcutting was practiced.[23] But it was the *combined* farm, range, mining, and forest activities that proved so disruptive to stream and riverine ecology in the region.

Untreated industrial wastes, urban sewage, and logs dumped directly into the region's rivers and streams further added to the degradation of water quality and salmon breeding habitat. Such practices prompted the Oregon Board of Health early in this century to declare the lower portions of the Willamette River "an open sewer." The board's report for 1911 disclosed that pollutants in the river in some instances made fish unsuitable for food; indeed, the dissolved oxygen content of water in the Portland Harbor area was so low that trout died within minutes when they were lowered into the water in wire cages. *The Oregon Sportsman,* the official publication of the Oregon Fish and Game Commission, observed in 1914 that pollution in the Willamette River was destroying fish life: "Dumping the sewage of cities, the waste of our mills and factories and filth of all kinds into our public waters is a factor that will completely deplete our streams of fish, if it is allowed to continue." The state agency concluded: "These things are wrong, both morally and legally."[24]

Elsewhere in the Columbia country large-scale industrial mining activity produced huge piles of tailings that in subsequent decades would release toxic metals (especially lead) into tributary streams. The U.S. Fish Commission reported in 1894 that placer mining on the upper Boise River had seriously depleted the salmon runs. On other tributaries—the Yakima, Snake, and Owyhee—early reclamation projects began diverting water to irrigate semiarid lands; tributary streams sometimes dried up because of the volume of water used to irrigate fields. Unscreened canals posed another problem, providing passageways for aquatic life, unnatural waterways that often left fish stranded in a farmer's fields. Moreover, the mere expansion in reclaimed agricultural acreage added to the sediment load in streams.[25] And all of this preceded the building of the gigantic Grand Coulee project, a high dam that effectively eliminated forever about 1,100 linear miles of salmon spawning grounds.

And then there were the numerous small dams—seemingly everywhere in the Northwest—that obstructed the passage of fish to upstream breeding grounds. The dams, especially those that blocked access to lakes, were particularly detrimental to sockeye salmon, a species that requires lake systems for the young to mature. Some of those early dams stored water for purposes of irrigation; others, especially those built after the turn of the century, were designed to produce hydroelectricity. Even before the giant concrete behemoths of the 1930s came on line, one fishery authority observed that dams had made inaccessible nearly 50 percent of Columbia Basin salmon habitat.[26] While that estimate may be exaggerated, it does testify to extensive alterations to natural stream flows in the region at the onset of the Great Depression; it also served as a harbinger of the future when large main-stem dams increasingly began to dot the countryside.

The point to this discussion is to indicate the wide-ranging, systemic, and multifaceted environmental changes that were taking place everywhere in the region. Singularly, none of those industrial practices threatened salmon over the entire Columbia system; collectively, they would eventually imperil *all* anadromous fishes. The roots of those changes resided in the acquisitive, commodity-oriented perspective of a modernizing Eurocentric vision that viewed the alteration of stream flows and the "development" of landscapes in terms of progress and human improvement. For most of the nineteenth century, stories about the Great River described a setting where humans remained subservient to the forces and power of water and landscape; with the advent of newer, more invasive forms of technology, however, that sense of humility and respect toward the river began to erode.[27]

The application of steam power to the movement of commodities by rail and river on the Columbia system marked the onset of a new age. The opening of The Dalles-Celilo Canal on May 15, 1915 provides an excellent moment to examine the rhetoric that accompanied that transformation. Attended by politicians, prominent newspaper editors, influential businessmen, and developers, the event was accompanied by lofty speech making and celebratory breast beating. The imagery and symbolism evoked in that rhetoric also signified what would become standard fare for defining the future of the Columbia River—the manipulation of its contours to the technical and instrumentalist designs of the dominant culture.[28]

For Marshall N. Dana, editor of the Portland *Oregonian* and one of the speakers at the ceremonies at Big Eddy, no achievement could compare with "such a project of community benefit as the open river." The engineering expertise for the development of the Columbia River required "big men capable of doing things in a big way." The opportunity for the future of the Columbia Basin, Dana told the crowd, was "almost beyond computation. Civilization may well make here its most splendid achievements." Portland corporation lawyer, progressive political figure, and erstwhile conservationist Joseph Nathan Teal viewed the improved transportation on the river as a means to "unshackle" the waterway from both physical obstacles and extortionate toll charges. "Our unyielding purpose," he enthused, was "to secure a free river from the mountains to the sea." With the opening of the canal "the shackles are broken. The river is free at last." The further "improvement" of the Columbia and Snake rivers would make the Inland Empire "an empire in fact as well as in name":

> an empire of industry, of commerce, of manufacture and agriculture; and the valleys of the Columbia and Snake will have become one vast garden, full of happy homes and contented and industrious people.[29]

As the twentieth century advanced, distant markets, an industrializing economy, the emergence of electrical power as a source of energy, the stability of the national political economy, and the logistics of foreign policy were the key factors driving the manipulation of the Columbia River system. The imagery and legal prescriptions accom-

A ten-story advertisement on the side of Portland Railway Light and Power's downtown office building was part of the marketing of electricity in the 1930s.

panying those imperatives found expression in artistic imagination, in ethnohistorical scholarship, in the compelling folk lyrics of Woody Guthrie, and finally in the imposition of legal forms that severely constrained the rights of native people. The consequences included the dramatic alteration of the river's landscape and the continued decline of the anadromous fish.

That new celebratory body of writing—heralding the achievements of human energy and ingenuity in "harnessing" the "untamed" power of the Columbia—has dominated historical narrative for most of this century. With the establishment of the Bonneville Power Administration in 1937, federal and regional authorities had a formal institutional vehicle to propagate the emerging truth through film and other public relations media. From the time of Franklin Roosevelt's great public works programs of the 1930s until the present, that interpretation of the "working river" has enjoyed the elevated status not only of history, but of myth and nostalgia. Bunyanesque in its claim to legendary and heroic achievement, the conventional account of the "development" of the Columbia River and its tributaries—until recently—served as a model regional success story.

Tall, angular, and bespectacled, Richard Neuberger is one of the region's venerated political and journalistic heroes, rising through news-reporting and writing skills to a leadership position in the Oregon legislature and subsequently election to the United States Senate. From the time he converted to New Deal liberal activism in the mid-1930s, Richard Neuberger became one of the foremost proponents for transforming the region's "almost limitless . . . undeveloped natural resources" into productive public use; most of his attention (and admiration) focused on the giant engineering projects on the Columbia River. Describing the great waterway's passage through the desertlike Columbia Basin as "a living force in a dead land," Neuberger praised the giant federal works projects on the river and argued that water would transform an area that supports "only desert weeds and bushes, and coyotes and rattlesnakes and prairie dogs" into a land of poplar trees, corn fields, farmhouses, and small communities.[30]

Neuberger's descriptions of the physical and cultural world of the Columbia River are consistent with those of the dominant political and economic interests of his time. "Still in the dawn of its impact on civilization," he pointed out, the Great River of the West had the potential to irrigate immense basins, to light cities, to run factories, and to mechanize farms. The sole requirement was a public will to "tame the wild torrent and put it to work."[31] Insofar as Richard Neuberger defined nature as the servant and handmaiden of humankind, he was at one with the larger economic culture that saw nature as capital to be put to productive use.[32] His writing reflected what he deemed the virtues and civic duties of the larger social good. As such, he was the exemplary spokesperson for his age, giving emphasis to values and attitudes that found expression in the transformation of the once free-flowing Columbia River into a managed, regulated, and techno-dominated waterway.

His language and that of his contemporaries was one of neither caution nor reflection, but of unabashed buoyancy and a firm belief in willful human dominion over the natural world. As the writer Marc Reisner observes, the amazing thing about Grand Coulee—and the great dam-building projects on the Colorado, Missouri, and other waterways—is "that people just went out and built it, built anything, without knowing exactly how to do it or whether it could be done." Through the entire dam-building era there were no detailed studies of consequences, of environmental effects, or alternative approaches; rather the promoters saw themselves as practical-minded doers, problem solvers, people who were assured and confident in their ability to control the future. Between 1928 and 1956, Reisner notes, "the most fateful transformation that has ever been visited on any landscape, anywhere, was wrought."[33] The Columbia River and its extensive tributary system was an integral part of the human reconfiguration of those landscapes.

To be sure, there were protests along the way, naysayers who feared that altering the flow of the Great River would be the final *coup de grace* to the already declining salmon runs. Fisheries biologists, naturalists, sports fishers, and Indian groups testifying at extensive public hearings during the 1930s and 1940s questioned the soundness of building dams on the main-stem Columbia and its major tributaries. And even its proponents agreed that the fish ladders at Bonneville Dam, the hatchery at Leavenworth below Grand Coulee, and the prospect of the successful downstream migration of juvenile salmon were experiments. Frank Bell, the U. S. Commissioner of Fisheries and a supporter of Bonneville, admitted in 1937 that the "development of the Columbia River for power and agriculture imperils an ancient industry, the salmon fisheries." Stanford University ichthyologist Willis Rich was even more ambivalent: "The future outlook for the salmon fisheries of the Columbia River is not bright, but neither is it hopeless." And before the salmon migration figures for Bonneville Dam were available, Oregon's master fish warden, Mike Hoy, remarked: "We're going to learn whether fish . . . can exist in a river system extensively developed for power, industry and reclamation."[34]

As a group, the constituencies opposed to the dams were over-whelmed and politically impotent compared to the massive influence of metropolitan chambers of commerce, development interests, public power advocates, farmers, and a panoply of other promoters. The supporters believed in the efficacy of engineering the mid- and upper Columbia to control flooding, to generate hydroelectrical power, to

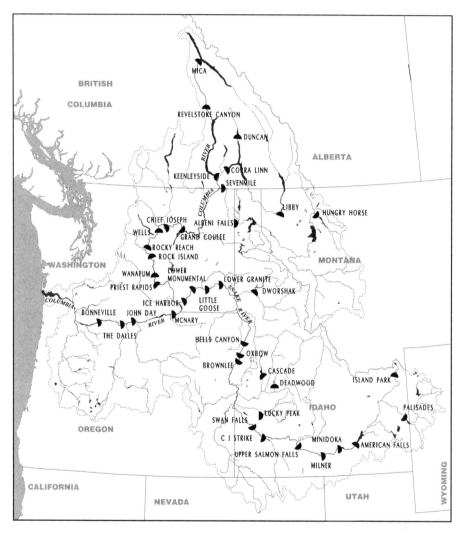

The major dams of the Columbia River basin provide benefits for people but cause many problems for salmon.

improve navigation, and to provide water for irrigation. Their power-ful political representatives in the region employed a loftier rhetoric, citing the exigencies of the Great Depression, World War II, and the Cold War to push home the need to develop the Columbia. And the dams went up: first Bonneville, then Grand Coulee, and, following the war, several main-stem and tributary dams that turned much of the Columbia system into a series of slack-water reservoirs.

Although he was mostly a booster of those projects, Richard Neuberger raised the appropriate questions about the future of salmon in *The Saturday Evening Post* just as the gates were being closed at Grand Coulee Dam in 1941:

> Are enough Chinooks getting upstream past Bonneville Dam? Will the fingerling fish . . . scoot safely through Bonneville's turbines or will they be mangled by the whirring propeller blades? What will be the effect of additional dams projected for the Columbia's tributaries—the Snake, the Umatilla, the Willamette? Will Congress accept the recommendations of the Army engineers for seven more big dams across the main stem of the Columbia?

The Oregon journalist raised other questions that proved ominous for the future: Would salmon survive polluted rivers and increased timber harvesting? Would irrigation ditches continue to serve as death traps for misdirected salmon? Would fingerlings be able to escape predators in the large lakes behind the dams? Was it possible to pro-tect Idaho's Salmon River, "the last untouched spawning area" in the region? And, finally, could fish and civilization mix successfully?[35]

What the widely read Neuberger presented was a synthesis of sorts, a composite of the arguments posed by sports and commercial fish-ers, by treaty Indians, by skeptical scientists, and by others who were concerned about the future of Columbia River salmon. But Neuberger, who was an ardent supporter of Franklin D. Roosevelt's New Deal (including the great public works projects on the Columbia), muted those queries as the 1940s advanced and extolled the virtues and ben-efits of the region's growing industrial prowess, a line of reasoning that saw positive benefits in the dams.[36] In brief, Neuberger's writing increasingly followed familiar themes, testimonials that praised the virtues of engineering and managing the natural world for human benefit.

The boom years following World War II witnessed the culmination of the water development projects on the Columbia system. Reflect-ing in part America's postwar hegemony in world affairs, Northwestern congressmen marched with the battalions that pushed huge engineering projects at home and abroad. The speeches and writings of Washington's senators Warren Magnuson and Henry Jackson and Oregon's Wayne Morse mirror a culture whose collective ethos equated hydropower, reclamation, and flood control as the route to the good society at home and international prestige abroad. According to that collective mind-set, historian Richard White argues, the "working river" would restore equilibrium to the social order, bring freedom and dignity, and cure environmental problems.[37]

With the completion of the last major dams on the Columbia system—say by the close of the 1960s—the river was stabilized; it no longer "ravaged" adjacent landscapes during the peak of the spring runoff; it produced a surplus of hydropower that could be marketed outside the region; and it provided irrigation water for millions of acres.[38] The latter "benefit," according to one scholarly enthusiast, is "an outstanding example . . . of the application of geotechnics—the process of making the earth more habitable."[39] It was an orderly, managed, regulated, and human-dominated waterway, one designed to maximize production for most of its industrial users. Indeed, the Columbia fits historian Donald Worster's prescription of engineering a common efficiency on an otherwise discordant landscape: it is "a techno-economic order imposed for the purpose of mastering a difficult environment."[40]

"Dams do literally kill rivers," Wallace Stegner tells us, "which means they kill not only living water and natural scenery but a whole *congeries* of values associated with them." The naturalist Robert Pyle, who lives immediately adjacent to the Great River in the small town of Grays River in southwestern Washington, made a similar argument: "Things go wrong with rivers, and much of what could go wrong with the Columbia already has."[41] For anyone familiar with the headlines in regional newspapers, those commentaries are not particularly new. Hence, the era of the modern "working river" has multiple meanings for the Pacific Northwest: without question, it has vastly speeded the demise and extinction of salmon populations; it has abrogated legal and moral guarantees to Native American people whose subsistence and spiritual life center on the salmon; and in the present it threatens to engulf the region in a legal and political struggle among a variety of interest groups over who is to benefit from the river. And this has taken place in a very brief period of time, especially given the thousands of years of relative ecological and social stability along the Great River of the West.

One of my graduate students wrote in a recent essay that she would give up luxuries and creature comforts if she could "see the Columbia River before it was *damned* to servitude."[42] Molly McFerran's remark echoes the sentiments of writer Barry Lopez:

> One of our deepest frustrations as a culture, I think, must be that we have made so extreme an investment in mining the continent, created such an infrastructure of nearly endless jobs predicated on the removal and distribution of trees, water, minerals, fish, plants, and oil, that we cannot imagine stopping.[43]

Notes

1. "How Coyote Made the Columbia River," in Ella E. Clark, *Indian Legends of the Pacific Northwest* (Berkeley: University of California Press, 1953), 88.
2. Eugene S. Hunn, *Nch'i-wana "The Big River": Mid-Columbia Indians and Their Land* (Seattle: University of Washington Press, 1991), 20-21, 148-49.
3. C. Melvin Aikens, *Archaeology of Oregon* (Portland, Ore.: Bureau of Land Management, 1984), 41-42; Hunn, *Nch'i-wana "The Big River,"* 19-21; and Don Holm, "Where Rolls the Columbia," *The Oregonian,* July 20, 1975, pp. 6-7.
4. Anthony Netboy, *The Columbia River Salmon and Steelhead Trout: Their Fight for Survival* (Seattle: University of Washington Press, 1980), 4-5; *Journal Kept By David Douglas during his Travels in North America, 1823-1827* (New York: Antiquarian Press, 1959), 127; and Holm, "Where Rolls the Columbia," 6.
5. Hunn, *Nch'i-wana "The Big River,"* 148; and Randall F. Schalk, "Estimating Salmon and Steelhead Usage in the Columbia Basin Before 1850: An Anthropological Perspective," *The Northwest Environmental Journal* 2, no. 2 (summer 1986), 14-15, 21.
6. Schalk, "Estimating Salmon and Steelhead Usage in the Columbia Basin Before 1850," 6.
7. Hunn, *Nch'i-wana "The Big River,"* 151; Netboy, *Columbia River Salmon and Steelhead Trout,* 11; and David Johnson, "Salmon: A Legacy of Abundance," *What's Happening* (Eugene), January 31, 1991, p. 6.
8. Gary E. Moulton, ed., *The Journals of Lewis and Clark,* vol. 5 (Lincoln: University of Nebraska Press, 1988), 287-88.
9. Moulton, *The Journals of Lewis and Clark,* vol. 5, pp. 327, 335. The estimates of the number of fishing stations encountered by Lewis and Clark is in Netboy, *Columbia River Salmon and Steelhead Trout,* 13.
10. Donald Worster, *Dust Bowl: The Southern Plains in the 1930s* (New York: Oxford University Press, 1979), 5-6.
11. Alexander Ross, *Adventures of the First Settlers on the Oregon or Columbia River, 1810-1813* (1859; Lincoln: University of Nebraska Press, 1986), 108; Philip Aston Rollins, ed., *The Discovery of the Oregon Trail: Robert Stuart's Narratives* (New York: Charles Scribner's Sons, 1935), 52; and "Occupation of the Columbia River, A Report of the Committee to Inquire into the Situation of the Settlements upon the Pacific Ocean," *Oregon Historical Quarterly* 8 (1907), 62.
12. E. E. Rich, ed., *The Letters of John McLoughlin from Fort Vancouver to the Governor and Committee* (Toronto: The Champlain Society, 1941), 37, 120-21, 124; and Schalk, "Estimating Salmon and Steelhead Usage in the Columbia Basin Before 1850," 13.
13. Johnson, "Salmon: A Legacy of Abundance," 6.
14. Netboy, *Columbia River Salmon and Steelhead Trout,* 19; and Charles Wilkes, "Report on the Territory of Oregon," *Oregon Historical Society* 12 (September 1911), 286-87.
15. George Catlin, *Episodes from "Life Among the Indians" and "Last Rambles"* (Norman: University of Oklahoma Press, 1959), 144.

16. Richard White, "The Altered Landscape: Social Change and the Land in the Pacific Northwest," in *Regionalism and the Pacific Northwest,* William G. Robbins, Robert Frank, and Richard Ross, eds. (Corvallis: Oregon State University Press, 1983), 112.

17. Holm, "Where Rolls the Columbia," 14; Netboy, *Columbia River Salmon and Steelhead Trout,* 20-21; and Carlos A. Schwantes, *The Pacific Northwest: An Interpretive History* (Lincoln: University of Nebraska Press, 1989), 164.

18. Lisa Mighetto, *Saving the Salmon: A History of the U.S. Army Corps of Engineers' Role in the Protection of Anadromous Fish on the Columbia and Snake Rivers* (draft report prepared for U.S. Army Corps of Engineers, Portland and Walla Walla, February 17, 1994), 20-21; and Courtland Smith, *Salmon Fishers of the Columbia* (Corvallis: Oregon State University Press, 1979), 30-33.

19. Johnson, "Salmon: A Legacy of Abundance," 7; and Netboy, *Columbia River Salmon and Steelhead Trout,* 20-21.

20. Netboy, *Columbia River Salmon and Steelhead Trout,* 21.

21. The quote is in Mighetto, *Saving the Salmon,* 21. Also see Schwantes, *The Pacific Northwest,* 164; and Netboy, *Columbia River Salmon and Steelhead Trout,* 34-36, 150-55.

22. See William G. Robbins, *Lumberjacks and Legislators: Political Economy of the U.S. Lumber Industry, 1890-1941* (College Station: Texas A & M University Press, 1982).

23. The argument presented in this section is based on two decades of research and writing about industrial practices and their social and environmental consequences in the Pacific Northwest and elsewhere. Among my publications that are relevant to these issues, see especially *Lumberjacks and Legislators; Hard Times in Paradise: Coos Bay, Oregon, 1850-1986* (Seattle: University of Washington Press, 1988); "Narrative Form and Great River Myths"; and *Colony and Empire: The Capitalist Transformation of the American West* (Lawrence: University Press of Kansas, 1994).

24. George Gleeson, *The Return of a River: The Willamette River, Oregon* (Corvallis: Water Resources Research Institute, Oregon State University, 1972), 101-103; David B. Charlton to the author, November 13, 1975; and *The Oregon Sportsman* (January 1914), 1.

25. Charles H. Gilbert and Barton W. Evermann, "A Report Upon Investigations in the Columbia River Basin, With Descriptions of Four New Species of Fish," U. S. Fish Commission *Bulletin* 14 (1894), 179; Oregon State Game Commission, *The Problems of Pollution of Oregon Public Waters and the Solution Offered Under the National Recovery Act,* Bulletin 1 (Portland, 1933); and Netboy, *Columbia River Salmon and Steelhead Trout,* 57.

26. Marshall McDonald, *Salmon Fisheries of the Columbia River* (report prepared for U. S. Commission of Fish and Fisheries, 53rd Cong., 2d sess., 1894 [Senate Misc. Doc. 200]), 155; Netboy, *Columbia River Salmon and Steelhead Trout,* 55; and Mighetto, *Saving the Salmon,* 28.

27. The argument in the remainder of this essay is adapted from my article, "Narrative Form and Great River Myths."

28. For an account of the addresses on the occasion, see the *Oregon Historical Quarterly* 16 (1915), 107-203.

29. *Ibid.*, 122-24, and 126-31.

30. Richard Neuberger, *Our Promised Land* (1938; Moscow: University of Idaho Press, 1989), 353-57.

31. *Ibid.*, 31-32.

32. The relationship between capitalism and the natural world is suggested in Worster, *Dust Bowl*, 6. For a different view, see Peter Berger, *The Capitalist Revolution: Fifty Propositions About Prosperity, Equality, and Liberty* (New York: Basic Books, 1986).

33. Marc Reisner, *Cadillac Desert: The American West and its Disappearing Water* (New York: Viking Penguin, 1986), 166 and 172.

34. The Frank Bell quote is in Richard L. Neuberger, "Climb, Fish, Climb," *Collier's*, November 6, 1937, 50. The Willis Rich and Mike Hoy quotes are in Neuberger, "The Great Salmon Mystery," *The Saturday Evening Post*, September 13, 1941, 21.

35. Neuberger, "The Great Salmon Mystery," 21.

36. For a flavor of Neuberger's essays in support of New Deal programs, see "Bridling Our Last Frontier," *New York Times Magazine*, May 31, 1936, 6-7, 21; "Power Giant of the Far West: Mighty Bonneville Dam," *New York Times Magazine*, May 16, 1937, 8-9, 28; "Columbia River Power," *The New Republic*, February 5, 1940, 177-78; and "Bonneville: The First Ten Years," *The Nation*, May 8, 1948, 502-4. A synthesis of these essays appears in Neuberger, *Our Promised Land.*

37. Richard White, "What Makes the Columbia River so Powerful," address to The Great River of the West Conference, Vancouver, Washington, May 2, 1992.

38. Schwantes, *The Pacific Northwest*, 349-50.

39. Ronald Albert Weinkauf, "The Columbia Basin Project, Washington: Concept and Reality, Lessons for Public Policy," (Ph.D. diss., Oregon State University, 1973), 2.

40. Donald Worster, *Rivers of Empire: Water, Aridity and the Growth of the American West* (New York: Pantheon Books, 1985), 6-7; and Worster, *Under Western Skies: Nature and History in the American West* (New York: Oxford University Press, 1992), 14. For an account of the politics and economics of river development on the Willamette system, see William G. Robbins, "The Political Economy of Water Resource Development: Oregon's Willamette Valley Project," *Pacific Historical Review* 47 (1978), 585-606.

41. Wallace Stegner, *Where the Bluebird Sings to the Lemonade Springs* (New York: Random House, 1992), 89; and Robert Michael Pyle, *Wintergreen: Rambles in a Ravaged Land* (New York: 1986), 41.

42. Molly McFerran, June 3, 1991.

43. Barry Lopez, "A Sense of Place," *Old Oregon* (autumn 1991), 16.

II. The Exploitation of Nature

Introduction

In 1855, Kamiakin, a leader of the Yakama* Indians, signed a treaty with the U.S. government, which primarily reserved to his people their

Kamiakin, as sketched in the 1850s by Gustavus Sohon, an artist accompanying Isaac Stevens at the 1855 treaty signings.

rights to fish and hunt. Kamiakin did not like the way the deal was struck and he was filled with foreboding. He said, "I have been afraid of the white men. . . . Perhaps you have spoken straight, that your children will do what is right. Let them do as they have promised."[1]

During the next half century many more promises were made to the Indians, while the natural resources of the Northwest came under increasing pressure. The documents in this section begin with the Indian treaties of the 1850s and continue with the rapid industrialization of the salmon fishery in the 1880s and 1890s. By one hundred years ago many knowledgeable observers were voicing strong concerns for the future of the salmon.

Notes

* In 1994 the Yakama Nation requested that this new spelling be used. We have honored this request, with the exception of quotations from historical documents, book titles, etc.
1. Click Relander, *The Yakimas* (Yakima, Washington: Yakima Tribal Council, 1955), 14.

Previous page: Few regulations prevented overfishing in the early decades. Pictured is one night's catch on the Coquille River, circa 1900.

CROSSCURRENTS:
SALMON IN THE WILD AND IN HATCHERIES

Document:	**Explorations on the Columbia River**
Author:	Livingston Stone, U.S. Fish Commission agent in the Pacific Northwest
Year:	1885
Description:	After exploring the Columbia Basin, a fisheries expert argues the need for hatcheries.

Livingston Stone, circa 1905.

OF COURSE THE COLUMBIA itself below Snake River, and Snake River anywhere near its mouth, are not to be thought of in connection with a salmon-breeding station, their great volume and width making it wholly impracticable to collect any large number of spawning salmon from them. Below Snake River on the north or Washington side of the Columbia there are many salmon streams flowing into it as Alder Creek, Klikitat River, Wind River, Washougal River, Lewis River, and Cowlitz River, besides many others; but, with the exception of perhaps the Cowlitz and Klikitat, they are all short, diminutive rivers which would never furnish breeders enough to supply any great number of eggs, and although the Cowlitz and Klikitat are of greater size and would yield a larger supply of eggs, they nevertheless could not furnish enough to warrant the establishment of a salmon-breeding station anywhere along their course. On the south or Oregon side of the Columbia its tributaries are much larger, but each one of them is open to some objection which would be fatal to the collecting and distributing of salmon eggs on a large scale.

The first river below Snake River, on the Oregon side of the Columbia, is the Walla Walla. This river, although on the same side of the Columbia that Oregon is, is nevertheless in Washington Territory, as the Columbia from the mouth of the Snake River to a few miles below Wallula lies wholly in Washington Territory. The larger affluents of the Walla Walla River rise in the Blue Mountains,

about 100 miles east of the Columbia. About 15 miles from the
Columbia they become united, and now, under the name of the
Walla Walla River, their combined waters empty into the Columbia
at Wallula Junction. Although several persons have recommended
the Walla Walla as a good river for our purpose, and although in
times of high water many salmon run up this stream, it is nevertheless, I am convinced, too small a river to conduct any large
operations on in the way of collecting salmon eggs. The river is
scarcely more than 60 feet in width at low water, and shallow a
quarter of a mile from its mouth; and a river of this size would not
carry a sufficient volume of water to induce salmon enough to enter
it to furnish any great number of eggs in these times of canneries;
for it should be remembered that the immense canning operations
carried on along the Columbia River have entirely revolutionized
matters, as far as the abundance of salmon eggs is concerned.
Twenty years ago, before the business of canning salmon on the
Columbia was inaugurated, salmon literally swarmed up all the
small creeks and little tributaries of the main river in such immense
quantities that several million eggs could, without doubt, have been
easily collected from the spawning fish at the head of comparatively
insignificant streams; but that day has gone by, probably forever.
The vast number of nets that are being continually dragged through
the water at the canneries on the main river during the fishing
season catch millions of full-grown salmon on their way up the
river to spawn, and of course reduce to a corresponding extent the
number of parent fish that reach the spawning-grounds. The
comparatively few that succeed in running the gauntlet of the
innumerable nets in the main river would, if they could be gathered
together at one spot, still be enough to supply a great many million
eggs; but those which ascend the river above the nets, instead of all
going to one place, separate and divide up among the hundreds of
tributaries, large and small, that help to form the great Columbia.
Consequently a very small percentage, indeed, of the few salmon
that get by the nets are to be found in any one manageable stream,
unless some peculiar natural causes exist at some specified place to
make that point an exception to the general rule. It is accordingly
useless to look now to small streams which are subject to ordinary
conditions for a large supply of salmon eggs, however abundant the
salmon used to be in them in the former and better days of these
salmon rivers. . . .

I wish to add, however, that if Washington Territory and the
State of Oregon, between which the lower Columbia flows, could

agree upon a code of good protective laws for the salmon, the Clackamas River would again teem with salmon as before, and in that event perhaps the best point for a breeding station would be on that river where the station of the Oregon and Washington Fish Propagating Company was built in 1877. Before the times of canneries and excessive netting of the salmon in the lower Columbia, the Clackamas in Oregon was as good a salmon river as the McCloud in California, and if the salmon should ever be allowed to reach it, it might be again.

> Livingston Stone, *Explorations on the Columbia River from the Head of Clarke's Fork to the Pacific Ocean, Made in the Summer of 1883, with Reference to the Selection of a Suitable Place for Establishing a Salmon-breeding Station* (Washington, D.C.: Government Printing Office, 1885), 241-43, 254.

Document:	**Salmon Fisheries of the Columbia Basin**
Author:	Marshall McDonald, U.S. Commissioner of Fish and Fisheries
Year:	1894
Description:	This report makes an early argument that overfishing must be addressed as a prime cause of salmon decline.

Conditions Determining the Salmon Production of a River Basin

THERE ARE FUNDAMENTAL conditions determining the salmon production of a river basin and the nature and extent of the fisheries which may be maintained without overtaxing the productive capacity of the river. All the species of salmon which are the object of the fisheries are alike under the constraint of a natural law, which compels them to enter the fresh waters for the purpose of spawning. Some species ascend to a relatively short distance above tide water. Others, like the chinook, push their migrations to the remotest sources of the rivers and tributary streams when not prevented by natural or artificial obstructions. Where the area of distribution is contracted by the erection of barriers, dams, or other obstructions which the salmon can not surmount, the production of the river is diminished *pro tanto,* for the reason that the young salmon remain for some months in the waters in which they are hatched—they must here find their food—and consequently the extent of the feeding-grounds open to them will be the measure of nature's ability to repair the waste occasioned by natural casualties and the fishing operations. If there be no contraction of the breeding area by artificial obstructions, but, on the other hand, the times, methods, and apparatus of the fisheries are such as to intercept or in a large measure prevent the run of salmon into and up the rivers, then a serious decline in the fisheries is inevitable.

It is possible by fish-cultural operations pursued on an adequate scale, by hatching and planting the fry in the head waters of the Columbia and its tributary streams, to realize the full productive capacity of the river, so long as eggs can be obtained in sufficient numbers to furnish a basis for the extensive operations required. This would not be possible, however, if the fishing operations in the lower river practically excluded the salmon from the streams to which it would be necessary to have recourse to obtain a supply of eggs. It is evident, therefore, that fish-cultural operations can not be relied upon exclusively or chiefly to maintain the salmon supply in the Columbia. The regulation of the times, methods, and apparatus of the fisheries should be such as to assure the largest opportunity practicable for reproduction under natural conditions. Artificial propagation should be invoked as an aid and not as a substitute for reproduction under natural conditions. . . .

Decrease of Salmon in the Head Waters of the Columbia River

The investigations made by Prof. Evermann and the parties under his direction establish conclusively the fact that there has been a very great reduction in the number of salmon frequenting the head waters of the Columbia River and its tributaries. This decrease is more notable in the main river. In the early history of the fishery salmon were found in the head waters in marvelous abundance. According to the information obtained by Prof. Evermann:

> They were abundant in the Columbia River at Kettle Falls as late as 1878. Since then there has been a great decrease. They have been scarce since 1882. Since 1890 there have been scarcely any at Kettle Falls. The Meyers Brothers say that they have been almost unable to buy any salmon for their own table from the Indians for three years. Certain Indians with whom we talked at Kettle Falls said salmon were once very abundant there, but that very few are seen now. Other persons testified to the same effect. Essentially the same information was obtained regarding the decrease of salmon in other parts of the upper tributaries of the Columbia, viz: at Spokane, in both the Big and Little Spokane rivers, and in the Snake River and its various tributaries.

Dr. O. P. Jenkins, an assistant of Prof. Evermann, makes the following report in reference to the Yakima River, Washington:

> The Yakima is the main stream of the valley. It receives many tributaries, the main ones being Manistash and Wilson creeks. The river near the city (Ellensburg) is 160 feet wide, by an average of 10 feet deep, and flows with a velocity of 1 foot per second. Temperature at 9:15 a.m., August 24, 1893, 60° F.; water clear. Those acquainted with the facts state that formerly, up to about 1885, salmon of three or four kinds, including the quinnat, ran up the stream to this valley and spawned in the river in great numbers; at present very few make their appearance.

> There is no reason to doubt—indeed, the fact is beyond question—that the number of salmon now reaching the head waters of streams in the Columbia River basin is insignificant in comparison with the number which some years ago annually visited and spawned in these waters. It is further apparent that this decrease is not to be attributed either to the contraction of the area accessible to them or to changed conditions in the waters which would deter the salmon from entering them. We must look to the great commercial fisheries prosecuted in the lower river for an explanation of this decrease, which portends inevitable disaster to these fisheries if the conditions which have brought it about are permitted to continue.

> Marshall McDonald, "The Salmon Fisheries of the Columbia River Basin," in *Report of the Commissioner of Fish and Fisheries,* Senate Mis. Doc. No. 200, 53rd Congress, 2d session, 1894, 3-5.

Document:	**Fish and Fisheries**
Author:	Reporter with the *Morning Oregonian;* as was the practice of the period, no by-line was given.
Year:	1896
Description:	In this newspaper interview, W. A. Wilcox, another agent of the U.S. Fish Commission, argues the need for hatcheries.

MR. W. A. WILCOX, the agent of the United States fish commission, of Washington, D. C., is in this city on his regular tour of inspection of the waters of the entire Pacific coast, from Cape Flattery to

San Diego. Mr. Wilcox is an interesting talker, and, when seen at the
Imperial hotel last evening, furnished some interesting information
about the fishing interest. This is his third trip out here, his first
tour of inspection being made eight years ago, and his last four
years ago. On each occasion he finds a wonderful increase in the
number of fisheries, and the fishing industry generally, and from all
reports he looks for a corresponding increase this year, as the result
of his tour. Dull times have tended to increase the number of
fishermen, perhaps for the reason, as Mr. Wilcox says, that with no
other avenue for work and needing but small capital many were
driven into it that perhaps under ordinary circumstances would not
have been in it. At any rate, there is room for all, he says, as the
demand for fish is wonderfully on the increase.

The result of my many investigations is showing clearly that the
demands for fish throughout the United States is increasing all the
time, and it is only by means of artificial propagation that it can be
kept up, and even with the best that can be done at that the demand continues in excess of the supply a large part of the time. . . .

Mr. Wilcox had just returned from a run down to Astoria, which,
as he says, he found exceedingly dull, as the result of the strike, and
with no packing going on. He knew nothing of the merits of the
controversy, and wisely refrained from even inquiring into it.

When questioned about the salmon of the Columbia and on the
Pacific coast, and its scarcity on the New England coast, Mr. Wilcox
said:

"It is not generally known by the present generation, and has
been forgotten by the older men, that in the early history of the
United States all the rivers of New England abounded with
salmon equal in quality to the best Columbia river salmon, but,
by reason of that country becoming densely populated and all
the waters of the rivers becoming polluted by sewerage, drainage
and factories, the salmon began to grow fewer each year, until
today salmon is a thing of the past. There are a few yet being
caught in the state of Maine, enough to furnish sport to anglers,
but nothing in a commercial way.

"The vast volume of fresh water coming down the Columbia will
make it almost impossible ever to pollute it sufficiently to drive
away the salmon, and it is hardly possible that civilization will
ever crowd its banks to an extent that will endanger that industry, so I suppose it is safe to say that Columbia-river salmon will
always continue to be a choice dish in all parts of the world.

"Of course, the increasing demand for fish and the growing
scarcity of the same will call for more aid toward artificial propagation in order to keep up the supply, and this is what the fish

commissioners are looking out for. They are doing all they can in this direction, and will continue doing so, consistent, of course, with the appropriation placed at their disposal for that purpose."

Mr. Wilcox, previous to being connected with the United States fish commission, was manager of the American fish bureau of Gloucester, Mass., and secretary of the Boston fish bureau. He has made fish and its culture the study of his life, and since his connection with the government has been traveling in all sections of the United States, investigating the fisheries of the Great Lakes, the Atlantic coast and inland rivers and streams.

> "Fish And Fisheries. Importance Of The Industry In The United States. Additional Hatcheries to be Erected on the Columbia—Interesting Talk with an Expert," *The Morning Oregonian*, 5 June 1896, n. pag.

Document:	**Local Populations and Conservation of Salmon**
Author:	Willis Rich, a biologist at Stanford University and the first chief of research for the Oregon Fish Commission
Year:	1939
Description:	In a benchmark essay in salmon biology, the author presents evidence that salmon species are organized into distinct local populations.

Willis Rich, while a professor at Stanford University.

THE STUDY OF the migrations of the salmon of Alaska and the Pacific states has been actuated by the conviction that a knowledge of the movements of these fish is essential to the formation of a sound conservation program. The conservation of any species may be defined as the maintenance of the abundance of that species at a level that, with due regard for the requirements of the future, appears to be the most desirable from the point of view of

Man. Such maintenance of a population, whether of mice or men or of fishes, requires that the births and deaths shall be equal over a period of time. It is the function of conservation efforts to produce this condition and it is the function of conservation research to provide the information necessary to guide these efforts. . . .

In the conservation of any natural, biological resource it may, I believe, be considered self-evident that the population must be the unit to be treated. By population I mean an effectively isolated, self-perpetuating group of organisms of the same species regardless of whether they may or may not display distinguishing characters and regardless of whether these distinguishing characters, if present, be genetic or environmental in origin. Given a species that is broken up into a number of such isolated groups or populations, it is obvious that the conservation of the species as a whole resolves into the conservation of every one of the component groups; that the success of efforts to conserve the species will depend, not only upon the results attained with any one population, but upon the fraction of the total number of individuals in the species that is contained within the populations affected by the conservation measure. . . .

Turning now to a consideration of the salmon of the Pacific states and Alaska, I shall take up first the evidence relating to the existence of local populations and then that bearing on the nature of the movements of certain of these populations.

Evidence of the existence of local populations of Pacific salmon may be considered under three heads: (1) morphological and chemical, (2) statistical and (3) experimental.

1. A list of demonstrated morphological and chemical differences between fish running into different streams would be long and varied. It can only be stated here that there have been shown to be constant differences in size, both with and without differences in age; significant differences have been observed in the size of the mature eggs; differences in chemical composition especially as regards the oil content of the flesh have been shown—differences that exist at comparable stages of the spawning migration and so cannot be ascribed to differences in the length of time elapsed after leaving the feeding grounds; small but statistically significant differences exist in respect of such characters as proportional measurements and counts of vertebrae, fin rays, etc. Of a somewhat different nature are the differences observed in the scale markings which, in effect, provide a permanent and continuous record of the rate of growth throughout the life of the fish.

2. What I have chosen to call the statistical evidences of local populations include the persistence over long periods of time of distinctive age group ratios (as determined from scale examinations) and of distinctive cycles of abundance. The two are often related especially in cases, as that of the famous Fraser River sockeye run, in which the size of the breeding population is the chief determinant of future abundance. Such distinctive cycles of abundance have been demonstrated with statistical significance for a number of Alaskan streams and for at least two species, the red and pink salmon (*O. nerka* and *O. gorbuscha*).

3. Experimental evidence of local populations of Pacific salmon rests chiefly upon the results of numerous large marking experiments involving an aggregate of some three or four million young salmon. These have been marked by clipping fins before or during the seaward migration and the adults were recovered from the commercial fisheries or from the spawning areas. I started a series of such experiments on the Columbia River in 1916 and since then hardly a year has passed in which additional experiments have not been started. Most of these have had to do with the Chinook salmon (*O. tschawytscha*) and the sockeye or blueback (*O. nerka*). The results have shown beyond any reasonable doubt that the marked fish return in overwhelming proportions to the stream and even to the tributary in which they spent the early part of their existence. Aside from the evidence indicating the return of the adults to their home streams these experiments have provided evidence on a number of other problems that do not bear so directly upon the main subject of this discussion. Other evidence, experimental in nature, is that provided by the establishment of salmon runs in streams where no runs previously existed; as in the case of the Chinook salmon run into Spring Creek and that of the red salmon runs that were maintained for a number of years in Herman and Tanner Creeks, all in the Columbia River basin; similarly the gradual rehabilitation of depleted runs when properly protected over a period of years. The mere fact that the run of one stream may be depleted by too intensive exploitation while that of a neighboring stream is not is strong evidence in favor of the existence of local populations. . . .

To summarize: Diverse evidence points so clearly to the existence of local, self-perpetuating populations in the Pacific salmon that any hypotheses that do not conform must be subject to considerable doubt. This, I believe, must be accepted as a proved fact regardless of what may or may not be discovered about the extent of the oceanic migrations, regardless of how the migrations and particularly the return to the home stream may be accomplished and regardless of the reasons why the movements are made. Practical conservation measures must be based upon the acceptance of the "home stream theory" as an essentially correct statement.

> Willis H. Rich, "Local Populations and Migration in Relation to the Conservation of Pacific Salmon in the Western States and Alaska," in *The Migration and Conservation of Salmon*, publication no. 8, American Association for the Advancement of Science (Lancaster, Pennsylvania: Science Press, 1939), 45-47.

Document:	**Future of the Columbia Fisheries**
Author:	Willis Rich (see previous document)
Year:	1940
Description:	A biologist makes an urgent call for restraint and "sacrifices" to ensure the fisheries.

THE SALMON RUNS of the Columbia River constitute one of the most important natural resources of the states of Oregon and Washington. Thousands of people are dependent, wholly or in part, upon these resources for their livelihood; and their welfare is dependent upon the maintenance of the salmon runs. It is to the special interest of these people that the salmon supply be maintained at the level of maximum productivity and, indirectly, it is to the interest of all the citizens of these states that this be done.

In recent years it has become increasingly evident that these resources, taken as a whole, are decreasing in productivity and it has been frequently pointed out that this decrease is due primarily to the operation of two factors—a very intensive fishery and a reduction in spawning and rearing areas due to the utilization of the water resources of the Columbia basin for other purposes. These influences, however, have affected the several species of salmon that are found in the Columbia River quite differently; the more valuable species, Chinooks and bluebacks, showing more evidence of depletion than do the other species, silver salmon, chums and steelhead. . . .

The future outlook for the salmon fishery of the Columbia River is not bright, but neither is it hopeless. The situation calls for energetic measures if further depletion is to be prevented to say nothing of attaining some measure of restoration. Much additional information will be needed if our efforts to maintain and improve the runs are to be efficient. It will be necessary to restrict the commercial fishery to reduce catches, to improve conditions on the breeding grounds and to be eternally watchful that in the further development of water resources due consideration is given *from the beginning* to the needs of salmon conservation. The effects of whatever measures are adopted must be continually studied in order that their efficiency may be accurately determined, that good methods may be improved and poor ones discarded. This will mean on the part of all elements in the salmon industry the sacrifice of immediate gain for the benefit of the future. It will even mean sacrifice on the part of some of the agencies whose duty it will be to impose restrictions and which depend upon taxation of the catch for their income. Such sacrifices require courage as well as foresight and will bring a certain amount of hardship: But, if the courage is lacking now to take the steps necessary to sensible conservation, we shall have the losses and the hardships eventually anyway; with the difference that, if action is delayed, depletion will have progressed further and rehabilitation made just so much more difficult. This will mean also unselfish cooperation on the part of all agencies directly concerned with the development and prosecution of a conservation program: They must be able to present a strong and united front to the opposing forces, and they must act promptly. A few more years of inaction, of failure to attack the fundamental phases of these problems, and the runs may well have been reduced to a state of commercial extinction from which, if recovery is possible at all, it can be accomplished only after a long time and at great expense.

Willis H. Rich, "The Future Of The Columbia River Salmon Fisheries," *Stanford Ichthyological Bulletin* 2(2) (1940): 37, 46.

Document: **Artificial Propagation in Oregon**

Author: George Staley, a contract writer for the Oregon Department
               of Fish and Wildlife

Year: 1982

Description: This unpublished study recounts the troubled history of the
               hatchery idea and its execution in Oregon.

THE IMPETUS FOR the artificial propagation of Pacific salmon began
thousands of miles away from the West coast along the Mirimichi
river in New Brunswick. In 1869, the large Atlantic salmon hatching plant exporting eggs to the United States was closed due to the
hostility of local residents to the carrying-off of their "salmon
seed." The final indignity being the price demanded by the Canadian government of $40 per thousand eggs, payable in gold.

Four years later, the American Fish Culturists Association (later
the American Fisheries Society) petitioned Congress to undertake a
program of food fish culture, especially the culture of salmon.
Congress acted on the petition by appropriating money to be
disbursed at the discretion of the United States Fish Commissioner,
Spencer F. Baird.

Commissioner Baird called a meeting of the Fish Culturists
Association to decide how the money would be best spent. The
group concluded that millions of salmon eggs could be taken from
Pacific salmon at a cost equal to the taking of only a few hundred
thousand Atlantic salmon eggs and Livingston Stone was dis-
patched to California to establish an egg-taking and eyeing station.

A Harvard graduate and ordained Unitarian minister, who had
retired from the church to take up the more healthful and invigo-
rating profession of trout culture, Livingston Stone established the
first salmon-breeding station of the United States on the McCloud
river on the morning of September 1, 1872. He successfully pioneered many of the hatchery techniques in use today and
succeeded in sending crates of eyed-eggs to the east coast by stage
and railroad.

In 1877, the Oregon and Washington Fish Propagating Co., a
group of cannery owners concerned with the declining salmon

Staley's unpublished typescript contains a number of typographical errors,
which we have taken the liberty of correcting. We have also omitted most
of the citations.—Eds.

pack, invited Stone to Oregon to assist them in setting up a salmon hatching plant on the Columbia. Probably the Company learned, as did others from the private-sector, that they could no longer carry on the work at the expense of the few for the benefit of the many, and the hatchery they built on the Clackamas river was ultimately leased by the Oregon Board of Fish Commissioners when that body was organized in 1887. The Oregon legislature, however, was disinterested in fish culture and failed to appropriate any money to fund the work so the hatchery passed into the hands of the U. S. Fish Commission.

The operation of the Clackamas Hatchery was soon interfered with by mills, timber cutting in the watershed and dams. A dam at Gladstone completely blocked the salmon run and the hatchery was idled while the Fish and Game Protector entered into an unsuccessful 1893 court fight to force the provision of fish-ways.

In many ways 1894 seemed the darkest of hours to the State's fish culturists. Despoliation of the rivers and blockage of the spawning runs were already beginning to take their toll on some stocks. At the same time the promise of artificial propagation seemed so bright, yet so distant. The legislature was aloof to the pleas of the hatcherymen; the Clackamas Hatchery troughs sat empty; the money the legislature had appropriated—$2,000—had been spent building a hatchery on the Siuslaw river, but no salmon ever arrived at the racks because fishermen downstream had stretched their nets completely across the channel. With the country in the grips of a depression resulting from the financial panic of 1893, probably little hope was held out for further funding.

"The helpless salmon's life is gripped between two forces—the murderous greed of the fisherman and the white man's advancing civilization," Stone had declared in an address before the American Fisheries Society in 1892, " . . . and what hope is there for salmon in the end?"

It was the wastage occasioned by the act of natural reproduction that so appalled the hatcherymen and spurred their efforts on behalf of fish culture. The Fish and Game Protector (1896) estimated that only 10 percent of naturally deposited salmon eggs ever so much as hatched. Livingston Stone was alleged to have excavated chinook redds in California, finding only 8 percent "vitalised."

Arguably, the mortality suffered by salmon in the early stages of life are the highest and most variable, but the process of egg fertilization and implantation in the gravel is more efficient than fish culturist[s] envisioned. Dill (1969) considered a 10 percent survival rate from egg deposition to fry emergence in natural streams to be about average for pink and chum salmon and Solazzi and Martin (1982) estimated a 5 to 20 percent survival to smolting to be within the normal range for spring chinook.

Nevertheless, the streams the hatcherymen were concerned with were often far from "natural," being choked with sediment and rotting sawdust, blocked by crude power dams, or diverted into a maze of unscreened irrigation ditches and dewatered. Improving on the economy of nature by increasing the reproductive success of the salmon was at least something that could be done to sustain the runs.

Experimental ponding and feeding of fry began around the time the "Central Hatchery" was built on Tanner creek at Bonneville in 1909. Heretofore, fry had been released soon after they absorbed the yolk-sac, but some of the more enterprising cannery men pointed out to the Fish and Game Commission that from thirty to fifty million fry were being released every year into the Columbia with no apparent effect and perhaps more care was required. At first, food consisted of beef liver, but later ground smelt, salmon offal, salt salmon, horse liver and offal, and even potatoes were used.

Returns to the hatcheries beginning in 1917 seemed markedly better, the feeding experiments deemed a great success, and the practice was adopted by the U. S. Government.

The State had begun to take an interest in the work of artificial propagation around the turn of the century and in 1909 had appropriated the $12,000 necessary to build the Bonneville hatchery. Bonneville was the flagship of the hatchery system from the very beginning. Given the encroachment of civilization upon the salmon spawning streams and the demonstrated success of transferring eyed-eggs, it became the policy of the department to ship the eggs from hatcheries on the spawning streams to the Central Hatchery to raise the fry. In this way the fry could be safely released below all the saw mills, irrigation ditches and power wheels, directly into the Columbia.

The McKenzie Hatchery, established in 1902 near Vida, began shipping eggs to Bonneville, as did hatcheries constructed on the Middle Fork of the Willamette in 1911 and on the North Santiam in 1913. Although the "home-stream theory" had begun to gain some currency by 1917, the policy of transferring most or all of the eggs away from the hatcheries on the spawning streams, first to Bonneville and later to both Bonneville and Klaskanine, persisted until 1921.

The early part of this century was marked by overzealous, often reckless, expansion of artificial propagation in Oregon. When a series of sudden, unprecedented floods interfered with racking operations on the Middle Fork of the Willamette river in 1912, the master fish warden, the chief fish culturist, and the superintendent of the McKenzie hatchery decided to rack the river at its confluence with the McKenzie river in order to turn the entire Middle Fork spring chinook run into the McKenzie river. There they would be held behind racks until the time of egg maturation.

Material was on the ground and the racks completed on May 20, 1913. The spring chinook began to appear, nosing the pickets, but on May 29, 1913, the river unexpectedly rose nine feet in 24 hours and, carrying large trees and other debris, swept away the racks and the fish escaped upstream.

The hatchery work and concomitant management of the fishery became so extensive that separate Game and Fish Commissions were organized in 1921. By at least 1937, fish culture was fully institutionalized and the Fish Commissioner of Oregon reported to the legislature that the efficiency of Oregon's hatchery system was without peer.

It was not a time for complacency, however; new and larger threats to the salmon resource had rumbled over the horizon. Rock Island Dam, the first mainstream dam on the Columbia had been completed in 1933, and water would soon start to pool behind Bonneville Dam. Already the ACE [U.S. Army Corps of Engineers] was surveying the Willamette basin for water development. In their first report to Congress on what was to be known as the Willamette Valley Project, the ACE noted that the greater part of the spring chinook run in the North Santiam, South Santiam, McKenzie, and Middle Willamette rivers were propagated artificially by the Oregon Fish Commission.

Since there was much doubt as to the feasibility of through migration of anadromous fish due to the proposed high dams, the ACE felt that extensive and modern hatcheries were required as a substitute for the natural spawning. A later FWS [U.S. Fish and Wildlife Service] report put it more bluntly: ". . . the Federal Government should not spend large sums of money on fish protective devices the success of which would be doubtful, in order to make available spawning areas which are now largely unused."

Even at this late date the hatcheries had not proven their worth to biologists and conservationists. Many felt the complacent confidence of fishermen, laymen, and administrators in the ability of artificial propagation to counterbalance the inroads of civilization was a serious stumbling block to the development of proper conservation programs. To the water development agencies of the Federal government, however, fish culture was a boon.

And what hope was there for salmon in the end? As water development got underway in the Columbia basin in the early 1940's, it seemed everyone was betting on the techniques of artificial propagation of salmon pioneered by Livingston Stone.

> George Staley, "The Growth of Artificial Propagation in Oregon," in *Oregon's Mitigation Experience. The Performance of Anadromous Fish Compensation Programs Operated by the ODFW*, (Oregon Department of Fish and Wildlife, 1982, photocopy), 8-13. (Citations omitted.)

Document:	**Review of Fish Production Facilities**
Author:	Columbia Basin Fish and Wildlife Authority, a consortium of state and federal fish and wildlife agencies and of Indian tribes
Year:	1989
Description:	The following documents a fish agency's account of the history, development, and management of hatcheries.

Development of Fish Culture Practices

WHILE ANADROMOUS FISH hatcheries have operated on the Columbia River for over 110 years, it is only in the last three decades that hatchery programs have become effective. Very little information on the biology and culture requirements of salmon and steelhead was available during the early years of fish culture. In the late 1800's and early 1900's most hatcheries only released unfed fry soon after the eggs were hatched. The young fish are particularly vulnerable at this stage and it is doubtful whether hatchery production contributed much in the way of adult returns because of poor survival. By 1905, annual hatchery production in the Columbia River had reached 62 million eggs and fry.

Most of the knowledge of fish culture in the early years was acquired through trial and error rather than by scientific methods. It was soon learned that increased survival and greater contribution to returns could be achieved by releasing fish that had been fed for an extended period. Ground liver, spleen, fish carcasses, animal by-products, and vegetable feedstuffs were used extensively for feed. This diet posed a number of problems that were not recognized at the time. For example, it was not known until the 1960's that salmon fed diets not fortified with proper levels of vitamins, anti-oxidants, and minerals could not effectively metabolize animal fats and that such hard fats caused anemia and degenerative changes to the fish's internal organs. Feed containing untreated salmon carcasses also spread tuberculosis, bacterial kidney disease, and other serious fish diseases.

Increased research efforts in the late 1950's and early 1960's revolutionized fish culture practices. The development of the Oregon Moist Pellet (OMP) feed was a breakthrough in fish nutrition. Fish fed OMP experienced much greater survival and contributed more to the fishery than fish fed the old meat diets. The development of vitamin fortifications made it possible to develop dry pelleted feeds which could be stored without refrigeration for extended periods and resulted in less feed wastage. Dry and moist pelleted feeds are now produced to specific standards for protein, mineral, vitamin, fat and fiber content geared to the specific needs of the fish although much is yet to be accomplished to provide improved diets.

In the early years, hatchery success was measured primarily by the total numbers of fish released. By the early 1960's, better diets and larger hatcheries made it possible to increase the size of the fish released and marking experiments showed that much better survival could be achieved in some cases by releasing larger fish. Marking experiments were also valuable in determining the best time to release the fish to optimize survival. Rearing and release strategies for hatchery fish also were improved because of advancements in understanding the process of smoltification. Smoltification is the combination of physiological and behavioral adaptations that enable juvenile salmon and steelhead to successfully migrate from their natal streams to the ocean and to survive and continue to grow in their new environment. While much is yet to be learned, substantial progress has been made in identifying factors that inhibit smoltification and seawater tolerance.

Advances in other areas of fish culture yielded a better understanding of optimum rearing densities, water treatment, and
facility design. The development of specialized analytical instruments enabled better monitoring of dissolved oxygen, pH and
other critical water quality parameters for rearing salmon and
steelhead in the hatchery environment. Substantial progress was
also made in understanding fish pathogens and parasites and in
developing means for their prevention, treatment, and control.
This knowledge focused on the need for pathogen free water
supplies and for additional rearing space rather than more intensive use of hatchery facilities already operating near capacity.

Past Management of Hatchery Stocks

The management of Columbia River fish stocks has changed
dramatically over the years, and has continued to change in response to declining fish runs, changing harvest patterns, expanded
hatchery production, the acquisition of new knowledge, and court
decisions. In the early years, the primary criteria for selection of
most stocks for hatchery production were the accessibility and
availability of broodstock and eggs and the relative commercial
importance of the stocks. Stock transfers among hatcheries were
very common and often were driven by the objective of meeting
full station production without giving adequate consideration to
the suitability of the donor stocks.

The stock concept had not evolved and salmon and steelhead
were thought to be very similar over much of their range. Only
after years of observation and lack of success with stock transfers
did recognition of the importance of individual stocks emerge. In
the meantime, basic knowledge of fish genetics was limited and it
was convenient to use the stocks that were readily available. There
also was little information available on the interaction between
hatchery and natural or wild stocks. As a result, hatchery fish were
planted throughout the Columbia River Basin without an adequate
evaluation of the potential impact on the genetic integrity of
native fish, competition for limited food resources, fish disease, or
suitability of the hatchery fish for their new environment. Even less
information was collected on the success or failure of these ventures.

The rapid increase in survival of hatchery fish that occurred in
the 1960's was a boon to the sport and commercial fisheries but
created new problems for fishery managers. Mixed-stock fisheries
that relied heavily on hatchery fish often overfished individual
natural stocks. One of the reasons this occurred was because any

future benefits that could be derived from protecting a single stock by severely limiting fishing appeared small in comparison to the immediate loss of harvest of the more abundant hatchery stocks. Lack of adequate data for identifying individual stocks in mixed-stock fisheries was also a contributing factor.

By the 1970's, increased knowledge of the genetic differences among the stocks of salmon and steelhead accumulated through analysis of migration, life history, biochemical, and morphological information. Genetic data and theory suggested that genetic differences affecting survival of stocks increased with geographic separation from the stream of origin. It was recognized that relocation of stocks from distant geographic areas reduced their survival potential. New information on fish health also raised concerns over the effect of stock transfers on the spread of fish diseases throughout the Basin. As a result, more restrictive policies were adopted by the fishery agencies that limited the transfer of stocks into and throughout the Columbia River Basin. In addition, some streams were designated for management of self-sustaining natural production, and release of hatchery fish was prohibited.

The use of native stocks in hatchery programs has increased in recent years and greater emphasis has been placed on operating and managing hatcheries to retain, as much as possible, the characteristics of the stock from which the broodstock was obtained. For example, the practice was adopted at most hatcheries of taking eggs from the entire run rather than from just one segment of the run in order to maximize genetic variability. Practices were avoided that resulted in selective breeding or increasing the rate of inbreeding; for example, most hatcheries now avoid using a small number of males for spawning with a large number of females which was a common practice in the past that could have caused a reduction in genetic diversity.

The emphasis of salmon fishery management in recent years also shifted more toward regulating the rate of harvest on individual stocks in mixed-stock fisheries. This resulted from an increased emphasis on protecting stock diversity, from improvements in management of ocean and in-river fisheries, and from Federal court decisions regarding Indian treaty fishing rights that guaranteed the tribes the right up to a 50 percent share of the harvest from salmon and steelhead runs destined to pass through their usual and accustomed fishing areas.

Columbia Basin Fish and Wildlife Authority, *Review of the History, Development and Management of Anadromous Fish Production Facilities in the Columbia River Basin* (1989), 19-24.

Commentary

THE TROUTS, SALMONS, AND CHARS emerged about forty million years ago during the Eocene. Six million years ago the salmonids and chars were still evolving into the species we know today. The ancestors of the John Day River spring chinook knew the saber-toothed tiger and saw the immense shadows of the hairy mammoth. Humans have appreciated the salmon in ritual and relied upon them for food for over ten thousand years. Salmon became embedded in Northwest Indian culture.

People of European heritage became acquainted with the salmon in the Northwest in the late 1700s and depended upon them for food as the country began to attract white settlers in the 1830s. The natural history of Pacific salmon was described as early as 1880, when A. C. Anderson, Inspector of Fisheries for British Columbia, introduced the idea that salmon are organized into separate stocks. As a fisheries scholar, J. McDonald, wrote in 1981, Anderson recognized that "salmon stocks to major B.C. rivers are discrete, that the supply of salmon available varies from river to river, and he notes the relationship between the number of parent spawners and the resulting return to the fishery."[1]

Anderson and his successor, John Peace Babcock, established stocks as the basis for managing British Columbia's salmon fishery. As McDonald observed, regulation of the fishery "reflected their views, and included limiting fishing effort, restricting seasonal and weekly fishing periods, and restricting fishing gear."

In the United States, however, biological knowledge and management evolved differently. Livingston Stone, who operated in Oregon and Washington in the 1880s as an agent of the U.S. Fish Commission, was probably the most influential of the early specialists in salmon management. He was apparently unaware of the observations of Anderson and Babcock in British Columbia. In the report of a survey of the Columbia Basin in 1883, Stone showed his belief that salmon ran up rivers randomly, being attracted most to large streams that entered the Columbia in a fast torrent:

> It may not be generally known that a strong, rapid current of cold water is the most effective agent there is for inducing breeding salmon to turn from their course up a large river. It is very much a matter of chance whether they enter a river, even a large one, which is still and deep at its mouth. Such tributaries will certainly not attract the salmon into them from any great distance out of the main river. [2]

Stone believed that for salmon to find a suitable spawning river, the river must make an "impression" on the fish to draw them up it. For example, because the Cowlitz and Willamette rivers were slow where they entered the Columbia, he did not consider them good salmon streams.

One consequence of Stone's misunderstanding of salmon biology was that artificial production of salmon in hatcheries took on a greater importance for salmon production than it otherwise might have. Stone was an influential advocate for salmon hatcheries. In 1877, he had developed the first hatchery in the Columbia River Basin. He was hired by the Oregon and Washington Fish Propagating Company, a consortium of salmon cannery owners, who were worried about the declining salmon pack. The hatchery was constructed on Oregon's Clackamas River, and its purpose was to increase the supply of salmon to the commercial fishery.

The decline of the Columbia River salmon runs had already begun. In 1874 a commercial fisher harvested 30,000 pounds of sockeye salmon from Idaho's Payette River, but by 1880 this run of sockeye had become commercially "extinct"—there were not enough salmon to make it worthwhile fishing. Downward trends were also being observed elsewhere, and by 1886 Columbia River chinook were showing signs of depletion and the cannery operators were alarmed.

In 1883, Stone, operating as a federal employee, was given the task of finding a suitable place for a "salmon breeding station" in the Columbia River Basin. Regulating the commercial harvest of salmon to perpetuate the fishery was apparently not an option. Instead, emphasis was placed on developing hatcheries to maintain the supply of salmon. Stone (p. 242) observed:

> Twenty years ago, before the business of canning salmon on the Columbia was inaugurated, salmon literally swarmed up all the salmon creeks and little tributaries of the main river in such immense quantities that several million eggs could, without doubt, have been easily collected from the spawning fish at the head of comparatively insignificant streams; but that day has gone by, probably forever.

Stone was not alone in lamenting the decline of the Columbia salmon fishery or in prescribing hatcheries as the primary solution. In 1894 several reports were issued by the U.S. Fish Commission presenting another inventory of the Columbia Basin. These reports focused on salmon abundance, distribution, and spawning habits and found that the salmon were already declining and were becoming depleted in many watersheds. Following on this inventory, W.A.

Wilcox, another agent of the U.S. Fish Commission, told the *Morning Oregonian* in June 1896 that "the growing scarcity" of salmon "will call for more aid toward artificial propagation in order to keep up the supply."

Some scientists, however, were not so optimistic about hatcheries as the solution. One was Marshall McDonald, U.S. Commissioner of Fish and Fisheries, and Wilcox and Stone's superior. In 1894 McDonald wrote that "Until the States interested [in building more salmon hatcheries] adopt measures to restrain net fishing, so as to permit a portion at least of the salmon entering the river to pass up to their spawning-grounds, it is not deemed wise or expedient to attempt to increase or extend the work of artificial propagation of the salmon" (p. 18).

McDonald recommended against establishing further hatcheries in the Columbia River Basin. Nevertheless, more hatcheries were built—and the salmon continued to decline. Not until the 1930s was there another attempt to inventory the Columbia Basin salmon runs to determine their life history, abundance, and distribution, and the condition of their habitat. This time the provocation was dams.

In 1933 Rock Island Dam was completed on the Columbia above the Snake River; construction of Bonneville Dam and Grande Coulee Dam was underway. In 1934 the U. S. Bureau of Fisheries, the successor of the U.S. Fish Commission, began the inventory. The study was to include a detailed survey of all streams of the Columbia Basin that supported or had formerly supported salmon and steelhead. The goal was to determine the condition of these tributaries and provide the basis for improving their condition so they could be made more productive for fish. As of the mid-1930s "nearly all of the populations of salmon and steelhead trout in the Columbia Basin were depleted," the Bureau of Fisheries noted.

Salmon biologists were plainly alarmed by the prospect of dam construction throughout the region. Willis Rich, the first chief of research for the Oregon Fish Commission, noted that the builders of Bonneville Dam provided "no assurance" that "the provisions to be made for the passage of fish past the dam would prove successful." As the main-stem dam nearest the ocean, Bonneville was clearly crucial to upstream migration for many populations. But at the time, ten more dams were planned for the Columbia River, nearly as many for the Snake River, and a series for the Columbia's largest Oregon tributary, the Willamette River. Rich warned that "[e]ach [dam] will challenge the knowledge and ingenuity of the fishery conservationists and, perhaps even more, will test the courage and spirit of those administrators whose duty it may be to preserve and maintain our fishery resources."

As it turned out, sometimes the administrators saw their duty differently. When Frank Thomas Bell was appointed United States Commissioner of Fisheries in 1933, fisheries scientists threw up their hands in despair. Bell was a real estate developer who promoted Columbia Basin development and specifically the construction of Grand Coulee Dam. He offered bland assurances that nothing would go wrong:

> Contrary to the impression created by certain self-constituted critics who, although uninformed as to the true situation, have aired their pessimistic views in the press, we have no reason to believe that the Columbia River salmon are in danger of extinction. We feel confident that the preservation of the great national resource of Columbia River salmon is assured.[3]

If Bell was a shill for development interests, developers themselves could be more blunt. As J. F. Hosch, a New Deal leader in the Oregon legislature, remarked to journalist Richard Neuberger, "Must the Willamette Valley forever remain a wilderness so that the supply of salmon may be maintained?" Representative Hosch accused his critics of being "unquestionably more concerned about a few fish than about the people who inhabit our land."

In this political climate, hatcheries were again seen as the solution to continued salmon production. As George Staley makes clear (in his unpublished 1982 paper on salmon mitigation), "To the water development agencies of the federal government fish culture was a boon. In the Columbia Basin in the early 1940's it seemed everyone was betting on the techniques of artificial propagation of salmon pioneered by Livingston Stone."

The salmon managers should have known better and might have acted differently. In 1938, Willis Rich had published the first research paper for the Oregon Fish Commission, on the conservation of Pacific salmon. He had conducted a decade of study of salmon migration, through the use of tagged fish, and had determined that the "evidence shows clearly the existence of local, self-perpetuating populations of salmon." "Practical conservation measures," he wrote, "must be based upon protection of local populations." He stated his principles plainly. "In the conservation of any natural, biological resource," he wrote, "the population must be the unit to be treated. By population I mean an effectively isolated, self-perpetuating group of organisms of the same species. It is obvious that the conservation of the species as a whole resolves into the conservation of every one of the component groups." With this essay, Rich rediscovered the original insights of Anderson and Babcock in British Columbia a half-century earlier. Rich called his version of the stock concept the "home stream theory" of salmon conservation. "Practical conservation measures must be based upon the acceptance of the 'home stream theory,'" he wrote.

However, Rich's views were not shared by fishers, fisheries administrators, and the dam builders, who were convinced that hatcheries would protect and recover the fisheries. His ideas lay fallow for another twenty years, when the Columbia River Fisheries Development Program timidly proposed the restoration of natural salmon populations. The program, funded by Congress in 1957, presented plans to set aside streams as fish refuges. But this idea met with little success in the Oregon and Washington legislatures. Instead, the major consequence of the program was the building of twenty-one salmon and steelhead hatcheries in the lower Columbia River.

What does this history teach? Each time a crisis in salmon abundance has occurred in the last hundred years, the response of society has been to ignore long-term natural remedies to the crisis and opt for short-term technological fixes. That preference has resulted in the endangered species alarm of the 1990s. Whether populations of native salmon will ultimately fare any better now depends upon society's ability to overcome the legacy of failed salmon management.

The current crisis had its beginnings in the 1870s, propagating today's list of extinct salmon runs, a degraded salmon ecosystem, and squandered public benefits. The institutions society built to manage salmon have had 130 years to bring us to this juncture. It will take knowledge, commitment, and precious time to bring the salmon safely beyond it.

—Bill M. Bakke and Joseph Cone

Notes

1. J. McDonald, "The Stock Concept and Its Application to British Columbia Salmon Fisheries," *Canadian Journal of Fisheries and Aquatic Science* 38 (1981): 1657-64.
2. Livingston Stone, *Explorations on the Columbia River from the Head of Clarke's Fork to the Pacific Ocean, Made in the Summer of 1883, with Reference to the Selection of a Suitable Place for Establishing a Salmon-breeding Station* (Washington, D.C.: Government Printing Office, 1885), 6.
3. Frank T. Bell, "Guarding the Columbia's Silver Horde," *Nature*, January 1937, 46.

HATCHERIES: AN ARTIFICIAL SOLUTION

Document: **The Fish Supply**

Author: John Hittell, a prominent California journalist, wrote books on the resources and economic potential of California.

Year: 1882

Description: This excerpt from an 1880s examination of West Coast commerce extols the potential of hatchery production.

The Fish Supply.
Division V.—Fisheries, Etc.
Chapter XIX.—The Fish Supply.

FISH ABUNDANT.—The waters of the North Pacific, and especially those on the American side, are wonderfully rich in many valuable kinds of fish. Most of the species are different from those of the Atlantic, but the important kinds are well represented here, including the cod, halibut, mackerel, herring, salmon, smelt, sardine, flounder, and sturgeon. Of the kinds less valuable commercially, we have some that the Atlantic has not, and lack some that it has. Many intelligent observers, familiar with the fisheries of Europe, have expressed surprise at the greater abundance of fish on our coast. . . .

PISCICULTURE.—Congress provided, about 1870, for the appointment of a national fish commissioner, who should import valuable food fishes, and distribute them to the various States and Territories. . . .

In California nearly a dozen varieties of fish have been introduced by the commission, and with but one exception, the eel, they are increasing rapidly. The success in catfish and shad has been remarkable. The former, unknown here previous to its introduction by the commissioners, is now so abundant that the annual sales amount to double the appropriation made by the State for the propagation of fish. The new varieties which the commission are about to introduce are the gourami, from Cochin China, and a larger and better variety of shad from China, called there samli.

With a view of increasing the supply, the commissioners have had a standing arrangement with LIVINGSTON STONE, Deputy United States Fish Commissioner for California, to hatch out and put into the Sacramento River and its tributaries the McCloud and Pit, 1,500,000 or 2,000,000 salmon every season. . . .

Pit River near Fall River has a fall of 41 feet. At this fall a fish-ladder, about 450 feet long, has been blasted out during the past season, opening new spawning-beds, 280 miles in extent—an area more than equal to that of the McCloud and Upper Sacramento together. The appropriation of $5,000 should be doubled, and a hatchery built on the Pit; but the commission will not ask for this money, because they claim that their work speaks for itself.

The salmon-hatching establishment on the McCloud River, under the superintendence of Mr. STONE, produces from 600,000 to 10,000,000 young fish annually, and is the most extensive institution of the kind on the globe. It sends eggs in large numbers to the Atlantic States, Europe, and Austral-asia; and through its help the Californian salmon will probably at no distant time be introduced into every large river in the temperate zone. A mature female salmon lays 20,000 eggs annually, and from all these, when left to the ordinary course of nature, not more than one female, on an average, survives to lay another lot of eggs. By the art of the pisciculturist, the proportion of eggs that will hatch into fish, and of young fish that will reach an age to take care of themselves until they reach a size useful to man, will, it is supposed, be increased at least 50 fold. . . .

In 1879, 150 striped bass (Roccus lineatus) were imported by the fish commission and placed in the Strait of Carquinez, and are probably increasing.

Twenty-four mature lobsters, to which were attached about 2,000,000 eggs, were brought from the Atlantic in 1879, and placed in a sheltered cove near the Golden Gate. None have as yet been caught, but as all conditions seem favorable, the young are probably growing, and it is hoped that Californian lobsters will soon be found in the market.

The Eastern and Californian trout have been introduced into several places, notably the north fork of the American River, and in Alameda Creek. These rivers which, above the falls in each stream, originally contained no fish, are now well stocked with both kinds of trout. Several small streams through the State, which contained no fish a few years since, have also been stocked, and are doing remarkably well.

John S. Hittell, *The Commerce and Industries of the Pacific Coast of North American* (San Francisco: A. L. Bancroft, 1882), 321, 325-28.

Document: **Artificial Propagation of Salmon**

Author: Livingston Stone, who developed the salmon hatchery on California's McCloud River in 1872.

Year: 1896

Description: The principal government innovator in fish propagation gives a historical overview of salmon breeding along the Pacific.

A Brief History of the Salmon-Breeding Work of the United States Fish Commission on the Pacific Coast, with Especial Reference to Operations at Baird Station, California

IN 1864 THE NEW HAMPSHIRE legislature had the intelligence and fore-sight to appoint a fish commission—the pioneer fish commission of the United States—at the suggestion of Hon. Henry A. Bellows, of Concord. Two years after, in 1866, the commission sent Dr. W. W. Fletcher to New Brunswick to procure salmon eggs for Merrimac River. This was the first effort ever made in America in the direction of salmon breeding. Only two or three hundred fry were actually known to have resulted from this expedition, but it was a begin-ning—a small beginning, it is true, but one which opened up a field of operations that has since been enlarged beyond the most san-guine expectations. . . .

. . . Baird station of the United States Fish Commission was founded in August, 1872. It was known as McCloud River station until 1878, when the writer, having succeeded in getting a post-office established on the river, named the post-office "Baird," after the distinguished first Fish Commissioner of the United States, Hon. Spencer F. Baird, since which time the station has been called Baird station.

The first plant on McCloud River was a very modest affair. It consisted of a rough-board, one-room cabin, 10 by 14 feet, and 24 hatching-troughs in the open air, each covered, of course, but with no roof over them. The results of the first year were modest enough, too. The whole net product of the season's operations was only 30,000 salmon eggs, costing over $100 per 1,000, and when these were shipped across the continent to their destination in New Jersey 24,000 were lost in transit, leaving only 6,000 good eggs to be hatched and planted in the tributaries of the Atlantic. Neverthe-less, two important facts were established by the experiment, compared with the value of which the cost of the enterprise was trifling. The experiment established the fact that salmon eggs could be obtained in future from the Pacific Coast, and probably in large quantities, and also the fact, most important of all at that time, that salmon eggs could be shipped alive across the continent. The last fact was the more valuable, because up to that time salmon eggs had never been subjected to a long journey by rail, and serious doubts had been often expressed by experts as to the possibility of getting salmon eggs alive from the Pacific to the Atlantic. . . .

The foreign demand for ova had increased to such an extent by 1877 that during that year salmon eggs were sent from the McCloud to Prussia, Germany, the Netherlands, England, France, Canada, Australia, and New Zealand. The experience acquired in packing and shipping the eggs enabled us this year to get them to their destinations with very slight loss in transit. . . .

Owing to the destruction of the salmon by the railroad workers, Professor Baird discontinued operations at the salmon-breeding station on McCloud River in 1884, and they were not renewed till 1888, when the writer was made field superintendent of the Pacific Coast, and instructed by Hon. Marshall McDonald, then United States Commissioner of Fish and Fisheries, to push vigorously the salmon-breeding work on this coast. The writer reopened Baird station in the spring of 1888, and leaving Mr. George B. Williams, jr., in charge as temporary superintendent, proceeded to Oregon to carry out the instructions of the Commissioner to secure for the United States the salmon-breeding station on Clackamas River, Oregon. This station, which the writer built for the Oregon and Washington Fish Propagation Company (cannery owners on the Columbia) in 1877, was still owned by them, but had been leased to the State of Oregon. The company at first wanted $10,000 for the station, but after several weeks of consulting and negotiating they consented to deed the place to the United States for nothing, and the Oregon commissioners gave up their lease on the reimbursement to them by the United States of the actual cost of improvements they had just made. The transfer was practically made July 1, 1888, on which day the splendid salmon-breeding plant on Clackamas River became a station of the United State Fish Commission. . . .

[Concerning t]he Clackamas station, in Oregon, I will say that unfavorable conditions have already set in there and seriously interfered with the operations of the station. When it first passed into the hands of the United States Fish Commission it yielded 5,000,000 salmon eggs a year, but it was too near civilization to prosper long as a salmon-breeding station, and gradually mills and dams, timber cutting on the upper waters of the Clackamas, and logging in the river, together with other adverse influences, so crippled its efficiency that it was given up this year as a collecting-point for salmon eggs, but several million eggs have been sent there from Baird station and Battle Creek, so that a very respectable number of salmon eggs will doubtless be hatched for the benefit of Columbia River this season. . . .

When the work of the United States Fish Commission in salmon breeding was begun on the Pacific Coast, it was supposed that that coast had enough salmon to spare, and it was the intention of the Commission to increase the salmon on the Atlantic Coast by restocking its depleted salmon rivers. The highest hopes were entertained of doing this. After it had become an accomplished fact that millions of salmon eggs had been procured on this coast, and that they had been safely transported across the continent to the Atlantic rivers, I doubt if there was one person who had heard about it in America, whether interested in fish-culture or not, who did not believe that salmon were going to become abundant again in the Atlantic rivers on account of the introduction of the Pacific Coast fish; and not only this, but many persons believed that several southern rivers that had never had salmon in them before, would now become prolific salmon streams, when they were well stocked with this new California salmon that abounded in warm latitudes on the Pacific Coast. That this did not prove to be the result was a stupendous surprise and disappointment. The eggs hatched out beautifully. The young fry, when deposited in the fresh-water streams seemed to thrive equally well. They grew rapidly and when the proper time came were observed to go down in vast numbers to the sea. What afterwards became of them will probably remain forever an unfathomable mystery. Except in very rare isolated instances, these millions of young salmon were never seen again. . . .

This, however, is only one side of the case. As soon as the requisite space of time had elapsed after the United States Fish Commission began to return young salmon fry to the Sacramento, the fishes of that river showed a great increase. New canneries sprang up every succeeding year. The market for fresh and salted salmon in San Francisco felt the effects of the salmon-breeding work on the McCloud. . . .

It thus appears that although nature has evidently designed that the quinnat-salmon shall not take up its abode on the American shores of the Atlantic, the breeding of this fish seems to serve a legitimate and very valuable purpose in keeping up the supply of its species in its native waters of the Pacific Slope; especially in view of the enormous drafts made upon these fish by the canneries and by the yearly increasing consumption of fresh and salted salmon.

> Livingston Stone, "The Artificial Propagation of Salmon on the Pacific Coast of the United States, With Notes on the Natural History of the Quinnat Salmon," *Bulletin of the United States Fish Commission* 16 (1896), 205, 208, 213, 216-20. (Citations omitted.)

Commentary

THE HUMAN EXPERIMENT of the last ten thousand years has been to modify and simplify ecosystems. Agriculture succeeds by taking diversity out of an ecological system, at least for a short period of time, and by focusing ecosystem productivity on a selected crop. Fish propagation is a similar system. Four hundred years ago, Francis Bacon argued that human societies could develop the knowledge to control nature. Newcomers to the West Coast brought the Baconian philosophy and technologies to achieve control over this untamed environment. Entrepreneurs, politicians, and scientists led the way in rearranging the ecosystem to make it more productive and to yield the products people desired.

For a century the salmon managers of the Pacific Northwest felt they could control and introduce desirable changes to the ecosystem. This is reflected in the experiments of R. D. Hume. Hume left the Columbia after 1876 and moved to the Rogue River because he felt the Columbia was overfished. To keep productivity high on the Rogue River, Hume established a hatchery and experimented with hatchery methods. As with current experiments, it is unlikely that Hume controlled enough variables to scientifically document the effectiveness of hatcheries. The excerpts from John S. Hittell and Livingston Stone show both the promise of pisciculture, or artificial propagation, and some of the unintended consequences. Human societies continue to simplify, rearrange, add to, and enhance the productivity of ecosystems. These excerpts show the confidence people had in the nineteenth century—and that many retain today—that the environment could be made better if one species were added here and another moved over there. Each change was made without regard to the impact on the whole system.

Livingston Stone, a pioneer of fish propagation, notes that artificial fish breeding on the West Coast was financed by the federal government, which hoped to improve the depleted salmon resources on the East Coast of the United States. The first problem Stone had to solve was the transportation of salmon eggs across country. He accomplished this using the new transcontinental railroad and refrigeration technologies put together by the entrepreneurial robber barons. This technology facilitated transportation in both directions. Hittell, who extolled the business opportunities on the Pacific Coast, notes the many introductions from the east to the west, including shad and striped bass, which took much better than did the salmon transported to the East. These rearrangements of ecosystems did not stop with East-West transfers. As Stone notes, salmon were also introduced into South America and New Zealand.

The single-element, pieces-of-systems approach still characterizes our strategies for dealing with fisheries. Even the management approaches used until very recently looked at one species at a time. Fishery managers have no control over forest practices, land use planning, power development, and many other activities that affect the viability of fish runs. It is also interesting to note Stone's initial disappointment with the cost of salmon transport to the East Coast. A recurring theme is how the cost effectiveness of the salmon-rearing operations drove many of the decisions.

Managing fish and forests through the concepts of maximum sustainable yield has for half a century raised hopes for maintaining environmental quality while producing sustained growth. In the 1930s E. S. Russell introduced into fisheries concepts about maximizing agricultural production. W. E. Ricker defines maximum sustainable yield as, "The largest average catch or yield that can continuously be taken from a stock under existing environmental conditions."[1] Maximum sustainable yield management is institutionalized in legislation establishing fishery management practices. The Magnuson Fishery Conservation and Management Act of 1976 requires that fishery management plans "assess and specify the present and probable future condition of, and maximum sustainable yield and optimum yield from, the fishery" (16 U.S.C. 1853). The optimum yield is the maximum sustainable yield modified by relevant ecological, economic, and social factors. Subsequently, "sustainable" has become a fashionable modifier for "agriculture," "development," "economics," "energy," "environment," "fisheries," "forestry," "futures," "growth," "livelihoods," and "world." Most meanings of "sustainability" suggest that we can continue living in a habitat or using a resource in the same way well into the future.

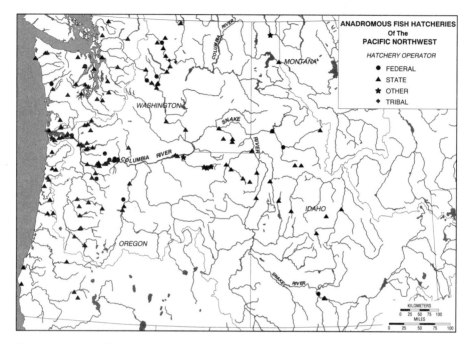

Hatcheries in the Columbia Basin, though numerous, have not stopped the salmon decline and in some ways have contributed to it.

Sustainable yield management has been successful in few fisheries. Most fish stocks are overfished and not close to levels that fishery biologists think could be sustained. Why, after fifty years of sustainable yield management, are fish stocks in such poor condition?

The answer lies in the Baconian belief that people can develop the knowledge to control nature. Sustainable yield management assumes that if we only had enough knowledge we could manage the system for the benefit of human beings. Bacon also emphasized that with adequate knowledge humans could experience progress, a general betterment in their quality of life. Because of the cultural priority given to progress, sustainable yield management is a continual struggle to hold off the environmental threats posed by the pressures of economic growth. Fisheries, then, represent on a smaller scale the problem society faces as a whole. If sustainable yields cannot be achieved for fisheries, then how will sustainability be successful in much more complex systems?

The problem with simplifying ecosystems, as we do when we attempt to manage them for human benefit, is that when niches are rearranged some species benefit while others lose. We have yet to invent the technology to predict the results of simplifying very complex systems. Complexity, then, is one factor that makes the managing of ecosystems problematical. In addition, as Livingston Stone's experience on the Clackamas shows, other uses of rivers—mills, dams, timber practices—adversely affect salmon runs. Indeed, the Clackamas hatchery was forced to receive salmon eggs from other areas less affected by the changes of "civilization."

Continuing the Baconian legacy, new concepts of ecosystem management, biodiversity, ecosystem health, habitat restoration, and sustainable development hold the same promise—-with more knowledge we can make things better. The experience of a century and a half of simplifying, modifying, and moving around salmon species, however, is that the condition of the fish stocks does not meet our goals. Hatchery stocks are now too abundant and wild stocks too scarce.

—Courtland L. Smith

Notes
1. Ricker, W.E., *Computation and Interpretation of Biological Statistics of Fish Populations* (Ottawa: Fisheries and Marine Service, 1975), 4.

THE CREED OF A SALMON CAPITALIST

Document:	**Salmon of the Pacific Coast**
Author:	R. D. Hume, a leader among the first generation of salmon cannery owners and hatchery operators in the Northwest
Year:	1893
Description:	An early entrepreneur discusses the natural history of salmon, the effects of human development on the fish, and propagation techniques for salmon.

Salmon cannery magnate R.D.Hume.

The Salmon of the Pacific Coast
I. Their Influence upon the Industries and Share in the Development of the Northwest

To give the reader a clear idea of the salmon industry of the Pacific Coast, and the influence it has had in the development of the Northwest, it will be necessary to give a brief history of the salmon canning business, the advent of which practically begins the salmon fishing era of the Pacific Coast; although prior to that time the taking of salmon had been done to considerable extent to supply the market with fresh fish, and a moderate quantity had been salted. But in comparison with the canning business, the quantity taken for these purposes was of little importance.

The business of canning salmon on the Pacific Coast was begun in the spring of 1864, at the town of Washington, Yolo county, California, on the banks of the Sacramento river, opposite the foot of K street, Sacramento city, by the firm of Hapgood, Hume & Co., the firm consisting of Andrew S. Hapgood, George W. and William Hume, with the writer as "sub" under small pay, but with large expectations of a partnership interest, to be realized whenever the business should prove the success anticipated. The pack of the first year amounted to about 2,000 cases, and the trials and difficulties attending their production are almost impossible to realize and describe, after the lapse of twenty-nine years, considering the improved methods of to-day. . . .

In the next two years the amount packed per annum was not much increased, on account of the scarcity of salmon in the Sacramento, and in the spring of 1866 William Hume went to the Columbia to see what could be done. Upon his return with favorable reports, G. W. Hume also went to the Columbia, for the purpose of selecting a site and building a cannery and other necessary buildings, that should be ready for the reception of the others, who went there some time in October of that year. The point selected by him was at Eagle Cliff in Wahkiakum county, Washington, and part of the cannery now owned and operated there by Wm. Hume is the original building erected by him. During the winter of 1866-67 we put our machines in order and made the nets and cans for the spring season of 1867, at which time we packed 4,000 cases of 48 cans each. . . .

In a lapse of ten years, what a change! Portland has by this time become a city of importance, and Astoria has stretched itself along three miles of water front; while instead of four small landings along the main Columbia, between Astoria and Portland the number has increased to more than forty, and instead of one small steamer making tri-weekly trips, we have four elegant steamers running between these places daily, besides about a dozen running in the fish carrying trade for the use of the canneries, and in place of a product of 4,000 cases of 48 tins each, we have a product of 450,000 cases, of the same number of tins, and we have our wheezy and dilapidated old mills running night and day to supply the demand for lumber to build new canneries, and where desolation ruled before we find signs of the greatest activity. We find all trades and professions plunging to get a whack at this new El Dorado, all seeking a fortune to be made from the capture of the scaly beauties. What a mine of wealth, that even all who might plunge might be enriched. But all good things which nature has furnished have a capacity beyond which they cannot be strained, and the year 1883 brings Columbia its maximum, when the vast quantity of 630,000 cases was reached; and from this time begins the decline of the salmon product of that wonderful stream. . . .

What a contrast between the years 1867 and 1892, as regards the industry. At the first date one cannery, with its small product, having great difficulty in obtaining sufficient employees to prosecute the business, while in 1892, in addition to the large number of canneries in British Columbia and on the Columbia river, which were employing thousands of people, there was not a stream putting into the ocean along the Oregon and California coast, which can be entered even by the lightest draught vessels, that has not one or more canneries located on its banks, . . .

The salmon industry of the Pacific coast has furnished lucrative employment to thousands, and has been both directly and indirectly the means by which very many have made fortunes, and who without its benefits would perhaps find themselves out of employment and lighter in pocket.

In view of the great importance of this industry, it would seem the imperative duty of all engaged or in anywise interested in the business to protect and preserve, so far as is possible, the source from which the essential factor springs, namely, the salmon of the Pacific coast; and the best efforts of the minds of those who are in any manner familiar with the conditions which are favorable to that end should be turned in that direction. The writer, firmly believing in the principles set forth in this section, although well aware that there is much yet for him to learn regarding the matter, proposes to give to the public as the result of the observations of a lifetime, a series of articles, wherein will be contained a history of the experiments made and experience gained by constant contact with the business in its various forms, hoping thereby not only to add his mite to the general fund of knowledge of the subject, but also to call forth from others such information as may have been gained by their experience, in order that, ere the streams of our State have been exhausted, and while such information may be of practical use, that the public may receive the benefit.

2. Their Value as a Food Product and the Proper Methods for their Protection

For many years prior to the advent of salmon canning on the Pacific Coast, owing to the scarcity of these fish in other parts of the civilized world, salmon had become a luxury of which none but the wealthy could partake, and the writer, when a small boy, heard two of the wealthiest citizens of his native town (Augusta, on the Kennebec river, in the State of Maine) argue for half an hour as to how a salmon of ten pounds weight should be divided so that each should get a fair proportion of the fat, and which should have the head part; and finally, after appealing to the large crowd of bystanders for their opinions regarding the question, at length settled the matter by cutting the fish on an angle, from belly to back, so as to give the one with the tail portion a fair share of the belly; and then paid $1 per pound for their portion, and went home with smiles on their faces and eyes glistening in anticipation of the glorious feast they were to have on the morrow.

At this time, which was about the year 1853, the catching of a salmon at this point on the Kennebec river was of rare occurrence, usually the catch for a season being three or four, and a half dozen being a large take for the year. At this time the principal supply of salmon for the markets of the United States was procured from the Penobscot river in Maine and the waters of the British provinces, namely: Mirimichi river, and the rivers putting into the bay of Chaleur; and these could be obtained only in limited quantities, and at a great expense to the consumer. Up to the age of eighteen, the time the writer left home for the Pacific Coast, although some of his family were engaged in the fishing business, it had never been his fortune to taste salmon but once, and it is doubtful if but few in that State of his age had ever seen one. What a blessing came to the poor with the establishment of the salmon canneries, and with their progression, an increasing benefit, to that extent that in 1892, allowing one can for two persons, which is amply sufficient, one hundred and thirty-five millions of poor people could enjoy, once in a year, such a luxury—and considering the amount of nutrition and ability to satisfy the appetite, at less than the price of any kind of flesh food.

In the early days of the salmon business South America and Australia furnished the consumers for the product, but as the supply increased a market in England was sought, which at first did not take kindly to the American product; but by the persistent efforts of a few of the principal dealers in food products (one of the most active of which was the firm of Pelling, Stanley & Co., of Liverpool, now one of the largest distributors of canned salmon in the world) the article became known, and the people of Great Britain in a short time became the principal consumers. A great deal of the prosperity enjoyed by the business is due to the efforts of these gentlemen, who were pushing, progressive people, their perceptions being alive to the fact that in this new product was embodied a nutritious food supply for the masses at the lowest possible cost, as compared with the products of other descriptions. . . .

In view of the fact that the salmon supply is a matter which, as a figure in the food question of so many millions, is of much importance, as well as being the source of so much wealth to the Pacific Coast, it certainly would seem strange if the people of this country did not feel disposed to foster both the business and the source from which it derives its life. It is the desire of the writer to present such facts for the consideration of his readers as will shed some light upon a question which, although it has been treated in various forms by very able writers for more than forty years past, still, in view of the success made by the operation of any plans laid down in the various works upon the subject, or benefits derived from legislation upon the matter, seems yet to the great majority as being in an experimental state. The first point to consider in this connection is the question, What were the conditions of the various streams when the salmon supply was most plentiful.? And it is easily answered: There is no question but salmon were most plentiful before civilization had begun its work, and when dams, traps and other obstructions and hydraulic mines were unknown, when the sources of the river were unsettled and undefiled by the sewerage of the cities, the forests at the head waters still untouched by man, and the country yet in its natural state.

The effect of a change of conditions can be best indicated by a description of the situation on a few of the salmon streams that have been either wholly exhausted or rendered practically useless for commercial purposes in this branch of industry, and those that are rapidly approaching that condition.

Taking the Kennebec river, which was a fine salmon stream at the early settlement of the country, and reflecting upon the possibility of the supply being maintained under the conditions which were in effect in the year 1853, the mind is easily satisfied as to the causes which led to the almost total extinction of these fish. By this time cities were located within a few miles of each other all along the banks, discharging their sewerage and waste from gas and dye works into the stream, while at Augusta was situated a dam which was impassible for any sort of fish, no provision for a fish ladder having been made, until through the exertions of Seth Green (who has been justly termed the father of fish culture in America) about 1857 one was constructed, but was soon allowed to get out of repair, and was of no practical use. There were also a large number of sawmills delivering their sawdust and other waste into the river, the timber was being rapidly removed from the tributaries which formed the headwaters and spawning grounds of the stream, while the lower part of the river, in Merry Meeting bay and other favorable locations, was lined with traps to such an extent as to render the escape of a fish almost an impossibilty [sic], and only a very narrow channel was left for the passage of steamboats, and this running in such a serpentine course as to require a skillful pilot to work the vessel through.

The Sacramento river, prior to the introduction of hydraulic mining in 1853 was, during the running season, so plentifully stocked with salmon that no use could be made of but a moiety of the supply, and we have an illustration of the destructive force of this new agent when we consider the fact that eleven years after its introduction the Sacramento river was practically rendered useless for commercial purposes as a salmon stream.

The Klamath river furnishes another illustration of the destructive action of hydraulic mining upon the salmon streams of the coast. In 1850 in this river during the running seasons, salmon were so plentiful, according to the reports of the early settlers, that in fording the stream it was with difficulty that they could induce their horses to make the attempt, on account of the river being alive with the finny tribe. At the present time the main run, which were the spring salmon, are practically extinct, not enough being taken to warrant the prosecution of business in any form. The river has remained in a primitive state, with the exception of the influence which mining has had, no salmon of the spring run having been taken except a few by Indians, as a reservation by the government has been maintained, until within a few years, and no fishing has been allowed on the lower river by white men; and yet the spring run has almost disappeared, and the fall run reduced to very small proportions, the pack never exceeding 6,000 cases, and in 1892 the river producing only 1,047 cases.

The next and most important river on the coast to receive consideration is the Columbia, and this, though not yet exhausted, has shrunken its output since 1883, in the number of cases produced, more than one-third, and according to good authorities the product of 1892 was but little more than 150,000 cases of true adult Chinook salmon, the balance of the pack being steel-heads, blue-backs, and a small salmon of a variety which will later receive attention. This, if true, would show a fearful decrease in the past nine years, amounting to more than three quarters of the supply of the quality packed when at its best; and from both packers and fishermen comes the cry that, although the demand for the article is good, they are unable to make living profits from the prosecution of the business. A contemplation of this proposition leads one to inquire what have been the conditions that have brought about such a result, when since 1883 the number of canneries on that river have decreased considerably, and during the time a hatchery has been in operation, which has turned out millions of young salmon every year.

Prior to 1879 traps and fish wheels cut a small figure in the methods of taking salmon on the Columbia river, the few traps in operation being mostly in the vicinity of Oak Point, the lower river about Astoria being free from their influence. Since 1883, however, the number of traps at Astoria and fish wheels on the upper river have rapidly increased, with a corresponding decrease in both the quality and quantity of the salmon packed on that stream, as well as a rapid falling off of the profits of the business. The question will naturally be asked, in view of the difficulties surrounding the proposition, can the supply be maintained in such a manner as to protect the industry? This I answer in the affirmative, if the operations toward stocking the rivers are maintained in a proper manner, and the right sort of legislation is had upon the question of taking the product of the rivers. . . .

A careful attention on the part of the fish commission of the State regarding obstructions which prevent the salmon from reaching the natural spawning grounds, such as dams and traps, placed entirely across the streams, would be a powerful factor toward the preservation of the species; and the passage of a law which would make it a crime for taking or having a gravid or spawning salmon in possession, except for spawning purposes, with the assistance of the other factors mentioned above, assisted by the operation of such hatcheries as the importance of the business seems to justify, would enable the industry to remain as permanent a branch as that of agriculture.

Professor Baird often said that "one acre of water was worth seven acres of land, if properly cultivated," but I am convinced that the Professor erred only in this, that I believe one acre of the waters of any salmon stream in Oregon, if judiciously cultivated under favorable circumstances, and if not paralyzed by ignorant or vicious legislation, is worth more as a medium for the product of a food supply than forty acres of the best land in the State. The fact, however, that there are many different streams which produce salmon that have their runs at different times in the year, and also that the same river may afford runs of different kinds at various times in the year, makes any laws heretofore passed, which apply to the seasons they have sought to close, inapplicable to the necessities of the case, and productive of more harm than good. In view of this position of affairs I would submit the following plan to my readers, which to my mind, in addition to the preceding sections, seems the only way of taking a grasp of the whole question with any certainty of realizing a benefit:

Let an act be passed by the legislature which shall provide for the appointment of a Chief Fish Warden for the State, who shall have deputies in every county, whose duty it shall be to take note of the different runs of Salmon and Trout in his district, and report the same to the head of his department; and an act which shall provide that in parts of such streams, wherein lie the natural spawning beds, no fishing for salmon or trout shall be done for one month prior to, nor at any time during, the spawning time of the different runs, and making it the duty of the fish warden to close such portions of the stream by posting notices at various stations along the banks, denoting such portions as shall remain closed to fishing, and also to publish notices in the nearest newspaper to the same effect, and any violation to be punished by a heavy penalty. Also an act providing that no salmon of any variety in any of the rivers of the State of Oregon should be taken by traps, fish wheels or seines, of less than five pounds weight.

I will add that unless some such steps are taken, in less than ten years the packing of salmon on the Columbia river will have become impossible as a business proposition, and in much less time the truth of this proposition will become apparent. But by the passage of the laws mentioned, and the adoption of the suggestions herein contained, the salmon supply would be kept up without interfering with any other branch of industry, for reasons that will appear in future treatment of other branches of the salmon question.

3. A Short Treatise upon the Commercial Varieties and their Habits....

... With many of the theories that have heretofore been generally accepted, both regarding the habits and culture of salmon, I must disagree, as the light of my experience has shown their fallacies; and it is also with astonishment that I hear persons at this day, in view of the success made in other branches of pisciculture, and with the knowledge of the destruction caused by the encroachments of civilization, making the assertions that all that is required to keep up the supply is to allow a portion of the run to ascend to the spawning grounds, that have been, or are in the process of being, destroyed by every method known to civilization.

I contend that without reasonable exertion for the erection and operation of hatcheries, and the exercise of wise laws for the protection of the spawning grounds, and regulating the size of fish to be taken, the States of Oregon and Washington, which now enjoy a monopoly of the finest quality of salmon in the world, will have soon lost their heritage. The lack of interest manifested by those engaged in the salmon canning business on the Columbia, in the matter of their propagation, is surprising, when very many are aware how simple and inexpensive is the process of merely hatching the eggs—in fact, so simple that any cannery could have a small hatchery, and by obtaining eggs in which the eye spots were formed could finish the process, and when the fish were well developed distribute them with little trouble in the fresh water branches nearest their location. They could also procure eggs, if by concerted action they would establish ripening ponds at the mouths of some of the small streams that put into the lower river, similar in character to those in use at Gold Beach, a description of which will be given in a future discussion of the subject.

4. The Art of Salmon Culture. The Apparatus Necessary for Propagation

In order that any readers who may be stimulated by what is herein contained to undertake the propagation of salmon, may avoid the mistakes and difficulties which were made and encountered by the writer in his early attempts, and the very considerable expense consequent thereto, a short history of the early part of the undertaking may prove useful, as well as furnish some evidence to substantiate the conclusions to which I have arrived in former articles regarding other branches of the question. More than twenty years ago I suggested to the packers of the Columbia river that as other streams, which were formerly abundantly supplied, had at that time become pratically [sic] exhausted, something should be done toward stocking the river; but I was generally met, with the remark "that the salmon would last as long as they would need any." A few years, however, convinced them that they might be mistaken, and the result was the location of a hatchery on the Clackamas river in Oregon.

Hearing that salmon of a fine quality were very plentiful at the Rogue river, I purchased a location and built a cannery there the latter part of 1876, and in the spring of 1877, much to my surprise, packed only 3197 cases, which was all that could be obtained by the utmost exertion, which proved that the reports, except as to quality, were but echoes of the past; and thus I was furnished with the necessity as well as the opportunity to put into practice those crude ideas which had long been forming in my mind. As soon as I realized how few salmon the stream afforded, operations were begun towards stocking by excavating a pond for holding and ripening the adult fish, on a little spring branch which afforded about one thousand gallons per hour, during the dry season, that put into the river about a mile from the bar or entrance, and a small hatching house was built close by the pond. After completing the pond and house I stocked the pond with one hundred adult female salmon and fifty of the male species of the finest specimens that could be selected. After this was accomplished I made a trip over-land to the hatchery on the McCloud river, a tributary of the Sacramento in California, for the purpose of observing the opera-tion of spawning, etc., arriving there in the early part of August, and although the superintendent was away the men in charge kindly went through the operation for my benefit. After making note of the various items of interest I proceeded to San Francisco, where by the kindness of mutual friends I was introduced to the Hon. B. B. Redding, then secretary of the fish commission of the State of California, who proved to be very enthusiastic on the subject of salmon culture, and who, when I stated that I was in pursuit of information upon the subject, advised me to engage the services of a young gentleman by the name of Kirby B. Pratt, who had been employed at the McCloud hatchery for a number of seasons; and acting upon the suggestion I engaged Mr. Pratt, and we at once made our way to Rogue river, when Mr. Pratt took charge, and against all difficulties with which he had to contend, in spite of the fact that he had previously had no experience with fish that had been kept in retaining ponds for the purpose of ripening, from one hundred females, in the following spring succeeded in turning out three hundred and fifty thousand healthy salmon. After turning out the young fry, on account of poor health Mr. Pratt was com-pelled to seek a more genial climate, and thus we were deprived of a valuable assistant in our efforts.

Having made such a success in the beginning, the next season I determined to so prepare, that we should correct the weakness of our system of the year previous and make a much larger output, and with this in view made the pond larger, planked and tarred it, increased the water supply, cut away the timber that heretofore had shaded the place, and made quite a clearing, beside many other, as we thought, improvements about the place. When the season had arrived we placed a fine lot of salmon in the pond, but much to my surprise in a short time they began to swim about near the surface of the water, showing white patches in various parts of their bodies, which kept growing worse until they were covered by a growth of fungus, their eyes blinded, and finally nearly all died, leaving only enough to give us about fifty thousand eggs. At this result of what I

A 1912 publication showed a view of ponds and hatchery buildings at Oregon's Bonneville hatchery.

had considered would enable me to surpass any previous efforts, I was much disheartened, but finally concluded that the trouble came from the planking with which the pond had been enclosed, and that a liberal use of coal tar would correct that, and then everything would go along in good style. So the next year I tarred liberally, but on placing the fish in the pond the same thing occurred. By this time I was so much worked up over the question that I determined to make a radical change. I would no longer trust planked ponds, but build with stone, and as there was a point of solid ledge on the up-river side of the cannery I had the earth piped away from a portion of it down to the solid rock, and built a concrete wall around, enclosing a space forty by sixty feet, and turned in a much better water supply than ever before, believing that I had at last solved the question, and in my mind's eye seeing many young salmon ahead. You can imagine my disappointment and disgust when, after repeating the operation of the year before, the same result occurred. To add to my eagerness to succeed, the crop from the first year's planting came in that year, and for a time the river seemed alive with fish, while with all the force we could muster we were not able to take care of half that might have been caught.

The evidence of the value of propagation being so forcibly brought to my mind made me very anxious to succeed, and I would spend hours on the point above looking at the poor creatures paddling about the surface of the pond, and worry myself sick in the effort to discover a remedy. One day while occupied in this manner I began to reflect upon the propositon [sic], and asked myself the question, under what conditions was the greatest success of this undertaking made? And the recitals of conditions came in this order: a little pond, a little water, a great deal of mud, and so much brush and trees that the place never got the sun. "Eureka!" I cried, *"I've got it!* That is what has been the trouble!" I at once began the construction of a building over the pond that would close out the light, and when completed put in a new lot of salmon, with the result that they showed no signs of the previous trouble. When the building was closed the place became so dark that the fish remained perfectly quiet, probably having the idea that they were in a deep pool, while previously they were bruising themselves badly in their attempts to find an outlet. If the letting in of the sunlight would produce such an effect upon the fish that were in a pond, the bottom and sides of which were constructed from solid ledge and concrete, with the water at a depth of ten feet, and fed by a pure stream, would it not seem reasonable that the removal of the timber and undergrowth at the headwaters of a stream would produce the same result? Would it not also indicate the origin of the so-called salmon disease which has afflicted these fish in the rivers of Great Britain? . . .

5. The Art of Salmon Culture. Propagating the Fish. . . .
. . . It would seem that in view of the simplicity of the methods and certainty of success of salmon cultivation, good evidence of which is shown by the operations of our neighbor in the Dominion of Canada, who in 1887 had established nine salmon hatcheries, by which they have kept up the supply in the various sections of their country, together with the showing made by the writer, whose work has increased the supply of spring salmon in Rogue river nearly four fold, in spite of very adverse circumstances, the record showing that it is the only river in the world where fishing has been done steadily each season that has shown such an increase, while the fall run in the same river, which has not been propagated, has fallen off in as great a proportion, should satisfy any reasonable mind as to the value of salmon culture, and stimulate not only those engaged in the business of canning, but the State and general government, to assist and encourage in every way possible the cultivation of this excellent fish. If the writer, by the feeble efforts which appear in any of the preceding pages, is able to awaken any to the importance

of, and necessity for speedy action, he will have been amply repaid
for his exertion.

R. D. Hume, *Salmon Of The Pacific Coast* (San Francisco: Schmidt
Label and Lithographic, 1893), 6-20, 22-40, 47-52.

Commentary

 R. D. HUME was born in 1845 in Augusta, Maine, and lived
there for eighteen years. During that time he observed the
decline of Atlantic salmon in the Kennebec River. In 1864,
he joined his brothers William and George and a friend,
Andrew Hapgood, in Sacramento, California, where they established one of the first salmon canneries on the West Coast. After a
few years, the Humes believed the salmon runs in the Sacramento
River were in decline, so in 1867 they moved their cannery operations north to the Columbia River. In 1876, following the death of his
wife, R. D. Hume left the Columbia River and settled at the mouth of
the Rogue River along the southern Oregon coast, where he established another cannery. He remained on the Rogue River and ran his
cannery there until his death in 1908.

R.D. Hume was unique among the early cannery operators in that
he not only capitalized on salmon as a commodity, but he was also a
conservationist, at least by the standards of the time. He saw limits to
the resource when others acted as though the supply of salmon was
limitless. Hume constructed the first hatchery in Oregon to ensure a
supply of salmon for his business. He also tried to warn his contemporaries that the salmon were vulnerable to the destructive activities
of humans. To that end his pamphlet, *Salmon of the Pacific Coast,* published in 1893, has the following preface:

> To call the attention of both producer and consumer to the
> danger of the total extinction of this most valuable of food
> fishes, and provide a simple method for their preservation is the
> object of this *Little Work.*

It was appropriate that R. D. Hume dedicated his essay to Thomas
Pelling, an Englishman who helped establish a market for canned
salmon in the British Isles. Shipment of canned salmon to England to
feed factory workers changed the role of salmon in the Northwest
economy forever. For thousands of years salmon were a gift from the

sea in the natural economy of the Indians and were treated with the respect accorded a gift. Entrepreneurs like Hume and Pelling transformed the salmon to a commodity on the world market. They had little incentive to keep the demand for salmon in foreign markets within the sustainable productivity of the resource. The huge pristine runs of salmon were among the first victims of the global economy in the Northwest.

Pioneers from New England brought with them a long association with Atlantic salmon and were aware of the potential for depleting salmon. Hume recalls an incident from his home town on the Kennebec River in which two men fought over the division of a single salmon, presumably because there was a shortage. The vulnerability of the salmon to human actions was a theme that appears throughout Hume's essay. Like most other conservationists of his time, Hume saw only one way to maintain the production of salmon in the face of the inevitable declines caused by destruction of habitat or overfishing—the hatchery.

In 1872, Livingston Stone built the first salmon hatchery on the West Coast. Five years later Hume was constructing his hatchery on the Rogue River. Hume viewed hatcheries in terms of an agricultural model. He writes of the need to cultivate the rivers, estimating that the rewards from doing so would be forty times those achieved from cultivating the land. His misconceptions were not limited to the potential of hatcheries to increase salmon productivity. He also erred in believing that salmon survived after spawning, especially in the smaller rivers. However, he was a keen observer and experimenter, which led him to conclusions that were ahead of his time. For example, he carried on a running battle with Oregon's Master Fish Warden Henry Van Dusen over the proper size to release young salmon from the hatchery. Hume believed the fish should be held in the hatchery until they were five or six inches long before release, whereas the state released young salmon shortly after hatching.[1] Not until the 1940s did it become common practice to hold salmon to the larger size. Hume also observed that salmon were adapted to their home stream (pp. 24 and 40 of *Salmon of the Pacific Coast*). His statement that salmon should be planted only into streams with conditions similar to those of the stream from which they came was not generally accepted until several decades later.

Hume shared one important flaw with the other enthusiasts of artificial propagation: he trusted blindly in the ability of artificial propagation to reverse the adverse impacts of people on the salmon.

By 1930, John Cobb, in his survey of the Pacific salmon fisheries, commented that hatcheries were a major threat to the salmon industry.[2] Cobb's concern was not directed specifically at the hatcheries, but at the blind optimism with which the hatchery program was implemented. He believed it was the lack of any verification of the claims made by hatcheries that in the long run constituted a threat to the industry. Basically Cobb's observation was and continues to be correct.

The significance of Hume's essay is not in its technical facts, some of which are clearly wrong, but in the mind-set it reveals. Hume, like many others of his time, believed that technology in the form of hatcheries could make up for human destruction of the salmon's habitat. That attitude led us to ignore alternative management options that are now no longer a possibility. In the end, the enthusiasm for technology and blind faith in hatcheries did, as John Cobb predicted, contribute to the destruction of the industry.

—James A. Lichatowich

Notes

1. G. B. Dodds, *The Salmon King of Oregon* (Durham: The University of North Carolina Press, 1959), 147.
2. J. N. Cobb, *Pacific Salmon Fisheries,* U.S. Dept. of Commerce, Bureau of Fisheries Document No. 1092 (Washington, D.C., 1930).

THE SCRAMBLE TO REGULATE FISHERIES

Document: **Fish and Game Protector Reports, 1893-94 & 1895-96**

Author: Hollister D. McGuire, Oregon Fish and Game Protector

Year: 1894, 1896

Description: The reports of the Fish and Game Protector offer important government overviews of the serious problems in the Columbia River salmon fisheries, written less than thirty years after the start of commercial fishing. The later report includes recommendations.

Decadence of the Fisheries

IT DOES NOT REQUIRE a study of statistics to convince one that the salmon industry has suffered a great decline during the past decade, and that it is only a matter of a few years under present conditions when the Chinook salmon of the Columbia will be as scarce as the beaver that was once so plentiful in our streams. Common observation is amply able to apprehend a fact so plain. For a third of a century, Oregon has drawn wealth from her streams, but now, by reason of her wastefulness and lack of intelligent provision for the future, the source of that wealth is disappearing and is threatened with complete annihilation. No private individual so wasteful and improvident of his resources would receive the least sympathy from his fellows if he died in poverty and was buried in the potter's field. States like individuals should conserve their sources of income, else they neither deserve nor can expect to enjoy continued prosperity. Though this decadence of the fisheries is plain, a study of the statistics given elsewhere in this report will impress the matter more strongly upon the mind. It will then be seen that the deterioration is more marked and serious than the mere surface conditions indicate. In studying these statistics, it must be borne in mind that the period that elapses from the spawning of the young salmon until it returns to the river to procreate is four years, according to the opinion of pisciculturists; consequently, any interruption of natural propagation would not show its deleterious effects until four years had passed. Likewise, any measures to increase production, whether by natural or artificial means, would not show any apparent results in the increase of the number of fish in the river for four years. This means that the results of our past folly will continue to be felt for at least a period of four years longer, and that the measures now taken to retrieve our error must wait the necessary period for their full fruition. The five years from 1880 to 1884 inclusive was the period of the greatest activity in the canning of Chinook salmon, the pack ranging from 530,000 cases in 1880 to 620,000 in 1884, the highest point being reached in 1883, a total of 629,000 cases. The effects of this excessive fishing were felt as soon as the necessary four years had passed, and with 1885 the run of Chinook salmon began perceptibly to decrease. In five years, notwithstanding still more close and persistent fishing, the pack of Chinook had declined more than one half, and stood at 266,697 cases. For the next three years it was from 60,000 to 90,000 greater, but in 1893 had fallen to 290,000, and the past season was 351,082. The total pack of salmon on the Columbia has by no means fallen so low, as the figures will show, but the difference is made up of inferior fish. Salmon that ten years ago the canners would not touch now constitute from 30% to 40% of the pack. The famous Chinook, upon which the reputation of the Columbia rests, and whose higher prices in the market enables our canners to compete with those of other sections whose product is put up at a much less cost to the packers, has fallen off to less than two thirds the quantity of a decade ago, with the probability that it will still further decline before remedial measures can be made effective. In its place an inferior fish is being substituted, that may do irreparable damage to the reputation of the Columbia River before the average quality of the pack has been restored by an increase of the Chinook. There is another feature that is entitled to consideration. When the great pack was made a decade ago fishermen received less than one half they do now for fish and made more money. The price of Chinook fish to canners has gradually increased, and this season the canners paid five cents a pound, averaging $1.10 per fish. Meanwhile the price of canned salmon has declined in the market. With this increase in the price paid for fish and decrease in the value of their product, canners have only been able to continue in the business by the adoption of improved methods of operating and in effecting a saving in other directions sufficient to offset these disadvantages. The business has concentrated and the number of canneries has decreased one half. Whether they can continue to meet the conditions imposed by this decrease in the supply of fish is a serious question. Certainly a marked increase of fish in the river and a consequent reduction of the first cost to packers would place the industry on the Columbia in a better position to compete successfully with those of Alaska and British Columbia.

First and Second Annual Reports of the Fish and Game Protector to the Governor, 1893-94 (Salem, 1894), 7-8.

FOR IF IT [*THE SALMON*] is to be perpetuated it is absolutely essential, in my opinion, that the recommendations which I have made in my former reports be enacted into law. Let me repeat these recommendations:

First—Repeal all laws for the protection of salmon and enact a new law comprehending the entire subject.

Second—Make the close season for salmon on the Columbia and its tributaries from March 1st to April 25th, and from August 1st to September 25th.

Third—Prohibit the taking of salmon in the spawning streams or within half a mile of their mouths.

Fourth—Establish joint regulations with the state of Washington for fishing on that portion of the Columbia river forming the boundary line between the two states.

Fifth—Provide that all dams in streams ascended by salmon should be provided with fishways and that only such fishways as are designated and approved by the person to whom the enforcement of the fish law is intrusted, shall constitute a fishway within the meaning of the statute.

Sixth—Prohibit fishing for salmon in the Clackamas or Sandy rivers, or within half a mile of the mouths of said streams, except for the purpose of artificial propagation under state or national auspicies.

Seventh—Repeal the fish tax and branding statutes and enact a law levying a license tax upon all fishing gear, to provide a fund to be used to increase the facilities for artificial propagation of salmon, and for performing the work of operating hatcheries.

Eighth—Provide for the protection and restoration of the sturgeon fishing industry by making close season for same, limiting size of fish to be lawfully taken, and by prohibiting the use of Chinese sturgeon lines.

Ninth—Endeavor to secure legislation in the states of Washington and Idaho supplemental to and in harmony with that in this state for the protection of salmon on the breeding grounds.

Tenth—Provide for the building and operation of hatcheries by the state.

Eleventh—Provide for the protection of salmon and other fish by requiring all persons or corporations operating or having in charge any mill race, irrigating or mining ditch connecting with any river, lake, or other waters in the state, to put in and maintain, when required to do so by the fish commissioners, over the inlet of said ditch, canal, or mill race, a wire screen of such construction, fineness, and strength as will prevent any fish from entering such canal, ditch, or mill race.

Twelfth—Pass a law to encourage and promote the planting and cultivation of eastern oysters in the waters of our state and for the protection of same.

Thirteenth—Provide for the seizure and confiscation of fish, game, and deer hides taken in violation of the fish and game laws; also, for the seizure of boats, nets, and all fishing gear used in violation of fish laws.

Fourteenth—Provide for extending and improving the fishway at Willamette falls.

Fifteenth—Provide for the appointment of county fish and game wardens, as outlined in this report.

> *Third and Fourth Annual Reports of the Fish and Game Protector* to the Governor (Salem, 1895-96), 27-28.

Document:	**Fish Commissioners Reports**
Authors:	The 1887 and 1888 reports were prepared by Oregon Fish Commissioners F. C. Reed, E. P. Thompson, and R. C. Campbell. In 1891 George T. Meyers replaced Thompson.
Year:	1887 (published 1888), 1888 (published 1988), 1891 (published 1893)
Description:	These Oregon reports show that fishery regulations fell behind measures that would have protected the fish.

A GREAT DEAL OF fishing gear has been constructed during the past six years, or since the law was allowed to become inoperative, and had the literal law been enforced this year, private property to the amount of $200,000 would have been rendered worthless, and while owing to the wealth of the packers they could have bourne the loss without serious hardship, but it is not so with the fishermen who have their all in their fishing gear, and that being the only means of the support for their families. . . .

While the commission are not required by law to act as policemen, or empowered to make arrests, they have done all they could to have the law enforced, and accomplished it in a quiet way and with better success than if arrests had been made in all cases of violation. . . .

Again, in regard to the close time of August and September, the commission did all they could to have this part of the law enforced and met with much better success than we anticipated from the fact that there was only one of them that could attend strictly to the enforcement of the law. The President being constantly employed at the hatchery to see that the work going on there was done economically and well, and Mr. Campbell having business which called him away for several weeks, left this work almost wholly with Mr. Thompson, who performed effective work when we take into consideration the fact that his field of operation was large, and that it took several days to visit all points. But by going about it quietly, avoiding as much as possible the fact that the lash was in our hands, we saved much expense to the different counties, as well as the State, and succeeded in having all the canneries closed down in a few days.

A few fishermen may have taken fish after the canneries closed, but the amount so taken was small, and as in case of weekly close time we were advised not to look so much after the fishermen, but to stop the packers.

"Operations and Results of the Law," *First Report of State Board of Fish Commissioners to the Governor of Oregon, 1887* (Salem, 1888), 4-5

THE ARRESTS MADE for violating the close law are as follows:

A complaint was made against the owner of a pound-net in Baker's bay for fishing on Sunday. The party was arrested and taken before a justice of the peace in Astoria, and the evidence taken not being sufficient for conviction, the defendant was discharged.

There were five arrests made of parties fishing for salmon with gill-nets; two of which, while they were caught with their nets in the water on Saturday night after six o'clock, were discharged by the justice, as they had not caught any salmon, there being no penalty under the present law for fishing for salmon. The other three had actually caught salmon, so they plead guilty, paid their fine, and were discharged.

Early in August, after all fishing was stopped on the lower river, the commissioners proceeded to the Cascades, and finding all fishing suspended for the season in that vicinity, went on to The Dalles, and there also found the close time respected. While there we received information that a wheel at Celilo had been running and catching salmon in August, and complaint had been made against the owner. We went to Celilo by the next train, but on our arrival there the wheel was not running.

The party complained of was arrested the next day, brought to The Dalles and placed under bonds to appear before a justice of the peace the following day for a preliminary examination. Two days having been spent at this place, two of the commissioners were obliged to return, the other member remaining in order to be present at the trial before the justice. The testimony was taken on both sides and the defendant was bound over under the sum of $1000 to appear before the grand jury.

"Operations and Results of the Law," *Second Report of the State Board of Fish Commissioners to the Governor of Oregon, 1888* (Salem, 1888), 4-5.

WE FOUND IN some of the reports from the different state commissions that the McDonald fish-way was the best, and have written to the company for plans and cost of construction, but have been unable to get any reply. We wrote for a plan of the Rogers patent fish-way, which is a Nova Scotia patent, and got some plans which gave us an idea of its workings, but think it quite expensive, and could not recommend it until we have seen more of it and become better acquainted with its efficiency to obtain the desired results.

"Operations and Results of the Law," *Fifth Annual Report of the State Board of Fish Commissioners, 1891* (Salem, 1893), 4-8.

Document: **Regulation of Fishing Gear and Seasons**

Author: Henry O. Wendler, a biologist for the Marine Research Division
              of the Washington Department of Fisheries

Year: 1966

Description: A biologist summarizes the first hundred years of salmon
              fishery regulation on the Columbia River.

Table 2—Commercial gear regulations on the Columbia River, Oregon and Washington, 1859-1963 (abbreviated)

Year	Oregon	Washington	Regulation
1859		X	Nonresidents prohibited from taking fish on the beach of the Columbia River between Pt. Ellis and Cape Hancock.
1866		X	Unlawful to build a fish trap that would reach more than two-thirds of the way across or wholly prevent the passage of fish up and down the Walla Walla River.
1871		X	Unlawful to build or place a fish trap, weir, seine, or net that would reach more than two-thirds of the way across fresh-water streams or creeks, or that would wholly prevent the passage of fish either up or down. The above gear was not to be used in lakes.
1878	X		Specified minimum mesh sizes and spacing between slats on traps. Also required traps and weirs to have an opening permitting the free passage of fish during the weekly closed period.
1879		X	Passed legislation similar to the 1878 legislation of Oregon.
1890		X	Fixed appliances could not extend more than halfway across any channel or slough.
1891	X		Fixed appliances could not extend more than one-third the way across a channel or slough.

1893		X	Specified the maximum length of fixed gear and the minimum distances between such gear.
1897		X	Minimum size placed on mesh of fixed gear.
1898	X		A fish wheel could not be able to take fish during a closed season.
1899	X	X	Chinese sturgeon line prohibited.
1901	X		Gaffs, spears, and foul-hooks prohibited.
1907	X		Purse seines prohibited.
1909	X		Purse seines permitted in the Columbia River if licensed. . . .

Season Regulation

EARLY ATTEMPTS by each state to regulate commercial fishing on the Columbia River resulted in discontinuity and contradiction in seasons (Table 3).

Table 3—Seasonal regulations governing commercial fishing on the Columbia River by year, 1877-1908

Oregon	Washington	Regulation
	1877	March, April, August, and September closed to salmon fishing. May, June, and July had a weekly closing period from 6:00 p.m. Saturday to 6:00 p.m. the Sunday following.
1878		Same as above except that April was open to fishing subject to an unknown weekly closed period.
	1879	Regulations changed to agree with those of Oregon.
1880		Weekly closed period from sunset Saturday to sunset the Sunday following at any season of the year.
	1881	September opened to fishing. No weekly closed period provided.
	1890	Closed seasons from March 1 to April 10 and from August 10 to September 10.
1891		Closed seasons made to conform with those of Washington, Weekly closed period from 6:00 p.m. on Saturday to 6:00 p.m. the Sunday following.

	1895	Weekly closed period eliminated.
	1897	Illegal to capture or possess sturgeon between March 1 and November 1.
1899		Spring season closed from 12:00 midnight March 1 to 12:00 midnight April 15. Possession of sturgeon illegal from March 1 to November 1.
	1899	Closed season from 12:00 midnight March 1 to 12:00 midnight April 15, and from 12:00 midnight August 10 to 12:00 midnight September 10. No mention of weekly closed periods.
1901		Closed seasons from 6:00 a.m. March 1 to 6:00 a.m. April 15, and from 6:00 a.m. August 15 to 6:00 a.m. September 10. Weekly closed period from 6:00 p.m. Saturday to 6:00 p.m. the Sunday following from April 15 to August 15.
	1901	Fall closed season shortened 5 days by moving its starting time back to 12:00 midnight August 15.
1903		Weekly closed periods eliminated.
	1905	Spring closed season began 12:00 midnight March 15; the fall closed season began 12:00 midnight August 25. The fishing season was thus lengthened 25 days.
1908		Initiative petitions were passed at a general election which radically changed the seasons and legal gear, but these regulations were later repealed and were not enforced.

Henry O. Wendler, "Regulation of Commercial Fishing Gear and Seasons on the Columbia River from 1859 to 1963," Washington Department of Fisheries, *Fishery Research Paper* 2, no. 4 (1966): 24, 26.

Commentary

 REGULATIONS TO PRESERVE salmon stocks came after the development of the fishery. The Oregon fish and game protector's annual report for 1893-94 gives an overview of the problems in the Columbia River salmon fisheries less than thirty years after the resource was commercialized. As the summary shows, the latter part of the 1880s was a time of reduced salmon packs. Seeing lower catches, the use of smaller fish, and the substitution of fish that in the past would not have been used because they were not believed to be of high enough quality, the reports concluded that the salmon runs were overexploited. Something needed to be done. Knowledge was inadequate, but a start had to be made. Getting legislative action is difficult where there is uncertainty and knowledge is incomplete. As the excerpts from the annual reports of the Oregon Board of Fish Commissioners show, fishery management regulations, then as now, fell behind what was needed to protect the fishery.

From the first relatively simple and limited regulations to the present state and federal fishery management bureaucracy, the assumption has been that there is a set of regulations that will manage the salmon fisheries at a sustainable level. Experience proves this not to be the case. Fishery management regulations have a history of not catching up with conditions in the fishery. For example, the migration patterns of salmon have led to interstate and international commissions and treaties to extend protection to salmon and allocate the catch. Columbia River salmon spawn in Idaho and migrate through Canadian waters to Alaska. In the ocean salmon are subject to the gears of many nations. To deal with the interstate problems mentioned by the fish and game protector, the Columbia River Interstate Compact was approved in 1918. The 1985 U.S.-Canada treaty and agreements to suspend ocean drift netting deal with international problems. Nevertheless, the rules fail to keep up. Now, as in the late nineteenth century, legislators do not enact necessary laws early enough. Legislators accept the argument that more research is needed before they will give greater protection to the resource at the expense of economic opportunity.

Part of the problem is that the ecological system needed by salmon cuts across boundaries of the sociopolitical system. State and national boundaries were drawn and resources of the Columbia Basin were developed for purposes that did not take into account the needs of salmon and those staking their livelihoods on them.

The "hogline" is the traditional way anglers fish for spring chinook on Oregon's Willamette River, among other places.

Management regulations constitute the rules of the game: people fishing for salmon continually develop new offenses to catch more and defenses to restrict their competitors. Tables 2 and 3 from Henry O. Wendler's study show early types of rules used to regulate the fishery. Since the cost of scientific knowledge and refereeing must come, at least in part, from salmon profits, the referees for the system seldom have the resources to fully do the job. Both good rules and sufficient enforcement are requirements for successfully regulating a fishery. Even a few violators can be very expensive to deal with and can undermine well-conceived rules. Further, salmon do not always stay within the field of play controlled by the referees. New rules for U.S. players may merely provide new opportunities for those from other nations.

The object of the game is to take the most fish within the limits of the regulations. The game ends only when the salmon population becomes so scarce that something like the Endangered Species Act halts activities and forces consideration of all the factors affecting the viability of salmon.

—Courtland L. Smith

III. Contending with Technology

Introduction

STRONG THOUGH THEY ARE, resilient enough to withstand millennia of environmental change, salmon are still no match for humans. At a conference in January 1994, one witty fisheries scientist listed the "Top Ten Ways to Stop Salmon Runs," using the style of talk show host David Letterman:

10. Cut forests

9. Build dams

8. Fish hard

7. Introduce new predators

6. Dilute genes

5. Add cattle

4. Irrigate

3. Pollute

2. Manage by legislation

1. Wait until the experts agree

Most of the scientists and managers at the conference—the experts—laughed at the list, out of a sense of recognition. We've done it all. That was the sad part of the joke.

The documents and commentaries in this section reflect on the numerous ways that the Euro-American settlement of the Northwest has altered and compromised the natural habitat of the salmon. The most notorious example is the giant dams of the Columbia and Snake rivers, and much of the fisheries discussion since about 1930 has revolved around responding to the threats posed by the dams. For the most part, however, salmon advocates, as much as those whose activities they were trying to mitigate, seemed to believe in the power of technology. Somehow, they believed, we could manage technology and have it both ways: salmon and development.

Previous page: Grand Coulee Dam under construction, 1941.

WHAT HAPPENS WHEN THE PUBLIC MANAGES TECHNOLOGY

Document: **The Effects of the Partial Elimination of Fishing Gear**

Authors: D. R. Johnson, W. M. Chapman, and R. W. Schoning, researchers with the Oregon Fish Commission

Year: 1948

Description: An agency-supported study shows the effects on salmon conservation of fishery management dictated by a 1935 voter initiative.

Conclusions

IT APPEARS THAT the elimination of any one type of gear on the Columbia River has served only to increase the catch by other gears rather than increase the escapement. The trend of total annual production of chinook salmon in the Columbia River has not changed appreciably in the nineteen years under consideration (1928 through 1946). This is interesting in view of the fact that elimination of fixed gear (fishwheels, traps, seines, and set nets) in 1935, from the Washington side of the river was undertaken presumably to reduce the catch and increase the spawning escapement. The results have not been precisely as planned. While the Washington catch has dropped sharply since 1934, the Oregon catch, despite the slight decline in total production from the river, has actually increased. A probable reason for this is that the Oregon catch has been for many years principally from gill nets and seines, and although the best trap sites were on the Washington side of the river, many of the best gill net drifts and seine grounds were on the Oregon side. In such an intensive fishery as that practiced on the Columbia River, there is presumably competition between the different types of gear. The elimination of traps and seines from the Washington side of the river left more fish for the gill nets and Oregon seines to catch. There were insufficient gill nets in Washington to make up for the loss from traps and seines, but the continuation of the use of all gear on the Oregon side gave rise to an actual increase in Oregon's landings.

Various investigators have concurred in the above observations. For example, Rich had the following to say concerning the elimination of fixed gear on the Washington side of the Columbia: "It seems rather doubtful that these restrictions have actually had this result (increasing the escapement).... It may well be, however, that the elimination of these two forms of gear (referring in this case to fish wheels and traps) has only resulted in increasing the catch of other forms, without materially increasing the breeding stock."

In 1938 the Oregon State Planning Board studied commercial fishing operations on the Columbia River in order to determine general conditions of the fishery, the results of elimination of fixed gear on the Washington side in 1935, and whether or not such restrictions on the Oregon side were advisable. Concerning some of these things they wrote, in part: " . . . the abolition of a particular type of gear would probably not decrease the total catch by the quantity of fish previously taken by that gear." In addition, the Board stated, "The abolition of fixed gear on the Oregon side of the Columbia River . . . would not alone solve the problems of conserving the Columbia River salmon runs." Further, "The ban of any particular gear now in use would give a preference to fishermen operating with other kinds of gear. A group of commercial fishermen should not be discriminated against unless it is clearly demonstrated that their fishing operations injure or deplete the fisheries of a greater extent than other types of fishing. In considering different methods of commercial fishing operations, if no type of gear in use harms the resource (except that it catches fish) the activities of any particular group of fishermen should not in equity be curtailed without a corresponding curtailment in other groups."

While there is little doubt that certain components of the Columbia River salmon populations, particularly the spring chinook and blueback, are in dire need of protection, it is equally evident that the elimination of any one form of gear has not, and probably will not provide that protection. Fishery regulations designed to increase the escapement must operate on all gear used to take salmon during their entire life cycle in both fresh and salt water.

Summary
1. Six major types of commercial gear have been used to take salmon and steelhead on the Columbia River; namely, gill nets, set nets, seines, traps, fish wheels and dip nets.

2. The five important commercial species in the Columbia River are chinook, silver, blueback and chum salmon and steelhead trout.

3. In 1927 fish wheels were eliminated in Oregon. In 1935 fish wheels, traps, seines and set nets were eliminated in Washington.

4. The effect of the gear change in Washington in 1935 has been to increase the take in other gears, while the previous trend of total landings has not changed appreciably.

5. There is no conclusive evidence that the elimination of fixed gear in Washington increased the escapement of salmon and steelhead.

6. There is no conclusive evidence that any gear is injurious to the run except by subtracting fish from the run.

7. Measures designed to increase the escapement should apply to all gears and cover the entire life history of each species.

> D. R. Johnson, W. M. Chapman and R. W. Schoning, *The Effects on Salmon Populations of the Partial Elimination of Fixed Fishing Gear on the Columbia River in 1935* (Portland: Oregon Fish Commission, 1948): 31-32. (Citations omitted.)

Commentary

 Throughout this century, attempts to eliminate types of fishing gear because of their destructive influence on salmon stocks have failed to produce any conservation results. Before the initiative process was introduced in the Northwest, various mechanisms were tried to eliminate competing gears. For example, in the 1890s gillnetters tried to get salmon traps, which were built yearly in the lower Columbia, declared hazards to navigation.

In 1902 Oregon introduced an experiment in popular democracy, the initiative and referendum process. An initiative enables the public to write and enact laws its legislators have not. The referendum allows the public to rescind laws made by their legislators. Between 1908 and 1992 Oregon voters acted on twenty-three initiatives to manage fisheries (see table 1); only ten passed. Supporters of all twenty-three initiatives presented conservation as some part of their goal.

As a general pattern, those gears that are most efficient, requiring the fewest people for the amount of fish caught, get eliminated first. One of the biggest initiative petition fish fights occurred in the state of Washington, when Initiative 77 passed in 1935, banning fixed gear— fish wheels, traps, and seines. Fish wheels had been banned by an Oregon initiative in 1926. Traps and seines were eliminated at the same time, but the Oregon legislature, pressured by the cannery own-ers of the seines, reinstated them.

Each initiative places various groups in opposition to one another. Four of the seven postwar initiatives pitted anglers against gillnetters. Even before the initiative process, gillnetters from Astoria sought to eliminate the trapmen from Ilwaco, Washington. Early initiatives set lower river fishers against those upriver. During the Great Depression, it was corporately owned fixed gear against individually operated fishing boats. Since World War II, the conflicts have been between recreational and commercial interests.

The problem with ballot measures, as the study above shows, is that they merely reallocate the distribution of catch. They do not result in any significant long-term conservation. They give the illu-sion of action without creating any real change in the status of the salmon stocks.

—**Courtland L. Smith**

Table 1. Ballot Measures

Date of Election	Title	Vote
June 1, 1908	Regulating time of fishing in Columbia River and tributaries.	+46,582 -40,720
June 1, 1908	Prohibiting fishing for salmon in the narrows of the Upper Columbia.	+56,130 -30,280
Nov. 8, 1910	Prohibiting commercial fishing in Rogue River and tributaries.	+49,712 -33,397
Nov. 5, 1918	Closing Willamette River to commercial fishing south of Oswego.	+55,555 -40,908
Nov. 5, 1918	Prohibiting seine and set-net fishing in Rogue River and tributaries.	+45,511 -50,227
Nov. 7, 1922	Salmon fishing and propagation amendment.	(a)
Nov. 2, 1926	Fish wheel, trap, seine, and gill-net bill (prohibits use in Columbia River).	+102,119 -73,086
June 28, 1927	Nestucca Bay fish closing bill.	+53,684 -47,552
Nov. 6, 1928	Deschutes River water and fish bill.	+78,317 -157,398
Nov. 6, 1928	McKenzie River water and fish bill.	+77,974 -153,009
Nov. 6, 1928	Rogue River water and fish bill.	+79,028 -156,009
Nov. 6, 1928	Umpqua River water and fish bill.	+76,108 -154,345
Nov. 4, 1930	Rogue River fishing constitutional amendment.	+96,596 -99,490
Nov. 8, 1932	A bill prohibiting commercial fishing on the Rogue River.	+127,445 -180,527
Nov. 3, 1942	Bill restricting and prohibiting net fishing coastal streams and bays.	+97,212 -137,177
Nov. 5, 1946	Bill regulating fishing in coastal streams and inland waters.	+196,195 -101,398
Nov. 2, 1948	Prohibiting salmon fishing in Columbia River with fixed appliances.	+273,140 -184,834

Nov. 2, 1954	Prohibiting certain fishing in coastal streams.	+232,775 -278,805
Nov. 6, 1956	Prohibiting certain fishing in coastal streams.	+401,882 -259,309
Nov. 6, 1962	Restricting commercial fishing on Columbia River.	(b)
Nov. 3, 1964	Prohibiting commercial fishing for salmon, steelhead.	+221,797 -534,731
Nov. 5, 1974	Making steelhead a game fish.	+458,417 -274,182
Nov. 3, 1992	Restricting lower Columbia River fishing to most selective means available.	+576,633 -828,096

(a) Marion County Circuit Court declared the petition to be invalid because of an insufficient number of genuine signatures. Accusations were made that this initiative petition was designed to "hold up" the salmon packer's. See statement by Master Fish Warden C. D. Shoemaker, *Official Voters' Pamphlet* for November 7, 1922, p. 12.

(b) Ruled off the ballot by the Oregon Supreme Court because petitions were improperly titled.

Source: *Official Voters' Pamphlet* and *Official Abstract of Votes* by Oregon Secretary of State.

ARMY CORPS AND CONGRESS:
TRUE BELIEVERS IN DAMS

Document:	**Army Corps of Engineers Report**
Author:	The Corps of Engineers
Year:	1931
Description:	In 1927, Congress authorized the Corps of Engineers to prepare a feasibility study of developing the Columbia River for multiple uses. The Corps' seminal report recommended construction of a series of dams on the main stem of the Columbia River.

THE COLUMBIA RIVER and its tributaries are susceptible of being developed into the greatest system for water power to be found anywhere in the United States. The power can be developed at low cost. The sites determined by the Board of Engineers for Rivers and Harbors as most promising, all things considered, are at 10 localities. . . . The structures contemplated in the scheme for power development are all on a large scale, some on a grand scale, and the conditions at some of them as to foundations and flood discharge over the dams are without precedent. There is nothing however to cause a belief that the engineering difficulties cannot be surmounted. . . . The cost of this development will exceed that of any other single development of any kind for power that has ever been made. . . .

[T]he Board reports that, based on present information, the best general plan for the comprehensive utilization of the natural water resources of the Columbia River and for its ultimate improvement for the purpose of navigation in combination with the efficient development of the potential water power, the control of floods and the needs of irrigation is substantially as follows. . . .

A system of 10 dams. . . .
The Board further reports that in its opinion the Federal Government would not be justified at the present time in making any improvement of the river other than as authorized by existing projects, nor would it be justified in participating in the cost of any portion of the comprehensive plan above outlined other than to

bear the cost of the construction of the navigation features of the plan for the development of the river below the mouth of the Snake.

> H.R. Doc. No. 103, 73d Cong., 1st Sess. 2, 3, 12-13 (1933) (Reports of the Chief and the Board of Engineers for Rivers and Harbors).

Document:	**Bonneville Project Act**
Author:	U.S. Congress
Year:	1937
Description:	This statute authorized creation of the Bonneville Power Administration to market power, construct transmission lines, and set rates.

[F]OR THE PURPOSE of improving navigation on the Columbia River, and for other purposes incidental thereto, the dam, locks, power plant, and appurtenant works now under construction at Bonneville, Oregon and North Bonneville, Washington (hereinafter called Bonneville project), shall be completed, maintained, and operated under the direction of the Secretary of War and the supervision of the Chief of Engineers subject to the provisions of this Act relating to the powers and duties of the Bonneville power administrator . . . respecting the transmission and sale of electric energy generated at said project. . . .

. . . In order to encourage the widest possible use of all electric energy . . . and to prevent the monopolization thereof by limited groups . . . the administrator is authorized and directed to . . . construct . . . electric transmission lines. . . .

. . . In order to insure that the facilities for the generation of electric energy at the Bonneville project shall be operated for the benefit of the general public, and particularly of domestic and rural consumers, the administrator shall at all times, in disposing of electric energy generated at said project, give preference and priority to public bodies and cooperatives. . . .

. . . It is the intent of Congress that rate schedules for the sale of electric energy which is or may be generated at the Bonneville

Aerial view of the site of Bonneville Dam, prior to dam construction. View in this 1933 photo looks downriver, with Washington on the right.

Bonneville Dam (left) and powerhouse and navigation lock (right) at Columbia River mile 146. View looks upriver, with Washington on the left.

project in excess of the amount required for operating the dam, locks, and appurtenant works at said project shall be determined with due regard to and predicated upon the fact that such electric energy is developed from water power created as an incident to the construction of the dam in the Columbia River at the Bonneville project for the purposes set forth in section 1 of this Act.

> Bonneville Project Act of 1937, Pub. L. No. 75-329, ch. 720, § 7, 50 Stat. 731-33, 735 (current version at 16 U.S.C. §§ 832, 832a(b), 832c(a), 832(f)).

Commentary

 IN 1927, CONGRESS authorized the U.S. Army Corps of Engineers to prepare a feasibility study of developing the Columbia River for multiple uses. The Corps plan, which was completed four years later, recommended construction of a series of ten dams on the main stem of the Columbia. The report emphasized navigation, hydropower, and irrigation benefits associated with these developments, but the first project constructed under the plan, the Bonneville Dam, was begun in 1933 as an emergency public works project designed to provide jobs and stimulate the Depression economy. In the same year, construction began on the massive Grand Coulee project on the upper Columbia. However, the Corps report specifically declined to recommend development of the Snake River, the Columbia's principal tributary.

The federal role in damming the Columbia was part of the New Deal belief that the federal government could and should stimulate economic recovery through fiscal policy. Federal water projects could not only put people to work, they could encourage creation of public utilities. These would serve rural areas that private utilities would not as well as providing a "yardstick" against which to measure private utility rates and service. The public power movement was a chief beneficiary of the New Deal's heavy emphasis on federal water projects, which spent 40 percent of public works money on them.

One month before his election in 1932, Franklin Delano Roosevelt told eight thousand cheering public power supporters in Portland that, if elected, he would pursue a nine-part power program, including government ownership where necessary to secure lower electric rates.

The next year, Roosevelt's Public Works Administration began construction of the Bonneville and Grand Coulee dams. Although hydropower production was one of the benefits that Congress sought from these projects, power generation was clearly a secondary consideration to the dams' primary purposes of navigation (in the case of Bonneville Dam) and flood control, downstream flow regulation, and irrigation (in the case of Grand Coulee). Nevertheless, the allocation of the hydropower produced by the dams became an issue of considerable importance as the projects neared completion.

As construction of the Bonneville Dam drew to a close, how to market the "surplus power" authorized by the 1935 Rivers and Harbors Act became the subject of debate in the Northwest and Washington, D.C. The debate invoked old conflicts between urban and rural areas and public and private power partisans as well as new ones concerning bureaucratic power. Public power advocates sought creation of a Columbia Valley Authority, modeled after the Tennessee Valley Authority, with broad powers to operate the project, market power, construct transmission lines, and plan other projects. Local private utilities, however, opposed creation of an agency with such comprehensive powers; instead, they favored a limited federal role, with the Corps of Engineers as the project operator and few federal transmission lines.

The 1937 Bonneville Project Act was a compromise among these interests. It produced a Bonneville Power Administration (BPA) with limited authority, leaving the Army Corps of Engineers as project operator at the Bonneville Dam and the Department of the Interior's Bureau of Reclamation as operator of Grand Coulee. Congress authorized BPA to market power from the projects and construct transmission lines, but gave the new agency no comprehensive authority to develop new projects like that possessed by the Tennessee Valley Authority. Congress did include directives that BPA should encourage "widespread use" of power and give preference to power sales to public utilities, but the statute did not prohibit sales to private utilities or industries. The 1937 Act led BPA, within a decade, to electrify vast areas of the rural Pacific Northwest and to lure to the region electric-intensive industries like aluminum plants. BPA also kept rates low, making cheap electricity the fulcrum of the region's economy. Low rates also encouraged use of electricity for heat, an inefficient use of the resource, and discouraged conservation.

—Michael C. Blumm and F. Lorraine Bodi

SCIENCE IGNORED FOR DEVELOPMENT

Document:	**U.S. Commissioner of Fisheries Report**
Author:	The federal commissioner of fisheries, directed by Congress to assess the effect of Bonneville Dam on salmon runs
Year:	1937
Description:	This report anticipates many of the continuing problems for salmon associated with the Columbia Basin dams but concludes that somehow those problems will be resolved.

THE CONSERVATION of a great fishery resource involves a variety of circumstances, concerning which there is a dearth of information at the present time. . . . [T]he recommendations involved [in framing a conservation policy] can only be considered as preliminary until such time as more information has become available through the work of fishery scientists. Indeed, a policy of conservation can never be devised in final or absolute form. Policies announced and adopted today will be modified and extended tomorrow when additional information resulting from continuing studies is available. The resource we seek to conserve is itself a living and dynamic thing, developing and adapting itself to new circumstances and conditions resulting from natural growth and changing economic conditions. . . . Wildlife resources can be conserved only by eternal vigilance in balancing the productive forces of natural growth and replacement against the destructive forces of man's exploitation. The following chapters therefore will be a progress report on a frankly unfinished work which must continue for many years. . . .

Bonneville Dam has been considered rightly as a key to the continuing prosperity of the fishing industry of the Columbia River system. The dam is located about 146 miles from the mouth of the Columbia in the midst of the mighty thoroughfare of migrating salmon between the sea and their spawning places. It will interpose a barrier which, if not surmounted, will destroy the major portion of the fish supply. While the Willamette and other tributaries of the Columbia below Bonneville afford extensive spawning areas for certain species, the major spawning grounds for the salmon and steelhead lie in the higher tributaries of the Columbia and include the great Snake River drainage. The success of fish protection at

Bonneville Dam, therefore, will affect perhaps 75 percent of the total salmon supply of the region. For that reason every means should be employed to minimize the interference with salmon migration. . . .

The commercial fisheries of Washington and Oregon support an industry that ranks about fifth in magnitude among the other great industries of the Pacific Northwest. The fishing industry of the Columbia River district gives employment to approximately 3,250 fishermen whose annual catches of fish and shellfish average more than 30,000,000 pounds, bringing the fishermen themselves an income of 1 3/4 million dollars. . . .

Recommendations for Fishery Conservation On the Columbia River
The foregoing pages provide a view of the present status of the Columbia River salmon fishery, as influenced by natural conditions, individual activities, and the combined effects of an increasingly complex social order. They reveal an imperfect understanding of the natural requirements of the fishes upon which a great industry depends. They suggest something of the fortuitous and heedless development of industry, which has produced changes in the environment that are inimical to continued prosperity of the fisheries. They clearly demonstrate the present inadequacy of governmental machinery to protect a resource that is important, if not indeed essential, to continued social progress. They should impel action to correct a situation which cannot be viewed with complete optimism. . . .

Scientific Investigations
The Federal Government should finance and conduct through its Bureau of Fisheries an increased program of research on the natural history and ecological requirements of the various species of salmon and other commercial fish in the Columbia River Basin as a basis for a continued program of fishery management. During the past 3 years approximately $22,000 per year has been available for studies in this region. In earlier years research had been conducted in a desultory fashion at various times. Already a great deal of valuable data has been secured but, faced with the emergency presented by the construction of Bonneville and Grand Coulee Dams, fundamental information has been found to be so incomplete that vast programs of development were of necessity undertaken without assurance of their possible effects on the fish supply. The fish-carrying capacity of the various tributaries of the

Columbia River system has nowhere been satisfactorily determined, yet an extensive program of transplantation of millions of fry must be conducted within the next year or two on a trial-and-error basis. Stream surveys that have already been completed reveal extensive spawning areas that can be utilized more completely with a resultant increase in fish stock, but less than one-third of the total basin has been surveyed to date and the work of rehabilitating the runs in the remainder of the basin must either be neglected or undertaken without a knowledge of possible success or failure.

Large investments are soon to be made in fish-cultural apparatus and property; millions of fry will be produced by artificial propagation and rearing to compensate for the runs obstructed by Grand Coulee Dam. Many of the technical details of this program have been worked out on a basis of general experience in fish culture rather than on a basis of fact demonstrated by actual experiment. Continual improvements in methods of feeding salmon in hatcheries are being made, but better rations should be provided as our knowledge of fish nutrition increases. When large numbers of fish are gathered together in the hatchery, conditions favorable to the disastrous spread of disease occur, yet the prophylaxis and cure of fish diseases are a relatively unknown field. Finally, the effects of commercial fishing on the supply are shrouded in mystery. Statistics of landings show a well-marked downward trend in total yield, but the racial composition and final destination of hordes of salmon entering the mouth of the Columbia River to be caught by fishermen or to continue to their spawning grounds as fate may direct is unknown. As a result, aside from blind restriction of commercial activity, the protection of individual runs menaced by virtual extinction must at the present time be left to chance. The facts developed by these various lines of investigation all bear directly upon the ultimate objective of fishery conservation; that is, the management of the supply in such a way as to yield maximum and stabilized returns to the fishing industry and to maintain these historic runs of salmon as a food resource for national safety.

The Columbia River is an interstate stream. Canned salmon is a national food commodity. The recreational facilities of the Columbia River Basin attract visitors from all parts of the country. Therefore, the Federal Government could properly expend three or four times the amount now provided in acquiring the necessary technical information to protect and develop the fishery resources.

S. Doc. No. 87, 75th Cong., 1st Sess. 1-2, 4, 74-76 (1937).

Document:	**The Mitchell Act**
Author:	U.S. Congress
Year:	1938
Description:	This federal law authorized funding of measures to preserve and protect Columbia Basin salmon.

BE IT ENACTED by the Senate and House of Representatives of the United States of America in Congress assembled, That the Secretary of Commerce is authorized and directed to establish one or more salmon-cultural stations in the Columbia River Basin in each of the States of Oregon, Washington, and Idaho. . . .

SEC. 2. The Secretary of Commerce is further authorized and directed (1) to conduct such investigations, and such engineering and biological surveys and experiments, as may be necessary to direct and facilitate conservation of the fishery resources of the Columbia River and its tributaries; (2) to construct, install, and maintain devices in the Columbia River Basin for the improvement of feeding and spawning conditions for fish, for the protection of migratory fish from irrigation projects, and for facilitating free migration of fish over obstructions; and (3) to perform all other activities necessary for the conservation of fish in the Columbia River Basin in accordance with law.

Mitchell Act, Pub. L. No. 75-502, ch. 193, 52 Stat. 345 (1938) (current version at 16 U.S.C. § 755).

Commentary

FOUR MONTHS BEFORE enactment of the Bonneville Project Act in 1937, the Senate adopted a resolution directing the commissioner of fisheries to assess the effect of Bonneville Dam on the propagation of the Columbia River salmon runs and to recommend steps "to attain the full conservation of [the salmon] and the preservation of the fishing industry." The commissioner's report concluded that it would be years before the full ramifications of the dam would be known. However, he anticipated many of the problems salmon would confront in their efforts to coexist with water project development in the Columbia Basin.

Bypass problems for juvenile fish at the dams, unscreened irrigation diversions, unsophisticated hatchery technology, and mixed-stock ocean harvests were all noted in the report and were all to contribute to the decline of the Columbia salmon runs over the next half century. The commissioner emphasized funding scientific research into salmon migrations and the effects of the dam on the fish runs. Because of the vast areas traveled by salmon during their life cycle, there have always been great scientific uncertainties surrounding salmon migration, and these uncertainties have not disappeared, despite a half century of studies. It is interesting to note the commissioner's assumption that water project development would not be deferred pending completion of the studies, but would instead proceed. Unwilling to suggest a "blind restriction" on commercial harvests or dam operations, the commissioner reached the unsettling conclusion that "the protection of individual runs menaced by virtual extinction must at the present time be left to chance."

The 1937 report prompted enactment a year later of the Mitchell Act, which authorized funding of measures to preserve and protect Columbia Basin salmon, including hatcheries, fish ladders, irrigation screens, and habitat protection and restoration projects, as well as scientific studies. The act also contained a broad directive to the Secretary of Commerce to "perform all other activities necessary to the conservation" of Columbia Basin salmon, but the secretary never interpreted that authority to include altering the operation of Columbia Basin dams to facilitate salmon migration.

Over the years, concern over scientific uncertainty was turned into a "heads I win, tails you lose" proposition for Columbia Basin salmon. Not only would the dam building not stop while scientific studies were undertaken, but increasingly the federal operating and marketing agencies took the position that no changes in river operations could take place until they were grounded on scientific proof. Thus, while Congress never expressly indicated that the Columbia's salmon should be sacrificed in pursuit of navigation, irrigation, or hydropower, the federal agencies managing the dams effectively ensured the decline of the salmon runs by employing optimistic assumptions about the effects of the projects and by invoking the need for scientific study before making any operational changes. Although these agencies funded the work of numerous biologists to study various aspects of the salmon life cycle, the demand for scientific certainty inhibited meaningful protection and restoration efforts.

One activity that did proceed despite scientific uncertainty was the construction of hatcheries funded by the Columbia Fishery Development Program under the Mitchell Act. Most of the Mitchell Act hatcheries were situated in the lower basin, so that their fish would not be confronted with dam passage problems in the main-stem Columbia. This unfortunately produced unfair distributional consequences, as upper basin fishers, including Indian tribes and Idahoans, bore the brunt of the dam-related losses with little or no compensation for many years.

Even worse, there is now increasing recognition that heavy reliance on hatchery fish damages wild fish productivity through competition for limited food and habitat, transmission of disease, and loss of genetic integrity through interbreeding. Hatchery fish also perform poorly in the wild; one study has found wild salmon to be nine times more productive spawners than hatchery salmon. Many biologists now consider hatcheries to be a narcotic serving only to mask the magnitude of problems that dam-induced alterations in streamflow regimes present for salmon. There are growing doubts about whether hatchery fish can even assist in the rebuilding of self-sustaining fish runs that spawn naturally. Virtually no one any longer believes that hatcheries can substitute for river conditions that facilitate fish migration.

—Michael C. Blumm and F. Lorraine Bodi

DEVELOPERS CONSIDER COSTS AND BENEFITS

Document:	**Army Corps of Engineers Report**
Author:	U.S. Army Corps of Engineers, reporting to Congress
Year:	1938
Description:	This report describes development of the lower Snake River for hydropower and navigation.

FOR THE ULTIMATE DEVELOPMENT of the Snake River below Lewiston the division engineer has prepared plans for a complete slack-water improvement with a series of 10 locks and dams. While such an extensive development may be feasible in the far-distant future, he believes that planning at the present time may for all practical purposes be limited to slack-watering only those stretches which cannot be made navigable by open-river methods at reasonable cost. He therefore proposes the construction of four locks and dams at sites 4, 57, 93, and 135 miles above the mouth, supplemented by open-channel improvement to provide a minimum depth of 5 feet over a bottom width of 150 feet outside the pools. Navigation and fishway facilities would be similar to those proposed for the four middle Columbia River dams. The slack-water pools, totaling 60 miles in length, would drown out the more steep and hazardous sections where commercial navigation is now impracticable. The 81.4 miles of open river remaining between the mouth and Lewiston would have an average slope of 2.4 feet per mile, with maximum velocities of 8 miles per hour at low water and 9 miles per hour at medium stages. Through navigation would be possible with boats of adequate power during 10 months of the average year, and would be blocked by ice or floods during the remaining 2 months. Power could be generated at the lowest three dams, although at relatively high cost due to excessive reductions in head during high water. The total initial cost is estimated at $47,000,000 with power installations totaling 155,000 kilowatts, and $28,000,000 without power facilities. The division engineer presents this improvement, plus the four locks and dams proposed for complete canalization of the middle Columbia, as the best coordinated plan of improvement of the Columbia and Snake Rivers between The Dalles and Lewiston.

The division engineer states that the coordinated improvement described above would benefit navigation, irrigation, and power interests. Some degree of flood control could be effected through use of storage in the upper levels of pools, but this method of operation would either conflict with power use or entail increased costs, and is not justified by the relatively slight value of additional flood control on the lower Columbia. . . .

Construction of the proposed Arlington and Umatilla and the lower of the Snake River Dams would reduce the estimated annual costs for pumpage to these areas by $210,000, $145,000, and $220,000, respectively. *The total navigation and irrigation benefits discussed above amount to only 15 percent of the estimated total annual carrying charges for the coordinated improvement.* As no other major interest is materially affected, the remaining charges must be covered, if at all, by the value of the power generated. . . .

Dams were thrown up across the lower Columbia and Snake rivers rapidly from the 1930s to the 1970s, forcing salmon to run a concrete gauntlet. The dates indicate year of initial operation.

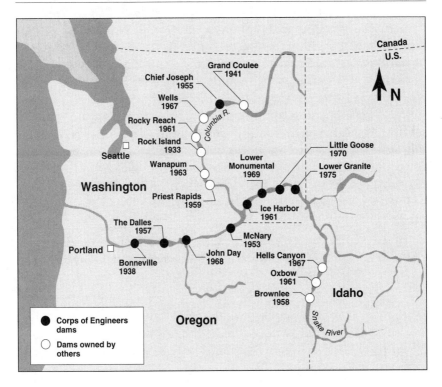

The division engineer concludes that further improvement of the Columbia River from The Dalles to the mouth of the Snake and of the latter stream below Lewiston should be considered a single project; that this potential trade route between tidewater and the interior of the Pacific Northwest cannot be made usable over its entire length by open-river improvement at reasonable cost; that construction of a high dam at The Dalles is neither advisable nor advantageous; and that the best coordinated improvement comprises a series of four locks and dams on each stream, with supplemental channel improvement on the Snake between the pools formed by the dams, all as outlined above; that the direct navigation and irrigation benefits to the general public are not commensurate with the cost of the coordinated improvement, and that it cannot now be safely assumed that sufficient power can be sold from the dams within the next 50 years to assure economic justification for the development in view of the large blocks of power available at Grand Coulee and Bonneville, although such a possibility exists; and that provision of low-cost water transportation between tidewater and the interior, which he considers more or less essential to success of the Federal projects already under way in the basin, will promote the economic security and future development of agriculture and industry in the Pacific Northwest, with indirect benefits which may be sufficient to warrant the initiation of construction work at the present time. He believes, however, that decision as to whether work should be started at this time, without waiting for further development of the power market, must be left to the Congress, and recommends that the coordinated plan presented by him for further improvement of the Columbia between The Dalles and the mouth of the Snake, and of the Snake below Lewiston, Idaho, be approved as a basis for modification of the existing projects for these waterways when such action appears to be justified, but that no modification in these projects be made at the present time.

> H.R. Doc. No. 704, 75th Cong., 3d Sess. 8-11 (1938) (Report of the Board of Engineers for Rivers and Harbors). (Emphasis added.)

Commentary

FOUR YEARS AFTER the Army Corps of Engineers 1931 report, Congress directed the Corps to review its plan for Columbia Basin water project development to take into account changed economic conditions and new streamflow information; this second report was completed in 1938. The 1931 plan had called for ten dams on the main-stem Columbia, four below the confluence of the Snake to serve both navigation and power purposes, and six on the mid-Columbia largely for power. Just two years before, in 1936, the Corps had specifically rejected developing the lower Snake, the Columbia's principal tributary, until the projects planned for the lower Columbia were completed, their navigation value was demonstrated, markets were developed for more hydropower, and more information was gained about the effects on salmon of the existing dam But in the 1938 report, the Corps shifted its attention to development of the lower Snake for navigation, giving two reasons for this change: (1) uncertainty about whether there were markets for more hydropower from the Columbia and (2) strong lobbying from local shipping and agricultural interests for the development of a Snake River slack-water navigation channel linking Lewiston, Idaho, with the ocean. The lobbying pressure was strong enough to overcome a fairly ludicrous cost-benefit ratio: according to the Corps, the navigation and irrigation benefits from constructing dams on the lower Snake were only 15 percent of their costs. Nevertheless, the Corps included the Snake dams in its 1938 report, leaving the question of their construction "to the wisdom of Congress."

In addition to shifting federal emphasis from the mid-Columbia (which ultimately was developed by nonfederal public utilities) to the lower Snake, and from power to navigation benefits, the 1938 Corps of Engineers report made two lasting contributions to the future of Columbia Basin water project development. First, the Corps rejected a high dam at The Dalles similar to Grand Coulee, instead favoring a series of low dams on the lower Columbia. In large part, this recommendation was due to the opposition of salmon advocates who opposed any dam that would block access to salmon spawning grounds. As a result, the Corps' division engineer recommended against a high dam at The Dalles because it "would destroy upstream salmon fishing" and urged that "adequate provision should be made at all dams for passage of fish."

The second lasting contribution of the 1938 Corps report was to recommend that all planned projects between The Dalles and Lewiston be considered as one integrated project. The net effect of subsequent congressional ratification of this recommendation was to preclude private water project development from the lower Columbia and lower Snake and to ensure that the federal government would remain the dominant force in the development of the Columbia Basin's water resources.

The Corps plan was not quickly adopted by Congress: World War II deflected attention to defense matters. But while the war postponed new water project development, it helped produce markets for hydropower. The promise of cheap electric power lured defense-related industries—such as shipbuilding, aviation, and aluminum manufacturing—to the region, and the Northwest's economy boomed. The war also induced the War Production Board to issue a series of directives to the Bonneville Power Administration (BPA) to coordinate operations with regional utilities to ensure that defense-related electric demands were satisfied. The war thus precipitated the "one utility concept" that remains the chief attribute of Northwest hydropower operations today.

With the end of World War II imminent, Congress passed its first omnibus Rivers and Harbors Act in seven years in 1945. Anticipating a large role for water project development to provide employment for returning soldiers and to stabilize the postwar economy, the 1945 Act adopted the recommendations for lower Snake River development contained in the 1938 Corps report. The statute authorized "such dams as are necessary" to provide slack-water navigation and irrigation. "Surplus power" from these projects was to be marketed by BPA.

The ultimate products of the 1938 Corps report and Congress' 1945 ratification were four lower Snake dams, the last of which was not completed until 1975. These dams transformed the lower Snake from a free-flowing river into a series of lakes. It is fairly clear that Congress did not, however, intend dam building on the lower Snake to extinguish the river's salmon runs. In the same statute that authorized construction of the Snake projects, Congress authorized McNary Dam, just below the confluence of the Columbia and the Snake, with express provision for the safe passage of salmon to their spawning grounds (see page 116).

—Michael C. Blumm and F. Lorraine Bodi

WHAT THE MITCHELL ACT PROMISED THE SALMON

Document:	**Agreement to Implement the Mitchell Act**
Authors:	Signed by the top fishery officials of Oregon, Washington, and Idaho and the director of the U.S. Fish and Wildlife Service.
Year:	1948
Description:	This agreement describes the actions the states of Oregon, Washington, and Idaho and the federal government agreed to take to conserve salmon in the Columbia Basin.

WHEREAS, the act of May 11, 1938 (52 Stat. 345), as amended August 8, 1946 (60 Stat. 932), authorizes and directs the Secretary of the Interior:

1. To establish one or more salmon cultural stations in the Columbia River Basin in each of the States of Oregon, Washington, and Idaho.

2. To conduct such investigations and such engineering and biological surveys and experiments as may be necessary to direct and facilitate conservation of the fishery resources of the Columbia River and its tributaries.

3. To construct and install devices in the Columbia River Basin for the improvement of feeding and spawning conditions for fish, for the protection of migratory fish from irrigation projects, and for facilitating free migration of fish over obstructions.

4. To perform all other activities necessary for the conservation of fishery resources of the Columbia River Basin.

5. To utilize the facilities and services of the agencies of the States of Washington, Oregon, and Idaho responsible for the conservation of the fish and wildlife resources in such States in carrying out the authorizations and duties imposed by the act, and

WHEREAS, a general program for the conservation of the fishery resources of the Columbia River Basin in accordance with the act of May 11, 1938, as amended, has been proposed by the States of Washington, Oregon, and Idaho, and the Fish and Wildlife Service of the Department of the Interior in cooperation with other agencies of the Federal Government, and . . . .

> Agreement Covering Participation of the States of Washington, Oregon, and Idaho in the Program for the Conservation of the Fishery Resources of the Columbia River Basin (n.p.: n.p., 1948), 1

Document:	**The Fishery Program in the Lower Columbia River**
Author:	Leo Laythe, regional director of the U.S. Fish and Wildlife Service
Year:	1948
Description:	This paper offers an interpretation of how the Mitchell Act's fishery provisions would be implemented in the Northwest.

The Organization of a Management Program

IN 1938, CONGRESS authorized the appropriation of $500,000 for surveys and improvements in the Columbia River watershed for the benefit of salmon and other anadromous fish (Public Law 502, 75th Congress). This authorization recognized that during the period of 1905 to 1931, inclusive, the Government had received more than $500,000 from the lease of seining grounds on Sand Island and Peacock Spit at the mouth of the Columbia River and, further, that because of the destruction of favorable environmental conditions by deforestation, pollution, dams for hydroelectric development, and diversion of water for irrigation, the salmon fishery of the Columbia River was in a serious and progressive decline. The purpose of this authorization was to reinvest the funds derived from the fisheries back into that resource. . . .

On August 8, 1946, the President approved a congressional amendment (Public Law No. 676, 79th Congress) to the Act of May 11, 1938, which removed the limitation on subsequent appropriations to be made by Congress for the development of the fisheries for anadromous species in the Columbia Basin. It enabled and authorized the Secretary of the Interior to utilize the facilities and services of the conservation agencies of the States of Idaho, Oregon, and Washington in developing the salmon resources of the Columbia Basin. The Act was an important step in the history of salmon conservation because it permitted closer cooperation between the Federal Government and the States and also permitted the transfer of monies to the States for specific work—an advantage that had not been previously authorized.

Intensive planning of water-development projects in the last few years has pointed to the need for a definite program of conservation, which would have as a goal the preservation of the fishery of the Columbia River. Dams such as McNary, Priest Rapids, and those on the Snake River have clearly indicated that the lower Columbia Basin is obviously the region in which to concentrate efforts toward maximum utilization of streams by fish. . . .

Inasmuch as the fishery-development program is financed by the Federal Government, the funds appropriated are transferred to the Fish and Wildlife Service by the Corps of Engineers for expenditure as budgeted. . . . The Fish and Wildlife Service will construct and enlarge a small number of hatcheries located in Oregon and Washington. . . .

To execute the objective of this fishery program the following phases of operation are designated: (1) removal of obstructions to permit passage of fish; (2) abatement of pollution; (3) screening of water diversions and constructions of fishways; (4) transplantation of upriver runs; (5) expansion of artificial propagation; and (6) establishment of fish refuges in which conflicting developments will not be permitted. . . .

. . . Fundamentally the transplantation of upriver runs would be similar to the salmon relocation program of salmon in the Grand Coulee salvage program. It would, however, be on a far greater scale, especially if additional dams in the main stem of the Columbia and its principal tributary, the Snake River, prove to be effective barriers to the migration of spawning fish. In spite of the indicated success at Grand Coulee it is realized that other transplantations may present greater problems and may even be complete failures. Transfer or restoration of the spring runs of king salmon will probably present the greatest problem. The intent is not to move all upriver fish to the lower tributaries, but rather to build up the existing runs in the lower basin to the maximum capacity of the streams utilized. Many streams, however, contained no salmon at all and stock may have to be obtained from upper tributaries. These transfers will be carried out at first on an experimental scale and later, on an intensified and productive basis.

Leo L. Laythe, "The Fishery Development Program in the Lower Columbia River." *Transactions of the American Fisheries Society* 78, no. 48 (1948): 50-51, 53.

Commentary

 THE MOST VITAL fisheries management decisions affecting the Columbia River system were made during the period 1941 to 1979. These decisions led to fish management as we know it today in the Columbia River Basin. Although decisions that affected the Columbia River fisheries include logging activities and the building of dams for irrigation and power, this commentary is concerned with fish management policies devised and followed by the fisheries agencies of the federal and state governments. These policies affected both the river fisheries and the ocean fisheries off the Oregon and Washington coasts. The history of this agency management has been one of mandates established and forgotten, laws created and ignored.

One of the most significant actions that had an impact on Columbia fisheries was the Mitchell Act of 1938, an attempt to halt the decline of salmon and to begin a program to restore them throughout the Columbia River system. The agreement covering participation of the states in the program was signed by the various fishery agencies in 1948. The Mitchell Act became the formal document under which these agencies operated.

Ten years after the enactment of the Mitchell Act, Leo Laythe, regional director of the U.S. Fish and Wildlife Service, explained how the act and the 1946 congressional amendment to the act would implement a fisheries restoration program in Oregon, Washington, and Idaho. In describing the fisheries program authorized by the act, Laythe, perhaps inadvertently, underlined a practice in Columbia River fish management: to set guidelines and then ignore them.

Laythe recognized the potential of the act for real conservation. The program he outlined called for construction of artificial propagation facilities in Oregon and Washington and listed specific sites. It also stipulated that certain rivers, including the Deschutes, the Cowlitz, and the Lewis, were to remain free of obstructions. The program also prescribed habitat improvement, construction of fishways, pollution abatement, and removal of obstructions in streams so that fish released from the hatcheries would enjoy usable habitat.

Another provision of the program was a plan to transplant upriver runs from Idaho rivers and streams to tributaries located below the site of McNary Dam. Laythe noted that the Grand Coulee restoration program had achieved success in transplanting of some stocks and particularly in supplementing and reestablishing runs in the natural habitat. "Supplementation" is the term used in fishery management to describe the release of fish into underutilized or restored natural habitats. The Mitchell Act called for extensive habitat work, including restoring damaged habitat, on many of the streams before even the artificial production facilities could be put on line.

Although such helpful measures as these habitat improvement plans were outlined by the U.S. Fish and Wildlife Service, and most did occur, two important promises were broken. No dams were to be built on the Deschutes, the Cowlitz, and the Lewis; but dams were constructed on those rivers. Upriver runs were to be transplanted to lower tributaries; however, the success of programs such as that at Grand Coulee was not repeated. These two broken promises would become pivotal in the change from managing salmon for natural/wild runs to managing for hatchery runs.

—Douglas W. Dompier

"WE'RE FROM THE GOVERNMENT AND WE'RE HERE TO HELP"

Document:	**The McNary Dam Authorization**
Author:	U.S. Congress
Year:	1945
Description:	This legislation authorized the construction of McNary Dam, near Umatilla, Oregon, and required that adequate provisions be made to protect salmon.

THE CONSTRUCTION of the [McNary] Dam for purposes of navigation, power development, and irrigation . . . In the design, construction, and operation of the [McNary] Dam adequate provision shall be made for the protection of anadromous fishes by affording free access to their natural spawning grounds or by other appropriate means.

> River and Harbors Act of 1945, Pub. L. No. 79-14, ch. 19, § 2, 59 Stat. 10, 22.

Document:	**Corps of Engineers Report**
Author:	The division engineer, North Pacific Division, U.S. Army Corps of Engineers
Year:	1948
Description:	This report not only recommended construction of The Dalles and John Day dams, but described a plan to compensate for the loss of fish caused by dam construction.

THE DIVISION ENGINEER proposes a carefully integrated, comprehensive plan of development, consisting of a system of dams and reservoirs, hydroelectric generating facilities, transmission lines, irrigation works, levees, fish facilities, and other works. . . .

   E. *Conservation of salmon and other migratory fish to the maximum practicable extent.*

F. Material assistance in meeting stream pollution and drainage problems of the basin and substantial contribution to the recreational opportunities of the region.

G. *Minimum interference* with the existing regional economy, *with fish and wildlife habitat*, and with the many scenic and recreational areas of the basin, such as those along the McKenzie River and in the Flathead Lake and Pend Oreille areas. . . .

129. The commercial aspect of the fish and wildlife problem is concerned with the preservation of migratory fish runs in the Columbia River system. The construction of large dams across the main stem of the river and lower reaches of the tributaries, by interfering with upstream migration, causing loss of fingerlings passing downstream through spillways and turbines, and inundating spawning grounds, will raise problems of far-reaching importance. Adequate fish ladders were provided at Bonneville Dam, 145 miles from the ocean, to accommodate the runs and these ladders have been outstandingly successful, so far as any depletion of subsequent runs is evident. The average number of salmon passing the dam between 1938 and 1947 was 570,357. Almost all chum, a large proportion of silver salmon, and considerable numbers of Chinook salmon and steelhead trout spawn in tributaries below Bonneville Dam, whereas blueback salmon spawn exclusively in upstream tributaries above lakes. Prior to the construction of Grand Coulee Dam, from 3 to 6 percent of the salmon and steelhead runs which escaped the fishermen in the lower river spawned upstream from that site. In order to preserve these runs after construction of the dam, the runs were successfully transplanted to Okanogan, Methow, Entiat, and Wenatchee Rivers, tributaries joining the Columbia River downstream from both Grand Coulee and Foster Creek dam sites. The counts of fish spawning in these streams and in the main-stem Columbia River above Rock Island Dam, located on the Columbia River 12 miles below the mouth of Wenatchee River, show an average of 40,931 salmon and steelhead passing the dam annually in the 5-year period 1943-47. This represents about 7 percent of those passing Bonneville Dam. The remainder go mainly into Snake River and tributaries.

130. The United States Fish and Wildlife Service, with assistance of funds and data furnished by the Corps of Engineers, has devoted much study to the fish problem. Definite conclusions have not been reached in most respects, due to the number of variables involved which makes the collection and analysis of specific data a slow process. Because so many uncertainties exist, and because the

McNary Dam, at Columbia River mile 292, near Umatilla, Oregon. Its concrete salmon ladder is in the foreground.

development of the river for other needed purposes cannot be delayed indefinitely until all fisheries problems in connection with dams are solved, a plan to improve the lower tributaries for salmon spawning has been advanced by the Fish and Wildlife Service in cooperation with the Corps of Engineers. In essence, this plan, . . . proposes to develop the salmon runs in the lower tributaries to the highest possible level of productivity by the removal of obstructions, abatement of pollution, screening of diversions, fishway construction, transplantation of runs, extension of artificial propagation, and establishment of fish refuges.

131. If the effects of proposed dams are as adverse as many fisheries authorities fear, this lower Columbia River fishery-development plan offers the only practical means for maintaining the valuable salmon resources. If, on the other hand, the problems of salmon migrations past the proposed dams prove less formidable than feared, or are successfully solved during the years that necessarily will elapse before many more dams are completed, then the lower river plan offers a means of augmenting the current salmon

industry and will be a desirable enhancement of the natural resources of the basin. Full support and cooperation in the lower
Columbia River fishery-development plan is proposed as an essential adjunct to the development of Columbia River water resources.
In addition, *continued research is proposed to determine the best possible
means for passing salmon upstream and downstream at the dam sites,
and ample provision for incorporation of every feasible facility* is carried
in the cost estimates. . . .

Associated Programs . . .

. . . The preservation of Columbia River fishery resources was
given serious consideration in the studies leading to selection of
projects included in the over-all plan of development of all the
water resources of Columbia River and its tributaries. Fish facilities
such as fish ladders, fish locks, supplementary fish hatcheries, fish
racks, and other related facilities will be provided as an integral part
of all projects. . . . It is, however, the opinion of aquatic biologists
that a succession of dams between the ocean and the greater part of
the more important spawning grounds may, even with appurtenant
fish facilities mentioned above, cause significant cumulative losses
of fish. Therefore, the lower Columbia River fishery plan as proposed by the Fish and Wildlife Service is a means of conservation,
rehabilitation, and enhancement of the fishery resource. . . .

101. The lower Columbia fishery plan includes the construction
of fish hatcheries, provision of fish ladders at natural falls, removal
of log jams, old dams, or other obstacles interfering with free
migration of fish, screening of water diversion, stream pollution
abatement, and proper management of water resources. The plan of
development would be accomplished in two periods of 6 years
each. The total capital cost of the plan for all tributaries of the lower
Columbia River is estimated to be about $20,000,000. The first 6-
year period would be one of intensive hatchery construction and of
extensive investigations, studies, planning, and engineering and
biological surveys. The capital cost, which includes cost of construction, planning, supervision, overhead, and operation and
maintenance during the first 6-year period is estimated to be about
$15,500,000. The annual operation and maintenance costs after the
first development period are estimated to be about $1,231,000.

> H.R. Doc. No. 531, 81st Cong., 2d Sess. 41-42, 97-98, 128-29
> (vol. I, 1950). (Emphasis added.)

Commentary

THE 1945 RIVERS AND HARBORS ACT essentially adopted the recommendations concerning the development of the Snake River contained in the Army Corps of Engineers 1938 report (see page 106). Along with the projects on the Snake, Congress authorized construction of McNary Dam, just below the confluence of the Columbia and the Snake, for navigation, hydropower, and irrigation. However, the statute expressly required that the project protect salmon migration, promising anadromous fish "free access to their natural spawning grounds."

This stands as the clearest expression of congressional intent that dam building was not to extinguish salmon runs. Moreover, by promising free access to natural spawning grounds, Congress could have been interpreted to have established a federal policy of ensuring that project operations produce maximum fish passage and of favoring wild fish protection over hatchery production. But those who managed the dams and the salmon never interpreted the statute this way. Instead, the operative assumption was that dam-related salmon losses could be offset through reliance on hatcheries. Relying on one technology to mitigate the impacts of another was to prove a faulty strategy.

Disastrous flooding in the spring of 1948—which, among other things, wiped out Vanport City on the banks of the Columbia adjacent to Portland—helped to create new demand for more dams. That year Congress directed the Corps to review its plan for the Columbia Basin, and the resulting report relied heavily on flood control as a rationale for the projects it recommended, including two main-stem projects on the lower Columbia, The Dalles and John Day dams. These dams would complete the navigation channel making Lewiston, Idaho, a deepwater port. But the Corps did not expect year-round navigation; in its 1938 report (see page 106) it had anticipated a two-month annual shutdown, which is precisely what would occur under the many proposals that have been made to draw down Snake River reservoirs to facilitate spring salmon migration.

Perhaps the most striking aspect of the 1948 Corps report was the attention it gave to anadromous fish, outlining a $20 million plan of fish ladders, irrigation screens, habitat improvement, and hatchery construction focused on the lower Columbia. Upriver losses were to be mitigated by "developing the salmon runs in the lower tributaries to the highest level of productivity." Thus, the Lower Columbia River Fishery Development Program was begun, devoting a significant amount of federal money to maintain salmon harvest levels by focusing almost exclusively on the lower river, especially on hatcheries. Fish biologists received research money to study hatchery technology, disease prevention, and nutrition; fish managers designed harvest seasons to avoid having too many returns to the hatcheries. Little thought was given to the effects of hatchery fish on wild salmon in terms of the carrying capacity of the rivers and ocean feeding grounds. Consequently, the federal money for the lower river fishery program was a Faustian bargain. And for the treaty Indians, whose fishing grounds were above the dams, the program constituted a blatant disregard of their treaty rights.

It is most interesting to note the Corps' commitments, in its 1948 report, to (1) "conservation of salmon and other migratory fish to the maximum practicable extent," (2) "minimum interference" with fish and wildlife habitat, and (3) incorporation of "the best possible means for passing salmon upstream and downstream at the dam sites." These standards were never taken seriously by project managers over the years. They became empty promises, forgotten in the increasing emphasis on generating every possible kilowatt from Columbia Basin dams.

—Michael C. Blumm and F. Lorraine Bodi

INTERNATIONAL AND REGIONAL COOPERATION
OVERLOOKS SALMON

Document:	**Columbia River Treaty**
Authors:	Governments of the U.S. and Canada
Year:	1964 (ratified by Congress)
Description:	Canada and the U.S. signed an agreement by which Canada obtained a share of the power production and flood control benefits resulting from the construction of new dams in Canada.

THE GOVERNMENTS of the United States of America and Canada

Recognizing that their peoples have, for many generations, lived together and cooperated with one another in many aspects of their national enterprises for the greater wealth and happiness of their respective nations, and

Recognizing that the Columbia River basin, as a part of the territory of both countries, contains water resources that are capable of contributing greatly to the economic growth and strength and to the general welfare of the two nations, and

Being desirous of achieving the development of those resources in a manner that will make the largest contribution to the economic progress of both countries and to the welfare of their peoples of which those resources are capable, and

Recognizing that the greatest benefit to each country can be secured by cooperative measures for hydroelectric power generation and flood control, which will make possible other benefits as well,

Have agreed as follows: . .

Article II
Development by Canada
(1) Canada shall provide in the Columbia River basin in Canada 15,500,000 acre-feet of storage usable for improving the flow of the Columbia River.

(2) In order to provide this storage, which in the Treaty is referred to as the Canadian storage, Canada shall construct dams:

      (a) on the Columbia River near Mica Creek, British Columbia, with approximately 7,000,000 acre-feet of storage;

(b) near the outlet of Arrow Lakes, British Columbia, with approximately 7,100,000 acre-feet of storage; and

(c) on one or more tributaries of the Kootenay River in British Columbia downstream from the Canada-United States of America boundary with storage equivalent in effect to approximately 1,400,000 acre-feet of storage near Duncan Lake, British Columbia.

(3) Canada shall commence construction of the dams as soon as possible after the ratification date.

Article III
Development by the United States of America Respecting Power
(1) The United States of America shall maintain and operate the hydroelectric facilities included in the base system and any additional hydroelectric facilities constructed on the main stem of the Columbia River in the United States of America in a manner that makes the most effective use of the improvement in stream flow resulting from operation of the Canadian storage for hydroelectric power generation in the United States of America power system.

(2) The obligation in paragraph (1) is discharged by reflecting in the determination of downstream power benefits to which Canada is entitled the assumption that the facilities referred to in paragraph (1) were maintained and operated in accordance therewith. . . .

Article V
Entitlement to Downstream Power Benefits
(1) Canada is entitled to one half the downstream power benefits determined under Article VII. . . .

Article VIII
Disposal of Entitlement to Downstream Power Benefits . . .
(4) The bypassing at dams on the main stem of the Columbia River in the United States of America of an amount of water which could produce usable energy equal to the energy component of the downstream power benefits to which Canada is entitled but not delivered to Canada under Article V . . . is conclusive evidence that such energy component was not used in the United States of America and that the entitlement of Canada to such energy component is satisfied.

> Treaty on Cooperative Development of the Water Resources
> of the Columbia River Basin, Jan. 17, 1961, U.S.-Can., art. II, III,
> V(1), VIII(4), 15 U.S.T. 1555, 1556-62.

Document: **Pacific Northwest Coordination Agreement**

Authors: The agreement was signed by the U.S. Army Corps of Engineers, the Bonneville Power Administration, and fourteen public and private utilities.

Year: 1964

Description: This agreement established detailed operating principles for Columbia River hydropower operations.

[T]HE PARTIES HERETO operate major electric plants and systems which serve the Pacific Northwest area and have in the past voluntarily cooperated in the coordinated operation of their facilities through the Northwest Power Pool and through various contracts and arrangements . . . and have thereby achieved substantial economies and additional firm power resources for the Pacific Northwest. . . .

. . . [C]oordination for the production of power must take into consideration non-power uses for water resources and must be achieved as a part of the comprehensive development and management of water resources for maximum sustained benefit for the public good. . . .

. . . Nothing in this agreement shall require a party to operate a Project in a manner inconsistent with its requirements for nonpower uses or functions, and no party shall be considered in violation of this agreement or suffer any penalty thereunder because of any Project operation undertaken in good faith for the purpose of preserving priority to such nonpower uses or functions, or of protecting against harm to human life or property. . . .

. . . This agreement is subject to the regulatory powers of any federal or state agency having jurisdiction.

> Pacific Northwest Coordination Agreement, Agreement for Coordination of Operations Among Power Systems of the Pacific Northwest, Contract No. 14-02-4822 at 3, 51 (1964).

Commentary

BY THE 1960s, most of the sites for large hydroelectric projects in the U.S. portion of the Columbia Basin had been developed or were under construction. But the basin extends well into central British Columbia, where it originates on the Columbia ice fields. The Canadian portion of the Columbia Basin, where the storage sites of the river's headwaters were situated, remained undeveloped in the 1960s. As a result, in high runoff years, much of the Columbia's spring freshet had to be spilled around dams in the lower basin, producing no power. Although the unharnessed freshet was worthless for power production, it was vital to the efficient transportation of young Columbia River salmon to the ocean each spring.

Harnessing the Columbia's freshet required the cooperation of Canada. Although negotiations began in 1944, they were unable to produce a treaty for two decades. Canada insisted on receiving a share of the downstream power and flood control benefits that Canadian storage projects would produce in the U.S. The U.S. position was that Canada was entitled to only monetary compensation for damages, not a share of downstream benefits. Canada finally broke the logjam in the late 1950s by threatening to proceed with an alternative, unilateral development plan on the Peace River. Consequently, the U.S. agreed to the downstream benefits principle, and the two countries signed the treaty in January 1961. The treaty called for Canadian construction of three large storage projects and authorized the U.S. to construct another project that would inundate Canadian lands.

A dispute between the Canadian federal government and the province of British Columbia over which government was to pay for project construction and where the power produced was to be marketed prevented ratification of the treaty until 1964. Together the Columbia Treaty projects would, when completed in the 1970s, add over 20 million acre-feet of storage, more than doubling Columbia Basin storage capacity and largely harnessing the river's enormous freshet.

Arguably, ratification of the Columbia River Treaty began the modern era of the Columbia Basin hydroelectric system. The four authorized storage projects were only the most visible manifestation of the treaty's effect on system operations. By doubling the basin's storage capacity, the treaty induced downstream project operators to install additional generating capacity to capture the river's increased power potential. These modifications increased the capacity of the projects to meet peak load demands. Unfortunately, peak loads in the

Northwest do not occur during the spring; consequently, hydroelectric managers seek to store the spring freshet for release later in the year when demand for power is high. But spring is when young salmon require high river flows for transport to the ocean. The treaty projects gave the system operators the means to change the hydrograph of the Columbia from a river with large spring flows to one where much of the spring freshet is stored for release in the fall and winter to meet power demands. This changed hydrograph is a reflection of hydropower's status as the de facto dominant use of the river. And the lack of high spring flows is a chief reason for depleted Columbia Basin salmon runs.

Nothing in the Columbia River Treaty elevates hydropower to the status of dominant use, however. No provision of the treaty purports to alter any of the purposes for which the lower river dams were authorized, and those purposes made hydropower a secondary purpose of the project. Yet the treaty is often cited as the authorization for hydropower's dominance of Columbia River system operations, and there is no question that the planning processes the treaty spawned largely ignore the needs of salmon.

Just as significant as the storage projects it authorized was the impetus the Columbia River Treaty gave to formalizing coordination among federal and nonfederal project operations downstream of the new projects. Project operators had been cooperating voluntarily for some time, but the premise of the treaty's principle of sharing downstream benefits was a fully coordinated system. As a result, shortly after the treaty went into effect, the Bonneville Power Administration (BPA), the Corps of Engineers, and fourteen public and private utilities signed the Pacific Northwest Coordination Agreement, a long-term agreement that established detailed operating criteria, power exchange principles, and a formula for allocating downstream benefits. Through this contract, the region's project operators ensured an integrated system of operations, generally referred to as the "one utility" concept.

Annual planning under the Pacific Northwest Coordination Agreement entails little or no consideration of environmental impacts or any public involvement and assumes that hydropower is the dominant use of Columbia Basin dams. Yet the Coordination Agreement itself expressly disclaims an intent to elevate hydropower over "nonpower uses," such as salmon flows, and can be interpreted to "preserv[e] priority to such nonpower uses." Unfortunately, the system's managers never interpreted the agreement in this way, and the planning process it set in motion was aimed almost exclusively at maximizing hydropower benefits.

One outgrowth of the Columbia River Treaty and the Coordination Agreement was confirmation of the central role of BPA in system operations. For example, BPA purchased the Canadian entitlement of downstream benefits from a consortium of U.S. utilities, which had bought it for a thirty-year term from British Columbia, which sold it to finance project construction. Thus, until 1998, BPA has complete control over the Canadian entitlement; but this control has done nothing to prevent the decline of Columbia River salmon runs.

Another example of the evolution of BPA as the central player in Columbia Basin hydroelectric operations is reflected in the construction of the BPA-administered intertie line that electrically connects the Northwest with California markets. Congress authorized construction of the intertie in 1964, shortly after ratification of the treaty, to ensure that there would be markets available for the additional power the treaty projects (and the additional generators downstream) would produce. However, construction of the intertie alarmed the Northwest aluminum industry, a principal beneficiary of the Columbia Basin's low-cost hydropower. The aluminum companies feared that California power sales might deprive the industry of the cheap power that drew them to the Northwest. The result was enactment of the Northwest Preference Act, signed into law only three weeks after Congress appropriated $45 million to fund the federal portion of the intertie that would, by 1967, connect Northwest dams to Los Angeles. The Preference Act limited Northwest power exports to power that was "surplus" to the needs of the Northwest.

Thus, the legacies of the Columbia River Treaty were many and varied. The treaty induced greater coordination of power sales, produced enhanced hydropower peaking capacity, began California power sales, and confirmed BPA as the region's principal hydropower agency. However, by harnessing the spring freshet upon which Columbia River salmon depended, the treaty and its aftermath sent the salmon runs on a decline from which they have yet to recover.

—Michael C. Blumm and F. Lorraine Bodi

JUSTICE DOUGLAS DECIDES FOR UDALL
AND THE CLEARWATER

Document:	***Udall v. Federal Power Commission***
Author:	The Supreme Court decision was written by Justice William O. Douglas.
Year:	1967
Description:	This interagency lawsuit resulted from the refusal of Interior Secretary Udall to allow construction of a dam that would have destroyed Idaho's remaining salmon runs. The Supreme Court sided with Udall.

THE OBJECTIVE of protecting "recreational purposes" means more than that the reservoir created by the dam will be the best one possible or practical from a recreational viewpoint. There are already eight lower dams on this Columbia River system and a ninth one authorized; and if the Secretary is right in fearing that this additional dam would destroy the waterway as spawning grounds for anadromous fish (salmon and steelhead) or seriously impair that function, the project is put in an entirely different light. The importance of salmon and steelhead in our outdoor life as well as in commerce is so great that there certainly comes a time when their destruction might necessitate a halt in so-called "improvement " or "development" of waterways. The destruction of anadromous fish in our western waters is so notorious that we cannot believe that Congress through the present Act authorized their ultimate demise.

> *Udall v. Federal Power Comm'n*, 387 U.S. 428, 437-38 (1967).
> (Notes omitted.)

Commentary

In the 1950s, the Eisenhower Administration sought to reduce the role of the federal government in hydropower and to increase the role of utilities. Spurred by favorable tax laws and increased demand from defense industries in response to the Korean War, utility-generated power in the Northwest nearly quadrupled during the decade. All nonfederal dams must be licensed by the Federal Energy Regulatory Commission, then known as the Federal Power Commission (FPC), under the terms of the 1920 Federal Power Act. In the Columbia Basin, the two principal areas of utility development were on the mid-Columbia, where five dams were eventually constructed by public utility districts, and on the middle Snake, where the Idaho Power Company built three dams just above Hells Canyon. The Idaho Power dams terminated the middle Snake's salmon runs when they were completed in the mid-1960s.

In the late 1950s, with the three Idaho Power Company projects under construction, a consortium of utilities proposed construction of a project below Hells Canyon, just below the confluence of the Snake with the Salmon River. This project, called the High Mountain Sheep Dam, would have extinguished Idaho's remaining salmon runs in the Salmon and Clearwater rivers, the last salmon spawning tributaries of the Snake in Idaho.

The FPC licensed the project over the objection of the Department of the Interior in 1964. The Interior Secretary, Stewart Udall, filed suit to stop the dam, an unusual action since one federal agency does not normally sue another. Although the license was upheld by an appeals court, the Supreme Court struck it down in a remarkable decision by Justice William O. Douglas.

The Supreme Court's decision in the Udall case overturned the FPC's license and sent the issue back to the commission for reconsideration. Justice Douglas interpreted the Federal Power Act to require the commission to consider alternatives to the utilities' proposal, including federal development and no development at all. This Supreme Court suggestion was one of the few times anyone in a position of authority seriously questioned whether more Columbia Basin hydroelectric construction was in the public interest.

Justice Douglas' often-quoted words not only constituted a pathbreaking interpretation of the Federal Power Act, they also effectively saved Idaho's remaining salmon runs from extinction, at least for a time. Eight years after the Udall decision, Congress included the proposed dam site in the Hells Canyon National Recreation Area, thereby

*Supreme Court Justice
William O. Douglas, photo-
graphed in 1948 near his
cabin at Lostine, Oregon.*

prohibiting the construction of dams and preserving the area's free-
flowing rivers and salmon habitat. However, the National Recreation
Area designation did nothing to restore the spring fish flows that young
Idaho salmon needed to survive the eight federal dams that now obstructed their journey from their spawning grounds to the ocean.

—Michael C. Blumm and F. Lorraine Bodi

THE PROBLEMS WITH HATCHERIES

Document: **AreWild Salmonid Stocks Worth Conserving?**

Authors: John Dentler and David Buchanan, members of the research and development section of the Oregon Department of Fish and Wildlife

Year: 1986

Description: This excerpt from a readily available information report by a state fish agency summarizes the major biological concerns associated with hatchery-raised salmon. The emphasis is on the potential negative effects of hatchery fish on naturally spawning fish.

DESPITE DECLINES in salmonid habitat, man's desire for salmonids has not abated. In many places natural production cannot keep pace with the sport and commercial harvest rates, and in some cases the development of land and water resources, such as hydro-electric dams or mineral extraction, precludes the production of wild salmonids. To satisfy fishery demands and to sustain salmonid populations, hatcheries have been constructed. Over 75 million salmonids were released from Oregon operated hatcheries in 1985.

Hatchery reared salmonids are qualitatively different from wild salmonids. They are usually less genetically diverse than wild populations. The founding stock of a hatchery is usually composed of a small portion of the original wild population, possibly resulting in reduced variability due to the so-called 'founder effect.' The protective and relatively constant hatchery environment may also result in the loss of much of the genetic variation of the wild population from which they originated.

Many hatchery produced fish may not return to the hatchery to spawn, but instead spawn with wild fish and thereby infuse hatchery-adapted genes into an otherwise wild-adapted population. A study of coho salmon in the Yaquina River in Oregon revealed that approximately 75% of the coho salmon spawning in that river were of hatchery origin, presumably from an ocean ranching operation situated on the Yaquina estuary. It is conceivable that such infusion could, under certain circumstances, enhance salmonid production; however, there is evidence to suggest that the progeny of hatchery X hatchery as well as hatchery X wild parents may be less fit for existence in the wild than the progeny of wild salmonids. Apparently the short-term productivity and degree of adaptedness of wild stocks can be reduced by such interactions. The long-term effects of these genetic interactions may be the reason that a wild stock of Nehalem coho salmon showed increased susceptibility to a disese [sic] produced by the myxosporidian *Ceratomyxa shasta*.

Hatchery produced salmon may compete for food and space with salmonids produced in the wild, or may prey heavily on wild salmonids. Hatcheries may also release high concentrations of pathogens in effluent water, which may inflect the wild populations downstream. For example, [a 1982 study] documented that the effluent of a salmon hatchery had the highest concentrations of *Flexibacter columnaris* in the Rogue River, Oregon. Hatchery fish derived even from native stocks may increase the potential for disease among wild fish by serving as carriers of disease organisms when living in the wild because of the failure of the immune system to develop or be selected for in the protected rearing environment of the hatchery. This may explain why . . . hatchery salmon returning from the ocean experienced higher mortality rates than wild adults during disease outbreaks among spring chinook in the Rogue River, Oregon. [A 1981 study] provided evidence that release of hatchery fish having high susceptibility to *C. shasta* was increasing the incidence of the disease in wild spring chinook in the Deschutes River, Oregon.

Perhaps the major drawback of hatchery production of anadromous salmonids results from mixed stock fisheries. The protected hatchery environment circumvents part of the natural mortality associated with juvenile rearing, whereas, the mortality rate for wild juveniles is generally higher. Hatchery populations can thus sustain a higher harvest rate. In mixed stock fisheries, it is difficult (if not impossible) to harvest one stock at the maximum level without over- or under-harvesting other stocks.

A comprehensive examination of the role of salmonid hatcheries and their relationship to wild salmonid stocks is needed. Hatchery production of salmonids is necessary in many areas and hatcheries will continue to be a useful tool of fishery managers in the future. However, a more cautious and critical examination might reveal ways in which to better integrate wild and hatchery salmonid production with associated fisheries.

John L. Dentler and David V. Buchanan, *Are Wild Salmonid Stocks Worth Conserving?* Information Report no. 86-7 (Oregon Department of Fish and Wildlife, 1986), 4-7. (Citations omitted.)

Document:	**Analysis of Supplementation**
Authors:	William H. Miller and others
Year:	1990
Description:	Under a contract to the Bonneville Power Administration, four fisheries specialists with the U.S. Fish and Wildlife Service undertook a comprehensive review of over three hundred projects designed to "supplement" salmon and steelhead in North America. The publication became widely cited in discussions of the issue.

THE UNPUBLISHED supplementation literature was reviewed primarily by the authors of this report. Direct contact was made in person or by telephone and data compiled on a computer database. Areas covered included Oregon, Washington, Idaho, Alaska, California, British Columbia, and the New England states working with Atlantic salmon. Over 300 projects were reviewed and entered into a computer database. The database information is contained in Appendix A of this report.

Our conclusions based on the published literature and the unpublished projects reviewed are as follows:

—Examples of success at rebuilding self-sustaining anadromous fish runs with hatchery fish are scarce. We reviewed 316 projects in the unpublished and ongoing work. Only 25 were successful for supplementing natural existing runs, although many were successful at returning adult fish.

—Successes from outplanting hatchery fish were primarily in harvest augmentation, a term we use to describe stocking where the primary purpose is to return adults for sport, tribal or commercial harvest.

—Adverse impacts to wild stocks have been shown or postulated for about every type of hatchery fish introduction where the intent was to rebuild runs.

—Reestablishing runs or introductions to areas not inhabited by wild/natural populations have shown good successes.

—The stock of fish is an important factor to consider when supplementing. The closer the hatchery stock is genetically to the natural stock, the higher the chances for success.

—Chinook are one of the most difficult salmon species to supplement. A return rate, smolt or pre-smolt-to-adult, of 3-5 percent is considered good by most managers for this species.

—Salmon species with the shortest freshwater life cycle, e.g., chum and pink, have shown higher success from supplementation, than longer freshwater cycle salmon.

—Short-run stocks of salmon and steelhead have responded more positively to supplementation than longer-run stocks.

—Wild/natural fish have consistently shown a much higher smolt-to-adult survival rate than hatchery fish.

—Overstocking of hatchery fish may be a significant problem in many supplementation projects.

—The use of wild broodstock by British Columbia has shown success in their chinook and steelhead supplementation programs.

—Both Alaska and British Columbia are having some success using streamside incubation boxes and subsequent outplanting of fry.

Overall, we concluded that protection and nurturing of wild/natural runs needs to be a top management priority. There are no guarantees that hatchery supplementation can replace or consistently augment natural production. For the Columbia River system, we concluded that all hatchery fish should be marked for visual identification. This will not only permit a more precise harvest management, but also better broodstock management and supplementation evaluation. Currently only hatchery steelhead are marked.

William H. Miller et al., *Analysis of Salmon and Steelhead Supplementation* (Portland, Oregon: Bonneville Power Administration, 1990), iii-iv, 1.

Document:	Techno-Arrogance and Halfway Technologies: Salmon Hatcheries
Author:	Gary K. Meffe, Savannah River Ecology Laboratory, South Carolina
Year:	1992
Description:	A biologist not employed in the Pacific Northwest penned an unusually blunt and impassioned critique of the region's reliance on hatcheries. The article was published in a professional journal read by biologists and conservationists.

FURTHERMORE, Nehlsen et al. (1991) identified 214 stocks of Pacific salmonids from California, Oregon, Idaho, and Washington that they considered to be of special concern, as they face a high or moderate risk of extinction.

A central feature of the mainstream solution to this debacle is technological: build hundreds of hatcheries to spawn thousands of fish and produce millions of eggs to stock back into the environment. There is a fundamental problem with this approach, however: much of the natural environment remains largely unsuitable for salmonid survival, reproduction, or migration, and continues to deteriorate. Millions of fish are being placed into degraded or even lethal environments and have little chance of survival to maturity and reproduction.

I maintain that a management strategy that has as a centerpiece artificial propagation and restocking of a species that has declined as the result of environmental degradation and overexploitation, without correcting the causes for decline, is not facing biological reality. Salmonid management based largely on hatchery production, with no overt and large-scale ecosystem level recovery program, is doomed to failure. Not only does it fail to address the real causes of salmonid decline, but it may actually exacerbate the problem and accelerate the extinction process. There are at least six reasons why the current use of hatcheries in salmonid management is counter-productive and should be reconsidered:

First, the data demonstrate that hatcheries are not solving and likely will not solve the problem of salmon decline. Salmonids have continued to decline throughout the Pacific Northwest, despite decades of hatchery production and the expenditure of millions of dollars. It should be obvious that this is not a reasonable solution to the problem, as it clearly is not working. For example, as of this

With other options seeming too expensive or too politically difficult, hatcheries became widely accepted as the method for maintaining salmon abundance. Here, workers at the Bonneville hatchery strip eggs and sperm from freshly killed coho salmon.

writing, the 1992 oceanic fishing season is in danger of being reduced or eliminated altogether, due to the now alarming decline of both natural and hatchery runs of fish.

Second, hatcheries are enormously costly to run. Severely limited state and federal monies spent on hatcheries could be redirected to local and ecosystem-level habitat restoration, or to prevention of further decline through land purchases. The latter would also benefit other species and maintain ecosystem services in the region.

Third, hatcheries are not sustainable in any long-term sense. They require continual infusion of energy and money, and they are only a piecemeal, year-to-year approach to the problem. Will hatcheries continue to operate in fifty years? Five hundred years? Five thousand years? At some point, for economic or other reasons, hatcheries will cease to operate, and the system will collapse. A long-term, self-sustaining solution is needed.

Fourth, hatcheries are a biologically unsound approach to management that can result in negative genetic changes in natural populations. The most basic concept in quantitative genetics is that an individual's phenotype reflects genotypic and environmental influences, plus interactions of these factors; hatcheries have never demonstrated the ability to properly manage either the genotype or the environment in any way that reasonably approximates nature. Although hatchery management practices have been changing to accommodate genetic concerns, most hatcheries have historically ignored basic principles of population genetics, such as genetically effective population size, and have purposely transferred stocks among subbasins and drainages, disregarding potential local adaptations and site fidelities. This has resulted in the genetic and ecological interaction of native and hatchery stocks, with repeated degradation or loss of native populations.

Fifth, hatchery production leads to greater harvest of salmonids, including those from natural populations, resulting in decline of the very stocks being protected. Hilborn (1991) stated that "There is wide concern throughout the Northwest that we have allowed our fisheries harvest rates to match the potential productivity of hatchery stocks, causing wild stocks to be over fished." He continues with an example: "Just north of Puget Sound . . . harvest rates on Coho Salmon are as high as 95%, sustainable only by the most successful hatchery stocks. The net result of these high harvest rates is that as hatchery production has increased, wild stocks have declined. But the Canadians have no more Coho now than they did 15 years ago. They have swapped hatchery fish for wild fish." Successful hatchery production seems to provide a psychological license to increase harvest rates, which reduces wild stocks, thus defeating the initial purpose of hatcheries

Sixth, hatcheries are at best a palliative that conceals from the public the real problems and dangers facing a valued resource. This, I believe, is the most serious objection to the hatchery approach. By financially supporting hatchery production as a standard mitigation practice, the hydropower companies and other development projects that are largely responsible for environmental degradation can "buy out" of their moral responsibilities for salmonid losses and habitat destruction by demonstrating their concern for and dedication to the declining resource. They, along with the fishing industry, have created a popular mythology, foisted on managers and the public, that hatcheries are a viable solution to environmental destruction and loss of salmon. This is an insidious deception of the public trust, and this particular mythology must be challenged. The taxpayer and voter is deceived (whether by commission or omission) into believing that technological advances can simultaneously allow environmental degradation and sustained production of an economically, aesthetically, and recreationally valuable resource. The public is also led to believe that their native salmonids are in reasonable condition and in good hands. Consequently, the public is insulated from the reality that their rivers and terrestrial ecosystems are rapidly degrading, and that native fishes, including the salmon they like to catch and eat, are disappearing.

The hatchery approach to salmon conservation is a good example of what Lewis Thomas (1974) has called "halfway technology," a reference to medical practices that treat symptoms rather than eliminate causes of disease. To quote Frazer's (1992) essay on sea turtle conservation,

> Thomas defined halfway technology as "the kinds of things that must be done after the fact, in efforts to compensate for the incapacitating effects of certain diseases whose course one is unable to do very much about. It is a technology designed to make up for disease, or to postpone death." In short, halfway technology does little or nothing to address the cause or the cure of disease. It's what we use to treat a disease when we don't really understand it.

Essentially, halfway technology in salmonid management recognizes the symptom (fewer fish) and treats that symptom (grow more fish) without making a concerted effort to identify and eliminate the underlying causes (environmental destruction and overexploitation). Hatchery rearing of millions of fish does nothing to address the causes of declining populations of fish but simply tries to make more fish available. A medical analogy would be to save the life of a bleeding patient by continual blood transfusions rather than by identifying and stopping the source of bleeding. . . .

[Literature Cited]

Frazer, N. 1992. Sea turtle conservation and halfway technology. Conservation Biology 6:179-184.

Hilborn, R. 1991. Hatcheries and the future of salmon and steelhead in the Northwest. The Osprey 11:5-8.

Nehlsen, W., J. E. Williams, and J. A. Lichatowich. 1991. Pacific salmon at the crossroads: stocks at risk from California, Oregon, Idaho, and Washington. Fisheries 16(2):4-21.

Thomas, L. 1974. The lives of a cell. Notes of a biology watcher. Viking Press, New York.

Gary K. Meffe, "Techno-Arrogance and Halfway Technologies: Salmon Hatcheries on the Pacific Coast of North America," *Conservation Biology* 6, no. 3 (1992): 351-52. (With four exceptions, citations omitted.)

Commentary

IT'S NOT HARD to understand the appeal of producing salmon under controlled conditions. Consider all the factors that increase the odds against naturally reproducing fish—all the problems of freshwater habitat loss and degradation, all the problems of ocean variability and omnipresent predators. Dams, where they exist. Fishers, wherever they can put themselves. Twentieth-century fish managers, groping for a way to respond somehow to this daunting array of problems, would probably have had to invent salmon hatcheries—artificial fish-production facilities—if that had not already been done in the last century.

For many concerned about salmon production, belief in hatcheries became an article of faith by the late 1800s. Raising fish in hatcheries was considered little different from raising other animals. People had been domesticating animals for centuries, and they thought that, for the most part, they had not only done right but done well. People got better animals, improving on nature; and they also helped ourselves.

The notion that humans can solve any environmental problem through technology has perhaps, however, begun to pass out of vogue. The latter part of our century has offered too many examples of the unhappy consequences of a blind faith in technology. Nonetheless, as the twenty-first century approaches, many would still place their faith in the belief that fish hatcheries will, somehow, continue to provide. Such faith and hope must fly in the face of a considerable body of scientific judgment and well-informed opinion. This position is represented in differing degrees and in differing tones in the three excerpts in this section, all written by fisheries scientists.

The main problem they see with hatcheries is their negative effects on wild fish. As the four authors of the Bonneville Power Administration report on supplementation wrote, "Adverse impacts to wild stocks have been shown or postulated from about every type of hatchery fish introduction where the intent was to rebuild runs."

Not discussed here is one last, completely separate, problem that hatcheries must contend with for the foreseeable future: publicly funded government hatcheries are subject to the changing budgetary priorities of agency officials, elected representatives, and the public. The expenses of operating hatcheries, particularly when those expenses result in biological returns deemed inadequate, ultimately may have more of an effect on the continued operation of hatcheries than any biological argument has ever had.

—Joseph Cone

A Fisher's Campaign for Conservation

Document:	**Fiftieth Anniversary Number,** *Pacific Fisherman*
Authors:	Miller Freeman, publisher of *Pacific Fisherman* from 1902 to 1955; other excerpts by staff contributors
Year:	1952
Description:	*Pacific Fisherman*, the era's flagship fishing publication, celebrated its golden anniversary by reaffirming its publisher's long commitment to conservation through excerpts taken from five decades.

"Wise Use" Conservation Ever First Responsibility

CONSERVATION OF THE FISHERY resources—conservation in its true sense, "wise use"—has been a cardinal objective of *Pacific Fisherman* throughout its 50 years.

This journal has not hesitated—does not hesitate today—to insist that *perpetuation of the resource is the first responsibility of all who live by it;* and that *understanding and acceptance of that responsibility by the industry—fishermen and packers—is infinitely preferable and infinitely more effective than governmental fiat.*

This attitude was made plain constantly through every year of the 50 from its first enunciation in 1904, when we find this editorial statement:

If the fish come, there is no doubt but that the largest pack in the history of fishing on the Sound will be put up. *Great care should be taken, however, to see that plenty of fish reach the spawning grounds, for in this lies the whole future of the industry.* (Emphasis added in 1952).

As early as 1908 packers were reporting to *Pacific Fisherman* that "The Columbia River harvest of spring-run Chinooks is getting more belated every year." Now we know from the studies of the Fisheries Research Institute that actually the heart was being fished out of the run, and that the pack was being made from the most productive fish, while the aberrant fore-runners and tailenders were escaping to produce a bi-modal run. . . .

Warped Concepts Common In First Decade Thinking

Concepts of the fishery resource were warped in the early days of the first decade. The very first issue of *Pacific Fisherman* quotes the Washington fisheries commissioner as saying of the Sockeye: "The day is not far distant when they will be extinct." . . .

In September, 1903, we reported:

> The Columbia River pack has exceeded all possible hopes. There appeared to be a solid body of fish entering the river in magnitude never before equalled. . . . Old fishermen acknowledge that it surpassed any year they had ever seen or heard of.

Incidentally, hatcheries were credited with producing this astonishing volume of fish after some very lean years. . . .

Conservation a Consistent Concern of "P. F."

From its beginnings this journal was concerned with conservation, and a consistent crusader against unsound investment in the fisheries.

An early 1916 editorial is typical of the firm position taken on both these points:

> *Pacific Fisherman* forcibly calls to the attention of those interested in the conservation of this great industry the need for some radical change in the near future if it is to be preserved for our children and grandchildren.

Warren's Salmon Cannery near Bonneville was one of dozens operating on the Columbia River during canning's boom years, 1880-1920. 1902 photo.

Too many canneries—lots of them ill-advised—was given as the reason for "the over-heavy drain on the fishery resources"; and this over-building was ascribed as due to the "entirely erroneous idea generally prevalent that it is a bonanza business, and that all one needs to do to get rich quick is to build a salmon cannery." . . .

Hatcheries Held End-All Of Salmon Problems
Before we leave this consideration of conservation we must refer again to persistence of the slavish devotion to the thinking that in hatcheries lay the salvation of the salmon, and that artificial propagation provided a panacea for all ills.

For example, when the Association of Pacific Fisheries was organized in 1914, Item 1 on its list of objectives was: "To encourage artificial propagation of various kinds of food fishes."

Again, American packers told an American-Canadian commission studying the Fraser River—in 1918: "Hatcheries would be the salvation of the industry."

It was the end of 1919 before the pages of *Pacific Fisherman* yield any evidence of doubt. Then, and from then on, there seemed to be a turning toward the thought that hatcheries are effective and justifiable only under special conditions, and that reliance upon them cannot replace research and provide panacea for the problems arising from rule-of-thumb regulation. . . .

Threat of Dams First Became Acute in 1924
Dams and the destruction of salmon spawning streams in 1924 touched off a controversy which persists today. Declaring that the proposed Priest Rapids dam—which was never built—"imperils the Columbia River salmon fishery," *Pacific Fisherman* published an editorial "Save the Salmon Streams." The Skagit was threatened also, and later in the year this journal carried an editorial titled: "Watch the Power Commission"—an injunction equally pertinent today, when 30 years have proven that the Federal Power Commission still needs watching. . . .

External Pressures Shaped the Fisheries of 4th Decade 1933-42
Fisheries of the Fourth Decade of our Fifty Years were shaped more by external pressures than by influences from within.

These were years when the industry—*all* industry actually—felt the molding pressures of enormous forces!

Depression—to depths beyond previous economic experience;

"Controlled economy" — and its search for economic panaceas;

Uncontrolled Bureaucracy—seeking new empires;

Imports—the world hunting markets in America;

War—with its shocking waste and sweeping changes.

These forces acted and reacted upon the fisheries in the years from 1933 through 1942.

The decade was not one of development in the sense that its immediate predecessors had been, but it was one of *change*—for the fishing industry of the Pacific, and for every human being upon Earth. . . .

Canada Abandons Hatcheries

Hatcheries for salmon were abandoned by Canada in 1936 after years of exhaustive study convinced the Dominion's scientists that they are an unsound substitute for natural propagation, save in the relatively restricted cases where adequate reproduction *cannot* succeed on a natural basis. With this stroke, advanced biological thinking broke away from the long years of supine enslavement to the bureaucratic doctrine that the hatchery is the panacea which solves all salmon problems. . . .

Decade 1943-52
Shaping the Course for the Years to Come

Future course for fisheries, intelligently laid on the basis of wise-use conservation and scientific fact determined by research, was the principal concern for the Fifth Decade—1943-1952—once victory had been won in World War II.

First years of *Pacific Fisherman's* Fifth Decade naturally were dominated by the demands of war—and the fisheries delivered those demands in full, despite the staggering loss of vessels to the military service, and the handicaps laid by the blunderings of bureaucracy and its callow, sophomoric economists.

With the war away, and its lessons still sharp in recollection, leaders of the Pacific fisheries along all the western coast of North America began to concern themselves with the courses the fisheries would follow in the long-pull years of the future.

The Course to Come

In no other decade of the 50 years which we have studied in detail as we have sought the fundamentals in this half-century of industrial history has there been comparable concern for the course of the years to come.

The 10 years closing with this have made long strides in industrial technology; and in them the fisheries have contributed heavily
to victory in war—but the distinguishing characteristic of this final
decade of our Fifty Years—its prime contribution—has been its
strides in the field of international understandings for development
and conservation, and in the realm of scientific research. . . .

Drain of War Demand Impairs Future of Fisheries

Thus far in our digest of the Fifth Decade we have been concerned
with its remarkable record of developments which may be expected
materially to shape the future of the fisheries; but we have not
forgotten that this was the decade of war, when the heaviest demands were made upon fisheries for food and vessels.

The decade opened with Harold Ickes—never a friend of the
fisheries—declaring: "There is a vital need for every possible pound
of fishery product," and he went out to get it by proposing that
"conservation regulations be relaxed to produce all available fish."
Always a great *professing* conservationist, he added: "But at the same
time to preserve the capital stock of the resource."

Pacific Fisherman never could stomach such compromises with
conservation, and responded editorially:

> Already there is heard a call for the relaxation of restrictions laid
> upon fisheries in time of peace for the purpose of conserving and
> perpetuating the resource . . . The fact of war should not be made
> an excuse for destroying the gains achieved through years of
> conservation, until and unless the need is positively proven . . .
> Expansion of the fish catch can be achieved better and more
> soundly through the use of species we have formerly despised
> than through the reckless exploitation of what we shall need in
> the long future.

> Fiftieth Anniversary Number, *Pacific Fisherman*, August 1952, 12,
> 11, 27, 29, 39, 51, 58, 69, 77.

Commentary

MILLER FREEMAN began publishing the *Pacific Fisherman* in 1902 and continued his association with it until his death in September 1955. To celebrate its fiftieth anniversary, the magazine published a summary by decade of "the interesting, the human, the *significant.*" Salmon, sardines, tuna, and halibut dominated coverage. The preceding excerpts emphasize *Pacific Fisherman's* perspective, particularly on the concept of conservation. Miller Freeman was acknowledged as a leader in looking to the industry's future.

"There can be no compromise with conservation," said Freeman. "To have a fishing industry, you must have fish; and if you use your fish wisely you can have them forever." He continually tried to keep people focused on the future of the Pacific Coast's fishing industries. Yet despite being an articulate spokesperson for conservation, Freeman did not realize his goal. "There will never be an end to the fisheries' problems," he forecast. "As solutions are found, new posers arise." The articles excerpted document several reasons for the failure of conservation.

The first problem is lack of knowledge. For example, in the past some people saw hatcheries as a panacea, but experience in British Columbia led to a turn to natural propagation there as early as 1936. The full life cycle of the salmon was not known, so although policymakers recognized the need for a long-term view, they had too little information on which to act.

A second problem is the complexity of the system of which salmon are but one part. Many other activities coexist with salmon and have an impact on the fish. The building of dams; irrigation, mining, and logging practices; and municipal waste disposal are some of the activities that affect salmon runs but which have rarely taken account of them. The early dams did not include fish passage. Logging did not protect stream corridors. After World War II municipal and industrial wastes reduced water quality to the point where the August pollution below Willamette Falls blocked fish passage. Farm irrigation sucked large numbers of smolts out of the streams and onto the land. These and other activities did not seek purposely to destroy the salmon runs, but their cumulative impact was destructive. Each activity was carried out in a way that was easiest, most efficient, and least disruptive to its own goals.

Third, individual and corporate incentives to grow also counteract conservation objectives. In the past the fisher who caught the most

The technique of gillnetting was imported to Astoria by the Scandinavian and Finn fishers who moved there by the hundreds starting in the 1870s.

and the canner who canned the most were celebrated. Those catching the most fish were acknowledged as "highliners." To be a highliner, fishers invented new gears and technologies. Motorized boats allowed one person fishing to catch as much as two had previously, since the puller was no longer needed. Each year the *Pacific Fisherman* reported the productivity success stories of fishers and canners. The canners continually tried to increase their productivity by canning more with less labor and at lower costs to the consumer. Now, as then, this attitude creates incentives to catch more and be bigger. The *Pacific Fisherman* articles suggest that government bureaucrats and scientists are no different. They seek to enlarge their programs. Fishers, canners, bureaucrats, and scientists each act within their own narrow range of incentives in a way that may run counter to the needs of the system as a whole.

The Columbia River Fishermen's Protective Union worked for conservation laws, as did the canners. But each group sought conservation that protected its own interests. The day-to-day incentives of each were to get as much from the resource as possible. Gillnetters invented trolling to get around the closed season. Canners bought salmon from coastal buying stations to keep cannery lines running during the closed season. Biologists, seeking to please government bureaucrats and the public, introduced salmon in places where they had not been before and eradicated salmon from places they thought were better for other uses. So despite good intentions, the cumulative result of people's actions was to put ever greater pressure on the stocks.

Fourth, unexpected events beyond local control frequently occur. The Great Depression, World War II, the competition of imports, and governmental mandates complicate the situation to which local fisheries must adapt. World War II, for example, had a tremendous impact on resources. Secretary Ickes angered Miller Freeman by saying that for the national security, "There is a vital need for every possible pound of fishery product." The dams built on the Columbia River provided the electric power needed for wartime production. The Fraser River blockage by the Hell's Gate landslide in 1913 was another unforeseen event to which the salmon industry had to adapt. So while the small, incremental changes add up to big problems for salmon, major events—political and ecological—also shock the system from time to time.

Finally, the sequencing of these events has worked against the salmon. The incremental effects of dams, irrigation, logging, and municipal waste take time to be seen. Knowledge about the system always lags behind. The cumulative effects of activities bring new questions that take time to study. The studies usually raise more questions than they answer. Legislation needs a climate of some research certainty. Freeman continually criticized rules made without proper scientific grounding. The laws came too late. New laws deal with yesterday's problems, but more important, new laws create new incentives. As those fishing were more constrained inshore, they moved farther offshore. There was a continual reaching out to find new stocks of salmon or to catch them earlier in their life cycle. Regulations called for closed seasons, then size limits. But each new regulation only addressed a past problem, not the future of the fishery.

Complexity, lack of knowledge, incentives, unforeseen events, and timing have all interacted to limit the success of good intentions. The goal may have been right, but in practice day-to-day events often add up to a different result.

—Courtland L. Smith

MANAGEMENT OF WOOD IS CRITICAL TO RIVERS AND SALMON

Document:	**Salmon Fisheries of the Coastal Rivers**
Authors:	John Gharrett and John Hodges, biologists employed by the Oregon Fish Commission
Year:	1950
Description:	This report was among the first to describe the problems caused for salmon by logging practices.

WITHOUT DOUBT, many of the streams have been heavily fished and perhaps overfished, but the failure of the salmon populations to respond to the restriction and in many instances the removal of the commercial fishery indicates the necessity of investigating other factors which may affect the populations. It is probable that even yet we do not understand or even recognize all the factors affecting the salmon runs. The ocean life of salmon and steelhead is still somewhat a mystery. It has only been in the past few years that concerted studies have been started on this phase of the life history of the salmon.

The point to the above discussion is that there is much more to protecting the fish runs than elimination of one type of fishing.

Other Factors Affecting the Populations
Watershed Cover
Logging operations have been carried out to various degrees on the watersheds of all the coastal streams. Needless to say, this has caused considerable changes in the characteristics of these streams. Forest fires, too, have taken their toll of the watershed cover, particularly in the Tillamook area where approximately 250,000 acres of the headwaters of the Trask, Wilson, Miami, Kilchis, and Nehalem Rivers were burned over. The effects of these changes on fish populations have been obvious in many respects. In others, the effects have not been so evident.

Stream surveys have shown that many miles of spawning area in the coastal streams have been made unavailable and removed from salmon production due to the formation of impassable log jams resulting from logging debris . . . . Similar jams have also resulted from debris accumulating in the streams in the wake of fires. The removal of the watershed cover has reduced its ability to hold moisture. Consequently violent fluctuations in stream flow occur. The high winter flows scour the gravel from the stream beds in the upper reaches of the river and cover with silt the spawning areas of the lower reaches. In the summer the water temperatures are excessively high due to the reduced stream flow and the lack of protection from the sun. None of these conditions are conducive to salmon production as is evidenced by the relationship found between logging and salmon catches.

Water Use Projects

Other water uses also have an adverse effect on the salmon production of the coastal rivers. Splash dams in the Coos and Coquille systems, built for the purpose of sluicing logs down the rivers, have blocked the salmon runs and eliminated the productivity of the streams above them. This practice has also resulted in the sluicing of the gravel and destruction of the spawning areas below the splash dams. Many impoundments for log ponds, power production, and irrigation have been created without providing the proper facilities for fish passage. These have eliminated the salmon runs in many river sections. . . .

Stream Improvement . . .

In recent years it has become obvious that, if the anadromous fish populations are to be maintained in the face of adverse conditions resulting from the industrialization of the Pacific Coast, every bit of spawning area in the rivers will have to be made available for the propagation of these species. As rapidly as funds permit, the Engineering Division of the Oregon Fish Commission is making available such areas to spawning fish by removing log jams from the streams and building fishways over falls and dams.

> John T. Gharrett and John I. Hodges. 1950. *Salmon Fisheries of the Coastal Rivers of Oregon South of the Columbia.* (Portland: Oregon Fish Commission), Contribution no. 13: 20, 27. (Citations omitted.)

Document:	**Prevent Logging Damage to Streams**
Author:	Canadian Department of Recreation and Conservation
Year:	1966
Description:	The damage that logging could cause to streams and fish led to government regulations and guidelines calling for logging-related wood to be kept out of and away from streams. In Canada such rules came as early as 1932, here forcefully restated in two extracts from a Canadian Department of Recreation and Conservation publication.

(3) No PERSON ENGAGING in logging, lumbering, land clearing or other operations, shall put or knowingly permit to be put, any slash, stumps or other debris into any water frequented by fish or that flows into such water, or on the ice over either such water, or at a place from which it is likely to be carried into either such water. 1932, c. 42, s. 33.

> Excerpt from the Canadian Fisheries Act, 1932, c. 42, s. 1, in Canadian Department of Recreation and Conservation, *Prevent Logging Damage to Streams: A Message to All Logging Operators* (British Columbia: A. Sutton, 1966), 6.

Our Streams Are Vulnerable

STREAMS DRAINING the forest lands of British Columbia produce vast numbers of high quality trout and salmon. Some early logging methods created havoc on the land and destroyed many streams. The area affected by these poor practices was only a small part of our forests and the loss in fish production went largely unnoticed.

Today, when most of our forested watersheds are being logged, even minor stream damage on this wide scale could result in serious loss to our commercial and sport fisheries.

WITH GOOD PLANNING and a reasonable amount of care, forests can be logged with little damage to streams. While sound planning of forest operations is common, care for protecting our streams is often lacking.

The purpose of this booklet is to encourage greater care in logging so that our high quality fisheries may be maintained. . . .

To Prevent Siltation

1. Do not use stream-beds, even dry ones, for skidding logs.

2. Avoid long skid-roads on steep slopes. Use gradients of less than 12 per cent if possible.

3. Locate roads so that overcast and fill material does not enter streams. Roads should be at least 50 feet away from stream banks wherever possible.

4. Provide adequate ditching and culverts.

5. Keep all ditches and culverts open.

6. Do not use stream-bed gravel for road construction.

7. Avoid streamside landings.

8. Keep heavy equipment out of streams. . . .

Logging Slash in Streams
How does it affect fish?
Stream Channel Damage

Slash and large logging debris can form jams around which or under which the stream must scour a new channel. The resultant violent movement of channel materials can kill eggs and food organisms in the gravel and cause deposition of silt below the jam.

Obstruction

In channels confined by bedrock or large boulders, jams of logging debris can block the migration of fish to and from spawning-grounds.

Organic Pollution

Bacterial decomposition of slash and small-wood debris in water results in a removal of oxygen, and this process may cause a deficiency of oxygen for fish, particularly during their prehatching stage in the gravel.

Good co-operation by logging operators in stream clean-up work has resulted in relatively few prosecutions for infraction of the Fisheries Act. However, clean-up operations using heavy equipment near stream banks or bulldozers in stream-beds can compound the stream damage, and it is difficult to tell which is more harmful, the slash or the clean-up.

Active prevention of the entry of slash to streams is the best way to control this form of stream damage.

(1) Fall all trees away from streams wherever possible. If tree tops and limbs do enter a stream, they should be removed from the stream as soon as possible, certainly no later than when the logs are extracted.

(2) Before logging crews move to a new setting, check the stream to ensure that slash from current logging is neither in the stream nor likely to enter the stream on high flows.

Where removal of logs from any area has been completed and recent logging slash remains in the stream, prosecution is called for if fish are present in the stream or in any of the downstream waters.

WELL MANAGED FORESTS can provide better stream conditions for fish than natural "unspoiled" forests.

INCREASED WATER YIELD by the gradual removal of mature timber can be beneficial to fisheries, especially when low summer flows are augmented.

> Canadian Department of Recreation and Conservation, *Prevent Logging Damage to Streams: A Message to All Logging Operators* (British Columbia: A. Sutton, 1966), 3-4, 7-8.

Document:	**Guidelines for Stream Protection**
Author:	Richard L. Lantz, Oregon State Game Commission
Year:	1971
Description:	The brochure outlines guidelines for logging operations.

THERE ARE GOOD and bad ways to clean out a stream. Method and timing are important. Clearance should not be done by running heavy equipment through the stream . . . , creating a channeled sluiceway, removing spawning gravel, and perhaps killing eggs in the gravel or small fish in the stream. The men on the ground doing the job must understand why debris should be kept out of the stream. This is a matter of better supervision since improper stream clearance has been a large problem in the past, and continues to be so in some areas. Consultation with the local fishery biologist can be important in determining what material should be removed. In some cases he can save the logging operator money by recommending that stabilized material in the stream channel be left to provide fish habitat.

> Richard L. Lantz, *Guidelines for Stream Protection in Logging Operations* (Portland: Oregon State Game Commission, 1971), 10.

Document:	**Field Guide to Oregon Forest Practice Rules**
Author:	Oregon Forest Protection Association
Year:	1972
Description:	The guide prescribes Oregon rules for logging practices near and in streams.

[24-541 (1)] *(F1) LEAVE HARDWOOD TREES,* shrubs, grasses, rocks, and natural "down" timber wherever they afford shade over a Class I stream or maintain the integrity of the soil near such a stream. . . .

[(2)] (b) Trees should be felled, bucked and limbed so that the tree or any part thereof will not fall into or across any Class I stream. Remove all material that gets into such a stream as an on-going process during harvesting operations. Place removed material above high water level.

Field Guide to Oregon Forest Practice Rules (Oregon Forest Protection Association, 1972), 36, 37-38.

Document:	**Land Use Planning**
Author:	U.S. Forest Service
Year:	1974
Description:	This manual contains U.S. Forest Service rules from the agency's Pacific Northwest (region 6), pertaining to "woody debris."

CLASS I. The following practices, although not necessarily all-inclusive, are suggested. . . .

Man-caused woody debris must not be allowed to enter the stream channel. Removal of existing stable, natural woody debris shall be done only in cases where fish migration is blocked, water quality impaired, excessive erosion is occurring as a result of the debris, or access for recreation purposes is hampered. Existing natural woody debris will not be removed in wilderness.

"Title: 8200—Land Use Planning," *Forest Service Manual*, R-6 Supplement, no. 2 (March 1974), 6.

Commentary

RIVERS SERVED as important transportation routes during early Euro-American settlement, including transporting logs in the early days of logging in the Northwest. With few roads and even fewer that were passable in all seasons, loggers were faced with the choice of taking the mill to the trees or bringing the logs to the mill. Both alternatives were used, depending on local conditions and the skills of the operators. Initially, the only avenue for transporting the logs to the mills was to float them down the rivers. Low streamflows in the summer created major problems for log drives, but this obstacle was overcome by building splash dams. Logs were felled or dragged into the river either downstream of the dam or in the pond behind the dam and were transported by the wall of water that ripped through stream channels when the floodgates were opened. These dams ranged in sophistication from rough piles of logs embedded with dynamite charges to highly engineered dams capable of repeated releases and flow control. Log drives commonly resulted in immense logjams. Operators and communities worked extensively to eliminate obstructions in the river channels to prevent the jams that halted log drives and damaged property. As a result, most rivers of the Northwest were simplified by blasting rapids and clearing snags and islands to make it easier to move logs down to the mills. Even small streams that could be jumped across were dammed to transport shorter pieces of lumber, called ship's knees, which were used for board walks, railroad ties, ribbing in ships, and shakes.

Other forms of transportation eventually made river drives outmoded and, over time, landowners along rivers became opposed to log drives, complaining about the bank damage caused by floating logs, and the fact that crews often crossed private property with teams of horses and equipment. In 1919 the Oregon legislature prohibited the driving of "free" logs down streams and rivers. Nonetheless, rivers were used for holding logs and transporting them in bundles for several decades to follow. Logs were tied together in "booms" and anchored to pilings along the margins and side channels of the major rivers. Opposition to log booms grew for two reasons—the effect of booms on the ecology of the rivers and questions about rights to the state's waterways. After prolonged use for log storage, river bottoms became blanketed with submerged logs and bark. Aquatic organisms were eliminated by the loss of oxygen caused by the rotting wood and by the leaching of toxic chemicals from the wood and bark. Eventually, log storage in public waters was prohibited in 1972, and this source of river simplification ended.

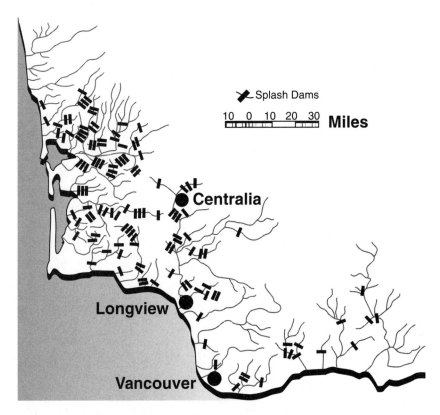

Splash dams were numerous in western Washington from 1880 to 1910.

The specter of floods, the nemesis of all river dwellers, has led to the straightening and simplification of stream channels during this century. After floods during World War II, the U.S. Army Corps of Engineers mapped out the distribution of the floods of the century since early settlement and called for several efforts to reduce the loss of property in future floods. The agency focused intensively on making river modifications and flood control dams in the headwaters. In response to the floods of the 1940s, they obtained funding from Congress for clearing snags from 300 miles of the Willamette River and its major tributaries.

The importance of navigation has precipitated numerous federal and state laws to remove or prevent obstructions in streams and rivers. These laws were used by the Army Corps of Engineers to prevent landowners from dumping brush and stumps into streams in Oregon at the turn of the century. Such statutes are clearly aimed at not only the larger navigable channels but also small tributaries that would transport logging debris into lower rivers during floods.

Snagging and stream clearing continues in all municipalities and residential areas along the region's rivers. City and county plans and ordinances, such as the 1981 Corvallis Drainage Master Plan, call for clearing woody debris from streams passing through towns and suburbs.[1] Logs are removed to minimize obstructions and route the water off the land as quickly as possible.

Woody debris in forests and streams was altered greatly by logging practices over the last century. Early logging operations tended to leave enormous quantities of large tree bases because the primitive mills had difficulty in cutting the uneven sizes of the boles. Equipment developments after World War II meant that fewer big logs were left on the ground after a logging operation, though great quantities of "slash," or small logging debris, ended up in the channels and deposited large amounts of sediment into streams. Often the first cut in a harvest unit was dropped into the stream, and cutting progressed uphill from that point to minimize breakage and rolling trees.[2] In spite of statutes that prohibited loggers from loading debris into natural stream channels, large quantities of organic debris and soil were left in many streams after logging.

Fishery biologists in the Pacific Northwest became alarmed at the degradation of fish habitat, barriers to migration, depletion of oxygen, and high stream temperatures. The Oregon Fish Commission surveyed coastal streams from 1945 to 1950 and, as reported by John Gharrett and John Hodges, noted numerous problems with logging debris. Impassable logjams led the list. Concerns over degraded habitat and migration barriers caused regional fishery biologists to call for stream cleaning. Such efforts were excessive in many cases throughout the Pacific Northwest, and they reduced the ecological functions and physical stability of wood in streams.

The Oregon Fish Commission, for its part, worked extensively to clear streams of accumulations of logging debris, believing this would help maintain anadromous fish populations. Naturally occurring debris undoubtedly was removed in the process.

A bulletin of the Fish and Wildlife Branch of the Department of Recreation and Conservation of British Columbia in 1966 illustrates the problem. The cover photo of *Prevent Logging Damage to Streams* shows the debris from road building strewn along the bank of a stream and in its channel. A later photo intended to represent appropriate practices shows a stream with bare banks and no wood in the channel. The attempt to promote sound management suggests:

When the water was abruptly released from a splash dam the pent-up logs flooded downstream toward lumber mills. Splash damming, in use until the 1950s in some Northwest streams, damaged streams and salmon runs.

WELL MANAGED FORESTS can provide better stream conditions for fish than natural "unspoiled" forests.

INCREASED WATER YIELD by the gradual removal of mature timber can be beneficial to fisheries, especially when low summer flows are augmented.

Experience has shown such optimism to be unfounded.

Aggressive stream cleaning in the period between 1950 and 1970 is frequently cited as an example of fisheries resource managers' swinging from one extreme to another in their recommendations. Not all agencies were calling for wholesale removal of all wood. The Oregon State Game Commission developed *Guidelines for Stream Protection in Logging Operations* in 1971. The focus of these directives was to prevent or remove small debris or slash from the logging operation, not to remove natural wood.

From 1950 to 1970, fisheries management agencies recommended greater protection of streamside vegetation for shade and erosion control and removal of slash after logging. Oregon was the first state to pass comprehensive forest practices legislation for private lands in 1971. The Oregon Forest Practices Act that went into effect in July 1972 was designed to improve reforestation and road construction and "protect soil, air, water and wildlife resources." The original rules required removal of all woody material from streams. At the same time, federal agencies were incorporating debris management into their management guidelines as well. The Land Use Planning section of the *Forest Service Manual* in 1974 provided for removal of logging slash but retention of natural wood.

In 1973, Henry Froehlich of Oregon State University's School of Forestry described the characteristics of natural woody debris and logging slash in streams. In his conclusions, he observed that

> Stream protection requirements in our timber producing areas are very much a part of the new "environmental awareness." Demands to maintain or even enhance conditions in the stream systems are likely to continue and will possibly become even stronger. Overcleaning channels may not be in the best interest of stream protection. We must recognize what the stream systems are like in their natural condition and also to understand the role of the organic debris in these channels.[3]

A September 1975 conference on logging debris in streams was held at Oregon State University (OSU) and proved to be a pivotal recognition of the ecology of woody debris. Researchers described the natural abundance of wood, its ecological roles in streams, and the changes caused by land use practices. James Hall and Cal Baker of OSU presented a paper in which they concluded:

We understand that current policy of most public timber management agencies requires the removal from major stream channels of any debris that enters the stream as a result of logging. The intent is to leave intact any natural debris that is firmly keyed into the channel and not expected to move. Unfortunately, in practice distinguishing between logging and natural debris often proves difficult. The result of the cleaning operation is often a channel almost completely devoid of debris. This may be another case in which we have oversold a problem in the past and need to take a more balanced view of the role of debris.[4]

Scientists soon found that most streams in the region (and around the world, for that matter) contained large quantities of wood, and removal of that wood decreased stream health. Wood played critical roles in forming channels, storing sediments, stabilizing banks, dissipating the energy of flowing water, storing food resources for aquatic and wood-feeding organisms, providing habitat for biota, and offering refuge during floods. Terrestrial researchers also found that woody debris played diverse ecological roles in upland forests. Within a decade, federal forests were managed to maintain natural amounts of woody debris both in streams and on forest floors.

Land use regulations in the 1980s recognized not only the need to maintain pre-existing wood in stream channels but also to retain large numbers of mature conifer and deciduous trees along streams and rivers to provide future inputs of woody debris. In 1990, the Willamette National Forest adopted a *Riparian Management Guide* that called for maintaining intact forests along all floodplains, perennial streams, and even ephemeral streams.[4] One of the key functions of these rules was to maintain long-term inputs of natural amounts, sizes, and types of wood. In the guide, the Willamette National Forest noted that "of all the ecological functions of riparian areas, the process of woody-debris loading into channels, lakes, and floodplains requires the longest time for recovery after harvest."

Recent development of forest policies for federal lands has incorporated ecological functions of woody debris into both upslope and streamside management (e.g., the 1993 report of the Forest Ecosystem Management and Assessment Team). This area of ecosystem management is unique in the rapid application of science into public resource policy and the lack of litigation demanding it. Woody debris management has become a cornerstone of ecosystem policy in the Pacific Northwest and throughout North America. Understanding of ecosystems is growing constantly, and policies must adapt to more rigorous information.

Direct falling of trees into the streams, clearcutting to the water's edge, and building roads immediately along channels are no longer acceptable. Human activities over the last 150 years have greatly altered the amount and functions of wood in streams and rivers. Recovery of these functions—the challenge for the next 150 years—will be determined by the evolution of public and private land use practices and the success of intensive restoration.

—Stanley V. Gregory

Notes

1. CH2MHill, The Corvallis Drainage Master Plan, May 1981.
2. Del Skeesick, fish biologist, Willamette National Forest, personal communication.
3. Henry A. Froehlich, "Natural and Man-Caused Slash in Headwater Streams," *Loggers Handbook,* 33 (Pacific Logging Congress, 1973), 84.
4. J. D. Hall and C. O. Baker, "Biological Impacts of Organic Debris in Pacific Northwest Streams," in *Logging Debris in Streams, Notes for a Workshop* (Corvallis: Oregon State University School of Forestry, 1975), 7.
5. Stan Gregory and Linda Ashkenas, *Riparian Management Guide* (Willamette National Forest, 1990).

DOES PLANNING HELP?

Document:	**Pacific Northwest Regional Plan**
Author:	Roy F. Bessey, a civil engineer with fifty years experience in government and private consulting
Year:	1963
Description:	The excerpts from this report prepared for the Washington Department of Conservation provide a model for how planning can improve livability in a region, but they also reveal the low priority given to sustaining salmon in the Northwest.

Preface
Introduction and Synopsis
THE DEVELOPMENT of the water and related land resources of the Pacific Northwest—with the Columbia River system at the core—is one of the world's greater undertakings of its kind and era. Over the past thirty years it has attracted the attention of planners, engineers, economists, politicians, and the general public of this and many other countries. . . .

. . . Over the thirty years of retrospect, the problem areas have remained much the same. The changes have been principally in degree or in phase. A population upswing has accented problems of urban concentration and proper use of land and other resources. It has also raised more primary questions as to whether the "explosion" and the concentration may not be too prolonged and too great. The employment stabilization problem remains although public concern has shifted from periodic mass unemployment to an expanding hard core of unemployment that persists through economic swings of lesser intensity and shorter duration. Perennial are the problems of too slow or too erratic economic and social growth in the face of galloping technological change, of too limited a protection and improvement of environment, and of too meager a strengthening of democratic and cooperative organization and procedure for conservation and development of our natural and human resources.

With such motives and conditions in mind, the within review is not presented as a comprehensive, detailed or definitive investigation of the whole Pacific Northwest resource development effort.

Rather, the purpose is to give a reasonably-connected narrative account of a regional planning movement from the necessarily limited perspective of a single witness. The hope is that the account will serve as a general guide to this planning experience, in spite of its limitations as history.

The period covered under the review is, in particular, the three decades extending from the beginning of the depression-induced planning of the early 1930's down to the present time of renewed movement toward comprehensive and coordinated resources planning. However, the view does extend further backward on significant evolutionary developments before this period. And, hopefully, it ventures to look a little ahead for needed further efforts toward the effective conservation and development and beneficial use of the resources of the Pacific Northwest. . . .

To a considerable degree, the perspective is a critical one—it is intended to provide or to invoke some evaluation of the Pacific Northwest experience with a view to improved designs in planning, programming, coordination, organization and procedures for effective resources and regional conservation and development. . . .

. . . Also deeply involved throughout are such fundamental concepts and principles as:

(1) The interrelationships and the unity of resources . . .

(2) Conservation: The husbanding, sustained yield, and wise and efficient use of resources.

(3) Optimum use, optimum benefit and distribution, in the development of resources.

(4) Comprehensiveness and multiple use of resources in conservation and development.

(5) Regionalism and "riverbasinism"—areal interrelationships, cohesion, integration, etc.—and their uses. (Not sectionalism or parochialism.)

(6) Cores or centers for research, planning and programming and their coordination.

(7) The planning problem and task, in its simplified, universal and perennial form: ". . . the wealth of nations depends on (a) the material resources of man's environment, (b) the biological resources of social personnel, (c) the social resources for mobilizing the common will to make the fullest use of the first two." (Lancelot P. Hogben in *Retreat from Reason.*)

(8) Planning philosophy, purpose and scope: Planning as the use of collective intelligence and foresight to chart direction, order,

harmony and progress in public activity relating to the human environment and general welfare. . . .

(9) Planning method: Essentially scientific method in conservation and development—consideration of purpose or direction, survey or fact-finding, estimate or appraisal, finding or hypothesis, plan formulation and comparison, conclusion or decision basis, and finally review of plan as it goes into effect, with feed-back in further planning. The method recognizes the nature of the development process with its somewhat diffused web of substantive or functional strands (basic data; land, water, materials and energy resources; economic and social facilities; etc.) crossed by overlapping sequential or phase strands (survey; planning and programming, design and technics development; management, utilization, information and education; program application and feed-back).

(10) The multiple-discipline involvement in research and appraisal, planning and development.

All of these purposes and principles have played important parts in the Pacific Northwest regional planning movement. Many of them had origins in the broad conservation movement that took at least intellectual form at the turn of the century. . . .

Finally, and again logically it is trusted, the review essays an appraisal of the current conditions, needs, and potentials. It seeks a view of prospects for well-led, well-coordinated, widely participated in, and effective regional and river-basin planning in the interest of the short- and long-run development of the resources of the Pacific Northwest region and the Nation. . . .

Prospects in Pacific Northwest Planning
Turning to a general appraisal of the situation and prospects for planning in the Pacific Northwest, the outlook might be characterized as more than ordinarily favorable. The setting is good— assuming national and regional will and drive—for renascent regional planning on a base stronger than ever, and with an increasing degree of coordination.

In looking for the more meaningful highlights of the regional situation, it is desirable to generalize upon both the state of development and the state of planning.

The population of the Pacific Northwest has grown from a little over three million to nearly six million since the early 1930's. The rate of growth has exceeded the national norm except for the decade 1950-1960 when it was slightly less. In the 1940-50 period the regional rate of growth was more than twice that of the country at large. If we look ahead a generation, the regional population is likely to be of the order of 10 million. Looking beyond the end of the century we may expect it to be about 15 million. If the national population should flatten out, as we might hope, the population seems likely to continue to increase in the less developed and less occupied Pacific Northwest.

In terms of metropolitan concentrations, we may expect, in effect, an almost continuous metropolitan complex extending through the Puget-Willamette trough from Vancouver, British Columbia, to Eugene, Oregon, as well as a marked expansion of inland metropolitan clusters such as that around Spokane. We should be prepared, in our planning for the end of the century, for a Puget Sound metropolitan constellation in Washington of the order of four million people and for another cluster of about half that around the juncture of the Columbia and the Puget-Willamette trough in Oregon and Washington. . . .

Traditionally also, the economy of the Pacific Northwest has been of an "immature" type in which outputs are dominantly raw and semi-processed (such as products of forests, agriculture and mines) and intakes from other regions dominantly manufactures. The condition has also been strongly reflected in employment patterns. Diversity has increased over the period of our review. . . .

The region's potentials in material, labor and technological resources are still relatively under-used and the region under-developed. But it seems likely that—on the basis of the drawing power of unused space and other natural resources coupled with the impulses from anticipated growth in national and West Coast population for at least a generation—a new wave of Pacific Northwest development should be planned for. The "pushes" and "spillovers" from the extraordinary growth of California may be of special significance. Of particular importance among regional "pulls" is the strategic combination of one of the Nation's greatest water-supply resources, its lowest-cost power supply, and economical marine and inland water transportation. . . .

Dams completed and under-construction or authorized will, in early years, have removed the swift or shallow-water bottlenecks to modern inland navigation on a 500-mile inland trunk across the waist of the region. . . .

Flood control will profit greatly from upstream storage developed for multiple purposes mentioned. The long-run justification of storage for water supply and pollution control purposes, superimposed on the traditional justification for power and flood control

a funny
thing
happened on
the way to
the office

*"Come to Oregon where the market is growing and the living is fun," said
the headline to this 1963 advertisement, run by Portland General Electric
Co. in* Fortune *magazine. The ad explicitly linked salmon to the quality of
life that would attract a business executive to the Northwest: "Mr. Carlson
is a nut on fishing. He can ... drive 20 minutes from his home in the heart
of Portland and spend a couple of hours trying to latch onto a salmon and
still be in the office by 9."*

itself, should have material effects on the volume of storage and
degree of flood control ultimately feasible. A replica of the 1894
flood would be reduced to a "no damage" stage while the stages of
the possible greater floods would be correspondingly reduced.

The greater flood control would permit a wider use of the flood
plains and would set a higher value on flood plain lands in agricultural, urban and metropolitan areas. However, a balanced regional
flood management program should be planned for—to include
protection and retardation works, flood-plain zoning, forecasting
and warning services—within the larger national flood manage-

ment policy. The state and local roles in flood protection and in flood-plain zoning should be more intensively developed under appropriate federal technical and financial aids. . . .

Very obviously, electric power development in the Pacific Northwest underwent a revolutionary expansion within the years of this review. Capacity increased from about 1 1/2 million kilowatts in 1933 to about 12 million in 1963. The initial impetus came from the public works of 1933—Bonneville and Grand Coulee—then quite widely hailed as "boondoggles.". . .

Turning to the forward look: the hydroelectric power capacity of the Pacific Northwest is still only about one-third developed. Under conservative estimates, requirements are expected to be of the order of 27 million kilowatts by the year 1980 and 56 million by 2000 [Corps of Engineers 1958 review report]. But resumed dynamic policies and programs in development, marketing and utilization might well increase such load estimates by a considerable margin. By 1980, a changeover from the all-hydro to a thermal-hydro system should be under way, with nuclear power playing an expanding role. . . .

The planning and development problems of water supply and pollution are very urgent and, moreover, of greater magnitude than generally supposed. Their effective solution, particularly through the safe disposal of growing volumes and varieties of wastes—solid, liquid, and gaseous, organic, chemically and radiologically active, quickly or slowly decaying—will have large bearing on the economic, social and environmental character and development of the region. . . .

Attention to fish and wildlife problems has grown greatly, over the years reviewed, in Pacific Northwest planning and development.

Large investments have been made in anadromous fish conservation measures at dams, beginning with pioneer fish passage facilities at Bonneville and with the relocation of runs barred by Grand Coulee dam. General programs of biological and engineering research and development in the fishery field by Federal and state agencies have also advanced very materially. A special Columbia River program in this field, designed to progress in parallel with the multiple-purpose river development, has been under way for nearly 15 years and has produced very valuable results; however, it has not had sufficient financial support to keep the pace. In more recent years an accelerated fishery research program has been in progress, with the particular view of providing a sound basis for decisions for the development of crucial Salmon and middle Snake reaches. At this writing, the "crash" investigations have not been completed.

These fishery research and development programs are broad in concept, looking to the safe passage of migrant fish at dams, removal of obstructions, restoration and improvement of spawning grounds, ponding, artificial propagation and rearing, and other measures, together with basic biological and engineering research and experimentation. Fundamental knowledge has been amassed, many designs have been developed, and significant experiments carried forward. But much more can be done with respect to the establishment or reestablishment of runs, spawning beds and channels, rearing ponds, predator and fishing controls and other means of increasing yield, as well as to the passage of mature fish and fingerlings at dams and other obstructions (including some heretofore considered as impassable).

The program scope should be broad, encompassing all feasible ways and means and covering geographically both lower and upper reaches of the Columbia system, and coastal and Puget Sound streams and bays. For the desired effect, other programs—as for the appropriate control of commercial and sports fishing and for abatement of pollution of various kinds—must be correlated.

The need for a renewed and strengthened fisheries conservation and development effort covering sea-run and resident fishes is great. The anadromous runs of the region have declined over a long period of years—antedating the main-stream dam building era here reviewed. The causes have been manifold, including many rooted in human activities in fishing, logging, pollution, water diversion, and the like, but perhaps others of more obscure biological character. The conservation measures should be equally diverse.

Rather similarly, a broad program of wildlife conservation and its corollaries should be strengthened as comprehensive water and land development programs are advanced. In water planning and development, positive and parallel plans for such needs as waterfowl nesting and resting, or big game range, must be met or compensated for. In land development, including irrigation, planning for upland game and birds should proceed in full concert.

Outdoor recreation clearly presents one of the fastest growing of our land and water conservation and development needs. Uses and demands, under the cumulative effects of added population, disposable income, leisure, and mobility, are expanding at rates far above those for population alone. Demands are particularly pressing with respect to water areas, where limitations are already severe, particularly in interior regions and in many metropolitan areas. . . .

Very material progress has been made over our three decades in the field of watershed management, but much remains to be done in strengthening its role—particularly along the line of comprehensiveness and intensiveness of coverage. Most notable advances have occurred in the management of forest lands under private as well as public ownership, on public range lands, and on the largely private agricultural lands under the soil conservation districts. . . .

. . . Watershed management should be applied from top to bottom, that is from hill to valley bottom, and from the wild lands, through agricultural to urban areas. None of the effects on land and water of the more intensive urban, industrial and transportation uses should be overlooked. . . .

The greatest need is for an over-all land use planning—for the establishment of rational patterns of land use according to character, quality and location and to the needs of people in their expanding urban and rural uses. . . .

Conclusion

For the writer, the deepest or most significant conclusion to be drawn from a review of a generation of regional planning is that there is a great need for new concepts and purposes in regional and national planning. A new kind of planning—less narrow and specialized, more comprehensive of resources and community planning, more directly orientated to human life and living—is needed to meet the needs of the next generation. The search for the right kind of planning for our democratic society is more practical than utopian under the forseeable pressures of an explosive population growth and urban and metropolitan concentration that is certain to continue for the next few decades.

From the viewpoint of this reporter, the national and regional planning movement begun in 1933 as a part of the New Deal was on a good road so far as it could go. Its combination of conscious and intuitive wisdom applied to the over-all problem of resources and their use has not been attained since, in the view of the writer. It encompassed in its study the various aspects of the economy and the society, bringing to bear many disciplines and schools of thought. . . .

The great planning need in this crucial time then is to resume the work of pulling the pieces together at the national, regional and local levels. . . . There are key purposes that can be widely accepted—a harmony of man and environment, improvement of an environment for free men with opportunity for material and spiritual advancement. And in the shaping of environment must be applied the fundamental and universal criterion of livability or habitability.

The point may be illustrated by one view of the Pacific Northwest problem expressed nearly a quarter century ago by Lewis Mumford. He had been asked by the Northwest Regional Council to look at the region and the planning movement and to give his considered views [Lewis Mumford, *Regional Planning in the Pacific Northwest,* Northwest Regional Council, 1939]. He strongly stressed the human, the cultural, and the environmental side of the problem, the great and beautiful natural heritage and its preservation, the need of rational distribution of people, and social purpose and achievement as the primary justification in the use of the land and resources. With his concern for the land and for the city, and with evidences of spoliation before him, he saw the need for a unified and human consideration: "The lure of metropolitan congestion is, one sees, the other side of the loneliness of the hinterland. And the two things must be treated together."

Roy F. Bessey, *Pacific Northwest Regional Planning—A Review,* Washington Department of Conservation, Division of Power Resources, bulletin no. 6 (Olympia, 1963), vii-xi, 151-55, 157-60, 171-72.

Commentary

 TABLE 1 SHOWS some of the organizational complexity that surrounds salmon management. The number of organizations that have an impact on salmon creates a need for integrative organizations and regional planning.

Planning for the future was an idea mandated by federal legislation in the 1930s. Roy F. Bessey, the veteran author of this report, demonstrates the belief that with forethought human societies can anticipate and avoid future problems. Bessey anticipates that the relationship between the region's metropolitan areas and its hinterlands will need to be holistically considered in regional plans. He also emphasizes planning to promote economic growth to solve regional problems. Throughout this report, Bessey argues for "better" planning. A continual theme of his work is that if we could only achieve the planning ideal, our problems could be alleviated and solved.

Many of the priorities Bessey and his contemporaries had a half century ago are different from those of today. We are more likely to question resource extraction and the expansion of a less-developed region. But concern for resources and the relation between metropolitan areas and rural places continue as important issues.

President Theodore Roosevelt, forester Gifford Pinchot, and geologist-hydrologist W. J. McGee sold the people of the United States the idea of conservation. Conservation meant wise use, scientific management, multiple use, and careful planning. Bessey (p. 6) quotes President Roosevelt, speaking to the Governor's Conference on May 13, 1908:

> We can enormously increase our transportation facilities by the canalization of our rivers so as to complete a greater system of waterways on the Pacific, Atlantic and Gulf coasts . . . . But these varied uses of our natural resources are so closely connected that they should be coordinated, and should be treated as one coherent plan, and not in haphazard and piecemeal fashion.

In the 1930s, urban planning and zoning began to take hold. As governor of New York, Franklin Roosevelt said, "In the long run, state and national planning is essential to the future prosperity, happiness and existence of the American people" (Bessey, p. 16). In the 1960s river basin commissions became the planning unit. The Pacific Northwest River Basins Commission emphasized concern for regional growth and maintaining the quality of the environment.

Most of the planning was aimed at developing the Columbia Basin for hydroelectric generation, irrigation, navigation, and flood control. Bessey's 200-page summary of Northwest planning contains little about fish; the excerpt above contains a large part of his discussion of fisheries. Elsewhere are page after page given over to questions of economic growth. The health of fish stocks was not given equal treatment with economic development and expanding settlement in the Pacific Northwest.

Implicit in all the discussions of planning is the belief that humans have the ability to foresee problems and to fix whatever they break, that if they plan carefully they can prevent, and if need be, correct their problems. As Bessey reviews thirty years of planning, we are struck by the failure to ever get ahead of the impacts. We see planning as a continually reactive exercise, never achieving its promise of anticipating the impacts of change.

—Courtland L. Smith

Table 1. Some of the institutions affecting wild salmon in the Pacific Northwest

Aluminum companies
Bonneville Power Administration
Bureau of Land Management
Columbia River Inter-Tribal Fish Commission
Columbia River Compact
City governments
Columbia Basin Fish and Wildlife Council
Commercial Fishers' organizations
Consumer groups
County governments
Environmental groups
Environmental Protection Agency
Federal Energy Regulatory Commission
Forest products companies
International Salmon Commission
Irrigation districts and associations
Northwest Power Planning Council
Pacific Fishery Management Council
Pacific Salmon Commission
Port districts
Public and private electric utilities
Public and private water utilities
Recreation boating industry
Recreational fishing groups
Salmon and Steelhead Advisory Commission
State fish and wildlife departments
State forestry agencies
State governments
Treaty and non-treaty Indians
U.S. Army Corps of Engineers
U.S. Bureau of Reclamation
U.S. Department of Agriculture
U.S. Department of Commerce
U.S. Department of Justice
U.S. Department of State
U.S. Department of Transportation
U.S. Fish and Wildlife Service
U.S. Forest Service

Sources: Philip R. Wandschneider, *Control and Management of the Columbia-Snake River System* (Pullman: Washington State University Agricultural Research Center, 1984). Northwest Power Planning Council, *1991 Northwest Conservation and Electric Power Plan,* 1 (Portland, Oregon: Northwest Power Planning Council, 1991).

IV. The Indian Experience

Introduction

"*THE WHOLE TREATMENT* of the government towards these Indians has been full of bad faith." That statement, made by the white Superintendent of Indian Affairs in Oregon in 1867, applies to much of the settlement of the Northwest. As instruments of the Euro-American settlers, local, state, and federal governments frequently took advantage, or sought to take advantage, of the native people of the Northwest. So, often, did the Euro-Americans themselves.

Indians marched through downtown Portland in a June 1981 protest over a bill, introduced by Washington Sen. Slade Gorton, that would have seriously affected Indians by ending their rights to sell steelhead trout.

The first reaction from the Indians, as they confronted an alien power and its indifference, is what anyone would expect. "Long time my heart has been sorry when I thought of my people." So spoke A-miltswot-na, a chief of an Oregon coastal tribe, in 1873. But later the Indians began to use the courts. Over the last century, the federal courts have sometimes shown a commendable decency in understanding the petitions and the positions of the Indians. The courts'

Previous page: The Indian fishery at Celilo Falls, circa 1950.

intertwined treatment of the Indians and the salmon is the recurring element in the documents in this section.

For non-Indians, it may be difficult to get a perspective long enough to put this recent history of America into a natural and native perspective. The salmon have been in the Northwest for millions of years. The Indians were here for about ten thousand years before Euro-Americans showed up. Somehow, during all that time, the Indians never placed the salmon in the jeopardy they are in today.

Some will argue that the main difference now is regional population size. When only Indians lived here, the human population was far smaller. If there had been as many Indians then as there are people in the Northwest now, so the argument goes, they would have depleted the fish just as rapidly as has happened since white settlement. Or, perhaps, the difference is technology. If the Indians had had modern technology, so this argument goes, they also would have used it and caused a drastic depletion of the fish. All one can do is speculate. The fact is, the Indians did not put the salmon in jeopardy.

But such speculation is, itself, arrogant and arid, imagining, as it does, that traditional Indian culture is moved by the same forces and restrained by the same values as Euro-American culture. The following section presents a powerful vantage point on the troubled history of both the Indians and the salmon, and offers insights into both Indian and Euro-American culture.

WHAT THE TREATIES PROMISED THE INDIANS

Document:	**Stevens Treaty Negotiations**
Authors:	The minutes of the treaty negotiations were recorded by agents of the U.S. government.
Year:	1854
Description:	These treaties, pressed by Washington territorial governor Isaac Stevens, extinguished Indian title to more than 64 million acres that now make up most of the states of the Pacific Northwest.

Governor Stevens...

MY CHILDREN. I have simply told you the heart of the Great Father and what are his wishes and desires. But the lands are yours and we swear to pay you for them. We thank you that you have been so kind to all the white children of the Great Father who have come here from the east. Those white children have always told you that you would be paid for your lands, and we are now here to buy them.

The white children of the Great Father, but no more his children than you are, have come here, some to build mills, some to till the land and others to build and sail ships. My children, I believe that I have got your hearts, you have my heart. We will put our hearts down on paper, and then we will sign our names. . . .

Seattle.

I look upon you as my father. I and the rest regard you as such. All of the Indians have the same good feeling towards you, and will send it on paper to the Great Father. All of them, men old men, women & children rejoice that he has sent you to take care of them.

> Minutes of the Treaty of Point Elliot (Jan. 22 1855, 12 Stat. 927), reprinted in Edward G. Swindell, *Report on the Source, Nature, and Extent of the Fishing, Hunting, and Miscellaneous Related Rights of Certain Indian Tribes in Oregon and Washington* (Los Angeles: U.S. Department of the Interior, 1942), 340-41.

Che-law-teh-tat.

I WISH TO SPEAK my mind as to selling the land—Great Chief! What shall we eat if we do so? Our only food is berries, deer and salmon—where then shall we find these? I don't want to sign away all my land, take half of it, and let us keep the rest. I am afraid that I shall become destitute and perish for want of food. . . .

Governor Stevens.

Are you not my children and also children of the great Father? What will I not do for my children and what will you not for yours? Would you not die for them? This paper is such as a man would give to his children and I will tell you why. This paper gives you a home. Does not a father give his children a home? This paper gives you a school. Does not a father send his children to school? It gives you mechanics and a doctor to teach and cure you. Is not that fatherly? *This paper secures your fish.* Does not a father give food to his children? Besides fish you can hunt, gather roots and berries.

Minutes of the Treaty of Point-No-Point (Dec. 26 1854, 12 Stat. 933), reprinted in Edward G. Swindell, *Report on the Source, Nature, and Extent of the Fishing, Hunting, and Miscellaneous Related Rights of Certain Indian Tribes in Oregon and Washington* (Los Angeles: U.S. Department of the Interior, 1942), 345-48. (Emphasis added.)

Washington Territorial Governor Isaac Ingalls Stevens

Document: **Treaty of Medicine Creek**

Authors: The treaty was signed by the U.S. Congress and various Indian tribes.

Year: 1854

Description: Article III of the treaty protected traditional Indian fisheries.

ARTICLE III. The right of taking fish, at all usual and accustomed grounds and stations, is further secured to said Indians, in common with all citizens of the Territory, and of erecting temporary houses for the purpose of curing, together with the privilege of hunting, gathering roots and berries, and pasturing their horses on open and unclaimed lands.

> Treaty of Medicine Creek, Dec. 26 1854, art. III, 10 Stat. 1132, 1133.

Commentary

 IN THE MID-1850S, rapid white settlement of the Oregon Territory created conflicts with the indigenous Indians. To avoid warfare, Congress affirmed its intent to take the Indians' land by treaty, not by force, no fewer than five times after the U.S.-Great Britain Treaty of 1846. Congress directed Isaac Ingalls Stevens, Superintendent of Indian Affairs for Washington Territory and its first governor, to negotiate treaties to avoid warfare. In late 1854 and 1855, in a period of seven months, Stevens, along with Joel Palmer, Superintendent of Indian Affairs for the Oregon Territory, signed nine treaties with more than seventeen thousand Indians. These treaties extinguished Indian title to more than 64 million acres that now make up most of the states of the Pacific Northwest.

Although both Stevens and the Indians appear to have conducted the treaty negotiations in good faith, Stevens was hardly a disinterested participant. A young and ambitious politician, he was determined to facilitate rapid white settlement of the region. To negotiate the treaties, he organized small bands of Indians into tribes, effectively creating new political entities that persist to this day. The "chiefs" that Stevens appointed were naturally those who were more receptive to the white newcomers. Prior to this intervention and the earlier interactions of the native people with the Hudson's Bay Company traders, Northwest Indian social organization had been less formal, and leaders did not have the degree of authority which we would associate with the term "chief." In addition, Stevens conducted the negotiations in Chinook jargon, a simple dialect containing about three hundred words from several Indian languages, with a sprinkling of French and English. Many of the Indians did not understand Chinook jargon, but Stevens' interpreter Colonel Shaw did, although there is some question about his facility with the Indian languages. Moreover, the treaties themselves were written in English and drafted before any formal meetings with the natives.

Despite all these bargaining disadvantages, and although some Indians were willing to give up most of their land, the tribes insisted on treaty language that would protect their traditional fishing practices, not surprising for a people who, in the words of a federal judge, shared an "almost universal and generally paramount dependence" on salmon. And the federal government not only agreed to this bargain, it promised federal protection for both the Indians' reserved lands and their reserved fisheries.

The protection of traditional Indian fisheries, a prerequisite to the signing of the treaties, was guaranteed by Article III of the Stevens treaties. This article assured the newly formed tribes of the exclusive right to fish on-reservation and also the right to fish "in common with" settlers at their traditional fishing grounds located off the reservations.

Governor Stevens recognized the critical importance the Indians attached to maintaining access to their traditional fisheries and, in fact, the Indian fishery was expected to be an important part of the region's economy, as the Indians would sell fish to the white settlers. Although it is true that the federal government sought to foster agrarian practices on the tribes' land reservations, there is no evidence that the government intended to restrict the tribes to agriculture or prevent them from continuing their commercial fishing practices.

Thus, the promises made in Article III of the Stevens treaties were central to the bargain. They formed the bedrock assumptions of one of the largest peaceful real estate transactions in Western history.

For some years following the signing of the treaties, there were few disputes over tribal fishing. White settlers had not yet attempted to exclude the Indians from their historic fishing grounds. The salmon remained relatively abundant, and there was little large-scale fishing by whites, mainly because of low market demand due to inadequate preservation techniques and slow transportation facilities.

By the late nineteenth century, however, a number of technological developments created increasing conflicts between the proliferating white settlers and traditional Indian fishing practices. Perfection of the canning process and the construction of transcontinental railroads made salmon available to eastern markets in the 1870s. By 1883, some forty canneries packed over six hundred thousand cases of salmon. With demand for salmon increasing, a non-Indian commercial fishery began to preempt fishing by introducing new fishing techniques, such as fish wheels and beach seining with horses. On the Columbia River, the whites also effectively preempted upriver Indian fishers by securing a locational advantage in the lower Columbia. Gasoline-powered engines, introduced around the turn of the century, introduced a non-Indian troll fishery in the ocean and in Puget Sound.

The Indian fisheries were also preempted by the political process. Especially after Washington achieved statehood in 1889, the state frequently enacted laws curtailing Indian fishing in the name of conservation. Designation of "salmon preserves" restricted tribal fishing in western Washington rivers, while largely ignoring ocean and Puget Sound salmon fishing by whites. Thus, by the late nineteenth century, technological and political developments had displaced much of the traditional Indian harvest.

—Michael C. Blumm and F. Lorraine Bodi

SUPREME COURT UPHOLDS INDIANS' RIGHTS

Document:	***United States v. Winans***
Author:	Justice Joseph McKenna, Supreme Court Justice, wrote the majority opinion in the case.
Year:	1905
Description:	The U.S. Supreme Court ruled in this case that the fishing rights the Indians had kept for themselves in the Stevens treaties could not be taken away by state licenses and federal grants. The Winans brothers operated state-licensed fish wheels on federal land grants, and they wanted to keep Indians away from their fishing sites.

[I]T WAS DECIDED [in the lower court] that the Indians acquired no rights but what any inhabitant of the Territory or State would have. Indeed, acquired no rights but such as they would have without the treaty. This is certainly an impotent outcome to negotiations and a convention, which seemed to promise more and give the word of the Nation for more. And we have said we will construe a treaty with the Indians as "that unlettered People" understood it and "as justice and reason demand in all cases where power is exerted by the strong over those to whom they owe care and protection," and counterpoise the inequality "by the superior justice which looks only to the substance of the right without regard to technical rules." How the treaty in question was understood may be gathered from the circumstances.

The right to resort to the fishing places in controversy was a part of larger rights possessed by the Indians, upon the exercise of which there was not a shadow of impediment, and which were not much less necessary to the existence of the Indians than the atmosphere they breathed. New conditions came into existence, to which those rights had to be accommodated. Only a limitation of them, however, was necessary and intended, not a taking away. In other words, the treaty was not a grant of rights to the Indians, but a grant of rights from them—a reservation of those rights not granted. . . . Reservations were not of particular parcels of land, and could not be expressed in deeds as dealings between private individuals. The reservations were in large areas of territory and the negotiations were with the tribe. They reserved rights, however, to every individual Indian, as though named therein. They imposed a servitude upon every piece of land as though described therein. There was an exclusive right of fishing reserved within certain boundaries. There was a right outside of those boundaries reserved "in common with citizens of the Territory." As a mere right, it was not exclusive in the Indians. Citizens might share it, but the Indians were secured in its enjoyment by a special provision of means for its exercise. They were given "the right of taking fish at all usual and accustomed places," and the right "of erecting temporary buildings for curing them." The contingency of the future ownership of the lands, therefore, was foreseen and provided for—in other words, the Indians were given a right in the land—the right of crossing it to the river—the right to occupy it to the extent and for the purpose mentioned. No other conclusion would give effect to the treaty. And the right was intended to be continuing against the United States and its grantees as well as against the State and its grantees. . . .

The extinguishment of the Indian title, opening the land for settlement and preparing the way for future States, were appropriate to the objects for which the United States held the Territory. And surely it was within the competency of the Nation to secure to the Indians such a remnant of the great rights they possessed as "taking fish at all usual and accustomed places." Nor does it restrain the State unreasonably, if at all, in the regulation of the right. It only fixes in the land such easements as enables the right to be exercised.

The license from the State, which respondents plead to maintain a fishing wheel, gives no power to them to exclude the Indians, nor was it intended to give such power.

United States v. Winans, 198 U.S. 371, 380-82, 384 (1905).
(Citations omitted.)

Commentary

CELILO FALLS, the great Indian fishing ground on the Columbia that was drowned behind The Dalles Dam in the mid-1950s, was the site of a turn-of-the-century conflict between Indian and white fishers that ultimately would be decided by the U.S. Supreme Court. In the 1890s, Lineas and Audubon Winans operated four state-licensed fish wheels near Celilo. They also possessed federal homestead patents to shorelands adjacent to the falls on the Washington side of the river. The Winans brothers invoked these authorizations to keep members of the Yakima (now Yakama) Indian Nation from fishing at their traditional Celilo grounds, and the brothers also destroyed the huts the Indians had built on the shorelands for curing their fish.

The local U.S. attorney, somewhat surprisingly, sued the Winans, claiming that their exclusion of the Indians violated the promise of Article III of the Stevens treaties. The lower court ruled that the treaty gave the Indians only a guarantee of equal treatment with white citizens; it did not assure them any special proprietary rights. Nine years later, in 1905, the U.S. Supreme Court reversed, agreeing with the federal government that the treaty right was a property right that could not be lost because of state licenses or federal homestead grants. In eloquent prose that survives the passage of years, Justice McKenna's opinion laid the foundation for rules of treaty interpretation that federal courts have employed to interpret treaty provisions ever since: (1) treaty promises are reserved rights—that is, reservations of rights not expressly relinquished; (2) treaty language is to be construed according to the understanding of the tribes, an unlettered people; and (3) ambiguities are to be interpreted liberally in their favor.

Sometimes lost in the eloquence of Justice McKenna's language is the fact that the Court determined that the treaty reserved to the Indians a property right in their historic off-reservation fishing grounds. The treaty imposed a "servitude on every piece of land subject to the treaty," a "right in land" that gave the Indians the right to cross over and occupy lands—even lands "owned" by private parties—in order to exercise their fishing rights. The Supreme Court also rejected the argument that Washington statehood, achieved in 1889, should be construed to terminate the tribal property right.

Unfortunately, by recognizing that the treaty did not "restrain the State unreasonably, if at all, in the regulation of the right," the opinion sowed the seeds of state regulation of Indian fishing under the guise of "conservation" that would be used to undermine the treaty

Fish wheels could capture 100,000 pounds of salmon in a season.

right for many years. For example, by the 1970s, the tribal share of the harvest in Puget Sound was just 2 percent. Such inequities prompted the federal government on behalf of the tribes to seek and obtain a judicially declared share of the harvest.

Despite the unfortunate dictum regarding state regulation, *United States v. Winans* remains truly a landmark case. Its articulation of treaty promises as reserved rights, its use of rules of treaty construction favorable to the tribes, and its rejection of the argument that statehood could divest treaty rights have become staples of Indian law. *Winans* was also the harbinger of another decision authored by Justice McKenna three years later that brought the reserved rights doctrine to water law (*Winters v. United States*, 207 U.S. 564 [1908]). Moreover, although *Winans* held only that the treaty right guaranteed physical access to historic fishing grounds, subsequent cases have employed the reserved rights principle to include tribal exemption from state license fees (*Tulee v. Washington,* 315 U.S. 681 [1942]); to insulate the tribes from discriminatory state regulation (*Puyallup Tribe v. Washington Department of Game,* 414 U.S. 44 [1973]); and to give the tribes a right to a harvest share (*Washington v. Washington Passenger Vessel Fishing Association,* 443 U.S. 658 [1979]). These progeny of *Winans* make it a case that every student of Indian fishing rights should recognize as articulating first principles.

—Michael C. Blumm and F. Lorraine Bodi

JUDGE BOLDT DEFENDS FISHING RIGHTS

Document:　　**United States v. Washington, Phase I**

Author:　　Judge George Boldt, federal judge for the western district of Washington State

Year:　　1974

Description:　　This crucial case opined that the Stevens treaties had reserved to certain Indian tribes the right to harvest up to 50 percent of salmon runs.

ALTHOUGH THERE IS no evidence of the precise understanding the Indians had of the treaty language, the treaty commissioners probably used the terms "usual and accustomed" and "in common with" in their common parlance, and the meaning of them as found in a contemporaneous dictionary most likely would be what was intended by the government representatives. . . .

[36] By dictionary definition and as intended and used in the Indian treaties and in this decision "in common with" means *sharing equally* the opportunity to take fish at "usual and accustomed grounds and stations"; therefore, non-treaty fishermen shall have the opportunity to take up to 50% of the harvestable number of fish that may be taken by all fishermen at usual and accustomed grounds and stations and treaty right fishermen shall have the opportunity to take up to the same percentage of harvestable fish, as stated above.

Judge George Boldt, circa 1955.

> *United States v. Washington*, Phase I, 384 F. Supp. 312, 356, 343 (W.D. Wash. 1974). (Note omitted.)

Document:	**Washington v. Passenger Fishing Vessel Association**
Author:	Supreme Court Justice John Paul Stevens wrote the majority opinion.
Year:	1979
Description:	In a ruling remarkably sensitive to the Indian position, the U.S. Supreme Court upheld Judge Boldt's 1974 decision in *United States v. Washington*.

To EXTINGUISH the last group of conflicting claims to lands lying west of the Cascade Mountains and north of the Columbia River in what is now the State of Washington, the United States entered into a series of treaties with Indian tribes in 1854 and 1855. The Indians relinquished their interest in most of the Territory in exchange for monetary payments. In addition, certain relatively small parcels of land were reserved for their exclusive use, and they were afforded other guarantees, including protection of their "right of taking fish, at all usual and accustomed grounds and stations . . . in common with all citizens of the Territory."

The principal question presented by this litigation concerns the character of that treaty right to take fish. . . .

The anadromous fish constitute a natural resource of great economic value to the State of Washington. Millions of salmon, with an average weight of from 4 or 5 to about 20 pounds, depending on the species, are harvested each year. Over 6,600 nontreaty fishermen and about 800 Indians make their livelihood by commercial fishing; moreover, some 280,000 individuals are licensed to engage in sport fishing in the State.

One hundred and twenty-five years ago when the relevant treaties were signed, anadromous fish were even more important to most of the population of western Washington than they are today. At that time, about three-fourths of the approximately 10,000 inhabitants of the area were Indians. Although in some respects the cultures of the different tribes varied—some bands of Indians, for example, had little or no tribal organization while others, such as the Makah and the Yakima, were highly organized—all of them shared a vital and unifying dependence on anadromous fish. . . .

All of the treaties were negotiated by Isaac Stevens, the first Governor and first Superintendent of Indian Affairs of the Washington Territory, and a small group of advisers. Contemporaneous documents make it clear that these people recognized the vital importance of the fisheries to the Indians and wanted to protect them from the risk that non-Indian settlers might seek to monopolize their fisheries. There is no evidence of the precise understanding the Indians had of any of the specific English terms and phrases in the treaty. It is perfectly clear, however, that the Indians were vitally interested in protecting their right to take fish at usual and accustomed places, whether on or off the reservations, and that they were invited by the white negotiators to rely and in fact did rely heavily on the good faith of the United States to protect that right. . . .

The Indians understood that non-Indians would also have the right to fish at their off-reservation fishing sites. But this was not understood as a significant limitation on their right to take fish. Because of the great abundance of fish and the limited population of the area, it simply was not contemplated that either party would interfere with the other's fishing rights. The parties accordingly did not see the need and did not intend to regulate the taking of fish by either Indians or non-Indians, nor was the future regulation foreseen.

Indeed, for several decades after the treaties were signed, Indians continued to harvest most of the fish taken from the waters of Washington, and they moved freely about the Territory and later the State in search of that resource. The size of the fishery resource continued to obviate the need during the period to regulate the taking of fish by either Indians or non-Indians. Not until major economic developments in canning and processing occurred in the last few years of the 19th century did a significant non-Indian fishery develop. It was as a consequence of these developments, rather than of the treaty, that non-Indians began to dominate the fisheries and eventually to exclude most Indians from participating in it—a trend that was encouraged by the onset of often discriminatory state regulation in the early decades of the 20th century.

In sum, it is fair to conclude that when the treaties were negotiated, neither party realized or intended that their agreement would determine whether, and if so how, a resource that had always been thought inexhaustible would be allocated between the native Indians and the incoming settlers when it later became scarce.

III

Unfortunately, that resource has now become scarce, and the meaning of the Indians' treaty right to take fish has accordingly become critical. . . .

A treaty, including one between the United States and an Indian tribe, is essentially a contract between two sovereign nations. When the signatory nations have not been at war and neither is the vanquished, it is reasonable to assume that they negotiated as equals at arm's length. There is no reason to doubt that this assumption applies to the treaties at issue here.

Accordingly, it is the intention of the parties, and not solely that of the superior side, that must control any attempt to interpret the treaties. When Indians are involved, this Court has long given special meaning to this rule. It has held that the United States, as the party with the presumptively superior negotiating skills and superior knowledge of the language in which the treaty is recorded, has a responsibility to avoid taking advantage of the other side. "[T]he treaty must therefore be construed, not according to the technical meaning of its words to learned lawyers, but in the sense in which they would naturally be understood by the Indians." This rule, in fact, has thrice been explicitly relied on by the Court in broadly interpreting these very treaties in the Indians' favor.

Governor Stevens and his associates were well aware of the "sense" in which the Indians were likely to view assurances regarding their fishing rights. During the negotiations, the vital importance of the fish to the Indians was repeatedly emphasized by both sides, and the Governor's promises that the treaties would protect that source of food and commerce were crucial in obtaining the Indians' assent. It is absolutely clear, as Governor Stevens himself said, that neither he nor the Indians intended that the latter "should be excluded from their ancient fisheries," and *it is accordingly inconceivable that either party deliberately agreed to authorize future settlers to crowd the Indians out of any meaningful use of their accustomed places to fish.* That each individual Indian would share an "equal opportunity" with thousands of newly arrived individual settlers is totally foreign to the spirit of the negotiations. Such a "right," along with the $207,500 paid the Indians, would hardly have been sufficient to compensate them for the millions of acres they ceded to the Territory. . . .

. . . Because the Indians had always exercised the right to meet their subsistence and commercial needs by taking fish from treaty area waters, *they would be unlikely to perceive a "reservation" of that right as merely the chance, shared with millions of other citizens, occasionally to dip their nets into the territorial waters.* Moreover, the phrasing of the clause quite clearly avoids placing each individual Indian on an equal footing with each individual citizen of the State.

The referent of the "said Indians" who are to share the right of taking fish with "all citizens of the Territory" is not the individual Indians but the various signatory "tribes and bands of Indians" listed in the opening article of each treaty. Because it was the tribes that were given a right in common with non-Indian citizens, it is especially likely that a class right to a share of fish, rather than a personal right to attempt to land fish, was intended.

In our view, the purpose and language of the treaties are unambiguous; they secure the Indians' right to take a share of each run of fish that passes through tribal fishing areas. But our prior decisions provide an even more persuasive reason why this interpretation is not open to question. For notwithstanding the bitterness that this litigation has engendered, the principal issue involved is virtually a "matter decided" by our previous holdings. . . .

. . . [T]hey clearly establish the principle that neither party to the treaties may rely on the State's regulatory powers or on property law concepts to defeat the other's right to a "fairly apportioned" share of each covered run of harvestable anadromous fish. . . .

The purport of our cases is clear. Nontreaty fishermen may not rely on property law concepts, devices such as the fish wheel, license fees, or general regulations to deprive the Indians of a fair share of the relevant runs of anadromous fish in the case area. Nor may treaty fishermen rely on their exclusive right of access to the reservations to destroy the rights of other "citizens of the Territory." Both sides have a right, secured by treaty, to take a fair share of the

Indian family, posed in canoe, wearing traditional dress. Celilo Falls, 1903.

available fish. That, we think, is what the parties to the treaty intended when they secured to the Indians the right of taking fish in common with other citizens.

V

We also agree with the Government that an equitable measure of the common right should initially divide the harvestable portion of each run that passes through a "usual and accustomed" place into approximately equal treaty and non-treaty shares, and should then reduce the treaty share if tribal needs may be satisfied by a lesser amount. . . .

It bears repeating, however, that the 50% figure imposes a maximum but not a minimum allocation. As in *Arizona v. California* and its predecessor cases, *the central principle here must be that Indian treaty rights to a natural resource that once was thoroughly and exclusively exploited by the Indians secures so much as, but no more than, is necessary to provide the Indians with a livelihood*—that is to say, a moderate living. Accordingly, while the maximum possible allocation to the Indians is fixed at 50%, the minimum is not; the latter will, upon proper submissions to the District Court, be modified in response to changing circumstances. If, for example, a tribe should dwindle to just a few members, or if it should find other sources of support that lead it to abandon its fisheries, a 45% or 50% allocation of an entire run that passes through its customary fishing grounds would be manifestly inappropriate because the livelihood of the tribe under those circumstances could not reasonably require an allotment of a large number of fish.

> *Washington v. Passenger Fishing Vessel Ass'n*, 443 U.S. 658 (1979).
> (Emphasis added; citations and notes omitted.)

Commentary

BY 1970, THE REGULATORY authority of the state of Washington had effectively preempted the traditional fishery of Puget Sound. The tribes were harvesting only about 2 percent of the salmon runs because non-Indian fisheries in the ocean and the sound left little salmon for the tribes. After allowing heavy non-Indian harvests, the state frequently imposed the entire conservation burden on tribal fishers to ensure a sufficient number of spawners.

As a result of these inequities, the federal government, as trustee for the tribes, filed suit, claiming that the state's discriminatory regulation violated the promises of the Stevens treaties, and that those treaties entitled the tribes to a "fair share" of the harvests. Only the year before, in *Sohappy v. Smith* (302 F. Supp. 899 [D. Or. 1969]), in a decision by District Judge Robert Belloni, the district court of Oregon held that the treaties reserved to the tribes a fair share of the harvests. Now, in the western district of Washington, the federal government argued that a fair share meant 50 percent of the harvestable salmon. Looking at the treaty negotiations, historic tribal fishing practices,

Judge Robert Belloni

and a contemporaneous dictionary, Judge George Boldt concluded that the government was right: the treaties reserved to the tribes the right to harvest up to 50 percent of the salmon runs.

Judge Boldt's decision was appealed a number of times in both state and federal courts. The federal courts affirmed Judge Boldt; the state courts found that the state lacked the authority to implement his decree. The state thus forced the judge to implement the decision himself. For a number of years Judge Boldt was in effect the "fishmaster" of the salmon runs of western Washington. Finally, after what one appellate judge termed "except for some desegregation cases . . . the most concerted official and private efforts to frustrate a decree of a federal court witnessed in this century" (573 F.2d 1123, 1126 [9th Cir. 1978]), the Supreme Court agreed to review the case. Five years after Judge Boldt's decision, the Court largely affirmed his historic decision.

The Supreme Court's affirmance of the Boldt decision was, according to the Court, merely a logical extension of its earlier interpretation of the tribes' Stevens treaty rights. For example, in *U.S. v. Winans*, the Court had ruled that the state or federal government may not deprive the tribes of access to their historic fisheries by property concepts or regulations such as licensing fish wheels, demanding license fees, or banning net fishing. Guaranteeing the tribes a fixed share of the harvest was, the Court ruled, only a means to carry out the central promise of the treaties: the right to fish "in common with" non-Indians.

The state's argument that the treaties gave the tribes only an equal opportunity to fish was rejected by the Court as insufficient compensation for the 64 million acres of land the tribes had conveyed to the U.S. Because of the vastly superior numbers of non-Indian fishers, the "equal opportunity" approach had been used in the past to, in the Court's words, "crowd the Indians out" of their historic fisheries. This was a violation of the treaties that the Court held promised the tribes more than the right to "occasionally dip their nets" and come up empty.

The result of this case was, of course, a considerable redistribution of harvests toward the Indian fishery. Significantly, the Court ruled the treaty right was a class right, a tribal right, not an individual right. This interpretation had an important effect on the revitalization of the Northwest tribes as political entities. The Court's decision made it clear that it was the responsibility of the tribes to allocate the 50 percent harvest share among their members. Thus, tribal members would become more interested in tribal deliberations; tribal council decision making became more critical to the livelihood of tribal members when the tribe had an economically valuable resource to allocate.

This "retribalization" also encouraged the tribes to develop expertise in harvest management and salmon biology. This expertise allowed the tribes to begin to interact with the states and federal government on a government-to-government basis. Tribal biologists added important new perspectives to the science of salmon management, helping to advance the state of the art, especially by focusing on the entire salmon life cycle instead of concentrating on hatcheries, which had been the center of attention of most state biologists. Within a few years of the Boldt decision, the tribes and state fish and wildlife agencies forged an alliance to demand better habitat protection and improved hydroelectric operations. This alliance would eventually help produce the fish and wildlife provisions of the Northwest Power Act. Thus, the ramifications of Judge Boldt's decision were far reaching; it is no exaggeration to suggest that the era of modern salmon management began with his historic decree in 1974.

—Michael C. Blumm and F. Lorraine Bodi

THE COURTS TACKLE HABITAT

Document:	***United States v. Washington,* Phase II**
Author:	Judge William Orrick, federal judge, sitting by designation in the western district of Washington State
Year:	1980
Description:	The Ninth Circuit Court ruled that the Stevens treaties protected fish habitat from state actions. This ruling was later vacated (overturned) on appeal.

At the outset, the Court holds that implicitly incorporated in the treaties' fishing clause is the right to have the fishery habitat protected from man-made despoilation. Virtually every case construing this fishing clause has recognized it to be the cornerstone of the treaties and has emphasized its overriding importance to the tribes. The Indians understood, and were led by Governor Stevens to believe, that the treaties entitled them to continue fishing in perpetuity and that the settlers would not qualify, restrict, or interfere with their right to take fish.

The most fundamental prerequisite to exercising the right to take fish is the existence of fish to be taken. . . .

[11] The treaties reserve to the tribes a sufficient quantity of fish to satisfy their moderate living needs, subject to a ceiling of 50 percent of the harvestable run. That is the minimal need which gives rise to an implied right to environmental protection of the fish habitat. Therefore, the correlative duty imposed upon the State (as well as the United States and third parties) is to refrain from degrading the fish habitat to an extent that would deprive the tribes of their moderate living needs.

The tribes' treaty allocation is currently set at 50 percent of each harvestable run. That the ceiling has been applied creates the presumption that the tribes' moderate living needs exceed 50 percent and are not being fully satisfied under the treaties. As the burden is upon the State to demonstrate to the Phase I court that the tribes' needs may be satisfied by a lesser allocation, the State must also bear the burden in Phase II to demonstrate that any environmental degradation of the fish habitat proximately caused by the State's actions (including the authorization of third parties' activities) will not impair the tribes' ability to satisfy their moderate living needs. Naturally, the plaintiffs must shoulder the initial burden of proving that the challenged action(s) will proximately cause the fish habitat to be degraded such that the rearing or production potential of the fish will be impaired or the size or quality of the run will be diminished.

> *United States v. Washington*, 506 F. Supp. 187, 203, 208 (W.D. Wash. 1980) (citations omitted), *vacated*, 759 F.2d 1353, 1360 (9th Cir. 1985).

Commentary

WHEN THE FEDERAL government filed suit in 1970 seeking a harvest share for tribal fishers, it also requested that the court declare that (1) the tribes' harvest share include both hatchery and wild salmon, and (2) the treaties entitle the tribes to a right to protect the habitat necessary for the fish to survive. Judge Boldt separated the latter two issues for consideration after he had decided the issue of whether the treaties guaranteed a harvest share. Unfortunately, he died before he could resolve the hatchery and habitat issues.

These two issues were at the center of the Phase II case, decided by Judge William Orrick in 1980. The judge had little difficulty ruling that hatchery fish were included in the tribes' 50 percent share, largely because "if hatchery fish were to be excluded from the allocation, the Indians' treaty-secured right to an adequate supply of fish—the right for which they traded millions of acres of land and resources—would be placed in jeopardy." Because of the ever-increasing proportion of hatchery fish, Orrick held that "the tribes' share would steadily dwindle and the paramount purpose of the treaties would be subverted. Contrary to what the Supreme Court held to be the parties' intentions, nontreaty fishermen would ultimately 'crowd the Indians out of any meaningful use of their accustomed places to fish.'" In the excerpt above, Judge Orrick addressed the issue of whether the treaties protected fish habitat from destruction by the acts of the state.

On appeal, the Ninth Circuit Court of Appeals affirmed Judge Orrick on the hatchery issue (759 F.2d 1353, 1358-60 [9th Cir. 1985] [*en banc*]), but vacated his ruling on habitat protection. An *en banc* (eleven-judge)

Logging often turned rivers into highways and holding ponds for logs. The resulting habitat degradation affected salmon runs and traditional Indian fisheries.

panel of the appeals court determined that establishing such an "environmental" right by declaration, without a concrete factual controversy, was an improper use of the judicial function (759 F.2d at 1357). The court expressed no opinion on the merits of Judge Orrick's opinion, simply ruling that he had no right to make the decision.

But a number of other decisions indicate that, where there are concrete factual disputes, the treaty promise does in fact contain a right to habitat protection. For example, the treaties have enjoined dam construction (*Confederated Tribes of the Umatilla v. Alexander*, 440 F. Supp. 553 [D. Or. 1977]), changed dam operations (*Kittitas Reclamation District v. Sunnyside Irrigation District*, 763 F.2d 1032 [9th Cir. 1985]), limited irrigation withdrawals (*Joint Board of Control v. U.S.*, 832 F.2d 1127 [9th Cir. 1987]), *United States v. Adair*, 723 F.2d 1394 [9th Cir. 1983]), and blocked construction of a marina (*Muckleshoot Indian Tribe v. Hall*, 698 F. Supp. 1504 [W.D. Wash. 1988]). Since the Supreme Court has ruled that the central purpose of the Stevens treaties is to provide the tribes with a livelihood, if the tribes can show that they are being prevented from earning a livelihood because of, for example, hydroelectric operations, they should be able to obtain judicial relief substantially altering the operation of Columbia Basin dams.

—Michael C. Blumm and F. Lorraine Bodi

An Early Instance of Supplementation

Document:	**The Great Salmon Mystery**
Author:	Northwest journalist Richard Neuberger wrote *Our Promised Land*, an account of the Northwest in the 1930s; he later became a U.S. Senator from Oregon.
Year:	1941
Description:	In this *Saturday Evening Post* article, an influential journalist describes attempts to perpetuate salmon runs after the construction of Grand Coulee Dam.

ONLY A PART OF the Columbia's salmon population heads for the 620 miles of river back of Grand Coulee. But that part includes the best Chinooks, the fish with the most endurance and vitality. It is this strain of salmon which must not be allowed to become extinct.

Uncle Sam's academy for fish starts enrolling pupils when these salmon thoroughbreds are trapped below Grand Coulee. Then they are rushed forty-five miles in tank trucks to ponds alongside the immense hatchery which Joe Kemmerich operates in the Washington town of Leavenworth. There the salmon are spawned artificially. After about a year in hatchery troughs and pools the resulting offspring, approximately six inches long now, are put in the trucks and turned loose in streams entering the Columbia River below Grand Coulee Dam. The theory is that if one generation of Chinooks had an irresistible urge to spawn in creeks above Grand Coulee because it was the scene of their early life, why will not the next generation of Chinooks go back to tributaries below Grand Coulee if that was where the were released as baby fish?

"Thus," announces the U.S. Fish and Wildlife Service reassuringly, "the hatchery-reared fish will return to the water in which they were planted, establishing new and natural runs in those streams."

Will this idea work? Government experts think so, but admit there will be no conclusive answer for four years—not until the salmon now being propagated artificially at Leavenworth come back up the Columbia to spawn. Will they continue on to Grand Coulee, over the route their ancestors traveled, and perish buffeting its cement ramparts? Or will they wind off toward their new habitats?

The ultimate outcome of this novel plan is only a single phase—albeit, a vital one—of the Great Salmon Mystery. All sorts of other questions must be settled too. . . .

The Washington Department of Fisheries is pressing for legislation to compel the screening of all irrigation canals and has set up nearly 300 filters already. Oregon's Fish Commission wants trolling in the ocean rigidly controlled, and its chairman, John C. Veatch, believes no commercial fishing should be allowed on the Columbia above Bonneville Dam. Senator McNary, of Oregon, believes that trolling at sea must be closely regulated. He has introduced a bill giving the Fish and Wildlife Service the right to prevent the catching of salmon under certain weights and sizes. "We know," he explains, "that the Chinooks attain most of their growth in the ocean. It is an economic waste to permit the catching of a nine-pound salmon which in three or four months might weight twenty-five pounds. The reduction of spawning grounds in the upper Columbia makes more imperative than ever that we get every possible ounce of food value from the salmon which are netted in the Pacific." McNary says he has assurances that Canada will parallel any such action taken by the United States. A number of wild-life experts hope to forbid Indians from spearing and netting the homeward-bound salmon at Celilo Falls, but others ask if we take away even this from the country's original owners, what are we accusing Hitler of, anyway?

Ever since the first cannery was built on the Columbia seventy-five years ago, salmon have been a red-hot political issue in the Pacific Northwest.

Richard L. Neuberger, "The Great Salmon Mystery," *Saturday Evening Post*, 13 Sept. 1941, 20-21, 44.

Commentary

THE RATIONALE for supplementation—releasing fish into underutilized or restored natural habitat—was clear enough, as journalist Richard Neuberger observed. If salmon were released as juveniles into tributaries below Grand Coulee Dam, why wouldn't the adult chinook go back to these tributaries to spawn? And indeed, the adult fish did come back and did reestablish runs in those mid-Columbia tributaries. Today people speak of the mid-Columbia stocks as "wild" fish. In fact, they are wild fish only because of the Grand Coulee supplementation program under which the habitat problems were fixed, the juvenile fish were reared and released into the habitat, and the adults returned to spawn.

Today many biologists maintain that habitat is not "available" for supplementation in the lower river tributaries below McNary Dam, though the habitat in that area was restored. The National Marine Fisheries Service in a 1989 document describes the habitat improvement projects carried out by the state fishery agencies under the Mitchell Act. Neuberger, too, in 1941 clearly pointed out that habitat was available in that section of the Columbia for supplementation. However, between the implementation of the Grand Coulee program and that of the Mitchell Act program, goals for production changed.

The ability of hatcheries to produce tremendous numbers of fish in a very short time led to management decisions to abandon attempts to reestablish the natural stocks. Hatcheries became production tools. It was far easier to build one more hatchery, add one more rearing pond, tinker with fish diets, and develop or register a new drug, than it was to try to maintain the productivity of the natural habitat.

The very fishery agencies that supposedly were going to redevelop the natural runs instead turned toward hatcheries. Once the agencies emphasized hatchery production, certain fish management techniques and philosophies followed. For example, a wild fish caught in the fisheries became an "incidental catch"—because the target fishery was the hatchery fish. The Endangered Species Act of 1973 should have changed that disregard of wild fish, but for some populations of wild salmon this has not occurred. As for trying to boost natural production through supplementation, the agencies remained noncommittal.

—Douglas W. Dompier

ATTEMPTS TO FOSTER SUPPLEMENTATION RUN AFOUL OF POLITICS

Document: **Columbia Basin Fish and Wildlife Program**

Author: Northwest Power Planning Council

Year: 1982

Description: This first version of the fish program established by the Northwest Power Planning Council reflected the concerns of Indian tribes about hatchery production.

(f) Hatchery Survey

(1) BONNEVILLE SHALL FUND a study to compile all available information on existing and potential sites for hatcheries. The survey on existing sites shall include data on their full propagation potential, impediments to achieving full potential, and steps that must be taken to improve propagation quality and quantity. Data shall be included on hatcheries not making full use of available water. At potential sites for hatcheries, site characteristics such as water quality and quantity shall be evaluated. This study shall determine whether available data is sufficient to allow proposals to be made to the Council for improvement to existing hatcheries or for development of new hatcheries. The study shall be completed by June 1, 1984. Proposals for further action, including any studies required to supplement available data, shall be made to the Council at that time.

(g) Release Sites for Hatchery-Reared Fish

(1) Bonneville shall provide funds to evaluate sites suitable for release of hatchery fish and the levels of release compatible with natural propagation and harvest management. Initial efforts shall focus on the needs of upriver stocks, which will be defined by the fish propagation panel under Section 704(f) (1). The basin wide studies shall be completed by April 1, 1984. Proposals for reprogramming hatchery operations and a release plan shall be made to the Council at that time. The Council will adopt a comprehensive plan for reprogramming lower river hatcheries. This shall be done by November 15, 1984. Where current knowledge is sufficient, certain stocks may be moved to particular upriver streams. The fish and wildlife agencies and the tribes will cooperate in this effort.

(2) Upon approval by the Council of the plan, Bonneville shall provide funds to transfer a portion of the fish from existing lower Columbia River hatcheries to release sites in the upper Columbia River system to assist in restoring naturally spawning stocks. The fish propagation panel will develop detailed recommendations on the selection of brood stocks, production levels, and release sites. The fish and wildlife agencies and tribes shall submit a status report to the Council by February 15, 1983.

Background. The Mitchell Act and John Day hatcheries were provided to mitigate fishery losses because of the hydroelectric development of the Columbia River. A reprogramming of hatchery operations and release strategies will rebuild upriver runs and improve tribal fisheries. The tribes already have submitted to the Council a detailed plan for reprogramming lower river hatchery releases into the upper Columbia. The Council strongly supports restoration of naturally spawning upriver stocks, but further consultation is required with the fish and wildlife agencies and tribes to determine a final release plan.

> Northwest Power Planning Council, *Columbia River Basin Fish and Wildlife Program* (Portland, Oregon: Northwest Power Planning Council, 1982), 7-13.

Document:	**Columbia Basin Fish and Wildlife Program**
Author:	Northwest Power Planning Council
Year:	1987
Description:	Five years after the first program, the wording of the "Background" section shows differences to which the tribes ascribe considerable importance.

BACKGROUND. The Mitchell Act and John Day hatcheries were provided to mitigate fishery losses because of the federal development of the Columbia River Basin for hydropower and other purposes (such as irrigation and navigation) for which these projects were authorized. Reprogramming hatchery operations by developing new release strategies is intended to help rebuild upriver runs and improve tribal fisheries. The Council strongly supports restoration

of naturally spawning upriver stocks, but further consultation with
the fish and wildlife agencies and tribes is required to determine a
final release plan.

> Northwest Power Planning Council, *Columbia River Basin Fish
> and Wildlife Program* (Portland, Oregon: Northwest Power
> Planning Council, 1987), 97.

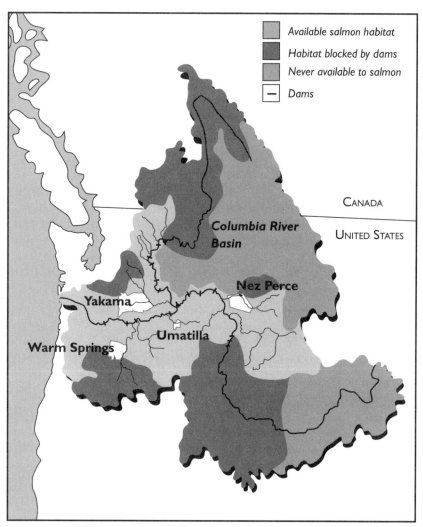

*The reservations of Columbia Basin Indian tribes are shown in relationship
to salmon runs, both historic and contemporary.*

Commentary

 I*N THE LAST FIFTEEN YEARS*, there have been continued attempts to supplement salmon runs. During the 1970s and early 1980s, the Columbia River treaty tribes in particular became very involved in developing programs that would have increased the natural spawning populations in areas they had historically fished. In 1982, the Northwest Power Planning Council adopted a fish and wildlife program that reflected the concerns of the tribes and in strong language called for a review of salmon production efforts.

The first amendment to the Power Planning Council's fish and wildlife program was made in 1984. In the 1984 document (not printed here), the language calling for reprogramming hatcheries remained intact. Three years later, however, the wording had changed to deemphasize the role of the tribes.

The chair of the Northwest Power Planning Council in 1982 was Dan Evans, an influential leader who had served as Washington's governor and who later became a senator from the state. He led a council that seemed to sense the need for change, perhaps even for a new vision. Members of the council put forth ideas that, although not new, had never had enough support to become policy. They were particularly interested in recommending changes in hatchery production, a subject of great concern to the tribes.

The tribes had coined the word "reprogramming" to describe the process of using hatcheries to put fish back in the habitat where they belonged rather than in the concrete cages of hatcheries. The council's 1982 fish and wildlife program called for "release sites in the upper Columbia River system" for hatchery-reared fish and reminded readers that two of the purposes of the Mitchell Act and John Day hatcheries were to "rebuild upriver runs and improve tribal fisheries."

The tribes appreciated the significance of finally seeing such words in a public document. The wording very nearly didn't make it. In 1981, in accordance with the Northwest Power Act, the Power Planning Council requested joint recommendations from the state and federal fishery agencies and the tribes. The agencies, however, refused to make joint recommendations if the tribes continued to insist on release sites in the upper Columbia. The tribes held the contract for developing and writing the recommendations. Five days before the joint recommendations were due, the tribes told the still intractable agencies that, in the absence of a joint decision, they would proceed with a report on their own. They felt confident that the council would

The first Northwest Power Planning Council, in whom great hopes were placed, was led by chair and former Washington Governor Dan Evans (dark hair, bifocals) and vice-chair Bob Saxvik of Idaho (to his right).

adopt their recommendations. Tribal optimism was not unfounded: at the time, Indian tribes were winning nearly every fisheries case they were involved in and there was strong public support for Indian causes. The day after the tribes' ultimatum, the agencies backed down and the joint recommendations were submitted on schedule.

By 1987, the Power Planning Council had a different chair and a different tone. In 1982, the Power Planning Council had given as its rationale for building the Mitchell Act and John Day hatcheries the desire "to mitigate fishery losses because of the hydroelectric development of the Columbia River." By 1987 the exclusive focus was no longer on hydroelectricity. Instead, the council's report states that the fishery losses that led to the building of the Mitchell Act and John Day hatcheries were caused by "federal development of the Columbia River Basin for hydropower and other purposes (such as irrigation and navigation)."

Gone also is the reference to tribal involvement in policymaking. This was not surprising, for two reasons. The council was becoming increasingly politicized, bending to the political whims of the states and their governors. In addition, between 1982 and 1987, state and federal fisheries agencies were strongly opposed to strengthening upriver runs. They found excuse after excuse not to act, among them that the hatchery fish would spread diseases to the wild stocks above the dams and that the genetic purity of the wild stocks would be sullied. Indeed, it was during this time that "genetic integrity" and "genetic diversity" became buzzwords on the Columbia River.

The politicization of the council continues. Members consult regularly with representatives from governors' offices. Furthermore, council members are now generally former state representatives or people who have been part of a governor's administration. In addition, in spite of repeated overtures to various governors, no tribal representative has ever been appointed to the council.

—Douglas W. Dompier

THE ROLE OF RACE IN SALMON POLICY

Document: **The Hutchinson Memo**

Author: Samuel J. Hutchinson, regional director of the U. S. Fish and
                Wildlife Service

Year: 1951

Description: A fishery agency official tells a reporter that salmon will fare
                better scaling The Dalles Dam than they did confronting the
                Indian fishery at the turbulent Celilo Falls.

[MR. LUNDY] ASKED as to the effects of The Dalles Dam. I stated that
the beneficial effects would compensate for the detrimental conditions that exist there at present. In brief, it would be easier for the
fish to go over a ladder in the dam than to fight their way over

*For thousands of years,
Indians had their main
Columbia River fishery at
Celilo Falls. The Dalles
Dam, completed in 1957,
submerged the falls,
eliminating the fishery
and its cultural
importance.*

Celilo Falls. The Indian commercial fishery would be eliminated
and more fish would reach the spawning grounds in better
condition.

He asked what effect Priest Rapids Dam would have on the
fishery and I said it would eliminate the red salmon runs going into
the upper Columbia.

He asked also if we were opposed to Ice Harbor, and I stated that
we definitely opposed the timing of Ice Harbor, but that we had
little if any objections to Hells Canyon Dam. . .

> Samuel J. Hutchinson, internal memorandum concerning
> conversation with Herb Lundy, 16 Jan. 1951 (Seattle: Archives of
> the National Marine Fisheries Service, photocopy).

Document:	**Columbia River Fishery Development Report**
Author:	U.S. Fish and Wildlife Service
Year:	1958
Description:	This report described actions undertaken by the Fish and Wildlife Service to implement the Columbia River Fishery Development Program.

THE INUNDATION of Celilo Falls in the Columbia River near The Dalles,
Oregon was a memorable event. Removal of this partial barrier by
backwater from The Dalles Dam eliminated forever an intensive
historic Indian fishery. The closure in February 1958 of all commercial fishing above Bonneville Dam has also had a very significant
effect upon the escapement to upstream spawning areas.

An unusual situation occurred relative to the spring chinook
salmon run of 1958. For some unaccountable reason most of the
fish of this early run remained in the lower river for an extended
period of time. During the first week of the commercial fishing
season more spring chinook salmon were caught than had been
taken in the entire spring fishing season period of 1957. About
100,000 fish were taken by the commercial fishery out of this year's
spring run and approximately 75,000 fish passed upstream over
Bonneville Dam. This resulted in a very poor escapement for
natural spawning. The situation which occurred this spring emphasized a very serious weakness existing in Oregon State law. As the

law now reads, 72 hours notice must be given prior to the calling of a public hearing by the Commission for any emergency closure.

Increased escapement of spring chinook salmon to the spawning streams of Idaho has triggered an accelerated increase in sport fishing. In the last several years this fishery has increased tremendously causing those who are concerned with management of the resource to review the total escapement above Bonneville Dam needed to provide fish for the sportsmen as well as for adequate seeding of the spawning areas.

> Fish and Wildlife Service, *Fishery Development Program of the Columbia River. Report of Activities to June 30 1958* (October 1958), 3-4.

In 1952, representatives of the government and the Confederated Tribes of the Warm Springs Reservation signed an agreement providing some compensation for Indian fishing sites to be lost at Celilo Falls. Avex Miller, the tribal council chairman, is seated at the right.

Document:	**Senate Appropriations Hearings**
Author:	U.S. Senate transcript
Year:	1960
Description:	U.S. senators quizzed Donald McKernan, the director of the Bureau of Commercial Fisheries, on the implementation of the Mitchell Act in Idaho.

SENATOR DWORSHAK. I am very much interested in this problem, as you know. Now at that point, may I ask you if in your planning there is any likelihood of a fish hatchery in the Middle Snake area? You have built about 24 or 25 hatcheries in the lower basin. Have you reached the point where you are planning to avoid repetition of the

Oxbow episodes, like last October.* In recognition of the accelerated upstream migration since Celilo fishing has been eliminated, do you feel that you should have some hatcheries in the Middle Fork area?

Mr. McKernan. There is very serious consideration and planning going on right at the present time with that as its objective.

Senator Dworshak. You have not any specific plans yet, but you do recognize the —

Mr. McKernan. No specific plan.

Senator Dworshak. The need of working toward the objective?

Mr. McKernan. Correct.

Senator Ellender. I notice here you have increased the number of hatcheries from 24 to 32.

Mr. McKernan. That involves planning on some hatcheries in this area that the Senator mentioned.

Senator Dworshak. And also some downstream?

Mr. McKernan. Correct.

Senator Ellender. Will some of these additional hatcheries be built in Idaho?

Mr. McKernan. Yes.

Senator Ellender. How many?

Mr. McKernan. That remains to be determined, Senator, after further study on these streams. We are not sure yet.

Senator Ellender. I see.

Cooperation from State of Idaho

Senator Dworshak. You are receiving, are you not, full cooperation from the State of Idaho Fish and Game Department so that there is no lack of interest carrying on this program effectively?

Mr. McKernan. Extremely good cooperation from all the State agencies, including Idaho. These men are working close together as a complete team. The Federal and State agencies actually have a sort of planning board of scientists and then another board of administrators to implement the recommendations from the scientists themselves, and it is working out very successfully.

Senator Ellender. Well, as you proceed with this program you are, of course, increasing the scope of it. Have you any legal impediments to this expansion, or can you just go on and expand it as large as you think necessary?

---

*The oxbow incident occurred when adult fall chinook that were being trapped below Oxbow Dam died before they could be moved above the dam. The fishery agencies blamed the Idaho Power Company for the loss.—Eds

Mr. McKernan. To my knowledge, there are no legal impediments to our present plan, sir.

Senator Ellender. You can just go on and do whatever is necessary to protect and preserve the fish in that area in order to conserve this resource and keep it to what it was before the dams were built?

Mr. McKernan. Yes, sir.

> U.S. Senate Subcommittee of the Committee on Appropriations, *Public Works Appropriations, 1960. Hearings before the Subcommittee of the Committee on Appropriations*, 86th Cong., 1st Sess. on H.R. 7509 (1960), 893-94.

Document:	**Report on the Lower Snake River Dams**
Authors:	National Marine Fisheries Service, U.S. Fish and Wildlife Service, Bureau of Sport Fisheries and Wildlife
Year:	1972
Description:	Federal agencies continued to support supplementation.

To maintain the representative number of steelhead trout in the Snake River system and to offset the loss of downstream migrants through the turbines at the four dams, artificial propagation facilities capable of producing 55,100 adults from 7,200 adults would be necessary. Acquisition of a hatchery site at the best available water supply in the upper Snake River system would be necessary. Smolts could be hauled to Snake tributary streams in Idaho, Washington, and Oregon for liberation, thus supplementing natural production and maintaining sport fishing for anadromous fish in streams affected by the projects.

Estimated capital cost for the steelhead trout hatchery and rearing facilities in $18,140,000. Estimated annual, operation, maintenance, and replacement costs are $834,000. These costs include the acquisition of 100 acres of land for hatcheries.

> National Marine Fisheries Service, Fish and Wildlife Service, and Bureau of Sport Fisheries and Wildlife, *A Special Report on the Lower Snake River Dams: Ice Harbor, Lower Monumental, Little Goose, Lower Granite. Washington and Idaho* (September 1972), 28.

Document:	**Endangered Species Act Workshop**
Author:	Howard Raymond, a research biologist with the National Marine Fisheries Service
Year:	1978
Description:	This document is part of a summary of a workshop at which biologists discussed the basis for protecting salmon under the Endangered Species Act.

THE OUTLOOK FOR SUMMER steelhead is good. Improved condition of smolts being released from hatcheries, positive benefits from mass transportation of steelhead, and good downstream survival in 1978 should result in a good run of 1—ocean fish in 1979 and 2—ocean fish in 1980. Continued improvement in hatchery techniques and mass-transportation technology to enhance downriver survival should soon bring back runs of steelhead to harvestable size.

Because of extensive water resource developments in the river, wild stocks are severely depressed. Even with improved downstream survival it is doubtful that these stocks will ever return to their former levels. With improved rearing techniques, hatcheries should provide an even greater contribution to the total run than is presently indicated. . . . Release of smolts throughout the watershed (in contrast to the present method of releasing at the hatchery) should ultimately provide a reasonable substitute for the original wild stocks.

> Howard Raymond (from panel discussion, "Status of Upriver Snake and Columbia River Stocks of Salmon and Steelhead," presented at a National Marine Fisheries Service workshop, *Biological Basis for Listing Species or Other Taxa of Salmonids Pursuant to the Endangered Species Act of 1973*, Portland, Oregon, 7-8 Dec. 1978), 70.

Document:	**Idaho Anadromous Fish Plan**
Author:	Idaho Department of Fish and Game
Year:	1984
Description:	This excerpt contains favorable comments about "supplementation" by a state fish agency.

ARTIFICIAL PROPAGATION will play a dominant role in restoration of anadromous fish resources during the remainder of this decade. Returns of adult fish from hatchery produced smolts to hatcheries and other terminal areas will provide most of the harvestable fish for the next several years and will support major fisheries. Release of smolts and/or sub-smolts into natural spawning and rearing areas is essential to full utilization of the available habitat and restoration of adequate spawning runs.

> Idaho Department of Fish and Game, *Idaho Anadromous Fish Plan 1984-1990*, draft (1 June 1984), 47.

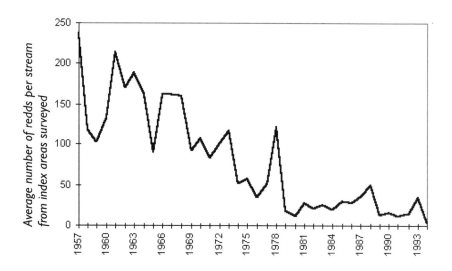

The average number of spring chinook redds (egg nests) has declined sharply in Idaho, a key indicator that these salmon are in jeopardy. Source: Idaho Department of Fish and Game.

212

Commentary

THE BUILDING of The Dalles Dam did not just close down what Hutchinson calls an "Indian commercial fishery"; it eliminated an important cultural tradition of the Indians of the area. The government, however, didn't see things this way.

In a 1951 memo written for the files, Samuel J. Hutchinson, the regional director of the Fish and Wildlife Service, recorded a conversation he had had with Herb Lundy, a reporter for the *Oregonian*. Lundy, who was preparing a story on the Lower Columbia River Program, which included construction of The Dalles Dam, was no casual reporter of the environmental scene. By 1951 he had been with the *Oregonian* fifteen years, writing on energy and natural resource issues.

As Hutchinson makes clear in his memo, he told Lundy that one of the "detrimental" conditions that existed at Celilo Falls was the presence of the Indian fishery. Furthermore, beneficial effects would result from the elimination of the fishery. That the acting director of the region's major fisheries agency could unhesitatingly say as much to a reporter of Lundy's credentials, who wrote for the state's most influential newspaper, reveals at least a lack of sensitivity toward Indians among government officials.

The tribes had more tangible reasons for viewing with alarm the actions of the government: agency support for dams and the government's reluctance to build hatcheries above the dams. Indian people wanted to believe that the fish agencies were fighting for the salmon, trying to help the Indians conserve the fish and maintain their fisheries. But even though the fish agencies typically blamed the dams for fishery problems, they were willing to support construction of The Dalles Dam. In this case, agency officials supported construction of the dam because it would eliminate the Indian fisheries. This particular aspect of fisheries management is one that is not discussed very often, even by fishery professionals, because it is disturbing. It tarnishes the profession.

Standing by itself, the first paragraph of the October 1958 Report of Activities, which describes the construction of The Dalles Dam, seems innocuous enough. However, taken in context, it reflects insensitivity toward tribal losses. The passage follows an account of the highlights of 1958, including experiments in dried fish food and the increased use of electronic fish counters to enumerate fish. The inundation of Celilo Falls is represented as just another achievement of the Fish and Wildlife Service, "a memorable event."

Nearly all the fish produced under the Mitchell Act agreement were raised below Celilo Falls, indeed, below Bonneville Dam, where the tribes do not fish. The only production facilities that were ever constructed as part of the Mitchell Act program above Celilo Falls were built after The Dalles Dam had eliminated the tribal fisheries there.

During the era of construction of The Dalles Dam, the Bureau of Commercial Fisheries (now known as the National Marine Fisheries Service) planned hatcheries for Idaho, as revealed in the 1960 Senate appropriations hearing discussion among Senator Henry C. Dworshak (Idaho), Senator Allen J. Ellender (Louisiana), and Donald McKernan, the director of the Bureau of Commercial Fisheries. Despite the optimistic tone of the discussion, Senator Dworshak did not get a hatchery in the Middle Fork area under the Mitchell Act program. He had to wait another ten years for the construction of the Dworshak Dam on the North Fork of the Clearwater River to receive not only a hatchery but a dam named after him.

In the 1960s, hatchery construction slowed down. The Corps of Engineers terminated funding of the Mitchell Act program. From 1949, when funding began under the Mitchell Act, until 1961, the Corps had paid for construction of all the hatcheries built by the program, as well as providing money for their annual operation and maintenance. But once the fishery agencies began talking about building hatcheries in Idaho, the Corps of Engineers stopped funding this program. Funds for building Idaho hatcheries under the Mitchell Act program—hatcheries that could have helped Indian fisheries—dried up.

Nevertheless, other hatcheries continued to be built and operational funds were still provided under the Mitchell Act. The stratagem was accomplished this way: some existing hatchery programs as well as some new ones were lumped as "complexes" and therefore qualified for funding under the Mitchell Act. For example, if one of the fishery agencies had previously built a hatchery and was using its own funds to operate the facility, it would combine the hatchery with a Mitchell Act hatchery and then refer to the facilities as a complex. This allowed agencies to use Mitchell Act funding to operate the complex. When all of the hatcheries and rearing ponds that are still being operated using Mitchell Act monies are counted, the number is close to forty-one even though the National Marine Fisheries Service in its official documents routinely only acknowledges that it is funding twenty-two hatcheries and three rearing ponds.

From the Grand Coulee program to the Mitchell Act and right up through the 1980s, fishery managers recognized the potential of supplementation. Fishery agencies also talked positively about supplementation, as shown in the 1972 report on the lower Snake River dams, the 1978 Endangered Species Act workshop reports, and the 1984 Idaho Fish and Game plan. Indeed, supplementation was carried out and was very successful in the mid-Columbia tributaries, and the fishery agencies planned further programs. But these programs were not implemented. Why?

One reason is the agencies' attitude toward Indian fisheries. Supplementation was intended to benefit natural production and the sports fishery, not the tribal fishery. The elimination of tribal fisheries has, arguably, always been a primary objective of the fishery agencies. Tribal fisheries were not thought of very highly by the agencies. Had the hatcheries been constructed in the upper river, rather than below the dams, and a supplementation program carried out, the natural runs would have been maintained and tribal fisheries that had flourished for thousands of years would have continued.

Perhaps a second reason why supplementation plans were not implemented is that the Mitchell Act hatchery program drained many of the available funds. Officials protected existing hatchery programs rather than risking the change to a potentially better program. People are always afraid of change. Status quo management is easier: the money is assured, programs are assured, fisheries seem assured.

—Douglas W. Dompier

A Case Study of a People and Their Resources

Document:	**Rogue River Treaty**
Authors:	The treaty was signed by representatives of the Rogue River band and the U.S. government.
Year:	1853
Description:	The Rogue River tribe was one of six western Oregon tribes to cede aboriginal lands by ratified treaty in exchange for a permanent reservation. The tribes retained the right to remain on temporary reservations within the ceded territories until a suitable selection was made for their permanent residence.

ARTICLE 2. It is agreed on the part of the United States that the aforesaid tribe shall be allowed to occupy temporarily that portion of the above-described tract of territory bounded as follows, to wit: Commencing on the north side of Rogue River, at the mouth of Evan's Creek; thence up said creek to the upper end of a small prairie bearing in a northwesterly direction from Table Mountain, or Upper Table Rock, thence through the gap to the south side of the cliff of the said mountain, thence in a line to Rogue River, striking the southern base of Lower Table Rock, thence down said river to the place of beginning. It being understood that this described tract of land shall be deemed and considered an Indian reserve, *until a suitable selection shall be made by the direction of the President of the United States for their permanent residence and buildings erected thereon, and provision made for their removal.*

> Treaty with the Rogue River, 1853 [Sept. 10, 1853]. 10 Stats. 1018. Ratified Apr. 12, 1854. (Italics added.)

Document:	**Notice of Intent to Establish Coast Reservation**
Author:	Joel Palmer, Superintendent of Indian Affairs of Oregon
Year:	1855
Description:	An official for Indian affairs gives notice to whites that he is setting aside a joint reservation for tribes from the coast and the Willamette Valley. This notice describes an area covering 1.1 million acres.

Indian Reservation

NOTICE IS HEREBY given that I have designated as an Indian Reservation for the Coast and Williamette [sic] Tribes and such others as may hereafter be located thereon the following described district of country, to wit:

Beginning on the Shore of the Pacific Ocean at the mouth of a small stream about midway between Umpqua and Siuslaw rivers: thence easterly to the ridge dividing the waters of these streams and along said ridge or highland to the western boundary of the eighth range of township west of the Williamette meridian: thence north on said boundary to a point due east of Cape Look Out: thence west to the ocean and thence along the coast to the place of beginning.

The tract described presents few attractions to the white settler, while it is believed to be better adapted for the colonization of the Indians than any other portion of territory west of the Cascade Mountains affording so few facilities of settlement to our citizens.

The object of this notice is to inform the public that this reservation will not be subject to settlement by whites.

     signed JOEL PALMER
     Superintendent.

Dayton, O.T.
April 17th, 1855

Letter from Joel Palmer, 7 April 1855, in "Letters Received by Comm. of Indian Affairs 1855," RG 75 National Archives. Also found in Court of Claims Case #4531 *Rogue River Tribe et al. vs United States.*

Document:	**Executive Order Establishing Coast Reservation**
Author:	President Franklin Pierce
Year:	1855
Description:	This executive order, in response to Palmer's notice (above), officially created the reservation.

November 9, 1855.

The reservation of the land within the blue shaded lines is hereby made for the purposes indicated in the letter of the Commissioner of the General Land Office of the 10th September last and letter of the Secretary of the Interior of the 8th November 1855.

FRANKLIN PIERCE

> United States Presidents, *Executive Orders Relating to Indian Reservations, 1855-1922* (1912-22; reprint, Wilmington, Delaware: Scholarly Resources, 1975), 152.

Document:	**Executive Order Reducing Coast Reservation**
Authors:	Joseph Harlan, Secretary of the Interior, wrote the supporting memo, and President Andrew Johnson signed the executive order.
Year:	1865
Description:	In response to increasing white pressure for overland and ocean access to Yaquina Bay, the President reduces the Coast Reservation by 200,000 acres. This was the first of a series of reductions in the Coast Reservation.

Department of the Interior
Washington, D.C., December 20, 1865.

SIR: PURSUANT TO a recommendation of the Secretary of the Interior of the 8th of November, 1855, the President of the United States, by an Executive order dated the 9th of that month set apart conditionally the tract of country on the coast of Oregon, extending from Cape Lookout, on the north to a point below Cape Perpetua on the south . . . for an Indian reservation.

It is represented by the Oregon delegation in Congress that this reservation is unnecessarily large, and that by reason of its access to the harbor of Aquina Bay by the numerous settlers in the fertile and productive valley of the Willamette is prevented.* They ask for a curtailment of this reservation, so as to secure to the inhabitants of the Willamette Valley the much-needed access to the coast, and for this purpose propose that a small and rugged portion of the reservation in the vicinity of Aquina Bay, not occupied or desired by the Indians, shall be released and thrown open to occupation and use by the whites. The Commissioner of Indian Affairs is of the opinion that the interests of the citizens of Oregon will be promoted by the opening of a port of entry at Aquina Bay, and that their interest is paramount in importance to that of the Indians located in that vicinity. Concurring in the views expressed by the Hon. Messrs. Nesmith, Williams, and Henderson, and the Commissioner of Indian Affairs, I respectfully recommend that an order be made by you releasing from reservation for Indian purposes and restoring to public use the portion of the said reservation bounded on the accompanying map by double red lines, and described in the communication of the Oregon delegation as follows, viz: Commencing at a point two miles south of the Siletz Agency; thence west to the Pacific Ocean; thence south along said ocean to the mouth of the Alsea River; thence up said river to the eastern boundary of the reservation: thence north along said eastern boundary to a point due east of the place of beginning; thence west to the place of beginning.

I have the honor to be, very respectfully, your obedient servant,
JAS. HARLAN, *Secretary.*

The PRESIDENT.
EXECUTIVE MANSION, *December 21, 1865*

The recommendation of the Secretary of the Interior is approved, and the tract of land within described will be released from reservation and thrown open to occupancy and used by the citizens as other public land.
ANDREW JOHNSON, *President.*

> United States Presidents, *Executive Orders Relating to Indian Reservations, 1855-1922* (1912-22; reprint, Wilmington, Delaware: Scholarly Resources, 1975), 152-53.

*This is the wording of the original document.—Eds.

Document:	**Annual Report on Indian Affairs**
Author:	J. W. Perit Huntington, Superintendent of Indian Affairs in Oregon
Year:	1867
Description:	The Superintendent of Indian Affairs in Oregon reports on the state of coastal Indians in the two years since President Johnson's executive order reduced their reservation by 200,000 acres.

Siletz Agency

MY ANNUAL REPORT for 1866 gave a very full description of this reservation, and some parts of that report will be reported in this, for as they are located at this point the largest number of Indians in the superintendency, and they have received up to this time by far the least attention from the government and have been treated with injustice and bad faith in some respects, the subject is of sufficient importance to occupy considerable space and time.

The "coast reservation" was originally a tract about 100 miles in length north and south, bordering on the Pacific ocean, and of an average width of about 20 miles. The land is all fertile, much of it exceedingly so, and mainly free from rock, but it is nearly all covered with an extraordinary growth of timber, mostly evergreen, fir, pine, hemlock, and spruce, with dense undergrowth and generally broken and mountainous. The few small prairies contained within its limits do not comprise more than a hundredth of its area. It has a cool and remarkable healthy climate, it is well watered with the purest springs and streams, and its numerous creeks, bays, and inlets are bountifully stocked with fish. The climate is damp, and therefore not well adapted to the production of cereals, although moderate crops of all grains except wheat can be raised with extra care, but for esculent roots, carrots, potatoes, turnips, all plants of the brassica tribe, and for nutritious grasses, I doubt if any soil in the temperate zone can excel it.

In 1864 application was made to the Secretary of the Interior for the vacation of a part of the coast reservation. Inquiry having been made by that office. I submitted a report upon the subject, which was printed in the report of the Commissioner of Indian Affairs for 1865 . . . and I again ask attention to that report in view of what has followed.

In that report I urged the importance of providing for a removal of the Indians located upon and about the bay before the land was thrown open to settlement. My suggestions in this respect were

The clearing of forested lands for homesites, farming, and ranching began in earnest in the 1860s in much of the Pacific Northwest. These changes often affected anadromous fishes, but the effects were not often noted at the time.

totally disregarded, and a district about 25 miles north and south by 20 miles east and west, beginning two miles south of Siletz agency, and including the whole of the Yaquina bay, was thrown open to settlement by an executive order.

Upon this tract were located some Indians who had been encouraged to open farms, erect buildings, and establish themselves permanently. The effect upon them and upon the other Indians was most disastrous. They had all been promised protection in the possession of their lands, and that protection had hitherto been afforded them; but now the agent was powerless, and whites occupied the lands as they pleased. There were also some public buildings upon the reservation and some boats belonging to the Indian department, but these were of comparatively small consequence. Common justice required, and still does require, that some compensation be made these Indians, and that provision be made for their removal to land not occupied by whites.

After the promulgation of the order by which the tract was thrown open to settlement, (which I may remark was very sudden, and gave no time for preparation on the part of the government or the Indians,) the whites rushed in upon the tract, seized upon the Indian farms, occupied their houses, in several instances ejecting the Indians who had built the houses by force, and immediately commenced the settlement of the country. The effect was deplorable. The Indians were dispossessed of their homes and property, and at the same time were afforded facilities for obtaining whiskey. They were discouraged because they could not feel any assurance that they would be protected in any other settlement they might make. They had no incentive to labor. A part were induced by Agent Simpson to remove above (north of) the vacated tract, and are now opening farms near the Siletz agency, but they are doing so timidly and haltingly, and during a late visit to them I constantly met with the inquiry "when the whites were coming there to settle." It is idle to expect any improvement in a people so harassed and discouraged. But a large part of them did not choose to trust again to the public faith of the whites. They scattered out among the white settlements or returned to their old country down the coast. Sub-agent Collins is now down there with a few assistants endeavoring to secure their return; with what success I am not yet informed.

The whole treatment of the government towards these Indians has been full of bad faith.

> Excerpt from Letter of J. W. Perit Huntington, Superintendent [of] Indian Affairs in Oregon, 20 August 1867 in the *Annual Report of the Oregon Superintendency of Indian Affairs*, U.S. Serial Set, House Exec. Doc. #1, 40th Cong., 2d sess., 1326.

Document:	**Report on Conditions of Siletz Agency Indians**
Author:	E. C. Kemble, U.S. Indian inspector
Year:	1874
Description:	Minutes of a meeting held between a U.S. inspector and the headmen on the Coast Reservation. The comments of the headmen show their deep fear of losing the lands that had been selected by the government for their permanent reservation.

I CONVENED the members of the several tribes at Siletz on the occasion of my recent visit, and obtained a complete expression of their views, as also those of white persons living in their vicinity; concerning which I have the honor to report. . . .

It was not necessary for me to invite the expression of their wishes in regard to their lands, for they had long been waiting an opportunity to make them known to "Washington," and were very eager to talk. . . .

I find these Indians desirous, to a man, to retain their reservation and to obtain a title from the Government to the lands they occupy. The accompanying synopsis of their remarks at the council will show the desires of the Siletz Indians respecting their reservation. . . .

[The white men] with whom I conversed [could not] assign any reason why they [the Indians] should be removed save that their occupancy of the land was an impediment to the growth of the country and prejudicial to the interests of white men in that section. . . .

The simple facts are: The call for the removal of the Siletz Indians was started by a handful of speculators two years ago, as a part of a scheme to invite settlement and capital into this part of Benton County, it being represented that the Yaquina Valley was a natural highway to the sea. . . .

Minutes of council held at Siletz agency, Oregon, December 15, 1873, with the chiefs of the confederated tribes. . . .

[GEORGE HARNEY, Rogue River Indian, head chief of the confederated tribes]: . . . A long time ago the whites defeated the Indians in battle and brought them here. They are still troubling us. They have taken a part of our reservation, and now want the rest. . . .

Agents have often promised many things but never performed their *promises*. I want the President to give us a mill. I want the whites to stop troubling us about our land and about removing us. What have we done? We believe in God. We are trying to do good. Why should they want to drive us away? All that is sorry in my heart I tell you. I want you to tell President that the Indians desire to remain here. . . . We were driven here, and now this is our home, and we want to stay. . . .

[CAPTAIN, A-miltswot-na]: . . . Long time my heart has been sorry when I thought of my people. I do not know how to write, and can't send letters to Washington. Now I am glad to see and talk with you. We are all poor. Why does Government give us worthless things like tobacco, calico, &c.? We want wagons, teams, mills, tools, &c. We want something we can work with. I want you to tell the President this. I am sorry because the Yaquina whites trouble us. Government brought us here and gave us this land. . . . I don't want bad white men to drive us off our land. . . .

[JOHN, chief of the Chasta Costas]: I am very poor. *I have to eat oats* and tie my horse there and eat with him, and I am ashamed when I go outside. . . . I don't want to give up this land. The great chief gave it to us in exchange for our old country, and we don't want to leave it.

43d Cong., 1st sess. Senate Misc. Doc. No. 65. 1874, 3-6.

Document:	**Letter from the Commissioner of Indian Affairs**
Author:	E. P. Smith, Commissioner of Indian Affairs in Washington, D.C.
Year:	1874
Description:	The commissioner's letter, addressed to B. R. Cowan, acting Secretary of the Interior, accompanied the above report. Both were forwarded to the chair of the Committee on Indian Affairs. The commissioner himself seemed unaware that most of the tribes removed to the Coast Reservation hadratified treaties.

SIR: I HAVE THE HONOR to submit herewith, for the action of Congress, a copy of a report from United States Indian Inspector E. C. Kemble, in relation to the condition of the Indians of the Siletz agency in Oregon, together with a copy of the proceedings of a council held with them, in which their wants are stated.

On the 11th August, 1855, a treaty was concluded with said Indians, providing for the establishment of a reservation, and the appropriation of certain funds for the erection of buildings, fencing, and opening farms; the purchase of teams, farming implements, tools, and seeds; for the erection of saw-mills, school-houses, blacksmith-shops, &c., with a view to their advancement in the arts of civilization.

This treaty, however, failed of ratification, leaving the Indians without a desirable title to their reservation, and depriving them of the funds necessary for the purchase of the articles above referred to, in view of which, it will be observed, the Indians bitterly complain.

I have, therefore, respectfully to recommend that Congress be requested to pass such an act as will carry out, to some extent at least, the intention of the Government toward said Indians when such treaty was negotiated.

For this purpose it is respectfully recommended that provision be made for the confirmation of the title in said Indians of the lands now occupied by them. These lands were secured for their use and occupation by an Executive order, issued in 1855, shortly after the date of the unratified treaty.

43d Cong., 1st sess. Senate Misc. Doc. No. 65. 1874, 1-2

Document:	**Looters of the Public Domain**
Author:	Stephen A. Douglas Puter, a former logger who spent seventeen months in jail for conspiring to defraud the government of public lands
Year:	1908
Description:	A convicted felon describes the well-orchestrated, illegal land transfers that whittled away the Coast Reservation at the turn of this century.

NO SOONER WAS A TOWNSHIP surveyed than it was quietly gobbled up by alleged settlers under the special homestead Act created by Congress for their so-called benefit. The whole proceedings looking to the disposition of these lands was a mistake from the beginning. In the first place, the country is of such general character that no person could ever make his living there by cultivation of the soil, as it would take a lifetime to develop any kind of respectable clearing. As a matter of fact, the region is a vast jungle, impenetrable to a greater degree than any portion of the heart of Africa, and it has been estimated that it would cost fully $300 an acre to clear the land.

It [the former Siletz Indian Reservation] is essentially a magnificent forest, and as such should have been preserved by the Government, allowing the few surviving Indians therein to retain possession of their own. They could do no harm by their occupancy, but on the contrary, were capable of accomplishing a great deal of good, as they would naturally take a pride in preserving it from devastating fires, thus affording a continuous protection to the watershed, and thus operating to the material benefit of the climate of the Western coast of the State. Provision should have been made for the sale of the ripened timber to the highest bidder in an open market, and in this way the Government could have secured a revenue sufficient to have maintained the reserve for all time. Wild game could thrive there almost unmolested throughout the closed season, and eventually the region would have become one of the world's greatest hunting grounds.

But there was design on the magnificent timber from the very start, and the proposition to throw the reservation open for settlement under the farcical Homestead Act quoted, was merely a ruse to cloak the real motives of those interested, who figured wisely that few honest claimants would attempt to comply with the prohibitive conditions of the law, and go there with the idea of making a home in every sense of the word. . . .

If necessary, I could cite numerous instances in the Siletz country alone where the General Land Office, under the Ballinger and Dennett administrations, has strangely shut its eyes to glaring frauds, and passed entries to patent that it must have known should have been canceled. This condition applies only to the Siletz country, and whether or not it extends in other directions, I am in no position to state.

In the case of the Siletz entries, it is a matter of record that in nearly every instance the claims were transferred to speculators as soon as final certificates were granted by the local Land Office, and that the holders of title were exceedingly active in securing the issuance of patents.

The trial of Willard N. Jones, Thad S. Potter and Ira Wade during 1905, wherein the two former were convicted and the latter acquitted, developed enough evidence to show that hardly an entry in the former Siletz Indian Reservation was made in good faith. Naturally, there are some exceptions, but they are so scarce as to render them unworthy of notice.

S. A. D. Puter, *Looters of the Public Domain* (1908; reprint, New York: Arno Press, 1972), 471, 480.

Document:	**Letter from Siletz Tribal Council**
Author:	Daniel Orton, Secretary-Treasurer of the Siletz Indian Tribal Council
Year:	1948
Description:	In a letter to the Oregon State Fish Commission (later the Oregon Department of Fish and Wildlife), the Siletz tribe expresses its concern at the destruction of habitat and the decline of salmon runs on the Siletz and its tributaries.

DEAR SIRS:

The Siletz Indian General Council at their meeting at Siletz, Oregon, on October 24th last instructed me to write you and call your attention to the following in the interest of fish conservation on the Siletz river and tributaries.

In years past a great many fish migrated up the Siletz river and spawned in its many tributaries. Later commercial fishing was banned on the stream to permit greater migration and spawning in the upper reaches.

In the later years logging operations removed much timber from the Siletz river area and through negligence or what not of operations many of the smaller streams that feed the river were completely clogged with waste logs, chunks and waste timber in general until at present it is almost impossible for chinook, silver-side, steelhead and other fish to go up these smaller streams and spawn as they have done for many many years.

Among the smaller streams affected as abovementioned we suggest that an investigation be made by your commission of the present conditions as mentioned in Thompson creek and Mill creek both below the town of Siletz, Dewey creek, Mill creek across the river west of Siletz, Logan creek near and south of Siletz, Klamath creek, Sam creek, Bentley or Baker creek, Spencer creek, Rock creek and Mill creek all above the town of Siletz. Many salmon have always spawned in the above streams in the past.

We suggest too that you look into pollution and dumping of saw-dust into the river proper and the mill that is operating on Sam creek a few miles above the town of Siletz. Also the retarding of fish migration in the river proper by the Camp 12 logging operators. Also the dam that exists and retards migration up stream on Bentley or Baker creek above Siletz.

Our Siletz Indians have lived in the above area for many years and fished all of the above streams and river and we know that there is a very great decline in fish migration up the above streams and we request that that [sic] above conditions that exist be looked into by the commission of fish conservation in the Siletz river area.
. . . [T]hanking you kindly in the matter, I am
Sincerely yours,
DANIEL ORTON, *Sec. Treas.*
Siletz Indian Tribal Council

> Letter from Siletz Tribal Council to the Oregon Fish Commission (10 Nov. 1948, photocopy), Archives, Confederated Tribes of Siletz Indians of Oregon, Siletz.

Document:	**Report on Siletz River**
Author:	Biologist John I. Hodges, a member of the Coastal Rivers Investigations group, part of the research section of the Fish Commission of Oregon
Year:	1948
Description:	In response to the complaint from the Siletz tribe, a state biologist inspected the Siletz and a number of its tributaries to determine reasons for the decline in salmon runs.

Preliminary Investigation of Conditions on Siletz River, December 7, 1948 Interviews.
1. LEE EVANS—Unable to contact—in Portland hospital.
2. Wolverton Orton—Mr. Orton is an Indian who has spent his entire life in the vicinity of Logsden. At present, he lives near the mouth of Sam Creek. His comments on the various streams mentioned in the letter of the Siletz Indian Tribal Council were as follows:
a) Thompson Creek—has been logged off and is now choked with logs. . . .
c) Dewey Creek—logged off long ago. Probably choked with logs.
d) Mill Creek (across the river, west of Siletz)—this is probably the same as Miller Creek as shown on map. Logged off long ago. Probably choked with logs.
e) Logan Creek—he was not acquainted with this stream.

Until comparatively recently roadbuilding and logging practices generally were not subject to regulations designed to protect fish habitat. Here, California fisheries workers view the effects of logging on a coastal stream in the 1950s.

f) Klamath Creek—there is a mill with a pond on this stream. He did not know whether there was a ladder at the dam.

g) Sam Creek—there is a mill at the mouth of the South Fork with a dam across the stream. This used to have a fish ladder. The lower stretches of Sam Creek are not choked with logs.

h) Bentley (Baker) Creek—choked with logs from old logging operation. . . .

i) Spencer Creek—Empties into Siletz River from north side, a short distance above Sam Creek. There is a mill with pond on this stream. He thinks there is probably no fish ladder.

j) Rock Creek—This stream is being logged at present time. . . .

All of the above streams were reported as having supported large runs of salmon years ago before being logged.

Mr. Orton said that Palmer Creek (about 3 miles above Logsden on north side of Siletz R.) used to have lots of salmon but is now choked with logs.

Mr. Orton said that the Camp 12 logging operators had not retarded the migration of fish in the main river as far as he knew but only in the tributaries where they are logging.

Concerning the dam on Bentley or Baker Creek, he said that quite a number of years ago, a dam had been built for power to light some one's home. He did not know whether the dam was still present on the stream.

His opinion was that these streams should be surveyed in the summer when the water is low.

When questioned about spring chinook in the Siletz, he said that chinook salmon used to show up in the river near Logsden in the month of June. He said he remembers them as a boy, and that he is 75 years old. . . .

Investigation of Mill at mouth of S. Fork of Sam Creek

The mill at the mouth of the South Fork of Sam Creek is owned by the Wienert Lumber Company. The South Fork of Sam Creek has been dammed to form a mill pond. The dam is approximately 8 feet in height and the water flows over this onto an apron forming a fast chute of water. It appeared that there had been a fish ladder at this dam at one time but it is now completely inoperative. This dam is a 100 per cent barrier to upstream migration of any species of salmon or trout.

The stream was spot checked by car for about 1 miles above the dam. The stream was high and muddy and flowing several hundred second feet. It appeared that this stream should be able to support salmon and Mr. Orton stated that it had had large runs in years past.

Sawdust and waste material is conveyed over the creek to the far shore where it is burned. Pollution from this source did not appear serious.

Recommendations:

1. That thorough summer surveys be made of all of the above tributaries to the Siletz and in addition any others that are reported to be impassable to the migration of salmon. This work should be done in the spring or early summer so that any serious conditions can be corrected by the time of the appearance of the fall runs.
2. That the Wienert Lumber Company be required to place an adequate fish way in operation at its mill at the mouth of the South Fork of Sam Creek.

Discussion

A survey was made of Mill Creek . . . by Mr. Rulifson and Mr. Clutter. Similar surveys should be conducted on the other tributaries. After completion of these surveys and the elimination of barriers to migration of salmon, a planting program should be undertaken to rebuild the runs in areas which have been blocked to migration and are found to have suitable spawning ground.

JOHN I. HODGES,
Aquatic Biologist

> Report by John I. Hodges (7 Dec. 1948, photocopy), from files of Robert Buckman, Oregon Department of Fish and Wildlife, Newport.

Document:	**Draft of Termination Act**
Author:	Bureau of Indian Affairs
Year:	1950
Description:	This draft is a preliminary version of the 1954 Western Oregon Indians Termination Act, which ended government-to-government relations between the Confederated Tribes of Siletz Indians and the United States. Justifications for termination were based on the diminished land and resource base of the Siletz Reservation and years of prior neglect by the Bureau of Indian Affairs, which gave the tribal members a certain amount of independence.

THERE IS NO LONGER any need for continuing government services to Indians of the jurisdiction, and it is therefore recommended that further obligation on the part of the Federal Government be formally terminated. The government has been fulfilling obligations assumed in numerous treaties since 1853 and as most Indians of the jurisdiction have no advanced to a point where they no longer need this guidance and protection, the program should be discontinued. It is therefore felt that, along with plans to discontinue their ward and trust status, special legislation should be proposed which would extend to them all the rights and privileges now enjoyed by other citizens and at the same time remove any and all special rights, privileges, exemptions, etc. now enjoyed by them. Such legislation should remove any further restriction against their purchase of liquor; it should end any special hunting and fishing rights; it should terminate benefits granted under the Reorganization Act.

> Bureau of Indian Affairs, *Program for the Early Termination of Selected Activities and Withdrawing Federal Supervision over the Indians at Grand Ronde-Siletz and Southwestern Oregon* (Portland, 1950), 17.

Document:	**Siletz Restoration Act**
Author:	U.S. Congress
Year:	1977
Description:	The Restoration Act, which reestablished the federally recognized status of the Confederated Tribes of Siletz Indians, was legally neutral on the question of hunting and fishing rights: it did not grant or restore any new rights, nor did it take away any rights that might have survived the Siletz tribe's long history.

(b) Restoration of rights and privileges

EXCEPT AS PROVIDED in subsection (c) of this section, all rights and privileges of the tribe and of members of the tribe under any Federal treaty, Executive order, agreement, or statute, or under any other authority, which were diminished or lost under subchapter XXX of this chapter, are hereby restored, and such subchapter shall be inapplicable to the tribe and to members of the tribe after November 18, 1977.

(c) Hunting, fishing or trapping rights and tribal reservations not restored

This subchapter shall not grant or restore any hunting, fishing, or trapping right of any nature, including any indirect or procedural right or advantage, to the tribe or any member of the tribe, or shall it be construed as granting, establishing, or restoring a reservation for the tribe.

> Pub. L., 95-195, § 3, Nov. 18, 1977, 91 Stat. 1415

Commentary

 THE ORIGINAL LANDS of the tribes and bands that became the Confederated Tribes of Siletz Indians of Oregon totaled about 20 million acres. They included all of that part of Oregon that lies west of the summit of the Cascade Range, and parts of the upper Klamath River and the Smith River regions in northern California. Each tribe hunted, fished, and gathered other foods within its territory according to tribal laws, customs, and ceremonies that protected the resources from mismanagement and unwise uses.

Subsequently, the land and its wealth were taken over by the U.S. government and its citizens. What followed is an old story, one that serves as a case history of abuse of native people, their land, and the salmon.

After 1850, as Congress encouraged U.S. citizens to move to the newly established Oregon Territory with legislation such as the Oregon Donation Land Act, the western Oregon Indians, like other Northwest tribes, were pressured into ceding their lands. All of the tribes signed treaties, most, but not all, of which were ratified (adopted into law) by the U.S. Senate. In all of the treaties from western Oregon that were ratified, the tribes reserved the right to stay within their ceded area until a permanent reservation was selected by the president of the United States.

On November 9, 1855, President Franklin Pierce signed an executive order that established the Coast Reservation at 1.1 million acres, as had been requested by Superintendent Joel Palmer in April of that year. In 1856-57 the western Oregon tribes and bands were removed to the Coast Reservation. They were destitute upon their arrival, having lost everything in the battle to keep their homelands, and they experienced much emotional and physical privation under the reservation system, as reported by Huntington and Kemble.

Confusion about how the reservation became established began soon after removal of the tribes to the reservation. The coastal tribes had signed a treaty with the U.S. government just weeks before the executive order establishing the reservation was signed. The treaty called for a smaller reservation. However, this treaty did not even arrive in Washington, D.C., until five days after the reservation had been established.

The treaty was never ratified by Congress, despite numerous requests by agents. The plight of the unratified treaty tribes became the focus of reservation correspondence and reports. A popular but erroneous interpretation developed: it was believed that the executive

233

order that established the reservation was signed as a temporary emergency measure only because Congress had refused to ratify the treaty. As a result of this inaccurate interpretation of events, people wanting to seize reservation lands argued that the tribe had no legal right to it.

By 1875 the U.S. government had reduced the reservation by 900,000 acres without the consent of the tribes or any compensation for the lands and resources that were taken. From 1875 to 1892 the reservation consisted of 225,000 acres between Cascade Head and Yaquina Head.

In 1892 the General Allotment Act took effect. Parts of the reduced reservation, now known as the Siletz Reservation, were surveyed into 80-acre parcels and assigned to individual tribal members. A section of the Allotment Act said that after each eligible tribal member had been assigned an allotment, the Secretary of the Interior could declare the rest of the reservation "surplus" and send a team of commissioners to "negotiate" for its purchase. About 85 percent of the land (192,000 acres) was declared "surplus." On October 31, 1892, after several meetings, the Confederated Tribes of Siletz Indians saw the futility of resisting the purchase. The unallotted lands were taken from the reservation for 74¢ an acre.

When tribal leaders told the commissioners that they knew that timber was as good as money to white people and should be considered in the sale price, they were told that timber values could not be considered here because of the remoteness and inaccessibility of the timber stands. However, when the commissioners reported to Washington, D.C., on the success of their mission, they praised the valuable timber stands throughout the sale area and the many rapid, running streams that would serve "as a means of getting the timber out." As an additional insult, they recommended to the commissioner of the General Land Office that future homesteaders within this sale area should pay a fee of no less than $2.50 an acre because of the value of the timber. (Homesteaders weren't "purchasing" lands, of course; they were merely paying filing fees on open, unclaimed government lands.)

Within the next several years, Siletz people began to request clear titles to their lands. Once they received these titles they would be considered citizens of the United States. Citizenship meant they would be out from under the trust restrictions that applied to their lands and other personal business. These goals were good, in theory, but having clear titles also meant paying taxes on their allotments, and those not able to pay their taxes were in danger of losing them to the county. Furthermore, in many instances Siletz people were tempted into mortgaging their property to pay for improvements or to take care of other bills, and ended up homeless. Encouraging this trend toward land alienation was the Siletz Indian Inherited Lands Act, passed by Congress in 1901, which essentially restricted the amount of land a Siletz Indian could hold in trust. By 1912, as agent Egbert noted, over half of the allotments originally assigned to the Siletz were owned by non-Indians.

By 1920 the Siletz Indian Reservation consisted of about 20,000 acres of the original 1.1 million acres. This land was not a contiguous mass, but consisted of scattered allotment and tribal parcels in a sea of non-Indian communities. The treaty agreements had promised a permanent reservation for the tribes to call their home, a place where they could continue, forever, their existence as Indian people. But federal policy directed them toward cultural assimilation with the mass population of the United States and took steps, such as assigning allotments, to ensure that tribal government and the traditional views of communal property ownership and resource rights were done away with on the reservations.

At about this time, the state began to enforce fish and game regulations in the Siletz area. Homesteaders and Indians were treated alike in all respects, even though the Siletz Indians had never consented to give up their aboriginal and treaty rights to hunt, fish, and gather other foods within their original reservation boundaries. Because tribal members were accustomed to the extreme nature of government controls and takings that had been the history of the Siletz Reservation, they offered no concerted resistance to these new regulations. After several years during which individual tribal members were arrested for "poaching game" and "illegal fishing" and complaints were made to the Portland office of the Bureau of Indian Affairs, the state began issuing metal tags to clip on gill nets. These tags were to be used by tribal members on trust allotments only.

This system was more or less a Band-Aid: it did not address the larger issue of treaty fishing rights, nor did it do much for the many tribal families with no allotment property adjoining the Siletz or Salmon rivers. Hunting issues were handled in a similar way. If a deer happened to walk onto a trust allotment, it could be taken, but the issue of hunting rights within the original reservation was not addressed. The cultural practices of procuring and storing subsistence foods suffered under these policies.

In the 1940s the Confederated Tribes of Siletz were notified of the statute of limitations on Indian land claims and other tribal grievances. All of the tribes were scrambling to file cases on the many ratified treaty and unratified treaty issues that the Siletz people were heirs to. These claims were heard by the Indian Court of Claims through 1950, but the decisions rendered in these cases were disappointing for the

Siletz people. The court failed to recognize and support the basic meaning and provisions of the ratified treaties. And in determining compensation for the loss of aboriginal lands—lands taken without a ratified treaty—the court ruled that a fair price was the value of the lands at the time of taking—1855—often with no interest.

Soon after the Indian Court of Claims had rendered its decisions on the Siletz cases, the Bureau of Indian Affairs announced its plan for the U.S. government to end its trust relationship with the Confederated Tribes of Siletz Indians. The government argued that because the Siletz tribe had a decimated and scattered land base and because very few federal programs served the Siletz area, the federally recognized status of the Siletz tribal government should be terminated.

The Western Oregon Indians Termination Act was passed in 1954. By 1956 the few remaining trust parcels were either deeded or sold by the Bureau of Indian Affairs. The few metal gill-net tags that had been issued were considered no longer valid as permits. Tribal life and culture were reduced to infrequent traditional dances, the occasional weaving of spruce root baskets, and story telling. If things were bad for the Siletz people before termination, the years as a terminated tribe proved to be rock bottom.

By the early 1970s some tribal members were talking about the impacts that termination had had on their people and were discussing possibilities for reversing the whole termination process. In 1977, after several years of intensive efforts, Congress passed the Siletz Restoration Act, which reestablished the federally recognized status of the Confederated Tribes of Siletz Indians.

There had been considerable opposition to the restoration efforts. Sportsmen's groups in the Pacific Northwest were concerned by the 1974 Boldt decision, which ruled that native fishers were entitled to up to 50 percent of the salmon harvest, and saw the Siletz restoration efforts as an additional threat to the dwindling fisheries resources. In response to the loud opposition, the restoration legislation was totally neutral on the issue of hunting and fishing rights. It neither granted new rights nor took away any hunting and fishing rights that might have survived the complex history of the tribe.

The Restoration Act stated that a proposal would soon be submitted for legislative action to establish a land base for the tribe. In 1980, the Siletz Reservation Bill was ready to be introduced. The tribe had identified about thirty small scattered parcels of Bureau of Land Management land in the Siletz area, totaling 3,600 acres. These parcels and the few acres that had been the old Siletz Agency site (which the tribe had turned over to the City of Siletz at termination time) were included in the proposal. As the tribe was preparing to have the legislation introduced, the opposition sprang up again with renewed force.

The groups opposing the Reservation Bill feared that returning lands to the Siletz tribe would greatly enhance the chances that tribal hunting and fishing rights would be recognized. It is worth noting that the Menominee and Klamath tribes both went to federal court during their years as terminated tribes, and both won their claims that termination did not also terminate their aboriginal and treaty rights to hunt and fish as guaranteed by their treaties with the United States government. It takes intentional and explicit action to reduce treaty rights, and Congress must then fairly compensate the tribes for reduction of those rights.

The federal legislator who was supposed to introduce the Siletz Reservation Bill sided with the opposition, announcing that the bill would not be introduced to Congress until the Confederated Tribes of Siletz Indians had first reached an agreement with the state of Oregon on hunting and fishing issues. With that coercive ultimatum, and with no clear understanding of what their aboriginal or treaty rights were, the Confederated Tribes acquiesced to an agreement with the state. The agreement, called the "Consent Decree," was referred to as a "friendly" law suit in federal court. It amounts to the following provisions: 200 salmon tags (each good for one fish) are issued to the tribe each fall; and 375 deer tags and 25 elk tags are issued in accordance with the regular Oregon State seasons. The Consent Decree also contains minor provisions for shellfish gathering and for issuance to the tribe of excess salmon carcasses from state-run fish hatcheries. These numbers are insignificant when we consider that the 2,400 members of the Confederated Tribes of Siletz Indians must *compete* for these tags.

The salmon, like the Siletz people, have paid a high price for settlement of former reservation lands. The Siletz people recognized this early on.

On November 10, 1948, Daniel Orton, Siletz Tribal Council Secretary/Treasurer, sent a letter to the Oregon State Fish Commission expressing concern about the declining salmon runs in the area and citing reasons for the decline. Since World War I large-scale commercial logging had been practiced in the areas mentioned. The careless practices of blocking stream channels, siltation, and degrading water quality were making their effects very apparent. These areas were all within the original boundaries of the Coast Reservation. All of the streams mentioned, in fact, had been part of the reservation until the General Allotment Act took effect at Siletz in 1892.

During the negotiations for the sale of the unallotted lands, the commissioners had promised the Siletz Indians that no white people would get any of the lands from the sale area unless they strictly observed the Homestead Laws of the United States. But the newly formed Lincoln County was thick with fraudulent homestead entries. Persons seeking to get rich off the old-growth timber paid other individuals to file entries and then had them transfer the title once it was cleared.

S. A. D. Puter, himself convicted of land fraud, wrote a book in 1908 called *Looters of the Public Domain*. Chapter 30 of that book is dedicated to the Siletz country, describing how it was taken from the Confederated Tribes of Siletz and how certain persons sought to acquire large portions of it illegally for their own benefit. A well-organized group carefully coordinated these illegal land transfers and several men were convicted of collusion to commit fraud. Many of the best timber stands in the Siletz River Valley were obtained for private exploitation this way. It is as a direct result of this history that the Siletz Tribal Council had to request an investigation into the disappearance of salmon runs from the Siletz River in 1948.

Puter wrote about the failure of the government to deal fairly with the tribes. He estimated that the 192,000 acres that were purchased for $142,000 had a conservative value of $8,000,000. He also observed,

> It is essentially a magnificent forest, and as such should have been preserved by the Government, allowing the few surviving Indians therein to retain possession of their own. They could do no harm by their occupancy, but on the contrary, were capable of accomplishing a great deal of good, as they would naturally take a pride in preserving it from devastating fires, thus affording a continuous protection to the watershed, and thus operating to the material benefit of the climate of the Western coast of the State (p. 471).

The devastating effects of the reservation reductions and the subsequent depletion of the resources have directly and deeply affected the lives and culture of the Siletz tribal members.

Cultural survival, more than monetary motives, spurs the Confederated Tribes of Siletz to do all in their power to stabilize the salmon runs within their lands and former lands. The true cause for the decrease in salmon runs is not the insignificant amount of cultural fishing that is practiced by the tribe. Rather the true causes lie elsewhere and must be determined and dealt with now, before the salmon disappears. The salmon has always meant life itself to the ancestors of the Siletz people; with any luck, their children will continue to know and honor the first salmon caught each season.

—Robert Kentta

Introduction

"EVERY SPECIES is destined for threatened, endangered or extinct status unless we regain environmental spiritualism," Yakama leader Ted Strong wrote in 1994.[1] Strong was the executive director of the Columbia River Inter-Tribal Fish Commission.

The experience of the last decade has ushered in a period of soul searching among natural resource managers. As the documents and commentaries in this section show, attempts—even very well-intentioned attempts—to improve the status of salmon have not been able to keep up with the conditions contributing to their demise. One example: the progressive legislation of the Northwest Power Act, which promised that Columbia Basin salmon would be treated as "coequals" with the hydroelectric use of the river, seemed to offer real hope for recovering salmon populations. But the administration of the act failed to prevent the listings of salmon stocks under the Endangered Species Act, a development that is also discussed in this section.

As the salmon crisis has accelerated and become more pronounced, many scientists and managers have begun to question the premises of the resource management they have been practicing. Attempts to force a complex natural world to provide what we want from it seem to have failed. If salmon and the rivers that support them are to persist over time and provide the benefits they have in the past, many people now believe it necessary for society to reexamine the approaches that have been taken to both biological management and resource politics.

Note
1. Ted Strong, *Columbia River Inter-Tribal Fish Commission Annual Report 1993* (Portland, Oregon: Columbia River Inter-Tribal Fish Commission, 1994), 5.

Previous page: Salmon fishing boats for sale were a common sight in the ports of California, Oregon, and Washington in the early 1990s.

SHOULD ECOLOGY RESTRAIN THE ECONOMY?

Document: **Ecology and Economy**

Author: Urban and Rural Lands Committee, Pacific Northwest River
                Basins Commission

Year: 1973

Description: This report wrestled with the idea that there might be
                appropriate limits to the human growth of the Pacific
                Northwest; salmon were interested bystanders in this analysis.

Chapter II
The Carrying Capacity Approach—One Alternative

ARE THE CURRENT efforts toward attaining a high quality environment
on a collision course with population growth and economic
growth? Economists and ecologists currently are debating the issue.
In an address to the World Affairs Council on March 29, 1972,
Russell Train, Chairman of the United States Council on Environmental Quality, called for a full public debate on national growth
goals. Economic growth objectives have dominated United States
policy since colonial days. Only within the last decade has appreciable attention been devoted to human ecology—the relationship
between human beings and their physical environment (including
biological components). Many "ecologists" or "environmentalists"
are concerned that the United States is approaching, or in some
areas, may have exceeded, the finite limits of land, water, and air
resources to sustain additional population and industrial growth.

A groundswell of interest and action is developing to protect and
improve the quality of our future environment in the Pacific
Northwest, as well as the rest of the nation. Northwesterners view
conditions in their region as among the best in the nation. The
outdoor environment is relatively unspoiled. Few leave except for
economic reasons. Historically there has been a substantial net in-
migration. But if effective counter-measures are not taken, increases
in population and industrialization may eventually result in drastic
degradation of the quality of the outdoor environment.

The Office of Business Economics, U.S. Department of Commerce, and Economic Research Service, U.S. Department of
Agriculture (OBERS), 1967 projections to the year 2020 include a
change in population for the Northwest region from 5.9 million in

1965 to 12.7 million (216%); and in per capita annual personal income, in constant 1965 dollars, from $2,785 in 1965 to $13,189 (474%). In per capita share of gross regional product the change would be from $3,520 to $16,700. Such increases would result in 10.2 times the production of goods and services that existed in 1965 or from $20.4 billion to $208 billion in constant 1965 dollars. The 1971 projections based upon 1967 data show population in 2020 as 11.97 million and per capita income as $13,181, in 1965 dollars. . . .

Historical trend economic projections, including some consideration of individual resource capability, frequently have been accepted by planners and decision makers as goals and are used to forecast the long range "needs" and "demands" for other national and local programs such as public lands and resources, transportation, energy supply, housing, health and education. The Battelle Memorial Institute and the Bonneville Power Administration have used such methods for projecting Pacific Northwest long range growth in population, employment, and income. This type of economic projection has proven to be a reasonably accurate forecast during the past 50 years and no other system for identifying goals has been readily available. However, it frequently ignores natural resource supply constraints, assumes unlimited growth, and fails to quantify either the combined capacity of all Northwest natural resources to sustain growth or the effect that the projected growth and economic development would have on the livability, the congestion, the air and water pollution, and the natural or the intangible values. . . .

During the first six decades of the 20th Century, primary attention in this nation has been focused piecemeal upon the short range uncoordinated planning, promotion, and development of individual components of the economy and the environment such as transportation, industrial production, agricultural production, forest production, energy supplies, water development, health, education, recreation, fish and wildlife, and wilderness preservation. The promotion, development and preservation goals have been further fragmented into small individual units by mission oriented private concerns, cities, counties, etc. Our decisions frequently have been based upon the perspective of individual disciplines with few cross ties to weigh the overall relevance of separate partial analyses. Little effort has been devoted to assessing the long range cumulative effects of all these activities upon the livability of everyone in an entire state, multi-state region, or the nation as a whole. Little effort has been devoted to influencing optimum long range growth trends.

Re-orienting Basic Assumptions about Growth

Until very recently orthodox economists here treated the environmental costs of economic growth as "externalities" far removed from their primary concerns. Most of the assumptions to date by economists and other planners have been that the future will be an extension of the past; that population increases and industrial growth inevitably will continue at an exponential rate and the proper course of action is to supply the highways, electrical power, water, urban expansion, etc., needed to accommodate this growth; that plans are needed only to organize the inevitable; that any problems which result from the growth will be solved by using science and technology—by substituting artificial human-control systems for natural ecosystems.

There is a rapidly developing differing view that:

(a) Many of today's problems are a result of successes as defined in yesterday's terms;

(b) An extension of the past is not the right prescription for the future;

(c) The primary planning goals for this nation should be altered—with high quality livability as the major long term objective (including a major improvement in the economic position of many of our citizens) and economic development shaped around this overriding determinant;

(d) Science and technology, if oriented toward harmony with nature, can, within limits, increase both the quality and the reliability of nature's carrying capacity and assist in reaching the highest attainable quality of life goals; in fact science and technology appear to be indispensable instruments for such a purpose;

(e) Through social and political action it is possible to encourage, modify, or block growth and development trends so that they are compatible with those long range goals which are supported by a popular consensus.

Unquestionably, the attainment of the present United States material standard of living coupled with a high level of personal freedom and leisure time has been a magnificent achievement—the envy of much of the world. But there were unforeseen and costly consequences too. Now there are new challenges. The foresight exercised in today's planning decisions and actions (or lack of

actions) will determine the quality of life (including material
standard of living) available for our children and grandchildren.
Land, water, and air resources must be recognized as inseparable
components of single life support system—not as independent
reservoirs for both raw materials and waste disposal to be appropriated and exploited at will. Some way must be found to balance and
harmonize both economic and ecologic goals while maintaining
our principles of democracy and personal freedom.

> Efficiency economics doesn't measure basic values which our
> society holds as its goals, such as preservation of human life,
> social justice, freedom, opportunity for individual expression and
> a chance to live a quality life in a quality environment . . . Blind
> adherence to the standards and methodology of efficiency
> economics has provided us with a set of decision-making tools
> which, in some respects, are poor tools.

Senator Henry M. Jackson
April 7, 1969

There are similarities between the present concern over livability
goals and the aspirations of Thomas Jefferson, other founding
fathers and 19th century leaders, for a pastoral society of peace and
contentment. As this nation's industrialization and westward
expansion were occurring, only the most astute grasped the contradiction between the kind of environment Americans said they
wanted and the kind they were actually creating. . . .

The remainder of this paper presents, within the limits of available information, the basic features of a prototype system for
identifying different combinations of population levels, economic
activity levels, and intangible value levels that are possible for the
Pacific Northwest—an approach that identifies both the limits of
basic natural resources of a region to support future growth and the
desirable and undesirable consequences of various levels of growth.
It is intended as a constructive alternative to the projection of
historical trends system which sometimes may have been misinter-
preted as being a forecast and frequently may have been adopted by
default as a long range goal. The purpose is not to set forth explicitly the means of attaining the long range goals that may be
selected. This is a vital next step after the goal setting process but is
beyond the scope of this particular effort.

It is important to recognize, however, that increasing mobility
will accompany increased affluence—that both the economy and
the ecology of the Northwest, the nation, and the world are interre-
lated. In the United States, people and industry will increasingly
tend to migrate toward locations such as the Pacific Northwest,

which at present has a generous endowment of natural outdoor values and an attractive balance between development and nondevelopment, until crowding has reduced quality enough to make the gradient disappear. It would be very difficult to counteract this trend. The material standard of living in the Northwest is approximately the national average and the chances of major improvements in the Northwest's relative position are not promising. However, the Northwest region may be enough of a geographic and economic entity that it would be possible to maintain the present advantage for certain intangible values (scenery, air and water quality, outdoor recreation, wildlife, etc.), at least temporarily—perhaps for twenty years. . . .

Many competent authorities believe that many cities and nations of the world are more densely populated than would be desirable in the long run. The judgment of the National Academy of Sciences in its 1969 publication "Resources and Man," is that "a human population (for the world) less than the present one would offer the best hope for comfortable living for our descendants, long duration for the species and the preservation of environmental quality." . . .

B. Basic Pacific Northwest Advantages

As a region for testing the carrying capacity concept in relationship to quality of life, the Pacific Northwest has many intrinsic advantages. One of the most significant is the fact that at a time when the public is becoming acutely aware of the ecologic consequences of uncontrolled growth, the Pacific Northwest region as a whole is relatively uncongested. In 1965 two of the subregions, Puget Sound and Willamette Valley, with 8.7 percent of the land area, had a population of 3.2 million or nearly 60 percent of the regional total. Puget Sound averaged 4-1/2 acres per capita and the Willamette Valley 6-1/3. For the remainder of the region the average was 60 acres per capita. The Northwest's high quality environment—land, water and air, is largely intact. Thus, there may be sufficient opportunity, time, and public will to guide both the future growth and distribution of Northwest population and industry in a manner that maintains high quality livability. . . .

The Environmental Approach

The policy of Congress as expressed in the National Environmental Policy Act is ". . . to create and maintain conditions under which man and nature can exist in productive harmony, and fulfill the social, economic, and other requirements of present and future generations of Americans."

Environmental quality, as conceived by the Council on Environmental Quality, encompasses the entire spectrum of man's surroundings—the social, economic, and commercial as well as the intangible—the necessities and the luxuries—the rural and the urban, the air, water, and land. In short, the attainment of high quality environment requires the harmonizing of the net effect of all man's activities with the basic natural laws that govern all life on earth. Confusion over the term "environmental quality" arises because of current emphasis upon elements that have been neglected in the past such as clean air, clean water, and scenic beauty. The wise use and development of natural resources and a healthy economy comprise a large and fundamental part of a high quality environment. But to achieve a more stable balance, the past overemphasis on single purpose short term exploitation of resources for their material values must be corrected and more attention paid to long term planning and to the intangible values.

Successful implementation of carrying capacity concepts for the Northwest region would appear to fulfill most, if not all, of the basic principles, precepts, and requirements of the National Environmental Policy Act. It would involve incorporating these principles and precepts in day to day decisions and operating procedures by public agencies, private concerns, and individual citizens. As these principles and precepts are adopted there could be a corresponding reduction in emphasis upon the environmental impact statements that many today consider an onerous burden and an obstacle to progress. . . .

The Northwest has certain inherent competitive advantages in manufacturing and marketing products and services based upon its native natural resources. But these resources are finite; their capacity to supply annually both the materials and the high quality working environment for management and employees that are the foundation for the Northwest economy is limited. With exponential growth rates these sustainable limits may be reached before the unwary realize what has happened. If the Northwest population should increase to the point that Northwest natural resources could not satisfy the demands on a sustained basis it might be possible to resort to importing more raw materials, resulting in a net import imbalance of natural resources, and "exporting Northwest labor." One point of view is that such an unfavorable natural resource trade balance would result in a reduction of per capita income as compared to competitive regions. Raw materials would be shipped in, manufactured locally, and the product shipped to other markets. Since the Northwest could maintain a technological edge only temporarily, the end result must be either abandonment of production or reduction of wages sufficient to meet world competition, plus shipping charges. Obviously this would be exclusive of industries that enjoy a contemporary competitive advantage because of Northwest low cost electricity, seaports, climate, high quality environment for management and employees, etc. It is highly improbable that an unfavorable natural resource trade balance would be or could be compatible with *optimum* livability for the Pacific Northwest. The study takes the position that in the final analysis there are no "non-extractive" industries. . . .

In summary, using the standards employed in this study, land and resources of the Pacific Northwest, if managed according to sufficiently comprehensive and farsighted planning, are adequate to permit use of the outdoor environment by 10 million residents, plus about 25% use by non-residents. Population growth beyond that point probably would be at the expense of the quality of life for the average resident. The most fragile areas, such as wilderness and wild rivers, would be the first to be overused (or use denied).

> Pacific Northwest River Basins Commission, *Ecology and the Economy: A Concept for Balancing Long-Range Goals, The Pacific Northwest Example* (Vancouver, Washington: Pacific Northwest River Basins Commission, 1973), 7-8, 10-15, 21, 32-33, 42, 51-52. (Citations and notes omitted.)

Commentary

THE PACIFIC NORTHWEST River Basins Commission's Urban and Rural Lands Committee, guided by Eugene K. Peterson, tried to incorporate into its planning a popular concept of the late 1960s—carrying capacity. The committee, representing over a dozen federal agencies, several state agencies, city and regional governments, private industry, and academics, came together to seriously look at the limits to growth in the Pacific Northwest.[1]

The committee's report, *Ecology and the Economy,* developed a carrying capacity recommendation for the Pacific Northwest based on the human population and on what the committee called the number of "servant machines" required to support each person, using per capita income as a proxy for this concept. The committee argued that by planning ahead the region could "not only keep but improve the present high quality Northwest livability for ourselves, our children, and grandchildren" (p. 1).

The committee did not think in the late 1960s that the Pacific Northwest had reached its carrying capacity. They estimated that the region could support 9 million people at 3.4 times the 1965 per capita income. In figure 3 of *Ecology and the Economy,* the committee projected regional growth to 2020, in population and per capita income. Extrapolating from the figure, we can compare their projections for 1990 to actual figures. The committee underestimated population growth by several hundred thousand (the latest census shows 8.7 million). Its projection for 1990 per capita income, on the other hand, was too high—$24,800. The actual per capita income was $16,200, or two times the 1965 per capita income corrected to 1990 dollars.[2] This figure is, however, affected by the fact that a greater percentage of the population is in the labor force, which lowers the per capita figure.

The Urban and Rural Lands Committee measured regional carrying capacity using gross regional economic product. Population times per capita income gives gross regional economic product. In 1990, gross product for Washington, Oregon, and Idaho was about half the level the Committee estimated as regional carrying capacity. With population growth and increased per capita income, the region closes in on the Committee's carrying capacity projection. Population and economic growth continue to dominate discussion of regional goals, while increasingly people question whether continued growth contributes to the high quality of Northwest livability.

One of the problems with carrying capacity as a concept for human populations is that technology and social organization make the limit a variable. With more efficient food production, manufacturing, transportation, communications, and human service technologies, more people can be supported in a given area. Conservation practices, planning in urban and rural communities, limited access systems to manage amenity use, vicarious experience with nature, and actions oriented to improving the environment mean that the possibility exists for having more people living at a higher quality of life. In addition, legitimate arguments can be made for establishing the carrying capacity limit at a variety of levels of quality of life.

Since the 1970s, discussions about carrying capacity have received much less attention. This was not due to new technologies and social organization that lessened concern for carrying capacity, but to sev-

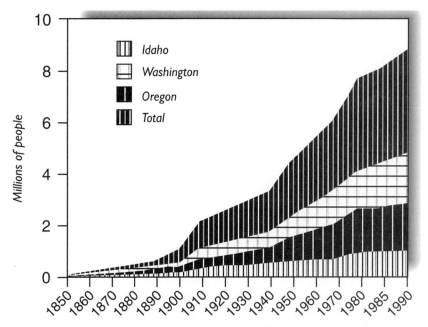

Population growth in the Pacific Northwest states, 1850-1990, has been marked by a 1.9% annual increase from 19940-1990. Source: Statistical Abstracts, USDC Bureau of the Census.

eral tests of carrying capacity that occurred after 1970. The oil embargo of 1974 challenged perceptions about carrying capacity. In the early 1970s the United States embarked on a policy of "energy self-sufficiency." The experience of the 1970s showed that markets could keep the U.S.'s appetite for oil fed, and in the 1980s national policy shifted to "energy security." In the 1980s, the Organization of Petroleum Exporting Countries lost its control of oil prices. North Sea, North Slope, Nigerian, and Mexican oil fields provided alternative supplies. The breakup of the Soviet Union and the aftermath of the Iran-Iraq and Gulf wars created conditions resulting in oil prices in 1990 that were as low in real terms as they have been since the end of World War II.[3]

The Pacific Northwest, which was embarking on a new generation of nuclear power plants to fuel its projected energy needs, found in the 1980s that conservation was faster and cheaper. With such economic and planning failures as the nuclear power ventures of the Washington Public Power Supply System, people were not as confident about any projection for the future. The bountiful times of the 1960s were replaced by new economic concerns, regardless of any effect on ecology, in the 1980s.

In 1980, Paul Ehrlich, with the help of colleagues, made a bet with Julian Simon on the 1990 price of five commodities. Ehrlich, adopting carrying capacity and limits to growth concerns, bet that the real prices of copper, chrome, nickel, tin, and tungsten would be higher in 1990 than 1980. Simon placed his faith in the long-term experience that over time resources generally become cheaper. Ehrlich lost his bet with Simon on all five commodities.

These and other experiences of the 1970s and 1980s did not justify much support for a carrying capacity approach but in the late 1980s people began to migrate from California to the Northwest in greater numbers again. As population growth rose in the Pacific Northwest, new concerns for carrying capacity emerged.

A practical problem has always dogged the implementation of a carrying capacity policy. What are the legal tools for controlling population and economic growth? How can the states of Washington, Oregon, and Idaho limit their population? All the incentives and pressures are to promote population and economic growth. No community is happy if its population base is not growing. How do communities get the financial resources necessary to fund municipal services? The traditional way is to expand the economy. The media also thrive on growth, and continually release population and economic statistics comparing those communities that are "improving" with those that are not.

As population and economic growth occur, salmon habitat is lost to urban growth, timber production, irrigation, electric power generation, and water supply competition. Technical fixes correct some of the habitat problems, but the experience for the Pacific Northwest has been a general loss of salmon habitat and a continuing decline in wild salmon runs.

—Courtland L. Smith

Notes

1. The concept of "limits to growth" had come from a book of the times, *The Limits to Growth* (New York: Universe Books, 1972), by Donella and Dennis Meadows, Jørgen Randers, and William W. Behrens, III.
2. A number of assumptions go into these calculations for which there is insufficient space to detail. It is the relative magnitude of the numbers given that is important.
3. Council of Economic Advisors, *Economic Report of the President* (Washington, D.C.: United States Government Printing Office, 1992).

A CALL FOR BALANCE

Document:	**A Question of Balance**
Author:	Ed Chaney, an Idaho conservationist
Year:	1978
Description:	In this brief study, the author envisions a new era of cooperation among fishery, hydropower, and irrigation interests on the Columbia, based on providing adequate river flows for anadromous fish, particularly the upriver runs.

BECAUSE THEY ARE like the neck of a funnel draining the Columbia Basin, the main-stem Columbia and lower Snake rivers reflect the cumulative effects of upper Columbia Basin water/energy management. Because they are the critical link between upper basin spawning and rearing areas and ocean feeding grounds, the survival of upper basin salmon and steelhead runs depends upon significant improvement in downstream migrant passage problems at main-stem hydroelectric dams and reservoirs.

Viewed from a regional perspective, the present Columbia Basin water management system—if it can be called that—has been aptly described as akin to issuing an unlimited number of blank checks to be unilaterally drawn on a limited fund of water. Consequently, there is not even a reasonably accurate estimate of how much unappropriated water is left in the basin to apportion among future competing uses.

Some analysts argue rather persuasively, and the status of upper basin salmon and steelhead runs seems to confirm, that the basin's water account is already seriously overdrawn. That it is simply bad business to make additional major commitments before conducting a basinwide accounting and devising a long-term, truly comprehensive water management plan to optimize the public benefits of a balanced array of water uses.

But in fact, there is nothing even approaching general unanimity on what constitutes a balanced use of the region's water resources. Or, for that matter, that balanced use is even desirable. Particularly if *balanced use* means altering long-term plans for hydropower production on the main-stem Columbia and lower Snake Rivers in order to protect salmon and steelhead runs of the upper basin.

The Army Corps of Engineers—which constructed and operates all main-stem dams on the lower Snake and Columbia below their confluence—and Bonneville Power Administration—which markets the power produced by them—repeatedly imply their mandates allow them to accommodate the main-stem flow needs of salmon and steelhead only so long as doing so doesn't significantly affect hydroelectric energy production.

Public utility districts operating main-stem dams on the Columbia above its confluence with the Snake are understandably reluctant to let the main-stem flow needs of salmon and steelhead interfere with energy production at their projects.

Hydropower interests exercise de facto control of all unappropriated water in the main-stem Columbia and lower Snake Rivers. However unacceptable that may be to salmon and steelhead interests, it is supported by the prevailing political wind. And the wind is rising.

It should not be inferred there is no cooperative effort underway to address means of accommodating the main-stem flow needs of anadromous fish. Representatives of basin water, power and fishery management agencies meet regularly to do just that. They are beginning to make substantial inroads into the *technical* aspects of main-stem flow water management for anadromous fish.

These genuinely cooperative, valuable efforts do not belie the fact, however, that traditionally prevailing main-stem water management policies and politics are essentially unchanged.

It should not be inferred there has been no effort to devise a basinwide water/energy management plan. To the contrary, current and projected levels of irrigation and hydropower development, particularly the latter, are the product of formal, long-term plans to maximize both.

In recent years there have been several major studies aimed at providing more comprehensive perspective into Columbia Basin water/energy issues and opportunities. These include major efforts funded by the Army Corps of Engineers, Bonneville Power Administration and Pacific Northwest Regional Commission. The most comprehensive effort has been conducted under auspices of the Pacific Northwest River Basins Commission. The commission is composed of representatives of virtually every state-federal water/energy interest in the Columbia Basin. Indian and non-Indian salmon and steelhead interests are not included.

These studies are the primary source of growing awareness that the days of "unlimited" cheap energy and free-to-cheap water in the Columbia Basin are numbered. That under *current* storage capability and *traditional* water/energy management practices, existing water supplies are not sufficient to serve all simultaneous demands during most years, and the shortfall is growing rapidly.

Ed Chaney, *A Question of Balance: Water/Energy—Salmon and Steelhead Production in the Upper Columbia River Basin* (n.p.: Northwest Resource Information Center, 1978), 26-27.

Commentary

 In 1975, THE LAST of the Corps of Engineers dams on the lower Snake River became operational. This completed the transformation of the lower Snake and lower Columbia from a free-flowing river into a series of lakes with an environment hostile to salmon survival. Two years later, a severe drought threatened wholesale destruction of upper basin salmon runs, and the region's governors managed to convince the Army Corps of Engineers to release water to provide fish flows for young salmon on a one-year, emergency basis. But the hydroelectric managers—the Corps and the Bonneville Power Administration—stated repeatedly that they lacked authority to change operations to benefit fish if those changes would reduce power production. In 1978, the year after the drought, Ed Chaney challenged that perspective in an influential analysis.

Chaney was among the first to suggest that the operational practices of the Columbia and Snake river dams were out of balance and inconsistent with a sustainable salmon resource. His claim that there was a water shortage in the Columbia Basin—despite the fact that there remained a significant amount of water for which no vested rights had been issued—challenged the conventional wisdom that the Northwest was a region with plentiful water supplies. And his charge that water management decisions were made with no involvement of the region's fish and wildlife agencies and Indian tribes was soon to be remedied by Congress.

The same year that Chaney wrote, the National Marine Fisheries Service and the U.S. Fish and Wildlife Service began a status report on the state of Columbia Basin salmon to consider whether certain runs should be listed for protection under the Endangered Species Act. Two years later, Congress began to give serious consideration to providing new legislative protection to Columbia Basin salmon, and the legislative history of what became the Northwest Power Act relied heavily on Chaney's analysis. Yet despite this congressional action, hydroelectric operations changed only marginally; hydropower never relinquished its position as the dominant use in Columbia Basin dam operations. Not surprisingly, therefore, the Endangered Species Act was to reappear a little over a decade after Chaney sounded the call of alarm.

—Michael C. Blumm and F. Lorraine Bodi

Northwest Power Act:
"Fish Coequal with Hydropower"

Document:	**Northwest Power Act**
Author:	U.S. Congress
Year:	1980
Description:	These excerpts from the legislative history and the statute reveal Congress' intent to elevate the importance of salmon in regional power planning, and make fish and wildlife "a coequal partner with other uses" of the Columbia River.

The Committee recognizes that the Federal agencies and others in the regin [sic] cannot correct past mistakes merely by enacting a new law, while many such mistakes unfortunately may be uncorrectable, others can clearly be corrected or avoided. Money, a reasonable amount of time, clear regulatory authority, and cooperative participation by the various interests will be needed to protect and rejuvenate the fish and wildlife resources of this region. It is not the Committee's intention to make fish and wildlife superior to power or other recognized needs. But it is the intention of the Committee *to treat fish and wildlife as a co-equal partner* with other uses in the management and operation of hydro projects of this region.

The Committee also believes that BPA and others in the region, including the so-called "power interests," concerned with meeting the power needs of the region have in recent times become more concerned about these valuable natural resources. They testified that they are anxious to accommodate fish and wildlife needs. The Committee believes that this is a hopeful sign and that this bill will help to achieve what appears to be a welcome common objective of protecting and enhancing this resource. . . .

Section 4(h) is designed to provide effective procedures and authorities whereby fish and wildlife of the Columbia River Basin will be treated *on a par with power needs and the other purposes* for which the hydroelectric dams of the region were built and are operated and maintained. This should ensure a balance for all uses of the river. . . .

. . . The objective is to give flexibility to all concerned to devise effective and imaginative measures that are also reasonable and will not result in unreasonable power shortages or loss of power revenues. Some power losses, with resultant loss in revenues, may be inevitable at times if these fish and wildlife objectives are to be achieved. . . .

Section (h) also provides a directive to BPA and other Federal agencies responsible for the management or operation or regulation of hydro facilities on the Columbia or its tributaries to adequately protect, etc., fish and wildlife affected by such facilities in a manner that ensures equitable treatment for fish and wildlife with other purposes for the facilities. This provision does not replace other provisions of law such as FERC's section 10 of the Federal Power Act, but supplements it. This provision is also *aimed at placing fish and wildlife on a par* with these other purposes.

> H.R. Rep. No. 976, 96th Cong., 2d Sess. 49, 50, 56-57 (1980).
> (Emphasis added.)

(h)(1)(a) The Council shall promptly develop and adopt, pursuant to this subsection, a program to protect, mitigate, and enhance fish and wildlife, including related spawning grounds and habitat, on the Columbia River and its tributaries. Because of the unique history, problems, and opportunities presented by the development and operation of hydroelectric facilities on the Columbia River and its tributaries, the program, to the greatest extent possible, shall be designed to deal with that river and its tributaries as a system. . . .

(5) The Council shall develop a program on the basis of [fish and wildlife agency, tribal, and public] recommendations, supporting documents, and views and information obtained through public comment and participation, and consultation with the agencies, tribes, and customers referred to in subparagraph (A) of paragraph (4). The program shall consist of measures to protect, mitigate, and enhance fish and wildlife affected by the development, operation, and management of such facilities while assuring the Pacific Northwest an adequate, efficient, economical, and reliable power supply. Enhancement measures shall be included in the program to the extent such measures are designed to achieve improved protection and mitigation.

(6) The Council shall include in the program measures which it determines, on the basis set forth in paragraph (5), will—

(A) complement the existing and future activities of the Federal and the region's State fish and wildlife agencies and appropriate Indian tribes;

(B) be based on, and supported by, the best available scientific knowledge;

(C) utilize, where equally effective alternative means of achieving the same sound biological objective exist, the alternative with the minimum economic cost;

(D) be consistent with the legal rights of appropriate Indian tribes in the region; and

(E) in the case of anadromous fish—

(i) *provide for improved survival* of such fish at hydroelectric facilities located on the Columbia River system; and

(ii) *provide flows of sufficient quality and quantity* between such facilities to improve production, migration, and survival of such fish *as necessary to meet sound biological objectives.*

(7) The Council shall determine whether each recommendation received is consistent with the purposes of this Act. In the event such recommendations are inconsistent with each other, the Council, in consultation with appropriate entities, shall resolve such inconsistency in the program giving due weight to the recommendations, expertise, and legal rights and responsibilities of the Federal and the region's State fish and wildlife agencies and appropriate Indian tribes. If the Council does not adopt any recommendation of the fish and wildlife agencies and Indian tribes as part of the program or any other recommendation, it shall explain in writing, as part of the program, the basis for its finding that the adoption of such recommendation would be—

(A) inconsistent with paragraph (5) of this subsection;

(B) inconsistent with paragraph (6) of this subsection; or

(C) less effective than the adopted recommendations for the protection, mitigation, and enhancement of fish and wildlife. . . .

(10)(A) The Administrator shall use the Bonneville Power Administration fund and the authorities available to the Administrator under this Act and other laws administered by the Administrator to protect, mitigate, and enhance fish and wildlife *to the extent affected by the development and operation of any hydroelectric project* of the Columbia River and its tributaries *in a manner consistent with* the plan, if in existence, *the program* adopted by the Council under this subsection, and the purposes of this Act. Expenditures of the

Administrator pursuant to this paragraph shall be in addition to, not in lieu of, other expenditures authorized or required from other entities under other agreements or provisions of law. . . .

(C) The amounts expended by the Administrator for each activity pursuant to this subsection shall be allocated as appropriate by the Administrator, in consultation with the Corps of Engineers and the Water and Power Resources Service, among the various hydroelectric projects of the Federal Columbia River Power System. Amounts so allocated shall be allocated to the various project purposes in accordance with existing accounting procedures for the Federal Columbia River Power System.

(11)(A) The Administrator and other Federal agencies responsible for managing, operating, or regulating Federal or non-Federal hydroelectric facilities located on the Columbia River or its tributaries shall—

(i) exercise such responsibilities consistent with the purposes of this Act and other applicable laws, to adequately protect, mitigate, and enhance fish and wildlife, including related spawning grounds and habitat, affected by such projects or facilities *in a manner that provides equitable treatment for such fish and wildlife* with the other purposes for which such system and facilities are managed and operated;

(ii) exercise such responsibilities, *taking into account at each relevant stage of decisionmaking processes to the fullest extent practicable*, the program adopted by the Council under this subsection. If, and to the extent that, such other Federal agencies as a result of such consideration impose upon any non-Federal electric power project measures to protect, mitigate, and enhance fish and wildlife which are not attributable to the development and operation of such project, then the resulting monetary costs and power losses (if any) shall be borne by the Administrator in accordance with this subsection.

(B) The Administrator and such Federal agencies shall consult with the Secretary of the Interior, the Administrator of the National Marine Fisheries Service, and the State fish and wildlife agencies of the region, appropriate Indian tribes, and affected project operators in carrying out the provisions of this paragraph and shall, to the greatest extent practicable, coordinate their actions.

Pacific Northwest Electric Power Planning and Conservation Act, Pub. L. 96-501, § 4(h), 94 Stat. 2697, 2708-11 (1980) (codified at 16 U.S.C. § 839[b][h] [1988]). (Emphasis added.)

Document:	**The 1982 Water Budget**
Author:	Northwest Power Planning Council
Year:	1982
Description:	This first rendition of an important part of the Columbia River Basin fish and wildlife program describes a plan to provide an additional sum of water (the budget) to help move juvenile salmon downstream through the Columbia dams.

AFTER CONSIDERING the sliding scale minimum flows recommended by the fish and wildlife agencies as well as the optimum flows recommended by the tribes, the Council has determined that increased spring flows are needed at Priest Rapids and Lower Granite dams to improve juvenile salmon migration. Power flows during the remainder of the year are generally sufficient to allow safe migration. In addressing the impact of water storage for hydroelectric generation upon migrating juveniles, the Council considers it most important to provide adequate flows during that portion of the spring when smolts are actually migrating downstream. For this reason, the Council proposes a "Water Budget" approach to improving spring flows. Under this approach, the fish and wildlife agencies and tribes would have the ability to shape flows during the period April 15 through June 15 by using a volume of water specified by the Council and called the Water Budget. Separate Water Budgets would be established for Priest Rapids and Lower Granite dams. No Water Budget would be established for The Dalles, since flows at Priest Rapids and Lower Granite determine the flow at The Dalles.

The size of the proposed Water Budget is derived from the flow recommendations submitted by the fish and wildlife agencies and tribes. First, the Council added the positive differences between the average monthly flows achieved under the fish and wildlife agency recommendations and the average monthly flows achieved during the 42-1/2 month critical period used for power requirements only. This calculation results in a total Water Budget of 67.8 kcfs-months (4.03 million acre-feet [Maf]), comprised of 40.2 kcfs-months (2.39 Maf) at Priest Rapids Dam and 27.6 kcfs-months (1.64 Maf) at Lower Granite Dam. (One kcfs-month is a flow of 1000 cubic feet per second for one month, or 0.0595 Maf.)

Computer simulations by the Instream Flow Work Group indicate that there is not enough water in the Snake River Basin during the critical period both to meet the recommended flows and to ensure that the system's reservoirs refill frequently enough to be of use for future power and fish flow purposes. To reflect these physical limitations, the Council has set the Water Budget for Lower Granite Dam in the Snake River Basin below that derived from the recommendations. Conversely, the Council has set the Water Budget for Priest Rapids Dam in the mid-Columbia above that derived from the fish and wildlife agency recommendations because the Council believes greater flows can be provided without significant adverse effects on the hydroelectric system. This larger Water Budget for Priest Rapids Dam increases the total size of the Water Budget from 67.8 kcfs-months to 78 kcfs-months and, together with shaping, improves the ability to meet optimum flows below the confluence of the Snake and the Columbia as requested by the tribes.

Through the use of the Water Budget, the fish and wildlife agencies and tribes will be able to increase spring flows for the downstream migration of juveniles. The Council has established a schedule of firm power flows for the period April 15 through June 15 to provide a base from which to measure Water Budget usage. The Water Budget may be used by the fish and wildlife agencies and tribes to implement any flow schedule which would assure juvenile salmon survival, provided the flows allow existing firm non-power commitments to be met. The Water Budget would not be used to achieve flows which are greater than the optimum flows (140 kcfs for both Priest Rapids and Lower Granite dams) recommended by the tribes. Water used for the Water Budget will create a reduction in firm energy load carrying capability throughout the year, with the concomitant benefit of improving juvenile migrant survival. . . .

304. Measures
(a) Establishment and Use of the Water Budget
(1) The federal project operators and regulators shall provide the fish and wildlife agencies and tribes with a total Water Budget of 78 kcfs-months (4.64 Maf). It is to be divided into 58 kcfs-months (3.45 Maf) at Priest Rapids Dam and 20 kcfs-months (1.19 Maf) at Lower Granite Dam. The fish and wildlife agencies and tribes will specify the use of the Water Budget during the period April 15 through June 15. The Water Budget may be used by the fish and wildlife agencies and tribes to implement any flow schedule which provides maximum juvenile salmon survival, within the limits of firm non-power requirements, physical conditions, and flows required for firm loads.

(2) To provide a base from which to measure Water Budget usage, the Council has established the "firm power flows" listed in Table 1. Water Budget managers will request flows for Priest Rapids and Lower Granite dams and dates on which these flows are desired. The flow requests must be greater than the firm power flows and less than 140 kcfs. Water Budget usage will be measured as the difference between the actual average weekly flows, which result from the Water Budget managers' requests, and the firm power flows.

Table 1. Firm Power Flows
(average weekly kcfs)

	Priest Rapids	Lower Granite
April 15 through April 30	76	50
May 1 through May 31	76	65
June 1 through June 15	76	60

(3) The federal project operators and regulators shall incorporate the Water Budget requirement in all system planning and operations performed under the Columbia River Treaty, the Pacific Northwest Coordination Agreement, all related rule curves, and in other applicable procedures affecting river operations and planning. All parties will act in good faith in implementing the Water Budget as a "firm" requirement. The Council expects that in order to reduce power system effects, thermal plant maintenance will be moved into the April 15 to June 15 period. The fish and wildlife agencies and tribes must give the Corps of Engineers three days' written notice of changes in the planned flow schedule under the Water Budget.

(4) The Water Budget is expected to result in an average annual loss of 550 megawatts of firm energy load carrying capability, which will be taken into account in the Council's energy plan as provided in the Act. The actual amount of power loss is dependent on actions taken by power managers to accommodate the Water Budget. Such actions may include extra-regional firm power exchanges and shifting of thermal plant maintenance schedules. . . .

(e) Dispute Settlement
(1) In the event that the fish and wildlife agencies and tribes are unable to agree on a flow schedule for the Water Budget, their Water Budget managers immediately will notify the Council, which

will assist them in promptly resolving the dispute. In the event that the dispute cannot be resolved, the Council may establish and transmit to the Corps of Engineers its own flow schedule for the Water Budget.

> Northwest Power Planning Council, Columbia River Basin Fish and Wildlife Program §§ 303-304, at 17-19, 22 (1984).

Commentary

IN THE LATE 1960s, with nearly all major dam sites developed or under development, regional utilities forecast severe electric shortages for the Northwest. In response, the Bonneville Power Administration (BPA) and the utilities formulated a program aimed at increasing the region's electric capacity by adding thermal (coal and nuclear) plants to hydroelectric generation. This "hydro-thermal" plan, which once envisioned twenty-six thermal plants, produced only about one-fourth of that number before it was enjoined, in 1975, by the courts for violating the National Environmental Policy Act. While BPA was preparing an environmental impact statement on the program (which took some five years), Congress began to consider legislation that would give BPA the authority to meet forecasted electricity shortages.

The legislation that emerged from Congress in 1980 did not, however, simply give congressional sanction to BPA's hydro-thermal program. Instead, the Northwest Power Act emphasized conservation programs over thermal plans and created a new interstate agency to forecast future electric needs and to devise an environmentally sensitive plan to meet forecasted demand.

Most significantly, Congress gave considerable attention to rectifying the hydroelectric system's adverse effects on Columbia Basin salmon. The legislative history, acknowledging "past mistakes," made clear that the aim of the statute was to elevate the status of fish and wildlife to that of a "coequal partner" with hydropower in the operation of the system "on a par" with other purposes for which the dams may have been authorized. The congressional architects recognized that this coequal partnership would require some power losses, but they were confident that "effective and imaginative measures" could avoid "unreasonable" power losses because power interests testified that they were "anxious to accommodate fish and wildlife needs."

The Northwest Power Act directed a new interstate agency, the Northwest Power Planning Council (NPPC), to develop a systemwide program to "protect, mitigate, and enhance" Columbia Basin fish and wildlife, especially its salmon. This program was to be developed with widespread public participation and be based on public recommendations, especially those from the region's federal and state fish and wildlife agencies and tribes. Congress also established a number of criteria the program was to satisfy, including (1) complementing existing and future activities of regional fish and wildlife agencies and tribes, (2) demanding the "best available scientific knowledge," (3) favoring biological outcomes over economic , (4) protecting Indian treaty rights, and (5) providing improved salmon survival at dams and salmon flows of sufficient quantity and quality to meet sound biological objectives.

Congress directed the NPPC to give deference to the expertise of the region's fish and wildlife agencies and tribes. The legislative history expressly warned the council against setting itself up as a "super fish and wildlife agency" (126 Cong. Rec. H10,683 [daily ed. Nov. 17, 1980] [remarks of Cong. Dingell]). Once developed, the program was to govern the actions of federal water management agencies: BPA must act "consistent" with the program, and other agencies such as the Corps of Engineers, the Bureau of Reclamation, and the Federal Energy Regulatory Commission must "take [the program] into account at each relevant stage of [their] decisionmaking processes to the fullest extent practicable."

Some five months after the Northwest Power Act was signed into law, a coalition of the region's fish and wildlife agencies and tribes submitted over seven hundred pages of recommendations to the council, including increased river flows, improvements in fish bypass at dams, habitat protection and restoration measures, and hatchery facilities. In November 1982 the council used those recommendations as the basis of its Columbia Basin Fish and Wildlife Program.

The Northwest Power Act and its fish and wildlife program dramatically changed salmon law and policy. Formation of the NPPC created an open regional forum where trade-offs between hydropower and salmon, as well as other restoration issues, such as the feasibility of relying on hatcheries to supplement wild stock runs, were discussed. The program's provisions calling for genetic sensitivity, main-stem dam bypass systems, and areas protected from future hydroelectric development (promulgated as a program amendment) made important contributions to salmon restoration efforts. Its systemwide focus created a new institutional framework in which federal and state agencies with varying missions were encouraged to act cooperatively to help the program achieve its goals, which included a doubling of the Columbia's salmon.

However, despite their innovations, the act and the program promised more than they delivered. For one thing, the act's limited scope—it focused on the hydroelectric system while overlooking harvest regulation, federal land management, and state water law—made a comprehensive approach to salmon restoration impossible. For another, the act's enforcement provisions—premised on ambiguous directives such as directing the Corps of Engineers to "take the program into account . . . to the fullest extent practical"—made program implementation problematic. For example, the Corps routinely refused to implement the program's main-stem passage provisions.

But the real Achilles heel of the fish and wildlife program lay in "the water budget." The council had rejected the fixed flows suggested by the agencies and tribes and instead adopted a water budget that dedicated a volume of water to help facilitate downstream salmon migration during spring. However, the amount of water dedicated to salmon on the Snake River was not as large as the agencies and tribes recommended because the council wanted to ensure reservoir refill. The council also rejected establishing a budget on the lower Columbia, limiting the budget to the upper Columbia and the Snake.

Moreover, the central premises of the budget concept—that it would (1) give representatives of the region's fish and wildlife agencies and Indian tribes control over flows when the fish needed them most, and (2) be in addition to, not a substitute for, base power flows—were flawed. The Corps consistently refused to supply flows when the agencies and tribes asked for them; base power flows turned out not to be reliable; and the council showed itself to be a poor program implementer. The result was that the water budget was regularly unmet; for example, in 1985, budget requests were satisfied only six of twenty-six days during the critical spring migration season.

For these reasons, the Northwest Power Act's promise of making salmon migration a "coequal partner" with hydropower generation went unfulfilled. Salmon became a topic of discussion among hydroelectric managers but hardly was treated "on a par" with other project purposes. The promise of power interests that they were anxious to accommodate salmon migration requirements seemed to wane rapidly after enactment of the statute. Neither Congress nor the council expressed much interest in seeing to it that these promises were carried out. Although the program did chart an innovative, systematic approach to salmon restoration, by failing to produce substantial improvement in salmon migration, it failed to achieve its basic goal.

—Michael C. Blumm and F. Lorraine Bodi

HATCHERY OPERATIONS SHOW BIAS

Document:	**Releases of Juvenile Salmon**	
Authors:	The Columbia River Fisheries Development Program (1987) and the National Marine Fisheries Service (1991)	
Year:	1987, 1991	
Description:	The two tables reveal a government preference for releasing hatchery fish into the Columbia River below The Dalles Dam. The releases were from hatcheries funded by the Columbia River Fisheries Development Program, the major source of juvenile salmon.	

	Above The Dalles Dam	*Below The Dalles Dam*
Spring chinook	300,000	7,742,000
Summer chinook	0	0
Fall chinook	1,100,000	67,652,000
Tules	0	56,966,000
Brights	1,100,000	9,586,000
Rogue River	0	0
Coho	1,504,000	24,553,000
Sockeye	0	0
Steelhead	180,000	3,107,000
Cutthroat	0	185,000
Total	3,084,000	103,239,000

Michael Delarm and R. Z. Smith, *Columbia River Fisheries Development Program Annual Report for F.Y. 1987* (Portland, Oregon: Columbia River Fisheries Development Program, 1988), 78.

Mitchell Act Release Programs
1991

	Above The Dalles Dam	Below The Dalles Dam
Spring chinook	1,387,000	7,137,000
Summer chinook	0	0
Fall chinook	1,891,000	85,633,000
Tules	0	66,595,000
Brights	1,891,000	18,252,000
Rogue River	0	786,000
Coho	1,446,000	21,619,000
Sockeye	0	0
Steelhead	180,000	2,626,000
Cutthroat	0	145,000
Total	4,904,000	117,160,000

National Marine Fisheries Service, *Report to Congress on Mitchell Act Hatchery Fish Releases* (n.p.: n.p., 1992), 96.

Commentary

THE COLUMBIA RIVER is divided into fishery zones. Zones 1 through 5, from the mouth of the river to Bonneville Dam, are fished by non-Indian fishers, both commercial and sport. The area known as zone 6, between Bonneville and McNary dams, is fished commercially by the Columbia River treaty tribes. (The first five zones and zone 6 are of approximately equal river mileage.) This arrangement was the result of an informal agreement between the tribes and the states (represented by the Oregon Fish Commission and the Washington Department of Fisheries) in 1969 after the inundation of the John Day pool. By that time, Bonneville, The Dalles, and John Day dams had been constructed, and all nontribal, commercial fisheries in these pools had ended. Specifically, according to their "gentlemen's agreement," the tribes said they would fish upriver of the dams and remain in zone 6 and the nontribal fisheries agreed to operate downriver of the dams.

The Mitchell Act, more than any other program, established the modern character of Pacific Northwest fish runs. The program was funded by the Army Corps of Engineers with money appropriated through the development of the principal dams on the main stem of the Columbia and Snake rivers. Mitchell Act funding passed through the Bureau of Commercial Fisheries (now known as the National Marine Fisheries Service—NMFS) to the states. The states, in cooperation with federal fishery agencies, developed the programs for managing the fish runs. Hatcheries were funded as the key to salmon production.

With such attention focused on the Columbia River fisheries, the tribes believed that the salmon would be sustained in fishable quantities.

Recent hatchery statistics give some indication of how the fish management of the Columbia has been shaped by the Mitchell Act. In 1987, approximately 107 million salmon were released by the Columbia River Fisheries Development Program; 103 million of these fish were released below The Dalles Dam. Where fish are released, so will they return. Thus, most of the adult returns were to areas below The Dalles Dam. In fact, they were never intended to return to the upper basin.

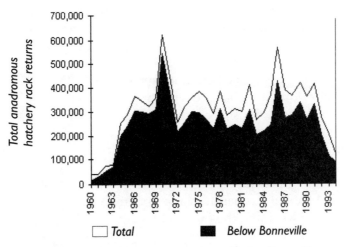

The returns of salmon to hatcheries are concentrated below Bonneville Dam. Source: State and federal fish agencies. The data from the 1960s and 1970s are incomplete for some hatcheries.

In 1987, no summer chinook or sockeye were released above the dams in spite of the fact that fisheries managers knew that certain upriver runs of these salmon were depleted. Chinook and sockeye have subsequently been listed as endangered in the Snake system. Instead, the major releases for the Mitchell Act were fall chinook and coho, the two fish that are the backbone of the ocean fishery. Without these releases, there simply would be no fall chinook or coho fisheries in the ocean or in zones 1 through 5.

By 1991, one might have expected some changes. For nearly ten years, the Northwest Power Planning Council, in its fish and wildlife program, had been arguing that fish should be released into the upper river. Four petitions had been made to list certain Snake River stocks under the Endangered Species Act. Unfortunately, no change in policy was occurring, as the 1992 *Report to Congress* indicates. Releases below The Dalles Dam in 1991 were 117 million salmon, an increase of roughly 14 million over those made in 1987. Releases above The Dalles Dam had increased to 4.9 million, only about 1.9 million more fish than in 1987. Once again, the major releases occurred below the dams. Once again, most of the releases were fall chinook and coho, the two programs that feed the ocean fishery.

On the lower Snake, a similar situation was occurring: some stocks of fish were enhanced at the expense of others. On the lower Snake, the state and federal fishery agencies had no programs for coho, sockeye, and fall chinook above Lower Granite Dam. The agenda in the Idaho program, apparently, was to feed the sports fisheries, in this case spring chinook and steelhead. Both on the Columbia and on the lower Snake, the agencies involved have catered to the most remunerative, high-visibility fisheries. The result in both cases has been a decline in the stocks that were not supplemented. In the lower Columbia, NMFS policies have, over fifty years, led to the decline of natural-spawning coho stocks. In Idaho, under NMFS policy, the decline of nonenhanced stocks—sockeye, coho, and fall chinook—is occurring at an accelerated rate because the dams cause severe losses. These runs are quickly disappearing.

The tribes' philosophy is this: we must put these stocks back into the natural habitat in quantities appropriate to their relative historic abundance. If we don't, the runs will be lost.

—Douglas W. Dompier

STATES MAY NOT HORDE NATURAL RESOURCES

Document: ***Idaho v. Oregon and Washington***

Author: U.S. Supreme Court

Year: 1983

Description: Idaho filed suit seeking an equitable apportionment of salmon under a principle that had previously been applied exclusively to water rights. The Supreme Court ruling against Idaho is excerpted.

[T]HE NATURAL RESOURCE of anadromous fish is sufficiently similar [to water allocation] to make equitable apportionment an appropriate mechanism for resolving allocative disputes. The anadromous fish at issue travel through several States during their lifetime. Much as in a water dispute, a State that over-fishes a run downstream deprives an upstream State of the fish it otherwise would receive. A dispute over the water flowing through the Columbia-Snake River system would be resolved by the equitable apportionment doctrine; we see no reason to accord different treatment to a controversy over a similar natural resource of that system. . . .

At the root of the doctrine is the same principle that animates many of the Court's Commerce Clause cases: a State may not preserve solely for its own inhabitants natural resources located within its borders. Consistent with this principle, States have an affirmative duty under the doctrine of equitable apportionment to take reasonable steps to conserve and even to augment the natural resources within their borders for the benefit of other States.

> *Idaho ex rel. Evans v. Oregon and Washington*, 462 U.S. 1017, 1024-25 (1983). (Citations and notes omitted.)

Commentary

 In 1980, the Supreme Court reversed a special master's ruling that Idaho's case should be dismissed because the federal government refused to be a party to the suit and—because it operated the main-stem dams, regulated the ocean harvest, and was trustee to the Stevens treaty tribes—its participation was indispensable to judicial relief. But three years later, when the case again reached the Court, the justices ruled against Idaho. The Court determined that Idaho had failed to prove by "clear and convincing evidence some real and substantial injury or damage" caused by overharvesting of salmon by Oregon and Washington.

This case failed to produce an equitable apportionment of salmon harvests for Idaho, but the Supreme Court's opinion did establish some important new legal principles. First, the Court determined that an equitable apportionment could have been made for salmon, had Idaho satisfied its burden of proving substantial damage by lower river overharvesting. This was the first time the Court applied the equitable apportionment doctrine to a resource other than water. Second, the Court linked equitable apportionment to the Constitution's commerce clause when it stated that the same principle animates both; that is, a state "may not preserve solely for its own inhabitants natural resources within its own borders." Further, the Court ruled that states have "an affirmative duty to conserve and even augment natural resources within their borders for other states."

This affirmative conservation duty, subsequently recognized by the Ninth Circuit Court of Appeals (*U.S. v. Oregon*, 913 F.2d 576, 583, 585 [9th Cir. 1990]) may prove to be the most enduring legacy of Idaho's attempt to secure an equitable apportionment of Columbia Basin salmon. Ironically, the principle could be used against Idaho. If the upriver state continues to resist additional storage releases or water transfers that could improve downstream salmon flows, Idaho would seem to violate its interstate conservation duty.

—Michael C. Blumm and F. Lorraine Bodi

COURT DEFINED "EQUITABLE TREATMENT" OF SALMON

Document:	***Yakima Indian Nation v. Federal Energy Regulatory Commission***
Author:	Ninth Circuit Court of Appeals
Year:	1984
Description:	This legal decision interpreted the meaning of a key phrase of the 1980 Northwest Power Act which promised "equitable treatment" to fish and wildlife.

THE [NORTHWEST POWER ACT] is specifically directed to the Columbia River system and, unlike the [Fish and Wildlife Coordination Act], it imposes substantive as well as procedural obligations. . . . One purpose of the [Northwest Power Act] is to place fish and wildlife concerns on an equal footing with power production. In this respect, the [Act] supplements the Federal Power Act. We have no doubt that if [the Federal Energy Regulatory Commission] failed its Federal Power Act obligation to consider fishery issues prior to licensing, it concomitantly failed to meet its obligation to give fish . . . "equitable treatment" under the [Northwest Power Act].

> *Confederated Tribes and Bands of the Yakima Indian Nation v. Federal Energy Regulatory Comm'n,* 746 F.2d 466, 473-74 (9th Cir. 1984).

Commentary

 THE FISH AND WILDLIFE provisions of the Northwest Power Act were not limited to the Columbia Basin Fish and Wildlife Program. One key provision, section 4(h)(11)(A)(i) of the act, directed the Bonneville Power Administration, the Corps of Engineers, the Bureau of Reclamation, and the Federal Energy Regulatory Commission (FERC) to give "equitable treatment" to fish and wildlife in carrying out all their other statutory responsibilities. Although the Northwest Power Act did not define the term, "equitable treatment" clearly meant more than the preexisting "equal consideration" required of the federal agencies by the 1958 Fish and Wildlife Coordination Act. How the equitable treatment mandate would be implemented was unclear until the Ninth Circuit Court of Appeals decided that FERC had violated the standard when it attempted to relicense the Rock Island Dam on the mid-Columbia River over the objections of several fish and wildlife agencies, Indian tribes, and environmental groups.

This case made clear that the equitable treatment standard is one that courts will enforce against federal agencies. FERC failed to demonstrate in its relicensing decision how the decision produced equitable treatment for fish and wildlife, and the court held that this failure violated the Northwest Power Act. The decision did not really help to define what equitable treatment requires of the federal agencies, but it did indicate that (1) federal agencies must develop administrative records explaining how and why their decisions will produce equitable treatment, (2) courts will review these decisions to ensure that the reasoning is not self-serving or unreasonable, and (3) "equitable treatment" means more than mere consideration of fish and wildlife—it requires substantive action.

—Michael C. Blumm and F. Lorraine Bodi

A Shared Resource:
The Tragedy of the Commons

Document:	**Pacific Salmon Treaty**
Author:	Governments of Canada and the United States
Year:	1985
Description:	The Pacific Salmon Treaty, an attempt by the U.S. and Canada to end decades of tension over communal fishing grounds, failed to halt interception fishing or to curtail activities that degrade habitat.

THE GOVERNMENT of the United States of America and the Government of Canada,

Considering the interests of both Parties in the conservation and rational management of Pacific salmon stocks and in the promotion of optimum production of such stocks;

Recognizing that States in whose waters salmon stocks originate have the primary interest in and responsibility for such stocks;

Recognizing that salmon originating in the waters of each Party are intercepted in substantial numbers by the nationals and vessels of the other Party, and that the management of stocks subject to interception is a matter of common concern;

Desiring to cooperate in the management, research and enhancement of Pacific salmon stocks;

Have agreed as follows: . . .

Article III
Principles
1. With respect to stocks subject to this Treaty, each Party shall conduct its fisheries and its salmon enhancement programs so as to:

(a) prevent overfishing and provide for optimum production; and

(b) provide for each Party to receive benefits equivalent to the production of salmon originating in its waters.

2. In fulfilling their obligations pursuant to paragraph 1, the Parties shall cooperate in management, research and enhancement.

3. In fulfilling their obligations pursuant to paragraph 1, the Parties shall take into account:

(a) the desirability in most cases of reducing interceptions;

(b) the desirability in most cases of avoiding undue disruption of existing fisheries; and

(c) annual variations in abundance of the stocks.

> Treaty Between the United States and Canada Concerning
> Pacific Salmon, TIAS 11091 (1985).

Commentary

 OVERHARVESTING of adult salmon has been a problem since the inception of non-Indian fisheries in the late nineteenth century. The onset of state fishery regulation in the twentieth century helped to curb overharvesting in rivers and the near offshore, but the migratory range of salmon extends well beyond the limits of state and even national jurisdiction. Thus, salmon harvesting presents a classic example of the "tragedy of the commons"—a situation in which there are strong economic incentives to seek individual gain by overuse of a common resource. In this case, the incentive is to intercept salmon spawned in another jurisdiction. This problem of "interception fisheries" has long been a source of contention among the Northwest states, Alaska, and Canada, particularly over Fraser River stocks, which migrate south across the international border into Puget Sound, and Columbia River stocks, which migrate north to Canadian and Alaskan waters. Management is further complicated by the intermingling of stocks from various river systems while in the ocean.

In 1930, the U.S. and Canada culminated fifteen years of negotiations by agreeing to the Fraser River Convention. The convention established the International Pacific Salmon Fisheries Commission and charged it with (1) restoring Fraser River sockeye salmon (which had been severely damaged by rock slides caused by railroad right-of-way blasting in 1913 and 1914) through hatcheries and habitat improvements, and (2) apportioning harvests equally between U.S. and Canadian fishers (in return for U.S. financial and technical assistance in the restoration efforts). Although the 1930 convention was extended to cover pink salmon in 1957, the agreement was not broad enough to deal effectively with the interception problem because it was limited to the Fraser River and to just two species of salmon.

As both nations extended their fishery jurisdiction in the 1960s and 1970s, in an effort to regulate offshore foreign fishing—from 3 to 12 to 200 miles—interest remained high in limiting and regulating cross-border harvests. But despite the fact that both countries supported the 1977 United Nations Law of the Sea Treaty's "state-of-origin" principle for anadromous fish (limiting harvests to countries where the fish spawned), salmon interceptions remained commonplace.

By the early 1980s, several developments on both sides of the border produced increased pressure for a salmon treaty. First, the 1974 Boldt decision (which allocated to Indian tribes 50 percent of the western Washington salmon harvest) encouraged the state to embark on a considerable expansion in hatchery production. Hatchery production was also increased dramatically on the Columbia in an effort to compensate for dam-caused mortalities. In addition, Canada was committed to an aggressive hatchery and habitat-improvement program that promised to double Fraser River sockeye runs. Neither country wanted the fruits of these investments harvested by the other's fishers. Moreover, in the early 1980s biologists noticed a startling decline in both U.S. and Canadian chinook and coho stocks, further illustrating the need for a joint management plan.

After more than a decade of negotiations, a draft interception treaty was signed in 1982. But objections by Puget Sound trollers and the state of Alaska, who feared that the treaty would require harvest reductions, blocked ratification. When Canada threatened to institute a "fish war" and Indian tribes filed suit to extend their 50 percent share to Alaskan waters, negotiations resumed and ultimately produced a revised treaty that called for harvest reductions in southeast Alaska, although not as severe as would have occurred if Alaska were subjected to the 50 percent formula. Congress ratified in 1985 by enacting enabling legislation, the Pacific Salmon Treaty Act of 1985 (16 U.S.C. §§ 3631-44).

The Pacific Salmon Treaty's two basic principles, set forth in Article III, are to (1) conserve the resource by preventing overfishing and providing optimum production, and (2) equitably apportion harvest rights by ensuring that each country obtains benefits equivalent to its salmon production. The second principle is a reformulation of the "state of origin" principle, which would restrict harvest rights to the producing country. To avoid the economic dislocation that would accompany a complete ban on interceptions, this "equity" principle promises to compensate each country for the benefits of its production efforts. To accomplish this goal, the treaty commits the two countries to generate and share data on run sizes, escapements, allowable catch, stock interrelationships, and management objectives.

Although the treaty obligates both countries to consider the desirability of reducing interceptions, the provision counseling against "undue disruption" of existing fisheries has circumscribed the ability of the Pacific Salmon Commission (created by the treaty to enforce its provisions) to curtail interceptions. Most of the commission's deliberations during its initial decade have concerned short-term harvest allocations, not long-term reduction of interception fisheries or rebuilding of depleted fish runs. Major intercepting fisheries have continued under the treaty, including those in southeast Alaska and off Vancouver Island, the latter apparently a Canadian retaliation for the former, resulting in significant interceptions of Columbia River stocks. Canada was so dissatisfied with the continuation of interception fisheries in southeast Alaska that, for a time in 1994, it charged high fees to fishing boats that used its waters to travel to or from Alaska.

Although the treaty commits the parties to a coastwide rebuilding program for chinook salmon, that provision has not been interpreted by either country to restrain habitat-degrading activities like logging practices, irrigation, and polluting activities. This lack of habitat protection, along with the commission's inability to significantly curtail interception fisheries, has led some to call for a renegotiation of the treaty.

—Michael C. Blumm and F. Lorraine Bodi

NEW REGIONAL PROGRAM
FAILED TO RESTORE RUNS

Document:	**The Failed Promise of the Fish and Wildlife Program**
Author:	Natural Resources Law Institute
Year:	1986
Description:	The *Anadromous Fish Law Memo*, a periodical covering efforts to restore salmon runs, analyzes the shortcomings of the Northwest Power Planning Council's program for salmon.

IT IS NOW EVIDENT that the Columbia Basin Fish and Wildlife Program, promulgated by the Northwest Power Planning Council to satisfy the mandate of the Northwest Power Act, is failing to make significant progress restoring upriver salmon and steelhead runs. That was the nearly universal sentiment expressed by fishery managers at a public workshop on Columbia Basin Program implementation held on September 27, 1986 in Portland. Repeatedly throughout the day-long workshop, fishery agency and tribal representatives catalogued instances in which federal project operators and regulators failed to implement program measures "to the fullest extent practicable." Worse, the Council has exhibited an increasingly lukewarm attitude toward such implementation failures. Moreover, the Council has tentatively rejected a number of program amendments recommended by the fishery agencies and tribes to make the program more effective and more enforceable.

Thus, 6 years after Congress made it national policy to preserve and restore the Columbia Basin's anadromous fish runs, 5 years after the fishery agencies and tribes made detailed program recommendations, 4 years after program promulgation by the Council, the program has yet to deliver on many of its promises.

> "The Failed Promise of the Columbia Basin Fish and Wildlife Program and What to Do About It," *Anadromous Fish Law Memo*, no. 38 (November 1986): 1.

Commentary

 In 1986 the Columbia Basin Fish and Wildlife Program was in its fourth year of implementation. By the mid-1980s, it was clear to some that the program was substantively inadequate to restore upper basin Columbia salmon runs and, worse, that the Northwest Power Planning Council was not interested in enforcing even the arguably inadequate provisions of the program. This lack of commitment was perhaps best evidenced by a 1986 decision of the council not to increase spill levels to facilitate salmon passage at main-stem dams without adequate juvenile bypass systems, as recommended by the region's fish and wildlife agencies and Indian tribes. (Spills, necessary to help juvenile salmon bypass dams, are distinct from flows, which transport salmon from upriver spawning grounds to the ocean.)

The council's decision was subsequently reversed as a result of the 1989 settlement agreement reached by the fishery agencies and Indian tribes and the region's power interests; this agreement increased spills in return for the agencies and tribes agreement not to challenge the environmental documentation of Bonneville Power Administration's proposal to expand intertie capacity. Although spill levels were increased, it was not the council's program but a lawsuit that prompted the change. By the late 1980s, the council seemed to have run out of imaginative and effective ideas for restoring Columbia Basin salmon and instead was relegated to ratifying agreements reached by others.

Michael C. Blumm and F. Lorraine Bodi

COURT SAYS COUNCIL VIOLATED LAW

Document: **Northwest Resource Information Center v. Northwest Power Planning Council**

Author: Judge Thomas Tang, for a three-judge panel of the Ninth Circuit Court of Appeals

Year: 1994

Description: The appeals court ruled that the Northwest Power Planning Council's 1991 "Strategy for Salmon" violated the Northwest Power Act by not deferring to the recommendations of the region's fishery agencies and Indian tribes.

SALMON AND HYDROPOWER are the two great natural resources of the Columbia River Basin. At odds for most of this century, congressional action in 1980 injected a needed resolve into the conflict, inciting a sense of optimism. Since that time, optimism has largely given way to the dynamics of a classic struggle between environmental and energy interests. The climax of this particular struggle may well be our review of the parties' efforts constituting what has been touted as the world's largest program of biological restoration. . . .

The flows of the Columbia River Basin are the linchpin of the Pacific Northwest's economy. More than one hundred and fifty dams are integrated to form the world's largest hydropower system, generating over forty percent of the nation's hydropower. The generation of kilowatts, however, is not the only reason for the Basin's importance; the Basin is the habitat for what were once the world's largest salmon runs.

Unfortunately, "[l]ike most of the American West, the Columbia River Basin has been developed, not managed as an ecosystem." Adverse impacts have resulted from deforestation, over-fishing, irrigation practices, mining, grazing, urbanization, and hydropower operations and development. Although precise estimates of the impacts of these activities are currently unknown, it is generally accepted that the Basin's hydropower system is "a major factor in the decline of some salmon and steelhead runs to a point of near extinction." . . .

As a result of human activities, anadromous fish runs in the Columbia River Basin have dwindled from an estimated ten to sixteen million fish annually, before European settlement in the Northwest, to about two-and-one-half million today. Of this annual loss, eighty percent is attributable to hydropower development and operation. . . .

. . . Recognizing the tremendous, detrimental impact of dams on the fish runs, Congress acknowledged "that no longer [should] fish and wildlife be given a secondary status." In 1980, Congress enacted the Northwest Power Act ("NPA" or "Act").

The NPA marked an important shift in federal policy. Continually declining fish runs had revealed the failures of previous legislative efforts requiring that "equal consideration" be given to fish and wildlife affected by resource exploitation. The NPA ensured the "equitable treatment" of fish and wildlife; it marked the shift of the burden of uncertainty—of proving specific harm to salmon from particular activities—from the salmon to the hydropower system, or so was its intent. In doing so, it created a new obligation on the region and various Federal agencies to protect, mitigate, and enhance fish and wildlife.

The Act created a "pluralistic intergovernmental and public review process." At the hub of this process, Congress established the Pacific Northwest Electric Power and Conservation Planning Council ("Council"), directing it to create "a program to protect, mitigate, and enhance" the Columbia River Basin's fish and wildlife "to the extent affected by the development and operation" of the Basin's hydropower system. In making fish and wildlife a "co-equal partner" with the hydropower industry, the NPA adopted several innovations, marking the Act for its legislative craftsmanship.

First, the Act expressly required "textual consistency"; that is, that its provisions, together with other applicable laws, specifically including environmental laws, be construed in a consistent manner. Second, the Act called for a systemwide remedial program to cover the entire Basin, rather than the more traditional approach of focusing on individual projects. Third, the Act shifted focus in wildlife mitigation from merely creating substitute resources, such as salmon hatcheries, to emphasizing changes in hydro project operations. Fourth, "Congress lowered the burden of proof for undertaking action by requiring that the remedial program (1) be based only on 'best available scientific knowledge,' not scientific certainty; (2) favor biological outcomes over economic ones, and (3) defer to the recommendations of agencies and Indian tribes with fish and wildlife expertise." Fifth, the Act tapped revenues of the Basin's hydropower system as a source for financing the biological restoration. Finally, the NPA called for energy conservation to be developed as a resource ahead of traditional resources.

Attempting to balance environmental and energy considerations, the Act states that fish and wildlife protection measures cannot jeopardize "an adequate, efficient, economical, and reliable power supply." Also, the Council's authority with respect to fish and wildlife measures is constrained; the Council "can guide, but not command, federal river management." On the other hand, the Act requires federal water managers to act in a manner consistent with the Council's fish and wildlife program. . . .

The Council promulgated the Columbia Basin Fish and Wildlife Program in November 1982. The Council rejected the recommended goal of run sizes equal to those predating 1953. Rather, the program directed BPA to study fish losses from hydropower development and operations, as well as current and potential carrying capacity. To judge the efficacy of the program, the Council directed the development of area-by-area and stock-by-stock goals by 1984. By mid-1986 these goals remained undefined.

The centerpiece of the 1982 program, however, was the Council's response to recommended mainstem flows. Rather than adopt a "sliding scale" of flows, "the Council avoided fixed flow levels and proposed a volumetric approach.". . .

Despite the Council's progress in ensuring the installation of bypass systems and sufficient spills, salmon and steelhead populations generally declined through 1987. This trend continued the next three years. As a consequence, the National Marine Fisheries Service ("NMFS") was petitioned in 1990 by special interests to list three Snake River stocks and one Columbia River stock under the ESA. Over the next two years, NMFS listed the three Snake River stocks and determined that the Columbia River stock was extinct.

The ESA proceedings spurred the region's political leaders to convene a "Salmon Summit" in 1990 of various agencies and interested groups to develop a regional plan to end the salmon decline. While the Summit produced several interim measures, the participants returned to the Council for direction.

In 1991, the Council adopted a four-phase decision-making process to amend the fish and wildlife program. The first three phases of this process culminated in the Council's adoption of the Strategy for Salmon on December 1992.

The Council received numerous proposals to its request for amendments to the fish and wildlife program. Fish and wildlife agencies and Indian tribes (collectively "agencies and tribes" or "fishery managers") emphasized two points: (1) that substantial increases in Columbia River and Snake River spring and summer flows were necessary, and (2) biological objectives, such as water particle travel time, were necessary to measure the efficacy of restoration efforts. These two ideas formed the basis of a comprehensive regimen intended to replace the Water Budget.

While fishery managers recommended significant changes— substantial increases in mainstem flows and the adoption of specific biological objectives—power interests and DSIs defended the status quo—conservation steps calculated to produce positive, albeit minor, improvements. In particular, these latter interests vigorously challenged the biological benefits of flows above 85 kcfs in the lower Snake River and 200 kcfs in the lower Columbia River.

During the second phase of the process, which focused on salmon survival and harvest, the Council rejected the consensus of agencies and tribes that flows should be significantly increased, and adopted flows very close to those recommended by power interests and DSIs. As for biological objectives, the Council deferred consideration until the third phase, which would deal with salmon habitat and production. . . .

. . . NRIC and the Yakima Nation mount a procedural challenge to the Program under [§ 4(h)(7) of the Act], alleging that the Council failed to explain, in the Program, a statutory basis for its rejection of river flow recommendations of fishery managers. . . .

The DSIs join NRIC and the Yakima Nation in arguing that the Council failed to explain its rationale for adopting the program measures of the Strategy for Salmon. The DSIs assert their challenge from a different perspective, however, arguing that the Council improperly tilted the balance between salmon and energy in favor of the salmon by failing to engage in a critical cost-benefit analysis of each program measure. . . .

Study of the Strategy for Salmon evokes an undeniable sense of the tremendous effort and commitment invested to create such a program. The Council has the unenviable task of sorting through the multitude of diverse recommendations and compiling measures that form the framework of an aggressive, effective, and balanced fish and wildlife program. To ensure a balance of interests in the program, the Act specifically requires the Council to explain, in the program, its reasons for rejecting recommendations. This requirement is critical to our review of Council decisions, but, more importantly, it forces the Council to hold out its *final* decisions and their rationale for public consideration and scrutiny. The Council neglected this mandate of the Act.

The Strategy for Salmon fails to explain the reasons for the Council's decisions rejecting recommendations of the agencies and tribes. . . .

In sum, [§ 4(h)(7)] requires the Council to explain, in the Program, a statutory basis for its rejection of recommendations. The Council failed to do so here with respect to the recommendations of agencies and tribes and was, therefore, not in accordance with the NPA. As a consequence, we remand this matter to the Council with instructions that it comply with the written statutory explanation requirement of [§ 4(h)(7)].

We note that the Council's failure to comply with [§ 4(h)(7)'s] mandate limits our ability to review the Council's actions in these appeals. . . . Therefore, we carefully consider the statutory interpretation issues with the expectation that our effort will aid the parties' efforts on remand. . . .

There is no question that [§ 4(h)(7)] requires that deference be given to the recommendations and expertise of agencies and tribes—the question is how much deference is due. . . .

The power plan provisions of the Act are cast in broad terms. . . .

These provisions grant the Council considerable flexibility in preparing a power plan; indeed, the Council's function under these provisions is essentially legislative.

In stark contrast are the fish and wildlife provisions of [§ 4(h)(7)]. To initiate the development of a fish and wildlife program, Congress required the Council to solicit recommendations from the region's fishery managers. . . . In short, the NPA requires the Council to develop the program from sources outside the Council. In doing so, the Council must adopt program measures that are consistent with the purposes of the Act—the protection, mitigation, and enhancement of fish and wildlife, "while assuring the region an adequate, efficient, economical, and reliable power supply." If reconciliation of recommendations is required, the Council must give "due weight" to fishery managers' recommendations, and may disregard such recommendations only after explaining in the program a statutory basis for its decision.

The difference between the power plan and the fish and wildlife provisions of [§ 4(h)(7)], then, is a contrast of generous discretion and bound discretion; the difference highlights the limited discretion of the Council under [§ 4(h)(7)]. . . .

We conclude that [§ 4(h)(7)] binds, more than unleashes, the Council's discretion with respect to fish and wildlife issues. Indeed, we are convinced that the fish and wildlife provisions of the NPA and their legislative history require that a high degree of deference be given to fishery managers' interpretations of such provision and their recommendations for program measures. . . .

. . . One of the primary purposes of the chapter is that "[t]he Council shall include in the [fish and wildlife] program measures which it determines" will meet the criteria set forth in [§ 4(h)(6)]. Inconsistencies between recommendations shall be resolved by the Council, "giving *due weight* to the recommendations, expertise, and legal rights and responsibilities" of agencies and tribes.

Congress's intent is manifest in the NPA's legislative history. Representative Dingell, one of the NPA's principal sponsors, emphasized, "[c]learly, the [C]ouncil should rely heavily on the fish and wildlife agencies of the State and Federal Governments and not try to become a superfish and wildlife entity." The House Committee on Interstate and Foreign Commerce stated:

> It has been suggested that the terms "protect, mitigate, and enhance" should be defined. The Committee did not choose to do so *in recognition of the fact that these terms are not new to those concerned with this resource,* and because such a definition might later prove more limiting than anticipated.

Hence, Congress realized that furtherance of the purpose of the Act, that fish and wildlife be on a par with energy, required that the Council defer to the recommendations of agencies and tribes. Of course, the reason for this deference to fishery managers is their unique experience and expertise in fish and wildlife. Congress intended that the Council not simply tap this resource of information and advice, but that it "heavily rely" upon it.

In promulgating [§ 4(h)], Congress anticipated the onus fish and wildlife issues would place on the Council in creating a hydropower plan that balanced fish and wildlife with energy. Congress recognized, in particular, that fish and wildlife issues were, and should be, outside the expertise of the Council and the hydropower regulating agencies. Nonetheless, the need for experience and expertise with respect to fish and wildlife was plain. Looking to those having responsibility for managing such resources, Congress found the experience and expertise on which the Council should rely to frame a fish and wildlife program. Accordingly, Congress required in [§ 4(h)] that fishery managers be given a high degree of deference in the development of a fish and wildlife program for the Basin.

In light of the NPA's legislative history and text, it follows that fishery managers, as well as the Council, be given deference in interpreting the fish and wildlife provisions of the Act. This conclusion is consistent with our holding in Public Util. Dist. 1. . . . that the BPA is due deference in interpreting the power plan provisions of the NPA because it was involved in the drafting of the Act. The role that fishery managers had in the promulgation of the NPA's fish and wildlife provisions demands no less of us here. Furthermore, the unique experience and expertise of fishery managers makes their interpretations of [§ 4(h)], especially [§ 4(h)(6)], particularly helpful. We find it inherently reasonable to give agencies and tribes, those charged with the responsibility for managing our fish and wildlife, a high degree-of deference in the creation of a program and the interpretation of the Act's fish and wildlife provisions. . . .

. . . [T]he Act's fish and wildlife provisions significantly temper the Council's discretion. At any rate, we do not decide here whether the Council abused its discretion in giving or failing to give proper deference to fishery managers because the record as it stands precludes such an inquiry. We note again that the Council failed to explain, in the Program, its reasons for rejecting the recommendations of fishery managers. This failure of the Council is disturbing given that it adopted, for the most part, the flows and measures recommended by power interests and DSIs, despite the overwhelming consensus among agencies and tribes in favor of significantly higher flows and more scientifically-based biological objectives.

We next turn to the nature of the [§ 4(h)(6)] criteria. . . .

The criteria in [§ 4(h)(6)] are mandatory. . . . As recognized above, the fish and wildlife provisions of the Act significantly circumscribe the Council's discretion with respect to fish and wildlife. . . .

We now focus on each of the criterion [sic] in this provision.

The first criterion requires that measures "complement the existing and future activities of the Federal and the region's State fish and wildlife agencies and appropriate Indian tribes." Since adoption of the Program, there have been various proceedings under the ESA concerning listed anadromous fish in the Basin. Several ESA actions have been filed, the lead case by the State of Idaho against NMFS and other agencies in 1992. That case challenges government actions in operating the Federal Columbia River Power System ("FCRPS") in 1993. . . .

Idaho Dept. of Fish and Game is relevant to the instant case not just because it involves, ultimately, the same issue—what to do about preserving and restoring the salmon—but because it urges policy and operations in a direction away from the status quo towards affirmative action. NRIC and the Yakima Nation press for the same direction from the Council, the instant case being their vehicle for doing so. While we do not now decide whether the Council's measures complement existing and future activities of fish and wildlife agencies and Indian tribes in the ESA actions, the Council's rejection of the agencies' and tribes' consensus as to increased flows and biological objectives does not appear to square well with these efforts.

The second criterion requires that measures be based on and supported by the "best available scientific knowledge." That the standard requires only the best available scientific knowledge ensures action in the promulgation and implementation of a fish and wildlife program. Textual consistency with [§ 4(h)(7)] requires that the Council defer to the agencies' and tribes' recommendations as to what is the best available scientific knowledge. Moreover, the standard requires only the best available scientific knowledge, not data. Section 4(h)(6)(B) suggests, therefore, that reasonable inferences and predictions may be drawn from the best available scientific knowledge. In this case, determining whether the program measures are based on and supported by the best available scientific evidence is prevented by the Council's failure to comply with § 4(h)(7)'s written statutory explanation requirement. . . .

Conclusion

The NPA adopted fish and wildlife restoration as a primary goal, leaving to the Council and interested parties the onerous burden of deciding how to restore such resourees. In doing so, the Act placed a premium on prompt action, allowing decisions to be made on the best available scientific knowledge. It also limited the role of economic considerations in decision-making. Most importantly, however, the Act acknowledged fish and wildlife as an irreplaceable finite resource.

Unfortunately, the record reveals few profound successes resulting from these innovations in thinking. The Council's approach seems largely to have been from the premise that only small steps are possible, in light of entrenched river user claims of economic hardship. Rather than asserting its role as a regional leader, the Council has assumed the role of a consensus builder, sometimes sacrificing the Act's fish and wildlife goals for what is, in essence, the lowest common denominator acceptable to power interests and DSIs. The Council has failed at least two requirements of the NPA in

The question of implementation by federal water managers arises from the statute's directives that BPA "act in a manner consistent with the program," and that BPA and federal agencies like the Corps of Engineers, the Bureau of Reclamation, and the Federal Energy Regulatory Commission take the council's program into account "to the maximum extent practicable" at each relevant stage of their decision-making processes (16 U.S.C. §§ 839b[10][A] and [II][A][ii]). Although these directives clearly forbid the federal agencies from simply choosing to ignore the program, whether they must actually implement the program is uncertain—the Ninth Circuit has ruled that "BPA must act consistently with the program but in the end has the final authority to determine its own decisions" (*Public Utility Dist. No. 1 v. BPA*, 947 F.2d 386, 392 [9th Cir. 1991]). The council has interpreted the statute to require federal agency implementation of its program unless the federal agencies supply a written explanation of why it is "physically, legally, or otherwise not practicable" to do so. Yet dam operators have essentially ignored the council's directive, contained in its "strategy for salmon," to implement reservoir drawdowns by 1995.

Thus, ultimately, even if the program is revised to eliminate the "lowest common denominator" approach of which the court complained, it is far from clear whether the federal agencies—which for a half century operated the Columbia Basin hydroelectric system with little regard for the needs of salmon—will implement a program calling for the kind of substantial changes the court thought necessary. The fate of the Columbia's salmon runs continues to rest uneasily on the shoulders of federal agencies that have long interpreted salmon restoration to conflict with their central missions. The Ninth Circuit's call for an end to incremental decision making must be tempered by that unsettling reality.

—Michael C. Blumm and F. Lorraine Bodi

THE ALARM THAT WAS HEARD:
THE CROSSROADS REPORT

Document:	**Pacific Salmon at the Crossroads**
Authors:	The Endangered Species Committee of the American Fisheries Society
Year:	1991
Description:	A paper by three biologists gives an eye-opening and influential description of the status of salmon stocks in the Northwest and California.

IN THE 1990S, native anadromous Pacific salmonids *(Oncorhynchus* spp.) are at a crossroads, the habitats of these once wide-ranging fishes are severely curtailed, many stocks are extinct, and many remaining stocks face a variety of threats. Since the 1850s, development activities such as hydropower, fishing, logging, mining, agriculture, and urban growth have caused extensive losses in salmon and steelhead populations and habitats. In most cases, enough of the native resource remains to allow a variety of remedial actions. If the salmon and their habitat continue to diminish, however, available options for present and future generations will diminish or disappear. The challenge for the 1990s is to take maximum advantage of technical, legal, and management avenues available to us now.

The task ahead is critically important. Salmon and steelhead are a cornerstone of West Coast industry, recreation, and culture. Native stocks are needed and will be needed in the future to (1) maintain natural genetic diversity within and among fish stocks needed to respond to major ecological and climatic changes, (2) provide the basis for re-establishing natural stocks where opportunities occur, (3) optimize natural production in streams, (4) support natural ecosystem function, (5) re-establish genetic variability in existing hatchery stocks, and (6) provide the basis for new hatchery stocks. While much progress has been made in artificially producing these fish, artificial production in itself cannot sustain them, and may contribute to the decline of native populations (Goodman 1990).

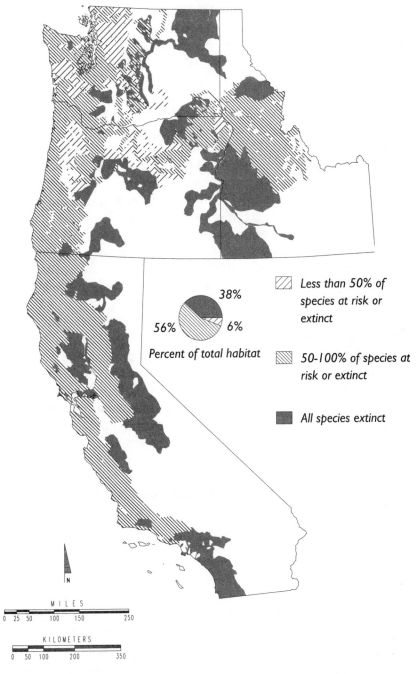

The condition of Pacific salmon stocks about 1993 was not very good. In only 6 percent of their regional habitat were most salmon in comparatively good condition. Source: The Wilderness Society, with data partly from the Crossroads report.

We identify 214 native naturally-spawning Pacific salmon and steelhead stocks in California, Oregon, Washington, and Idaho that appear to be facing a high or moderate risk of extinction, or are of special concern. . . .

The Stock Concept

Anadromous salmonid species comprise populations that originate from specific watersheds as juveniles and generally return to their natal streams to spawn. This life cycle results in a large degree of reproductive isolation of interbreeding individuals or stocks (Ricker 1972). Because Pacific salmon species comprise stocks adapted to local environmental conditions, the loss of stocks is more likely to lead to changes in genetic composition and reduction in genetic diversity in Pacific salmon than in species not stock-structured (Thorpe et al. 1981). This suggests that stocks are the basic building blocks of the Pacific salmon species. It is at the stock level that conservation and rehabilitation of salmon, if it is to be successful, will take place (Rich 1939).

The term "stock" was adopted 51 years ago (McIntyre 1983) shortly after the first attempts to describe stocks of Pacific salmon and discuss their importance to management of the species. Willis Rich was one of the earliest proponents of management based on the stock concept. After reviewing the results of early marking experiments, Rich (1939) concluded that Pacific salmon were divided into many local populations or what we now refer to as stocks (Ricker 1972). . . .

Stocks

We use the word "stock" in the sense of Ricker (1972) to describe the fish that spawn in a particular river system (or portion of it) at a particular season, and that do not interbreed to any substantial degree with any group spawning in a different place, or in the same place at a different season. Ricker acknowledged that what constitutes "a substantial degree" is open to investigation, but clarified that he did not mean to exclude *all* exchange of genetic material between stocks. Our identification of stock units does not necessarily imply that all these stocks are synonymous with "distinct populations" as provided for in the Endangered Species Act of 1973. In some cases, we may have aggregated more than one population within a drainage because existing data were inadequate to separate them.

Native (descended from original stocks present prior to development), naturally-spawning anadromous fish stocks are found in a variety of circumstances, ranging from stocks having no known interactions with nonnative fish to those that coexist with nonnative hatchery stocks in the same stream. Potential interbreeding with nonnative fish did not disqualify a stock from our list because substantial native character may remain. However, in many cases it is not known whether any fish of native or largely native character persist in such mixed populations. . . .

Status Descriptors
Information on the status of salmon and steelhead stocks was obtained from the published literature, fish management agencies, Indian tribes, Oregon and Idaho Chapters of the American Fisheries Society, and sportfishing and conservation groups. We reviewed all available data, e.g., spawning escapements, redd counts, adult counts, recreational catch, dam counts, and anecdotal observations. We relied primarily on spawning escapement data where these were available, but note that these data can be misleading because factors such as changes in methods, environmental and habitat conditions, harvest rates, and personnel can affect the data. More intensive analysis of such factors would be required to confirm population trends.

Based on these data, we then identified native stocks that fell into three categories: (1) at high risk of extinction, (2) at moderate risk of extinction, and (3) of special concern. The status descriptors are based on the NMFS (1980) working policy position papers for biological thresholds of endangerment. The policies are now being reviewed by NMFS as a result of recent petitions for endangered species listing of salmon stocks. New or refined criteria may emerge as a result of this review.

At high risk of extinction: Populations whose spawning escapements are declining. Fewer than one adult fish returns to spawn from each parent spawner. Populations having recent (within the past 1 to 5 years) escapements under 200, in the absence of evidence that they were historically small, also were placed in this category because of the genetic and environmental risks they likely face. NMFS, considering the status of Sacramento River winter chinook, cited the genetic evidence that 200 returning adults per year are needed to avoid irretrievable genetic losses, and recommended that 400-1,000 is a more realistic minimum for wild fish (NMFS 1987). The minimum number of adults needed depends on the size of the watershed, the extent of gene flow among stocks, and the history of the stock. We apply the "200 adults" threshold, recognizing that it is too stringent in some cases and not stringent enough in others.

A stock in this category, if intensive analysis confirms its population status and identity as a "distinct population segment," has likely reached the threshold for listing as endangered under the Endangered Species Act.

At moderate risk of extinction: Populations whose spawning escapements appear to be stable after previously declining more than natural variation would account for, but are above 200. Approximately one adult per spawner is returning to spawn. A stock in this category, if intensive analysis confirms its population status and identity as a "distinct population segment," has likely attained the threshold for listing as threatened under the Endangered Species Act.

In many cases it was difficult to distinguish a declining population from one that has stabilized after a period of decline, because of an insufficient period of record. In these cases, population size was also taken into account. Populations having larger escapements (around 1,000) were more weighted toward the *at moderate risk* category, while those having smaller escapements were weighted toward the *at high risk* category.

Of Special Concern: Populations for which:

1. Relatively minor disturbances could threaten them, especially if a specific threat is known.

2. Insufficient information on population trend exists, but available information suggests depletion.

3. There are relatively large ongoing releases of nonnative fish, and the potential for interbreeding with the native population exists.

4. The population is not presently at risk, but requires attention because of a unique character.

Our stock status criteria, which rely primarily on recent trends in escapements, may result in under-representing the number of at-risk stocks. . . .

Identification of Nature of Threat

We identified the major factors that threaten these at-risk populations, based on published information and the judgments of those who provided the stock status information. The population of anadromous fish returning to its home stream is the result of complex interactions during an entire life cycle. As one or more of these biological, environmental, or management-related factors changes, the abundance of the returning stock of fish will change (Nicholas and Hankin 1988). Although in nearly all cases several factors are contributing to the depletion of a population, we listed only those that our sources considered to be the most constraining.

The nature of threat refers to current problems, not necessarily the historical cause of the decline. A threat is identified even if efforts have begun to remedy it, if the status of the population has not yet shown improvement. The nature of threat is numerically coded according to the following key:

1. The present or threatened destruction, modification, or curtailment of its habitat or range. (In addition to habitat damage, this category includes mainstem passage and flow problems, and predation during reservoir passage or residence.)

2. Overutilization for commercial, recreational, scientific, or educational purposes. (This category includes overharvest in mixed-stock fisheries.)

3. Disease.

4. Other natural or manmade factors affecting its continued existence (hybridization, introduction of exotic or translocated species, predation not primarily associated with mainstem passage and flow problems, competition). (This category includes negative interactions with hatchery fish, such as hybridization, competition, and disease. Also included here are poor ocean survival conditions.)

Willa Nehlsen, Jack E. Williams, and James A. Lichatowich, "Pacific Salmon at the Crossroads: Stocks at Risk from California, Oregon, Idaho, and Washington," *Fisheries* 16, no. 2 (1991): 4-5, 7-8.

Commentary

 Publication of an article in a professional journal rarely creates much stir outside the circle of professionals whose own work it touches. Sometimes there is little even to stir that group. Such was not the case with the March 1991 publication of "Pacific Salmon at the Crossroads" in *Fisheries*, the journal of the American Fisheries Society (AFS).[1] The article created an immediate sensation, not only within the fisheries profession but in the wider public and political realms. The reasons are not hard to find.

As its title provocatively declared, the essay showed that people had serious decisions to make about Pacific salmon. If the residents of the region continued to treat salmon as they had during recent years, the Northwest would lose them. Salmon, inhabitants of the region for millions of years, were in danger of extinction in many locations.

Many fisheries professionals found this prospect unacceptable, and the essay provoked their concern. But even more important, the findings of the study alerted the entire Northwest public, including conservationists, fishers, Indians, and elected officials, to the very serious danger that salmon populations faced. Conservationists began taking political and legal action based on the information in the report. They filed to list certain salmon populations under the Endangered Species Act (ESA). The alarm was heard. The region would never be the same.

The origins of the "Crossroads" paper, as it immediately became known, date to 1987. Willa Nehlsen, acting as the salmon research coordinator of the Northwest Power Planning Council in Portland, had been asked by council member Kai Lee, of Washington, to review the status of salmon stocks returning to spawn in the Snake River. These salmon had the longest migrations to and from the ocean of any Northwest stock and hence were particularly vulnerable to the development of the Columbia-Snake River basin. In fact, many populations of Snake River salmon were in decline in the 1970s.

A decade before, the National Marine Fisheries Service (NMFS), the agency responsible for salmon under the federal Endangered Species Act, had become concerned enough over the status of Snake River salmon to have begun its own review. However, as the Power Planning Council—charged with restoring salmon populations diminished by the hydroelectric development of the Columbia and Snake—began developing its fish and wildlife program in 1982, NMFS deferred to the council and suspended its status review.

Nehlsen's review presented a disturbing picture. Not only had certain Snake River populations not fared better under the council's regime, but several, including some chinook and sockeye, were in serious jeopardy. Worse, one formerly sizable coho salmon population, on the Grande Ronde River, had become extinct.

When news of Nehlsen's report for the council reached Jack Williams, he asked if she would be willing to expand the geographic scope of her inquiry to include the entire Northwest. Williams, at the time an expert on endangered fish with the U.S. Fish and Wildlife Service, was the chair of the AFS' Endangered Species Committee. This committee had published a report on the status of freshwater fish species in 1989 and had pledged in that paper to review anadromous fish stocks in subsequent efforts.[2] The interest of the AFS was piqued by their involvement in a recent lawsuit to force NMFS to list the winter run chinook salmon of California's Sacramento River as a threatened species. This became the first salmon population to be listed under the ESA.

Both Nehlsen and Williams recognized that the salmon project would not be an official activity of either of their government agencies, but instead they would undertake it in their capacities as members of the AFS. Nehlsen agreed to lead the study, and she and Williams began the painstaking task of obtaining information from local fisheries biologists and others about the status of salmon runs with which they were familiar. James Lichatowich, a former director of salmon research for the Oregon Department of Fish and Wildlife, joined the study in 1989. During more than three years of research, the authors contacted dozens of fisheries experts in Oregon, Washington, Idaho, and California, compiling information about the condition of local salmonid populations. Local information was all they could hope to obtain. Until the Crossroads paper was published, no individual possessed the overview of the problem it presented.

The way the three researchers began their paper signaled the seriousness with which they viewed their historic task. They quoted a fisheries expert from the 1930s, M. C. James, who had presented an optimistic assessment of the prospects for Columbia Basin salmon. Fishers and others had "expressed alarm at the possibility of disastrous effects upon the fish through the erection of the tremendous dams at Bonneville and the Grand Coulee," James had written. He continued:

> Aside from the fish ladders and [fish] elevators contemplated [for development at the dams], there is a program for artificial propagation set up. . . . No possibilities, either biological or engineering, have been overlooked in devising a means to assure perpetuation of the Columbia River salmon.[3]

Nehlsen, Williams, and Lichatowich were fisheries specialists of another generation, one no longer inclined to put blind faith in technology to solve complex environmental problems. The facts of the salmon decline were too stark.

The Crossroads paper showed that anadromous salmonids (both the five species commonly known as salmon and the two sea-run trouts) were at risk throughout Idaho, Oregon, Washington, and California. The biologists listed 214 native, naturally spawning stocks that were depleted. Of these, they considered 101 at high risk of extinction, 58 at moderate risk of extinction, and 54 in the less-threatened category labeled "of special concern." About one-third (76) of the stocks were native to the Columbia and Snake rivers, while the remaining 138 stocks were found throughout coastal watersheds from the Canadian border to southern California. The article also listed 106 stocks that were already extinct.

The authors linked their risk categories to standards developed by NMFS for the ESA. Nehlsen and her colleagues defined "high risk" as stocks whose numbers of spawners showed a declining trend. Such stocks were candidates for "endangered" status under the ESA. "Moderate risk" stocks were candidates for "threatened" ESA status. They considered 159 stocks in these two categories as candidates for federal protection.

As to the causes of the decline, the authors drew up a list familiar to anyone who had been following the fortunes of the salmon for any time. "Habitat loss and damage, and inadequate passage and flows caused by hydropower, agriculture, logging, and other developments" led the list. Overfishing was another serious problem, as were poor ocean survival conditions and competition and hybridization with hatchery-raised fish. At the end of the essay the authors tried to sort out which threats were important to which stocks, listing all 214 stocks and the known threats they faced.

Beyond specifying the causes of the salmon crisis, the Endangered Species Committee proposed a framework for solutions. "A new paradigm that advances habitat restoration and ecosystem function rather than hatchery production is needed for many of these stocks to survive and prosper into the next century," they wrote. Native stocks—wild stocks—were the cornerstone of restoration, they were convinced. Much of the narrative of the paper is a lesson in the history of the science of salmon biology.

The insights of Willis Rich, who proposed the stock concept in 1939, were held in high regard by the authors, and they quoted his seminal 1939 article:

> Given a species [such as the salmon] that is broken up into a number of such isolated groups or populations, it is obvious that the conservation of the species as a whole resolves into the conservation of every one of the component groups.[4]

Native stocks were needed to maintain the natural genetic diversity that would allow stocks to survive major ecological and climatic changes. They were needed to reestablish natural stocks where possible. They were needed for the genetic viability of hatchery programs. Recovery could not be sustained without them.

The Crossroads paper was intended to be a scientific benchmark. It was that and more. The authors themselves hoped that it would influence public discussion. "We believe that this report is a necessary first step in addressing the deteriorating status of native anadromous fish stocks," they wrote. "Broad concern for the anadromous fish resource now must be translated into on-the-ground actions."[5]

The report had been reviewed before publication by about sixty fisheries experts as well as numerous state and federal agencies, so when it was published its credibility was strong and biologists and managers took notice of it. Fishery professionals immediately began citing the article in other professional papers: articles in five of the twelve monthly issues of *Fisheries* in 1993, for example, contained references to the Crossroads paper that, according to the editor of *Fisheries*, rapidly became "one of the most heavily-cited publications of the American Fisheries Society, ever."[6] The authors received numerous requests to write summary papers or follow-up reports, agreeing as a team to write articles for several professional publications.

Attention to the paper was not confined to the profession, however. The same month the report was published, NMFS proposed the listing of Snake River sockeye as an endangered species. That two hundred other salmon stocks were prospective candidates for protection was a fact not lost on journalists, who saw that this looming endangered species crisis would easily dwarf the long-running drama of the spotted owl. The Crossroads paper quickly became a topic of numerous news stories in the print and broadcast media. Major articles based on the paper appeared in such environmental and fishing magazines as *Wilderness, Audubon, Defenders,* and *Pacific Fishing.* The magazine *Trout,* a publication of the organization Trout Unlimited, republished the original article in its entirety—the first time the popular magazine had ever done this with a professional article.

The article's influence was perhaps greatest, though, on policymakers. Williams, who became the science advisor to the director of the Bureau of Land Management (BLM) in 1993, noted the far-reaching effect the paper had on government agencies:

> For land management agencies, the Crossroads paper basically changed our approach to aquatic and riparian management in the Northwest and California. As the Chief of the Forest Service

often said, the AFS report was a "wake-up call" for the agencies. The report inspired the Forest Service to prepare a new strategy for land management—that became known as PACFISH. BLM joined with the Forest Service on this effort in March 1993. The report basically showed that the salmon problem was not an isolated "endangered species" issue, but was so broad as to reflect a general decline in health of our streams and watersheds.[7]

The influence of the report was also felt in the development of President Clinton's Northwest forest management plans, which relied on the PACFISH strategy, with its broad emphasis on restoring healthy stream conditions.

The Crossroads paper prompted further reviews of the status of salmon in northwestern California by the regional AFS chapter, in coastal Oregon by the state fish agency, and in Washington by that state's fish agency. These studies confirmed the broad decline recognized in the Crossroads paper.

"The phrase 'endangered species' was not part of the language of most salmon watchers in 1987," Willa Nehlsen wrote in 1992. "Today the phrase 'endangered species' is not only part of the language of salmon watchers, it is the watchword."[8] For that change, the greatest amount of credit goes to the Crossroads paper.

—**Joseph Cone**

Notes

1. Willa Nehlsen, Jack E. Williams, and James A. Lichatowich, "Pacific Salmon at the Crossroads: Stocks at Risk from California, Oregon, Idaho, and Washington," *Fisheries* 16, no. 2 (1991): 4-21.
2. Jack E. Williams et al., "Fishes of North America Endangered, Threatened, or of Special Concern: 1989," *Fisheries* 14, no. 6 (1989): 2-20.
3. Quoted in Nehlsen et al., 4.
4. Nehlsen et al., 5. Citing Willis H. Rich, "Local Populations and Migration in Relation to the Conservation of Pacific Salmon in the Western States and Alaska," in *The Migration and Conservation of Salmon,* Publication no. 8, American Association for the Advancement of Science (Lancaster, Pennsylvania: Science Press, 1939), 45.
5. Nehlsen et al., 19.
6. Kristin Merriman-Clarke, personal communication, 21 June 1994.
7. Jack E. Williams, personal communication, 8 April 1994.
8. Willa Nehlsen, "The Story Behind the Story," *Trout,* Winter 1992, 52.

WILD FISH RECEIVE SPECIAL CONSIDERATION

Document: **Wild Fish Management Policy**

Author: Oregon Fish and Wildlife Commission

Year: 1992

Description: These excerpts show the provisions of Oregon's policy giving preferential treatment to wild fish.

General Policies of Wild Fish Management
635-07-526

(1) PROTECTION OF genetic resources shall be the priority in the management of wild fish to assure optimum economic, commercial, recreational, and aesthetic benefits for present and future generations of Oregonians.

(2) It is the policy of the Department to implement the Wild Fish Management Rules for all populations of wild fish except those populations specifically exempted by the Commission in accordance with OAR 635-07-528.

(3) It is recognized that management of some populations may not currently be fully consistent with these rules. However, it is the Department's long-term goal to bring these populations into compliance, with the exception of populations specifically exempted by the Commission in accordance with OAR 635-07-528. FWC 6-1990, f. & ef. 1-29-90

Operating Principles for Wild Fish Management
635-07-527

The Department recognizes that the operating principles developed to implement this policy are associated with varying levels of uncertainty. These principles shall be continuously revised as better information becomes available. In addition to the operating principles of the Natural Production Rules (OAR 635-07-521 through 635-07-524), the operating principles set forth in this section apply to the management of populations of wild fish.

(1) Wild populations of the following species shall be managed under these operating principles:

(a) *Oncorhynchus clarki,* commonly known as cutthroat trout;

(b) *Ocorhynchus keta,* commonly known as chum salmon;

(c) *Oncorhynchus kisutch,* commonly known as coho salmon;

(d) *Oncorhynchus mykiss,* commonly known as steelhead (anadromous form) or Rainbow trout (non-anadromous form);

(e) *Oncorhynchus nerka,* commonly known as sockeye salmon (anadromous form) or kokanee (non-anadromous form);

(f) *Oncorhynchus tshawytscha,* commonly known as chinook salmon;

(g) *Salvelinus confluentus,* commonly known as bull trout;

(h) *Prosopium williamsoni,* commonly known as mountain whitefish;

(i) *Acipenser transmontanus,* commonly known as white sturgeon;

(j) *Acipenser medirostris,* commonly known as green sturgeon;

(k) All fishes that have been designated as sensitive, pursuant to OAR 635-100-040; or threatened or endangered, pursuant to ORS 496.172 through 496.192 and OAR 635-100-100 through 635-100-130;

(l) Other wild fishes as information on their status becomes available.

(2) INTERBREEDING OF HATCHERY AND WILD FISH: The interbreeding of hatchery fish with wild fish of the same taxonomic species poses risks to conserving and utilizing the genetic resources of wild populations. To reduce this risk, naturally spawning hatchery fish, whether originating from on-site releases or from strays from other release sites, shall be limited by both number in the natural spawning population and genetic characteristics. . . .

(6) HABITAT: Degradation of habitat that reduces the potential for fish production, causes population fragmentation or adversely affects fish migration routes poses a risk to conserving and utilizing the genetic resources of wild populations.

(a) The Department shall oppose habitat degradation that causes a population to experience a decline in abundance that if continued would likely reduce the number of spawners to 300 breeding fish. In addition, the Department shall advocate the restoration of degraded habitat that has depressed a population to a level of 300 or fewer spawners. Populations that are declining toward, or have reached, 300 breeding fish shall be considered to be inconsistent with these rules, except under the conditions specified in section (10) of this rule.

(b) The Department shall oppose habitat degradation or the construction of artificial blockages that cause a population to be subdivided into fragments. If population fragmentation does occur, the fragments shall be treated as separate breeding populations and managed according to the standards of this policy. In addition, where population fragmentation is identified as a problem, the Department shall advocate and seek the restoration of degraded habitat or consider advocating the removal of artificial barriers that have the potential for reestablishing genetic exchange between the populations. . . .

(8) HARVEST: Providing the opportunity for optimum harvest benefits is consistent with wild fish management. However, an extreme level of harvest poses a risk to conserving and utilizing the genetic resources of a wild population. The Department shall oppose harvest strategies that are the major cause for a population to experience a decline in abundance that if continued would reduce the number of spawners to 300 breeding fish or that would cause a population to be subdivided into fragments. In addition, the Department shall advocate the termination of harvest strategies that have depressed a population to a level of 300 or fewer spawners. . . .

Implementation of Wild Fish Management Rules
635-07-529

(1) In implementing the Wild Fish Management Rules, the Department shall select strategies that are feasible and biologically sound, and shall consider both cost and social and economic impacts.

(2) The Department shall not impose fishery restrictions for the purpose of implementing the Wild Fish Management Rules by processes other than described in OAR 635-07-529(7) (Wild Fish Management Implementation Report), OAR 635-11-050 (Statewide Angling Regulations), OAR Chapter 635, Divisions 3, 41, and 42 (Commercial Fishery Regulations), or other formal actions of the Commission.

(3) Within one year of the effective date of these rules, the Department shall develop, for approval by the Commission, a provisional statewide list of populations of wild fish. This list shall be made available to the public for review prior to Commission consideration and approval.

Oregon Fish and Wildlife, "Wild Fish Management Policy,"
Division 7: Oregon Administrative Rules (1 June 1992), 9-15.

Commentary

 Why, after all, are "wild" fish important? Why is it important to preserve fish that spawn in rivers naturally, the offspring of generations of fish that have spawned and developed in the same location? The answer is adaptation: such fish are adapted to local conditions; these adaptations are reflected in their genetic makeup. Protecting these genetic resources, biologists believe, is the only guarantee of fish in the future.

Until very recently management of salmon and steelhead has focused on the short-term production of fish for consumption. This focus has resulted in the decline of the fish because their biological requirements have not been met. Local economies that depend in part on salmon and steelhead fisheries are in jeopardy.

Long-term sustainability of fish populations, on the order of two hundred years, should be the focus of management. State and federal agencies must begin with the premise that wild populations of salmon and steelhead and the habitats that sustain them should be the foundation of management programs.

The Oregon Department of Fish and Wildlife (ODFW) has become a leader in developing a policy framework for the conservation of native fish populations. This framework offers an institutional response to the conservation of native fish in the state—if it is adequately funded, if the staff expertise is made available, and if a link is maintained between the natural production program and agency policy and management. No other agency, state or federal, has been able to develop this important institutional capability.

The ODFW commission first adopted its wild fish policy in 1978, revising and re-adopting it in 1990. The updated policy is an administrative rule, developed through lengthy public meetings and negotiations with local government interests, commercial and sport fishing representatives, and conservation groups. These representatives, meeting together and with ODFW staff, developed a consensus position that was presented to the ODFW commission before the vote on the policy.

The wild fish policy is essential to the health of salmon populations, but it is not a panacea. The mission of ODFW is to provide sustainable fish resources for the benefit of Oregon residents. But ODFW cannot fulfill this mission on its own. All the natural resources agencies of the state share the responsibility for sustainable fish resources through their actions—constructive or not—on three crucial tasks. They must protect fish habitat, ensure the escapement of spawners, and protect the genetic resources of fish populations. Their record of accomplishment is mixed.

Habitat protection is necessary to allow adequate survival and production in all stages of a fish's life cycle. In Oregon, the state departments of forestry, water, agriculture, environmental quality, state lands, and geology are all involved in regulating the uses of the land and water upon which fish depend. Furthermore, the actions of federal land and water management agencies, including the Forest Service, the Bureau of Land Management, the Soil Conservation Service, the Environmental Protection Agency, and the Bureau of Reclamation, also affect the habitat of Oregon salmonids.

ODFW has no authority to regulate habitat. It serves only in an advisory capacity to these other agencies. Its ability to protect salmon habitat, and ultimately salmon themselves, depends on the consent of land and water management agencies. A 1995 report by the National Research Council (NRC) concluded: "The current set of institutional arrangements contributes to the decline of salmon and cannot halt that decline."[1]

The number of adult salmon that survive the fisheries—the escapement—must be sufficient to provide the next generation of fish. ODFW has the authority to manage salmon fisheries within 3 miles of shore to secure such an escapement. But it does not act alone. Annual negotiations with Canada under the U.S.-Canada Pacific Salmon Treaty and with other states under the auspices of the regional Pacific Fishery Management Council determine how many fish can be caught in the ocean fishery out to 200 miles.

The ability of ODFW to secure an adequate spawner escapement for Oregon salmon is dependent, therefore, to a significant degree, on Washington, Idaho, California, the U.S. Department of Commerce (which oversees the management council), and the government of Canada. Adequate spawner escapement, not surprisingly, has not always been achieved. Escapement targets for Oregon coastal coho salmon, for example, have not been met since 1986. The NRC reported too few spawners are being allowed to return to spawn. They recommended escapements should be increased and that a shift must be made from focusing on catch to focusing on escapement of wild salmon.

Maintenance of a diverse population of wild fish is the third condition for ensuring the perpetuation of native fish resources. The agency's wild fish policy sets forth the means by which this objective may be achieved. If Oregon's wild fish program is strong enough, populations listed under the Endangered Species Act could be recovered and further listings made unnecessary.

One action ODFW has control over is the operation and use of hatcheries within the state. Replacing native salmon stocks with hatchery stocks is a failed policy. It has led to the loss of biological diversity and has failed to compensate for the loss of wild salmon stocks.

The NRC report said that hatcheries should be used only when they will cause no harm to natural populations. All hatchery programs should adopt a goal of maintaining genetic diversity among and within both hatchery and wild populations. According to the NRC, the new role of hatcheries is to support the productivity and recovery of wild salmon, rather than focusing on increasing abundance for fisheries.

An ideal native fish conservation program would contain the following measures:

(1) Identify the conservation management units:

What is it we are trying to manage and protect? It should be the stock and substock structure in each river basin. This would mean that each river is assumed to have a distinct stock unless proven otherwise. The purpose of management would be to maintain, for the long term, the stock and its substock structure in terms of its genetic and life history identity, its productive capacity, and the evolutionary potential within its life cycle habitats.

(2) Establish management objectives to maintain the stock identity and its ecological requirements:

Identify the biological characteristics of the stock, including its genetic and life history attributes, and establish biological objectives to maintain those attributes over the long term. By doing this we establish a biological reference point that can be used to determine whether biological objectives are being achieved and whether characteristics of a stock are changing over time as a result of management actions. To persist, a stock must be able to adjust to a fluctuating habitat, so the purpose of management is to establish objectives that maintain the adaptive capacity of the stock.

(3) Evaluate the program to determine whether management objectives are being achieved:

The key to a successful salmon management plan is monitoring and evaluating management objectives to determine whether the biological organization of the stock is being maintained through management. Evaluation creates a feedback loop that can be used to change objectives based on the response of the stock to management actions.

(4) Conduct an independent scientific audit:

Independent scientific review is routinely used to evaluate experiments. Salmon conservation and recovery measures are experimental and therefore require scientific evaluation if they are to remain effective. An independent scientific review of management actions will bring new ideas and information to solve problems. The results of these annual audits should be made available to the public.

These four steps are necessary to address the problems humans have created for salmon and to find solutions. These measures address all management actions, including harvest, hatchery operations, and the protection and restoration of the habitats salmon require throughout their life cycle. The Oregon wild fish policy, if implemented, would accomplish most of these tasks.

But there is still much left to do to implement the policy. It is critical that the natural production program have a close linkage with the policy development component of the agency and not be relegated to the research section, thus effectively eliminating the institutional effect of the program. However, in mid-1994 ODFW programs that provide the institutional momentum to sustain healthy fish and wildlife populations began to face marginal, uncertain funding. The agency's biodiversity policy, the nongame program, and the wild fish policy are not funded adequately. By failing to support these vital programs, particularly as more species enter federal protection under the Endangered Species Act, ODFW is, in effect, transferring its management authority to the federal government.

—Bill M. Bakke

Note

1. Committee on Protection and Management of Pacific Northwest Anadromous Salmonids, Board on Environmental Studies and Toxicology, and Commission on Life Sciences, *Upstream: Salmon and Society in the Pacific Northwest.* (Washington, D.C.: National Research Council, 1995), 320.

SNAKE RIVER SALMON LISTED UNDER ENDANGERED SPECIES ACT

Document:	**Endangered and Threatened Species: Final Rule**
Author:	U.S. Secretary of Commerce
Year:	1992
Description:	A federal agency presents the official reasons for listing Snake River sockeye and chinook salmon under the federal Endangered Species Act.

Status of the Snake River Sockeye Salmon

HISTORICALLY, SOCKEYE SALMON were produced in Idaho in the Stanley Basin of the Salmon River in Alturas, Pettit, Redfish, Yellowbelly and Stanley Lakes and may have been present in one or two other Stanley Basin Lakes. . . . Outside of the Salmon River Basin, but within the Snake River Basin, sockeye salmon were produced in Big Payette Lake on the North Fork Payette River and in Wallowa Lake. . . .

Escapement of sockeye salmon to the Snake River has declined dramatically in recent years. Counts made at Lower Granite Dam (the first dam on the Snake River downstream from the confluence of the Salmon River) have ranged from 531 in 1976 to zero in 1990. . . .

During the spring of 1991, a fraction of the juvenile *O. nerka* [sockeye salmon] outmigrants from Redfish and Alturas Lakes were collected and transported to Eagle Hatchery, Eagle, Idaho, to provide a potential source of broodstock for future sockeye production. Four adults (three males and one female) returned to Redfish Lake in 1991 and were captured and held in special facilities at Sawtooth Hatchery near Redfish Lake. These fish were successfully spawned and the resulting progeny will be used to maximize sockeye production.

Summary of Factors Affecting the Species

The ESA requires a determination of whether a species is threatened or endangered because of any of the five factors identified in section 4(a)(1). This determination is based on the "Summary of Factors Affecting the Species" section in the proposed rule and on comments received on the proposed rule. A brief description of these factors follows.

A. The Present or Threatened Destruction, Modification, or Curtailment of Its Habitat or Range

Hydropower development has resulted in blockage of habitat, turbine-related mortality of juvenile fish, increased delay of juvenile migration through the Snake and Columbia Rivers, increased predation on juvenile salmon due to residualism in reservoirs and increased predator populations due to ideal foraging areas created by impoundments, and increased delay of adults on their way to spawning grounds. Water withdrawal and storage and irrigation diversions and blockage of habitat for purposes such as agriculture have also contributed to the destruction of Snake River sockeye salmon habitat.

B. Overutilization for Commercial, Recreational, Scientific, or Educational Purposes

Data specific to the exploitation of Snake River sockeye salmon are limited, but available information indicates that commercial fisheries in the lower Columbia River, and harvest on the spawning grounds, were primary factors in the decline of Snake River sockeye salmon.

The recreational harvest of sockeye salmon in the Columbia River is negligible. There is no information available to indicate that ocean harvest of Columbia River (including Snake River) sockeye salmon is significant.

C. Disease or Predation

Sockeye salmon are exposed to numerous bacterial, protozoan, viral, and parasitic organisms in spawning and rearing areas, migratory routes, and the marine environment. Even though [sockeye salmon] is susceptible to these, their effect on Snake River sockeye salmon is not documented.

Predators, particularly northern squawfish, *Ptychocheilus oregonensis*, and avian predator populations have increased due to hydroelectric development that created impoundments providing ideal foraging areas. Turbulent conditions in turbines, dam bypasses, and spillways have increased predator success by stunning or disorienting passing juvenile salmon migrants.

Marine mammal numbers, especially harbor seals and California sea lions, are increasing on the West Coast and increases in predation by pinnipeds have been noted in all Northwest salmonid fisheries. However, the extent to which predation is a factor causing the decline of Snake River sockeye salmon is unknown.

D. Inadequacy of Existing Regulatory Mechanisms
A wide variety of Federal and state laws and programs have affected the abundance and survival of anadromous fish populations in the Columbia River. These regulatory mechanisms have not prevented the decline of Snake River sockeye salmon.

E. Other Natural and Manmade Factors
1. Natural Factors. Drought is the principal natural condition that may have contributed to reduced Snake River sockeye salmon production. Annual mean streamflows for the 1977 water year were generally the lowest recorded for many streams since the late nineteenth century. The 1990 water year became the fourth consecutive year of drought conditions in the Snake River Basin.

2. Manmade Factors. There is no direct evidence that artificially propagated fish have compromised the genetic integrity of Stanley Basin sockeye salmon. Supplementation of kokanee salmon occurred sporadically, beginning early in this century. In most cases, the origin of the donor stocks is unknown. Preliminary electrophoretic analyses of 19 different sockeye and kokanee salmon samples from Idaho, Washington, and British Columbia (these include the most likely sources for donor stocks) indicated that Redfish and Alturas Lake kokanee populations are genetically different from the other populations sampled. Adult salmon returning to Redfish Lake were unavailable for sampling. Artificial production of other species may have an adverse impact on Snake River sockeye salmon as they jointly migrate through the rivers, estuary and ocean, and may compete with sockeye salmon for food.

Determination
Based on its assessment of available scientific and commercial information, NMFS is issuing a final determination that the Snake River sockeye salmon (*Oncorhynchus nerka*) is a "species" under the ESA and should be listed as endangered under the ESA.

Conservation Measures
Conservation measures provided to species listed as endangered or threatened under the ESA include recognition, prohibitions on taking, recovery actions, and Federal agency consultation require-

ments. Recognition through listing promotes conservation actions by Federal and state agencies and private groups and individuals.

For listed species, section 7(a)(2) requires Federal agencies to ensure that activities they authorize, fund, or conduct are not likely to jeopardize the continued existence of a listed species or to destroy or adversely modify its critical habitat. If a Federal action may adversely affect a listed species or its critical habitat, the responsible Federal agency must enter into formal consultation with NMFS.

Examples of Federal actions most likely to affect Snake River sockeye salmon include authorized purposes of mainstem Columbia and Snake Rivers hydroelectric and storage projects. Such authorized purposes include hydroelectric power generation, flood control, irrigation, and navigation. Federal actions including COE section 404 permitting activities under the Clean Water Act, COE section 10 permitting activities under the Rivers and Harbors Act, and FERC licenses for non-Federal development and operation of hydropower may also be affected.

> Endangered and Threatened Species; Endangered Status for
> Snake River Sockeye Salmon; Final Rule, 56 Fed. Reg. 58,619,
> 58,622-23 (1991). (Citations omitted.)

Status of Snake River Spring/Summer Chinook Salmon

HISTORICALLY, IT IS ESTIMATED that 44 percent of the combined Columbia River spring and summer chinook salmon returned to the Salmon River subbasin of the Snake River system. [Recent research] combined a number of estimates and concluded that in some years during the late 1800s, the Snake River produced in excess of 1.5 million adult spring/summer chinook salmon. By the 1950s, the abundance of adult spring/summer chinook salmon had declined to an average of 125,000 per year. Since then, counts at Snake River dams have declined considerably, from an average at Ice Harbor Dam of 58,798 fish during 1962 through 1970, to a low of 11,855 in 1979. Counts gradually increased over the next 9 years, peaking at 42,184 in 1988. However, in 1989, 1990 and 1991, counts dropped to 21,244, 26,524 and 17,149 fish, respectively. These numbers are illustrative of population trends, but are not indicative of wild fish abundance, because adult counts at dams since 1967 have been confounded by returns of hatchery-origin fish. . . .

. . . [T]he estimated number of wild adult spring/summer chinook salmon passing over Lower Granite Dam averaged 9,674 fish from 1980 through 1990, with a low count of 3,343 fish in 1980 and a high count of 21,870 fish in 1988. The estimated wild adult return in 1991 was 8,457.

Snake River redd counts in index areas provide the best indicator of trends and the status of wild spring/summer chinook salmon. In 1957, over 13,000 redds were counted in index areas excluding the Grande Ronde River. By 1964, the number of redds was only 8,542, including counts in Grande Ronde River. Over the next 16 years, annual counts in all areas declined steadily, reaching a minimum of 620 redds in 1980. Annual counts increased gradually over the next 8 years, reaching a peak of 3,395 redds in 1988. However, in 1989, 1990 and 1991, counts dropped to 1,008, 1,224 and 1,184, respectively.

Factors relevant to the determination of whether a "species" is threatened or endangered include current and historical abundance, population trends, distribution of fish in space and time, other information indicative of the health of the population, existing and potential threats to the species, and those efforts, if any, being made to protect the species. Nearly 95 percent of the total reduction in estimated abundance of Snake River spring/summer chinook salmon occurred prior to the mid-1900s. Over the last 30-40 years, the remaining population was further reduced. Currently, the abundance of these fish is approximately 0.5 percent of the estimated historical abundance. Furthermore, the 1991 redd count of (1,184) (index areas only) represents only 13.9 percent of the 1964 count (8,542). . . .

Status of Snake River Fall Chinook Salmon

Historically, fall chinook salmon were widely distributed throughout the Snake River and many of its major tributaries from its confluence with the Columbia River near Pasco, Washington, upstream 615 miles (990 kilometers (km)) to Shoshone Falls, Idaho. The most important spawning grounds for fall chinook salmon in the Snake River were between Huntington, Idaho . . . and Auger Falls, Idaho. . . .

During the early 1900s, a weir was placed in the Snake River downstream of Swan Falls Dam near Ontario, Oregon . . . to collect fall chinook salmon broodstock. Although only a portion of the returning fish were intercepted, more than 20 million eggs (a minimum of 4,000 females) were taken in a single year. This provides some indication of the distribution and large number of fall chinook salmon migrating into the upper reaches of the Snake River during this period.

Fall chinook salmon production [above river mile 456] was terminated in 1901 by Swan Falls Dam, which obstructed the passage of returning adults. Snake River fall chinook salmon abundance remained relatively stable until 1950, but declined substantially thereafter. The estimated mean number of fall chinook salmon returning annually to the Snake River decreased from 72,000 between 1928 and 1949, to 29,000 from 1950 through 1959. In spite of this decline in abundance, the Snake River remained the most important production area for fall chinook salmon in the Columbia River Basin through the 1950s.

The distribution of Snake River fall chinook salmon has been dramatically reduced and now represents only a fraction of its former range. The construction of Brownlee . . . (1958); Oxbow . . . (1961); and Hells Canyon . . . (1967) Dams inundated spawning habitat and prevented access to the primary production areas of Snake River fall chinook salmon when fish passage facilities at these projects proved to be inadequate. Snake River fall chinook salmon habitats were further reduced with the construction of Ice Harbor . . . (1961); Lower Monumental . . . (1969); Little Goose . . . (1970); and Lower Granite . . . (1975) Dams.

For Snake River fall chinook salmon, dam counts provide one indication of the population's recent abundance. Counts at the uppermost dam affording adult fish passage averaged 12,720 at Ice Harbor from 1969 through 1974, and 610 at Lower Granite from 1975 through 1980. However, the escapement of wild Snake River chinook salmon must be less than these figures since fish leaving the Snake River to spawn elsewhere are not accounted for in dam counts. Efforts were initiated in 1990 to estimate the number of hatchery-reared fall chinook salmon (initial returns to the Snake River were in 1983) and wild Snake River fall chinook salmon returning to Lower Granite Dam. This methodology was used to estimate wild and hatchery fall chinook salmon returns for the period 1983 through 1989, recognizing that site-specific straying rates were not calculable prior to 1990. Estimates of wild Snake River fall chinook salmon escapement to Lower Granite Dam varied from 428 adults in 1983, to 295 in 1989, to 78 in 1990. Wild escapement in 1991 was estimated to be 318.

Fall chinook salmon redds observed over the remaining 102 miles . . . of the Snake River available to fall chinook salmon for the period 1987 through 1991 were 66, 57, 58, 37, and 32 respectively.

Summary of Factors Affecting the Species
The ESA requires a determination whether a species is threatened or endangered because of any of the five factors identified in section 4(a)(1). These determinations are based on the factors reports for the Snake River spring/summer and fall chinook salmon, the proposed rules, and comments on the aforementioned documents. A brief description of these factors, for both species, follows.

A. The Present or Threatened Destruction, Modification, or Curtailment of Its Habitat or Range
Hydropower development has resulted in: Blockage and inundation of habitat; turbine-related mortality of juvenile fish; increased delay of juvenile migration through the Snake and Columbia Rivers; increased predation on juvenile salmon in reservoirs; and increased delay of adults on their way to spawning grounds. Water withdrawal and storage, irrigation diversions, siltation and pollution from sewage, farming, grazing, logging, and mining have also degraded the Snake River spring/summer and fall chinook salmon's habitat.

B. Overutilization for Commercial, Recreational, Scientific, or Educational Purposes
Historically, combined ocean and river harvest rates of Snake River spring/summer chinook salmon exceeded 80 and sometimes 90 percent. However, current ocean and river harvest levels have been greatly curtailed in the commercial, recreational, and Indian fisheries due to low escapements and efforts to protect these runs. The majority of current harvest occurs in the Columbia River net fisheries. Some harvest also occurs in Columbia River recreational fisheries. Columbia River fisheries directed toward other species can also impact spring/summer chinook salmon.

The total exploitation rate for Lyons Ferry Hatchery fall chinook salmon, which are assumed to have the same distribution as wild Snake River fall chinook salmon, is estimated to be 69 percent. These harvest rates may be higher than Snake River fall chinook salmon can sustain.

C. Disease or Predation

Both spring/summer and fall chinook salmon are exposed to numerous bacterial, protozoan, viral, and parasitic organisms; however, these organisms' impacts on Snake River spring/summer, and fall chinook salmon are largely unknown.

Predators, particularly northern squawfish, *Ptychocheilus oregonensis*, and avian predator populations have increased due to hydroelectric development that created ideal foraging areas. Numerous reservoirs provide preferred habitats, and turbulent conditions in turbines, dam bypasses, and spillways have increased predator success by stunning or disorienting passing juvenile salmon migrants.

Marine mammal numbers, especially harbor seals and California sea lions, are increasing on the West Coast and increases in predation by pinnipeds have been noted in all Northwest salmonid fisheries. For Snake River spring/summer chinook salmon, increased injuries attributable to marine mammals from a few percent annually to an average of 19.2 percent was noted at Lower Granite Dam in 1990 and reported in the factors report. The observed incidence of such injury in 1991 declined to approximately 15 percent. The extent to which predation is a factor causing the decline of spring/summer and fall chinook salmon is unknown.

D. Inadequacy of Existing Regulatory Mechanisms

A wide variety of Federal and state laws and programs have affected the abundance and survival of anadromous fish populations in the Columbia River. However, they have not prevented the decline of Snake River spring/summer and fall chinook salmon. Several of the more pertinent laws are summarized in the factors reports.

E. Other Natural and Manmade Factors

Drought is the principal natural condition that may have contributed to reduced spring/summer and fall chinook salmon production. Annual mean stream flows for the 1977 water year were generally the lowest on record for many streams since the late nineteenth century. The 1990 water year became the fourth consecutive year of drought conditions in the Snake River Basin. Drought conditions also prevailed in the Snake River Basin for the 1991 water year.

Artificial propagation programs were initiated following the major decline of Snake River spring/summer chinook salmon as an effort to offset juvenile and adult passage mortality resulting from

hydroelectric development. Although artificial propagation programs have maintained returns on some areas, Snake River spring/
summer chinook have continued to decline. Under this circum-
stance of low abundance, hatchery programs have contributed to
the further decline of wild Snake River spring/summer chinook
salmon through the taking of fish for broodstock purposes, behavioral and genetic interactions, competition, predation and the
spread of disease.

The only artificial propagation facility for Snake River fall
chinook salmon (Lyons Ferry Hatchery) initiated operation following the substantial decline of the species to offset impacts resulting
from the construction of hydroelectric facilities on the Lower Snake
River (Lower Granite, Little Goose, Lower Monumental and Ice
Harbor Dams). This facility was intended to preserve the integrity of
Snake River fall chinook salmon.

Artificial propagation activities have not been a primary factor in
the decline of Snake River fall chinook salmon. However, the taking
of Snake River fall chinook salmon for hatchery broodstock has
reduced natural escapements, and the recent straying of fall
chinook salmon from other areas into the Snake River threatens the
genetic integrity of wild Snake River fall chinook salmon.

Determination

Based on its assessment of available scientific and commercial
information, NMFS is issuing final determinations that Snake River
spring/summer chinook salmon and Snake River fall chinook
salmon are ESUs or "species" under the ESA and should be listed as
threatened. The ESU for Snake River spring/summer chinook
salmon is defined as all natural population(s) of spring/summer
chinook salmon in the mainstem Snake River and any of the
following subbasins: Tucannon River, Grande Ronde River, Imnaha
River, Salmon River, and Clearwater River. The natural population
consists of all fish that are the progeny of naturally spawning fish.
The offspring of all fish taken from the natural population after the
date of listing (for example, for research or enhancement purposes)
are also part of the ESU (natural population).

NMFS is now listing only the natural populations; however, it is
also important to address whether any existing hatchery population
is similar enough to the natural population that it can be considered part of the ESU and, therefore, potentially used in recovery
efforts. In general, hatchery populations that have been substantially changed as a result of artificial propagation should not be

considered part of the ESU. To address this and related issues, NMFS is developing a policy on the role of artificial propagation under the ESA for Pacific salmon, and will publish its proposed policy in the Federal Register for public comment. After issuing a final policy, NMFS will propose any revisions to the listed ESUs to include various existing hatchery populations, if appropriate. Pending completion of this process, NMFS is excluding from the Snake River spring/summer and fall chinook ESUs all fish in or originating from a hatchery at the time of listing.

> Endangered and Threatened Species; Threatened Status for Snake River Spring/Summer Chinook Salmon, Threatened Status for Snake River Fall Chinook Salmon; Final Rule, 57 Fed. Reg. 14,653, 14,659-61 (1992). (Citations omitted.)

Commentary

As EARLY AS 1978, the National Marine Fisheries Service (NMFS) and the U.S. Fish and Wildlife Service considered listing salmon for protection under the Endangered Species Act (ESA). After 1980, however, the federal fishery agencies suspended their status review to concentrate on efforts to implement the Columbia Basin Fish and Wildlife Program authorized by the Northwest Power Act in that year. But when the program failed to produce increases in river flows that were biologically justified, salmon advocates looked again to the ESA.

In March 1990, the Shoshone-Bannock Indian tribe petitioned the Secretary of Commerce to list the Snake River sockeye as endangered. Two months later, a coalition of environmental groups petitioned the secretary to list Snake River spring, summer, and fall chinook and lower Columbia coho for protection. On November 20, 1991, the secretary listed Snake River sockeye as endangered; five months later, on April 22, 1992, the secretary listed the chinook species as threatened (combining summer and spring chinook) but denied listing to the lower Columbia coho. The reason for this denial was the claim that wild runs of lower Columbia coho could not be distinguished from hatchery coho, of which there was an abundance.

The ESA listing process during 1990-92 prompted a flurry of actions in a vain attempt to ward off the listings. In 1991, Northwest

Conservationist and endangered-species petitioner Bill Bakke (bearded, at right) had a seat at the table at the Salmon Summit convened by Oregon Sen. Mark Hatfield in 1990. Deals were discussed at the summit, but a regionally determined salmon recovery plan did not emerge.

governors convened a grand round table on salmon issues, dubbed the "salmon summit." The summit inspired a proposal championed by Idaho Governor Cecil Andrus that would lower Snake River reservoirs during the spring salmon migration season by 25 feet or more to increase flow velocities. A lower reservoir has a smaller cross-section, so a drawdown of 30 feet, for example, would produce the same flow velocity at 85,000 cubic feet per second as 140,000 cubic feet per second at normal reservoir levels. Thus, the proposal could significantly reduce travel time for juvenile salmon with considerably less water from storage.

The Idaho drawdown proposal was newsworthy because it started from the premise of accomplishing a biological objective—reducing travel time for young salmon—and then investigated how to accomplish the objective in an economic and technically feasible manner. This approach represents a sharp break from the traditional approach of making incremental changes in the status quo that has dominated decision making by the Northwest Power Planning Council. The new approach is entirely consistent with the Northwest Power Act, however, which makes economic considerations a relevant but secondary factor to biological considerations.

Invocation of the ESA also induced the Northwest Power Planning Council to amend its Columbia Basin Program in late 1991 to provide increased protection for downstream migrating juvenile salmon. But the council failed even to set biological objectives or rebuilding schedules for listed stocks. Although the amendments contained a number of measures that could free up water previously thought unavailable for fish flows, on the Snake essentially all they promised was greater assurance that the existing water budget would be met. The ongoing ESA proceedings prompted project operators (principally the Army Corps) to finally, for the first time, satisfy the Snake River water budget in 1991.

The ESA listings had no effect on hydroelectric operations until the spring of 1992, when the federal project operators and regulators had to consult with NMFS to ensure that their actions did not jeopardize the continued existence of the listed species. However, NMFS ruled that 1992 hydroelectric operations satisfied the ESA because they promised improvements—due to the 1991 amendments to the Columbia Basin Program—over past operations. Despite the fact that 70 to 90 percent of juvenile salmon would perish on their downstream journey to the sea, NMFS issued a "no jeopardy" opinion, meaning that proposed hydroelectric operations would not jeopardize the continued existence of Snake River salmon. NMFS has, for over a dozen years, been calling for biologically based fish flows. Yet, when given decision-making authority by the ESA, the agency did not insist that the hydroelectric system achieve those flows. The result was that the ESA had little effect on basic Columbia Basin hydroelectric opera-

Idaho Governor Cecil Andrus aired his views about salmon and dams on a large billboard in Clarkston, Washington, July 1991.

tions until a court ruled that NMFS violated the ESA by issuing the no jeopardy opinion when the system required, in the court's words, "a major overhaul" (see page 322).

Because the objective of the ESA's consultation process is to prevent jeopardy to the species as a whole, NMFS possesses a considerable amount of administrative discretion, as reflected in the 1992 no jeopardy decision. The ESA's prohibition against "taking" listed species is, however, aimed at protecting individual members of the species and extends not only to federal agencies but also to states and private parties. However, decisions by NMFS have effectively circumvented this protection, too. NMFS characterized hydroelectric operations that kill juvenile and adult salmon as an "incidental take" and authorized them by a statement through the same consultation process that produced the no jeopardy opinion. Salmon harvests regulated by the federal government were similarly authorized.

Further, the "taking" of juvenile salmon for barge and truck transportation, a controversial surrogate for suitable river flows, in effect since 1981, requires a separate ESA permit, one authorizing activities to enhance the survival of the species. This permit requires, among other things, a finding by NMFS that barging and trucking salmon enhances their survival and is consistent with the preservation of river ecosystems upon which salmon depend. Barging and trucking have been implemented for over fifteen years as a substitute for biologically based flows—flows that are not now available because the hydroelectric system is driven by priorities other than providing river conditions suitable for salmon migration. In April 1993, NMFS granted a permit to allow the barging and trucking program to continue, a decision that environmentalists unsuccessfully challenged in court (*Northwest Resource Information Center v. National Marine Fisheries Service*, 56 F3d 1060 (9th Cir. 1995)).

Thus, the ESA has had remarkably little legal effect on Columbia Basin hydroelectric operations. The act does have the potential to affect a broader range of activities—harvest regulation, federal land management, state water rights allocation, to name a few—than does the Northwest Power Act. Some of this potential may be revealed in a salmon "recovery plan" due in 1996. However, as of this writing, the unsettling reality is that the salmon listings under the ESA have had only marginal legal effects on hydroelectric operations.

—Michael C. Blumm and F. Lorraine Bodi

OVERHAUL OF COLUMBIA RIVER OPERATIONS NEEDED

Document: *Idaho Department of Fish and Game v. National Marine Fisheries Service*

Author: Judge Malcolm Marsh, Federal District Court of Oregon

Year: 1993

Description: A federal judge rejected the National Marine Fisheries Service's biological opinion that Columbia River hydroelectric system operations posed "no jeopardy" to salmon.

I fiND THAT NMFS' selection of the '86-'90 baseline is arbitrary and capricious because the agency failed to consider relevant facts such as the drought condition and low run numbers of the species during the base period. NMFS also failed to articulate a rational connection between the facts, circumstances and myriad of factors contributing to the decline of the listed species and the choice of a standard by which to measure future success against. Instead, NMFS focussed on the system capabilities tending to the status quo rather than stabilization of the species. Finally, NMFS failed to conduct a reasoned evaluation of all available information when it adopted a standard which was based upon an undesirable period of years for the listed salmon. . . .

Based upon these results, NMFS concluded that 1993FCRPS [Federal Columbia River Power System] operations were "expected to result in a meaningful decrease" of 2.5% to 11.4% in mortality of spring/summer chinook relative to the base period and a "meaningful decrease" of 5.1-8.9% in mortality for fall chinook relative to the base period. In addition, NMFS noted that the 60-70% probability of achieving 1990 population levels for spring/summer chinook by 2008 represented a "reasonable certainty" of stabilization. Based upon these findings and conclusions, NMFS issued a "no jeopardy" BO [biological opinion] on May 26, 1993. . . .

Given the admitted high degree of uncertainty in the jeopardy analysis, there is no rational explanation for defendants to disregard only the low end, worst case assumptions. Further, the government offers no explanation for its failure to consider in-breeding and the "extinction vortex" as additional risks undermining confidence levels. IDFG and Oregon point to weaknesses in the BPA model results which might have supported dropping high range assumptions. Had NMFS not discounted the low range assumptions, the confidence levels would have been approximately 50% for spring/summer chinook instead of the 60-70% cited by NMFS in its conclusion. . . .

I find that NMFS arbitrarily and capriciously discounted low range assumptions without well-reasoned analysis and without considering the full range of risk assumptions. . . .

Federal defendants are under no legal obligation to listen and respond to salmon plans from every corner of the Northwest, but the ESA does impose substantive obligations with respect to an agency's consideration of significant information and data from well-qualified scientists such as the fisheries biologists from the states and tribes. See 16 U.S.C. § 1536(a)(2), ("Section 7(a)(2)") (each agency "shall use the best scientific and commercial data available"). . . .

NMFS has clearly made an effort to create a rational, reasoned process for determining how the action agencies are doing in their efforts to save the listed salmon species. But the process is seriously, "significantly," flawed because it is too heavily geared towards a status quo that has allowed all forms of river activity to proceed in a deficit situation—that is, relatively small steps, minor improvements and adjustments—when the situation literally cries out for a major overhaul. Instead of looking for what can be done to protect the species from jeopardy, NMFS and the action agencies have narrowly focussed their attention on what the establishment is capable of handling with minimal disruption.

> *Idaho Dep't of Fish and Game v. National Marine Fisheries Serv.*,
> 850 F. Supp. 886 (D. Or. 1994). (Citations and some acronyms
> omitted.)

Commentary

 DISSATISFIED WITH THE RESULTS of consultations under the Endangered Species Act (ESA), Idaho Department of Fish and Game filed suit against the National Marine Fisheries Service (NMFS), the U.S. Army Corps of Engineers, and the Bureau of Reclamation, claiming that 1993 Columbia River hydroelectric operations violated the ESA. Idaho, joined by Oregon and Columbia Basin Indian tribes, charged that NMFS' biological opinion arbitrarily concluded that hydroelectric operations would not jeopardize the continued existence of listed salmon runs. Judge Malcolm Marsh agreed with Idaho, Oregon, and the tribes and rejected NMFS' selection of a 1986-90 "base period" against which to measure whether the effects of planned operations would stabilize or restore the salmon runs. He concluded that the agency failed to consider matters such as drought conditions and low numbers in establishing the baseline. Judge Marsh also determined that the use of various computer models to predict the effect of proposed operations was arbitrary because they failed to consider the so-called "extinction vortex," a point at which fish numbers are so low that merely maintaining run sizes may in fact constitute a continued threat to the species' existence.

In rejecting NMFS' biological opinion on hydroelectric operations, the judge criticized the agency's adoption of assumptions that favored status quo operations when the salmon's situation "cries out for a major overhaul." For years a coalition of regional fishery agencies and Indian tribes has been advocating such an overhaul, including increased spring and summer flows, reservoir drawdowns, and strict limitations on barging and trucking of juvenile salmon, with little effect. Because Judge Marsh simply ordered a reinstitution of ESA consultation without attempting to direct river operations in the interim, federal water managers and NMFS would have another opportunity to overhaul operational practices to provide a river environment that avoids jeopardizing the Snake River salmon's continued existence.

—Michael C. Blumm and F. Lorraine Bodi

WHAT HAVE NORTHWEST RESIDENTS LEARNED?

Document:	**Oregon Voters' Pamphlets**
Authors:	Various individuals and companies, as listed
Year:	1908 and 1992
Description:	A comparison of statements on these initiative petitions offers some perspective on how far Northwest residents have come in dealing with salmon issues.

Submitted to Voters of Oregon June 1, 1908

*ARGUMENT
(affirmative)
Submitted by*

H. A. WEBSTER, formerly Deputy Fish Warden, State of Oregon, in favor of the measure designated on the official ballot, as follows:

PROPOSED BY INITIATIVE PETITION

For an act prohibiting fishing for salmon or sturgeon on Sunday from January first to October first, also in the Columbia River only from October first to December thirty-first, also in the navigable channels of Columbia River at night, also at any time in Sandy River and in Columbia River west of west line of range nine west, near Astoria, and east of west line of range sixteen east, near Celilo, and limiting seines anywhere in the State to one hundred and fifty fathoms long and four and one-sixth fathoms deep, and providing penalties.

Vote YES or NO.

318. YES.
319. No. . . .

The object of the proposed law is to replete a dwindling industry by checking the destruction of salmon, wrought by the various appliances. This bill will place limits on all classes of fishing gear without discriminating for or against any. Commercial greed has brought the noble Chinook, worth millions to our State, to deplorable plight. So many fish are caught that not enough now escape for purpose of propagation; the hatcheries, paid for at big expense

No matter that fish "traps" didn't look at all like the game traps pictured, this political ad from 1948 reflects the emotional heat associated with salmon ballot measures.

by taxpayers, are in some places closed and in others almost idle. Meanwhile the industry wanes. At present, there is practically no protection under the law; the closed Sunday has been abolished and the open season lengthened again and again, until now salmon are caught just as long as the fishermen desire to take them. These conditions are self-evident; authorities are agreed; the decline would prove it were there any dispute. The situation is best expressed by that great authority, Dr. Livingston Stone, U. S. Department of Fisheries, who says:

> Consider for a moment what the salmon has done for us, and then think how mercilessly we have treated him. Our salmon has been to us a source of national revenue, enjoyment, and pride, and what return have we meted out to him? He has been hunted pitilessly with hooks and spears, with all kinds of nets and pounds, with wheels and guns and dynamite, and there is not a cubic foot of water in the whole country where he can rest in safety. The moment he comes in from the ocean he meets the gill nets and the pounds at the mouth of the river, the sweep seines further up, the hook everywhere, and at last on his breeding-grounds, which at least ought to be sacred to him, he encounters the pitchforks of the white man and the spears of the Indian.

Relief must now be prompt if we would have a worthy inheritance to bequeath to our children. . . .

H. M. Lorntsen, Secretary Columbia River Salmon Protective Association, opposing the measure designated on the official ballot as follows: . . .

Argument Against Initiative Bill No. 318

This bill, while pretending to be for the protection of the salmon of the Columbia, is a bill which the few wealthy fishwheel owners of the upper Columbia are presenting to the voters in an endeavor to retain the unfair and destructive monopoly of catching salmon with fishwheels in the narrows and at the falls of the upper Columbia.

The initiative petitions for this bill were started after the Columbia River Salmon Protective Association was organized for the purpose of stopping fishing for salmon in the Columbia at head of tide; that is, where the river becomes so narrow that the fishwheels catch nearly every salmon that reaches these narrows and falls.

The fishwheel owners, realizing that throughout the State the sentiment for bona fide salmon protective legislation was growing, got up this trick bill for the simple purpose of confusing the voters. . . .

Submitted to Voters of Oregon June 1, 1908

Argument
(affirmative)
Submitted by

The Columbia River Salmon Protective Association in favor of the measure designated on the official ballot as follows:

Proposed by Initiative Petition

For an act prohibiting, after August 25th, 1908, fishing for salmon or sturgeon at any time, by any means, except hook and line, in the Sandy River or any of its tributaries, or in the Columbia River or any of its tributaries, at any place up stream from its confluence with the Sandy River, or with hook and line during the spawning season.

Vote YES or NO.

332. YES.
333. No. . . .

This bill provides that all fishing for salmon or sturgeon for commercial purposes shall stop in the Columbia or its tributaries, where the Columbia becomes so narrow that the salmon have no chance to get to the hatcheries and natural spawning grounds, if fishing is permitted.

Every Nation and State possessing salmon streams, seeing how salmon were being destroyed by fishing in the narrows of the rivers, has adopted the principle contained in this bill.

Oregon passed a law in 1901 which stopped fishing for salmon in its rivers with stationary appliances, and provided for dead lines against fishing where our rivers became narrow.

The Columbia was excepted from this law because the power and influence of the few rich men owning fish wheels in the upper Columbia prevailed against the logic and earnestness of the men who plead for the preservation of our salmon.

What has been the result of this failure to include the Columbia in this protective measure?

In the Columbia the salmon are steadily decreasing, especially our Chinook salmon, the king of all salmon. . . .

ARGUMENT
(negative)
Submitted by

SEUFERT BROS., WARREN PACKING COMPANY, AND P. J. MCGOWAN AND & SONS, for selves and others in interest opposing the measure designated on the official ballot as follows: . . .

This bill purports to have the support of a so-called Columbia River Salmon Protective Association. We do not desire to criticise the motives of the gentlemen comprising this association, but we feel that the use of their names has been secured by gross misrepresentations, and further, that, with exception of those hailing from Clatsop County whose motives are well known, not one is possessed of sufficient knowledge by personal research to be competent

Measure No. 8

authority. If you wanted medical attention you would not seek a
banker who had been told of appendicitis operations, nor for soil
needs would you consult a merchant, or for stock breeding a manu-
facturer.

For years lower-river interests have striven to eliminate all others
in favor of a monopoly of their own, a miniature Standard Oil,
fostered by a union, without union principles, which wants to
pursue salmon twenty-four hours a day, seven days in the week,
fifty-two weeks in the year, with no other protection than that to be
given at the expense of the other fellow, and, as before stated, this
union is backed as largest contributors by Astoria canneries and
further encouraged by one of the largest salmon trusts in the world
seeking to throttle legitimate opposition.

> *Pamphlet to be Submitted to Voters of Oregon June 1, 1908* (Salem,
> Ore., 1908), 47-48, 52, 107-8, 110.

Measure No. 8

STATE OF OREGON

*Proposed by initiative petition to be voted on at the General Election,
November 3, 1992.*

BALLOT TITLE
**8 RESTRICTS LOWER COLUMBIA FISH HARVESTS TO MOST SELECTIVE MEANS
AVAILABLE**

QUESTION—Shall state law restrict lower Columbia River fishing to
most selective means available, to allow release of non-targeted fish
unharmed?

SUMMARY—Act sets policy to harvest fish in lower Columbia River by
most selective means available. Harvest between Columbia mouth
and Bonneville Dam must be by most selective methods, to allow
nontarget fish to be returned to water unharmed. State must prepare management plans for species affected by harvest, oppose
some Columbia River gillnetting. Plan goals are to protect native
species, genetic diversity of those species. State may sell salmon if

numbers exceed goals, use proceeds to carry out Act. Act enforce-able by lawsuits against state.

ESTIMATE OF FINANCIAL IMPACT—In 1993-94, State expenditures will be $1.6 million for implementation. In 1994-95 and each year thereaf-ter, State expenditures will be $300,000 and State revenues will decrease $200,000. . . .

ARGUMENT IN FAVOR

We all know that salmon runs are declining at an alarming rate. There are many causes of this decline, and it is obvious that state and federal management policies are not working. The prime 4, 5 and 6 year old fish have been the target of the gillnet harvest. These are the larger, stronger fish, and should be used as brood stock. We should first obtain the *best stock* at the hatcheries to maintain the run. Then all surplus fish should be taken as a terminal *fishery—no waste.* The *incidental* taking of sturgeon would be stopped as their numbers are declining, The economic value of the spring Columbia salmon run is millions for the people of this state. The most press-ing problem we have is a duty to preserve some of our natural heritage for future generations. Our children and grandchildren have a right, and we are duty bound to preserve this resource for their use. The Columbia spring chinook is the most biteable fishery, and provides more recreation to the citizens of Oregon than any other segment of the salmon fishery. The close location of this fishery to the major population centers provides easy access for the fishing public. Recreation is vital to the area, and provides heavy economic income to moorages, motels, hotels, boat builders, motor sales, restaurants and numerous other businesses. The Oregon Department of Fish and Wildlife obtains a large share of its revenue from license and salmon tag sales. The gillnet fishery is a wasteful fishery and should be stopped. There is no quick fix for our salmon problems, but you have *a duty* to your children to try to protect declining runs.

Vote Yes on Measure 8

(This information is furnished by Oscar Thomsen, President, Oregon Division, Izaak Walton League of America.) . . .

In a professional capacity as Director of the Northwest Resource Information Center, President of Chinook Northwest Inc., and as a delegate to the Salmon Summit representing a broad coalition of Idaho conservation and environmental groups, I have spent 25 years fighting to protect Columbia River salmon and steelhead. Ballot Measure #8 is a politically divisive, anti-commercial fishing measure cloaked in fish conservation clothing. If passed, it will not restore salmon listed under the Endangered Species Act. It will only compound the damage to people and communities already victimized by the real fish killers, the Army Corps of Engineers and the Bonneville Power Administration.

(This information furnished by Ed Chaney, Director, Northwest Resource Information Center, Eagle, Idaho.)

Oregon Secretary of State, *Voters' Pamphlet* (Salem, 1992), 86, 88, 90.

Commentary

Is THERE MUCH difference in the intent of the 1908 and 1992 ballot measure statements? In 1908 both ballot measures passed, effectively shutting down the salmon fishery in Oregon by eliminating gillnetting, which was ineffective during the required daylight hours, and all the upriver fish wheels. Economic and jurisdictional concerns did not allow the fishery to be shut down for long. Those fishing from Washington were not covered under the Oregon laws. Oregon fishers argued that because of this the conservation intent of the laws could not be met, so they too should be allowed to fish. The courts agreed, and fishing continued.

The economic and ecological issues persisted in the 1992 ballot measure—economic value in the millions, the desire to protect spawners, and the belief that eliminating one group would solve the problem. Many of the problems facing the salmon fishery today were anticipated almost a century ago. For example, R. D. Hume warned of the impacts of dams in his 1908 article, as did Livingston Stone a decade earlier. Miller Freeman cautioned about too much dependence on hatcheries in the early 1900s. The Urban and Rural Lands Committee of the Pacific Northwest River Basins Commission asked whether the region could continue to grow without damaging its environment. Inadequate knowledge restricted actions in all periods. Management regulations were always behind what was needed to conserve threatened salmon runs.

Perhaps it is time to recognize that knowledge has never been adequate for crafting a scientific solution. Nor have people come to sufficient consensus to agree on a political solution. Ballot measures and the will of the people show no greater success than scientists and politicians. The system in which salmon live is complex, multijurisdictional, and influenced by events beyond local control.

Cassandras claim that new technologies are ruining life as we know it. Cornucopians claim we can have it all. Experience shows we face a future we cannot predict. Salmon and humans will coexist only as long as they can coevolve.

Each day fishers and farmers, potters and professors, writers and welders, home builders and the homeless try to maintain and improve their situations. Some days they achieve more than others, but on the whole, the ten-thousand-year human experiment has yielded more people who live longer, have more material goods, worry more about the future, revisit the past more often, and still do not know enough about the complexities of nature to subject her to their will.

Salmon have returned through thousands of life cycles. At times landslides, drought, and fire have blocked their passage. At other times nets, dams, pollution, and lack of water prevented salmon from reaching the spawning grounds. Our quest to learn enough to control salmon through their life cycle continues. Perhaps, now and then, reflection is as important as active research and restoration.

—Courtland L. Smith

INVISIBLE PARKS FOR NORTHWEST SALMON: NOWHERE TO RUN

Document:	**A National Salmon Park**
Author:	Livingston Stone, agent of the U.S. Fish Commission in the Northwest
Year:	1892
Description:	An essay written at the end of the nineteenth century calls for establishment of a salmon park.

I WILL SAY from my personal knowledge that not only is every contrivance employed that human ingenuity can devise to destroy the salmon of our West coast rivers, but more surely destructive, more fatal than all is the slow but inexorable march of those destroying agencies of human progress, before which the salmon must surely disappear as did the buffalo of the plains and the Indian of California. The helpless salmon's life is gripped between these two forces—the murderous greed of the fishermen and the white man's advancing civilization—and what hope is there for the salmon in the end? Protective laws and artificial breeding are able to hold the first in check, but nothing can stop the last.

To substantiate this statement, which may seem exaggerated, let me inquire what it was that destroyed the salmon of the Hudson, the Connecticut, the Merrimac and the various smaller rivers of New England, where they used to be exceedingly abundant? It was not overfishing that did it. If the excessive fishing had been all there was to contend with, a few simple laws would have been sufficient to preserve some remnants, at least, of the race. It was not the fishing, it was the growth of the country, as it is commonly called, the increase of the population, necessarily bringing with it the development of the various industries by which communities live and become prosperous. It was the mills, the dams, the steamboats, the manufacturers injurious to the water, and similar causes, which, first making the streams more and more uninhabitable for the salmon, finally exterminated them altogether. In short, it was the growth of the country and not the fishing which really set a bound to the habitations of the salmon on the Atlantic coast. . . .

But now the question comes up, "Will not protective laws and artificial breeding make the salmon secure enough?" My answer is that good laws and artificial breeding will do a good deal toward it, but not enough. Good laws can prevent overfishing, but no laws can arrest the encroachments on the salmon rivers of increasing populations and their consequent fatal results to the salmon. No laws could possibly have been enacted which for instance would have stopped the manufacturing enterprises on the Connecticut, or the vast water traffic of the great metropolis at the mouth of the Hudson which doubtless drove the salmon out of these rivers. Protective laws may regulate the salmon fishing of the Sacramento, but no laws can stop the mining, the logging and the railroad building that are destroying the spawning grounds of the tributaries of the Sacramento. It is not in the power of law enactments to save the salmon from all their dangers.

Artificial breeding can do a great deal, and has done a great deal, but it cannot be relied upon for a certainty. . . .

We must come to the conclusion then that even with the help and support of protective laws and artificial breeding, our salmon, like the buffalo of thirty years ago, are not safe. The destroying agencies of advancing civilization drove the buffalo to the last ditch, so to speak, and then the last survivors, or almost the last, were slain. They were obliged from sheer necessity to come to feed where from all directions the hand of man was raised against them. Whether they turned to the north or to the south, to the east or to the west, they went to their certain death, and in an incredibly short space of time they practically disappeared.

The story of our salmon is analogous. They are obliged to come inland to breed. They are compelled from sheer necessity to come up the rivers into the very midst of their human enemies. They cannot stay in the ocean like other fishes of the sea, where they are safe from the hand of man, but they must necessarily come, one might say, into his very grasp, and, like the buffalo, whether they turn to the north, south, east or west, they go into the very jaws of death; for what hope is there for a salmon to escape after he has entered a river, if man chooses to employ his most effective agencies for his capture? There is none. The salmon is doomed. There is no alter [sic] of refuge for the salmon in this country any more than there was for the buffalo.

Ought not something be done, then? Ought this state of things to continue? . . .

The locality which the writer has in mind is an Island in the North Pacific about 750 miles nearly due west of Sitka. Its name is Afognak, and it is the northernmost of the two largest islands of the group, called the Kadiak Islands. It lies just north of latitude 58° and between 152° and 153° west longitude. It is a small island, probably not over fifty miles across at its widest part, but there are several streams flowing from various points of the island to the surrounding ocean, and at the proper season contain salmon innumerable. . . .

The writer, however, would not urge the claims of Afognak or any other place to this distinction as against those of any locality that may be found to be better fitted for it. This island has been brought forward merely as showing that one place at least is known that would answer the purposes of a salmon park. There are doubtless others in our Alaskan possessions. There are possibly better ones. If a better place can be found, let us take it. If not, let us take Afognak Island; but at all events let some place be selected and set aside by the authority of the National Government. If not Afognak Island, let it be some other place. Provide some refuge for the salmon, and provide it quickly, before complications arise which may make it impracticable, or at least very difficult. Now is the time. Delays are dangerous. Some unforeseen difficulties may come up which we do not dream of now, any more than we did a few years ago of logging on the Clackamas, or railroad building on the upper Sacramento.

If we procrastinate and put off our rescuing mission too long, it may be too late to do any good. After the rivers are ruined and the salmon are gone they cannot be reclaimed. . . .

Consider for a moment what the salmon has done for us, and then think how mercilessly we have treated him. Our salmon has been to us a source of national revenue, enjoyment and pride, and what return have we meted out to him? He has been hunted pitilessly with hooks and spears, with all kinds of nets and pounds, with wheels and guns and dynamite, and there is not a cubic foot of water in the whole country where he can rest in safety.

Livingston Stone. 1892. "A National Salmon Park," *Transactions of the American Fisheries Society* (New York: D. S. Walton, 1892), 150-51, 154-57, 160-62.

Document:	**The Program for Anadromous Fishes of the Columbia**
Author:	Ross Leffler, Director of the U.S. Fish and Wildlife Service
Year:	1959
Description:	This article contemplates dedicating certain areas of the Columbia Basin to salmon conservation and development.

ONE OF THE GREATEST challenges facing the conservationist today is the preservation of the salmon and steelhead runs of the Columbia River. When I say "preservation" I mean the protection and even enhancement of the resource for perpetual use.

I believe the problem of preserving this fishery is unique on a national basis in that a very broad segment of our population and economy is involved. Problems and programs range from local to international in significance.

An example of the international aspect here is the Canadian proposal to divert the upper Columbia into the Fraser River. The interstate aspect is reflected in the coordinated regulation of the commercial fishery on the Columbia River through an interstate compact. . . .

In any event, it is clearly obvious to everyone in the fish and wildlife conservation field at the national level that the competition for water and related land resources between fish and wildlife and adverse developments for power, flood control and agriculture is keener in the Columbia River Basin than anywhere else in the Nation with the possible exception of the waterfowl production areas of the Northern prairie States. It is right and proper, therefore, that a large share of the Nation's investment in fish and wildlife conservation should be—and is—made in the Columbia River Basin. Given enough money, enough brains, enough of the spirit of cooperation among the agencies involved, and—most important of all, right now—enough time, we ought to be able to develop ways and means of preserving the living fishery resource of the Columbia River Basin, and still develop the river for the power, the flood control and the irrigation needs of the region. But short us on any one of these essential elements—money, brains, cooperation, or time—and needless destruction of resources is bound to result. . . .

I would like to leave with you also the thought that we will not have licked the fishery problem simply by solving the fish passage problem. It will be of little avail to pass the salmon and steelhead without being assured of means of maintaining essential spawning and rearing conditions, through either natural or artificial methods, for perpetuation of the resource.

I would also like to touch on another subject. This is something of which I spoke at your meeting in Glenwood Springs, Colorado, in 1957, when speaking on the subject "Can Western Wildlife Survive Today's Demands?" At that time I said, "Let's follow through with well-made plans for staking out appropriate areas of both land and water all over the west as being primarily suited for fish and wildlife—as being of more value for fish and wildlife than for any other purpose." I believe it is especially critical here on the Columbia River that we stake out a claim for an anadromous fish sanctuary in the Snake River basin. I am not prepared to say how extensive it should be, but certainly it should include the Salmon River in Idaho and parts, if not all, of such rivers as the Clearwater, the Grande Ronde, and the Imnaha. These rivers, particularly the Salmon, are the mainstay of the spring chinook and summer steelhead runs.

Last October, Secretary of the Interior Fred A. Seaton made a clear statement of policy on the critical Middle Snake River Area of the Columbia River Basin which has warmed the hearts of all fish and wildlife conservationists. Secretary Seaton called for deferment in the planning and development of high dams in the Middle Snake River Area, below the mouth of the Imnaha, pending a solution to the problem of fish passage and the preservation of the fishery value in connection with this type of river development. . . .

Nevertheless, we in the fishery conservation field must face up to the fact that we are expected by the people of the nation to come up with a satisfactory solution and that we cannot delay needed water resource development indefinitely or forever.

At the same time, we should not shy away from a vigorous advocacy of a share of the water resources pie for fish and wildlife conservation and development. If, in the end, we conclude that there cannot be any satisfactory solution to fish passage over high dams in important fish production streams, we can and should forthrightly declare that certain river basins of the Pacific Northwest should be dedicated to the conservation and development of fish and wildlife resources as their highest and best use. Certainly the recreational and commercial interests who depend on the fishery resources in the Columbia River have just as much right to an equitable share of the water resources of the Columbia as those interests who depend on the further development of the water resources for power and irrigation.

Ross L. Leffler. "The Program of the U.S. Fish and Wildlife Service for the Anadromous Fishes of the Columbia River," *Oregon State Game Commission Bulletin* (October 1959): 3, 6, 7.

Document:	**Forest Ecosystem Management**
Authors:	Forest Ecosystem Management Team
Year:	1993
Description:	The scientists who advised President Clinton on his 1993 Northwest forest plan propose refuges for salmon as a central element of their strategy to protect and restore the fish.

Key Watersheds

REFUGIA, OR DESIGNATED AREAS providing high quality habitat, either currently or in the future, are a cornerstone of most species conservation strategies. Although fragmented areas of suitable habitat may be important, Moyle and Sato (1991) argue that to recover aquatic species, refugia should be focused at a watershed scale. Naiman et al. (1992), Sheldon (1988) and Williams et al. (1989) noted that past attempts to recover fish populations were unsuccessful because the problem was not approached from a watershed perspective.

A system of Key Watersheds that serves as refugia is crucial for maintaining and recovering habitat for at-risk stocks of anadromous salmonids and resident fish species, particularly in the short term. These refugia will include areas of good habitat as well as areas of degraded habitat. Areas presently in good condition serve as anchors for the potential recovery of depressed stocks. Those of lower quality habitat should have a high potential for restoration and will become future sources of good habitat with the implementation of a comprehensive restoration program. . . .

Johnson et al. (1991) identified a network of Key Watersheds located on U.S. National Forest lands throughout the range of the northern spotted owl. These watersheds contain at-risk fish species and stocks and either good habitat, or if habitat is in a degraded

state, have a high restoration potential (Reeves and Sedell 1992).
U.S. Forest Service fish biologists have since deleted some watersheds identified by Johnson et al. (1991) and added others as new
information was incorporated and an overall design developed.
Watersheds on Bureau of Land Management land have also been
included as Key Watersheds. . . . A total of 162 Key Watersheds were
designated that cover 8.7 million acres or approximately one third
of the federal land within the range of the northern spotted
owl. . . . Option 7 is the only option for which Key Watersheds are
not designated.

The conservation strategy proposed here uses two designations
for Key Watersheds: Tier 1 and Tier 2. Tier 1 Key Watersheds are
specifically selected for directly contributing to conservation of
habitat for at-risk anadromous salmonids, bull trout and resident
fish species. The network of 139 Tier 1 Key Watersheds ensures that
refugia are widely distributed across the landscape. Twenty-three
Tier 2 Key Watersheds were identified. These may not contain at-
risk fish stocks, but were selected as important sources of high
quality water.

Because Key Watersheds maintain the best of what is left and
have the highest potential for restoration, they are given special
consideration.

Bibliography

Johnson, K. N.; Franklin, J. F.; Thomas, J. W.; Gordon, J. 1991. Alternatives
for management of late-successional forests of the Pacific Northwest. A
report to the Agriculture Committee and the Merchant Marine Committee of the U.S. House of Representatives. 59 p.

Moyle, P. B.; Sato, G. M. 1991. On the design of preserves to protect native
fishes. In: Minckley, W.L.; Deacon, J.E., eds. Battle against extinction:
native fish management in the American west. Tucson, Arizona: University of Arizona Press. 155-169.

Naiman, R. J.: Beechie, T. J.; Benda, L. E.; Berg, D. R.; Bisson, P.A.;
MacDonald, L. H.; O'Connor, M. D.; Olson, P. L.; Steel, E. A. 1992.
Fundamental elements of ecologically healthy watersheds in the Pacific
Northwest coastal ecoregion. In: Naiman, R. J., ed. Watershed manage-
ment: balancing sustainability and environmental change. New York,
NY: Springer-Verlag. 127-188.

Reeves, G. H.; Sedell, J. R. 1992. An ecosystem approach to the conservation and management of freshwater habitat for anadromous salmonids
in the Pacific Northwest. Proceedings of the 57th North American
Wildlife and Natural Resources Conference: 408-415.

Sheldon, A. I. 1988. Conservation of stream fishes: patterns of diversity,
rarity, and risk. Conservation Biology. 2:149-156.

Williams, J. E.; Johnson, J. E.; Hendrickson, D. A.; Conreras-Balderas, S.;
    Williams, J. D.; Navarro-Mendoza, M.; McAllister, D. E.; Bacon, J. E.
    1989. Fishes of North America endangered, threatened, and of special
    concern. Fisheries. 14(6):2-20.

> U.S. Department of Agriculture, U.S. Department of the
> Interior, U.S. Department of Commerce, Environmental
> Protection Agency, *Forest Ecosystem Management: An Ecological,
> Economic, and Social Assessment. Report of the Forest Ecosystem
> Management Assessment Team* (1993), V-46.

Document:	**Memo to Thomas E. Lovejoy, Smithsonian Institution**
Authors:	Willa Nehlsen and five other scientists
Year:	1994
Description:	This memo from a group of prominent fisheries biologists and ecologists supports the protection of certain key watersheds to benefit salmon.

From: Willa Nehlsen, Salmon Recovery Project Director, Pacific
Rivers Council

James R. Karr, Director, Institute of Environmental
Studies, Professor of Zoology and Fisheries,
University of Washington

Judy Meyer, Professor of Ecology, University of Georgia

Christopher A. Frissell, Research Assistant Professor,
Flathead Lake Biological Station, University of
Montana, Research Associate, Dept of Fisheries and
Wildlife, Oregon State University

Jack A. Stanford, Jessie M. Bierman Professor of Ecology,
University of Montana

To: Dr. Thomas E. Lovejoy, Assistant Secretary, Smithsonian
Institute, Washington, DC 20560

Dear Dr. Lovejoy:

THANK YOU for the opportunity to express our views on the scientific
basis for strengthening the President's plan for owl forests. From the
perspective of aquatic biodiversity and species recovery the central

weakness in the President's plan is the failure to adequately protect the health of existing aquatic refugia.

In keeping with sound conservation, the FEMAT Aquatic Conservation Strategy is predicated on a federal regionwide system of "key watersheds" whose role as refugia is considered "crucial" (FEMAT V-46). We agree with this approach, but suggest that while FEMAT prescribes such refugia, it fails to protect them. For such refugia to be effective over necessarily long recovery times (many decades to centuries) their integrity must be insured both in design and in implementation. The FEMAT preferred alternative does not provide that integrity, indeed it prescribes a rationale for introducing new human disturbance to those refugia. We find that the justification for such new disturbance highly speculative and its application entirely inconsistent with the conservation role of the refugia.

The intact (or more relatively intact) watersheds that form the refuge system are the last best places—they are the default refugia that remain in a highly altered landscape. Although they are disproportionately headwater areas, they are nevertheless the areas where:

1) land use, modification of flows, and non-native species have had the least impacts on the native biota;

2) connectivity is high;

3) the elements (genes, species, assemblages) and the processes (mutation/recombination, population demography, nutrient cycling) that are essential to the maintenance of these ecosystems are present, in contrast to the situation in lower reaches of the same systems; and

4) ecosystem function and habitat integrity are most likely to survive the next large magnitude flood.

Biotic recovery from disturbance is highly correlated with the presence of refugia, and inversely correlated with the distance to those refuges. A robust, secure, and well-distributed refugial system will be needed for a considerable span of time (many decades to centuries), even if the slow process of watershed recovery begins elsewhere promptly.

The FEMAT correctly observes that "stewardship of aquatic resources has the highest likelihood of protecting biological diversity and productivity when land use activities do not substantially alter the natural disturbance regime to which these organisms are adapted" (FEMAT V-29). We agree, but it is important to recognize that the vast majority of aquatic ecosystems are already operating under disturbance regimes permanently or persistently altered by human activities. Furthermore, under the preferred alternative the natural disturbance regime will not in fact be the basis of management even in the proposed key watershed refugia. Natural disturbance regimes are certain to be accelerated by past and continuing incursion of road construction and logging activities in these generally steep and very sensitive watersheds.

> Willa Nehlsen et al., memo to Thomas E. Lovejoy (March 1994, email copy).

Commentary

 FOR THE SALMON of the Pacific Northwest, 1892 could have been a momentous year. On the Columbia River and throughout the Northwest the salmon were contributing hugely to the material well-being of people. Approximately 3.2 million salmon and steelhead—weighing more than fifteen thousand tons—were caught on the Columbia River alone.[1] This was the largest catch until that time and the second largest ever.

The natural abundance of salmon had created wealth for some and employment for many. Astoria, for instance, was the second-largest city in Oregon in the 1890s, thanks mainly to the eleven salmon canneries in town and along the river nearby. So enormous was the catch of the region's salmon that knowledgeable observers were already speaking openly about the need to ensure the continued productivity of the species. Sixteen years earlier, in 1876, the first fish hatchery had been built on Oregon's Clackamas River, funded by cannery owners concerned about maintaining the supply of fish for harvest.

In 1892, Livingston Stone made the momentous suggestion that even as the salmon were providing for people, so people ought to provide for salmon if they wanted to ensure the fish's survival in the Northwest. Stone proposed the establishment of a national park for salmon.

Stone was no inexperienced conservationist when he made the proposal. fifty-seven years old, he had a long history of involvement with the biology and breeding of trout and salmon. Born in Massachusetts and educated at Harvard, Stone was one of the gentlemen-scientists who founded the American Fisheries Society in 1872. At the time, this professional society was dominated by proponents of aquaculture, "fish culture," as it was called. Stone had established a trout-breeding station in New Hampshire in 1866. In 1872 he was named a deputy commissioner of the newly formed U.S. Fish Commission, and that year he came west to develop hatcheries for salmon and conduct investigations of salmon fisheries.[2]

By 1892 his experience with these fisheries and his knowledge of the status of salmon from California to Alaska prompted him to present his case for a salmon park. He had seen the giant fish wheels on the Columbia River that were capable of catching thousands of fish a day. He had seen the fleet of fishing boats in San Francisco and Astoria. He had visited canneries on the Sacramento River, on the Columbia, and in Alaska, where tons of fish could be processed daily and where what couldn't be processed in time was simply wasted.

Stone's proposal was made at the annual meeting of the American Fisheries Society in New York City. He said that society was "destroying" the salmon, and not only through overfishing. Stone had the tragic foresight to recognize that "the white man's advancing civilization," in which all the Northwest settlers were implicated, posed the greatest threat. "What hope is there for salmon in the end?" he asked.

Or perhaps it was not so much foresight as a dry-eyed assessment of what had already occurred in his native New England.

> It was not the fishing, it was . . . the increase of the population, necessarily bringing with it the development of the various industries by which communities live and become prosperous.[3]

Stone had spent his adult years experimenting with, and to a degree succeeding in, artificially breeding salmon. Yet in his call for a salmon park, he recognized that "artificial breeding . . . cannot be relied upon for a certainty."[4]

The conclusion was, to him, inescapable. Drawing inspiration from the first national parks—Yellowstone (1872), the Adirondacks (1885), and Yosemite (1890)—Stone proposed that an island that he had visited off the central coast of Alaska would make an ideal salmon park. He told his New York listeners about the wonderful abundance of six species of salmon on Afognak Island:

> In 1889, the salmon was so thick in the streams that it was absolutely necessary in fording them to kick the salmon out of the way to avoid stumbling over them. I know that this story is an old salmon chestnut, but it . . . can be easily believed when it is remembered that 153,000 salmon were caught in one day at the mouth of the Karluk, which is a river only 60 ft. wide where it empties into the ocean.[5]

Although the salmon were present on Afognak "in as great numbers as could be wished," Stone was not committed to the island location itself but to the concept. As a native of New England, he was highly conscious of the need to act decisively and quickly. "After the rivers are ruined and the salmon are gone they cannot be reclaimed," he wrote.

Stone had been a Unitarian minister in Detroit and Philadelphia during the Civil War, and his skill as a preacher quite likely contributed to making converts to his cause. *Forest and Stream* magazine helped popularize his idea by reprinting the speech, and then quite suddenly, in December 1892, President Benjamin Harrison issued an executive order, proclaiming the Afognak Forest and Fish Culture Reserve. This was the first use of the presidential privilege to establish such a reserve, granted earlier that year in the Forest Reserve Act.[6]

The act had two interesting provisions relating to Alaska. One provided for sale of up to 160 acres of land at $2.50 per acre for individuals who planned to build salmon canneries. The other—perhaps in some effort to balance this first provision—allowed the U.S. Commission of Fish and Fisheries to establish fish culture stations on Kodiak and Afognak islands. A report of the commission, published in 1892, and to which Stone had contributed, advocated a hatchery there.[7] Perhaps Stone's speech to the American Fisheries Society meeting and the reprint in the magazine were part of a deliberate strategy. Fifteen years after the establishment of the reserve, in 1907, a salmon hatchery was built in the Afognak Fish Culture Reserve by the U.S. Fish Commission.

Despite the apparent success with the establishment of the park in Alaska, Stone's broader concerns about the encroachments of "civilization" and the impending demise of the salmon failed to win any greater protection south of Alaska. In hindsight, it might be argued that Stone made a tactical error by singling out an island in Alaska, if preserving salmon in the Columbia and Snake river basin or along the Northwest coast had also been his goal. This is probably unfair to him. In his proposal for the salmon park, it is clear that he does not advocate one particular location. Moreover, he seems to have been either ignorant of or unconcerned about the fact that salmon of the same species from widely different locations (such as Alaska and Idaho) will not transplant and establish themselves successfully. The scientific community was still decades away from understanding the differences between locally adapted populations of salmon. Nevertheless, Stone might have surmised that preserving salmon in Alaska was not a guarantee of preserving them elsewhere. After all, the attempts by him and his colleagues to establish transplanted Pacific salmon into East Coast streams consistently failed, as a 1906 Report of the U.S. Commissioner of Fisheries admitted.[8]

An ironic footnote here is that sockeye salmon from the Afognak hatchery were used in an attempt to restore decimated runs of the species at Lake Quinault following World War I. These sockeye of the Olympic peninsula were one of the most celebrated salmon populations south of Canada. The Alaskan fish, however, interbred with remaining wild-spawning Quinault fish, reducing their genetic fitness. In the hatchery, meanwhile, the Alaskan sockeye introduced a virulent fish virus, IHN, that infected the Washington stock, further depleting its numbers.[9]

All such qualifications aside, Stone probably thought that preserving salmon on Afognak was the best strategy for ensuring the survival of the fish in the Northwest. The Alaskan island was remote, largely uninhabited, and government owned:

> No complications now exist or can come up in the future, in regard to land titles in this island. The United States Government owns the land already like the rest of Alaska . . . (and) can set aside the island for any purpose whatever.

Stone's self-assured statement about island management later proved false. In the 1990s Afognak is in state, tribal, and private hands.[10]

Meanwhile, a salmon park along the lines presented by Stone has never been established in the Northwest. The idea of a salmon refuge has, however, continued to spark the thinking of salmon conservationists. In 1959, the director of the U.S. Fish and Wildlife Service in the Eisenhower administration, Ross Leffler, revived the idea. In a speech given at a meeting of the Western Association of State Game and Fish Commissioners, in Portland, Leffler proposed establishing an "anadromous fish sanctuary in the Snake River basin."

Like Stone before him, Leffler was no stereotypical dewy-eyed environmentalist when he made the proposal. Seventy-four years old, a former executive with Carnegie Steel, and a past national director of the Izaak Walton League, Leffler brought a lifetime of perspective in business and conservation to his presentation. He recognized that "adverse developments for power, flood control, and agriculture" in the Columbia River Basin made a fish refuge necessary.[11]

Although Leffler specifically mentioned a sanctuary that would "include the Salmon River in Idaho and parts, if not all, of such rivers as the Clearwater, the Grande Ronde and the Imnaha," because they were "the mainstay of the spring chinook and summer steelhead runs," he did not limit his agenda to those specific streams or those fish. If the problems of fish passage through the Columbia River dams could not be solved, he was unequivocal that "certain river basins of the Pacific Northwest should be dedicated to the conservation and development of fish and wildlife resources as their highest and best use."

Leffler's sanctuary idea was never implemented. Perhaps the problem was lack of time: the Eisenhower administration left office eighteen months after Leffler made the speech. Perhaps the problem was lack of a workable administrative framework: the diverse jurisdictions—local, state, federal, tribal—have always made salmon management problematic. The problems would no doubt only be compounded in making a preserve.

Nevertheless, the idea of creating a refuge for salmon on public lands has continued to occupy the planning of imaginative people in natural resources management. In 1993 government scientists prepared a report for the Clinton administration outlining options for the management of old-growth forest ecosystems within the range of the northern spotted owl. This report of the Forest Ecosystem Management Assessment team, led by Jack Ward Thomas, developed an "Aquatic Conservation Strategy" based on "key watersheds" that would act as refuges ("refugia") for salmon and other forest species. The scientists said:

> A system of Key Watersheds that serves as refugia is crucial for maintaining and recovering habitat for at-risk stocks of anadromous salmonids and resident fish species.[12]

However, the final version of the Clinton plan for these federal old-growth forests, released in April 1994, fell short of the scientists' recommendation. Key watersheds were part of the plan, but they were not refuges as such. Some logging would be permitted in these watersheds as would new road building. Many fish biologists and conservationists complained. Both road building and logging had long been implicated in the demise of salmon populations. More than one hundred years had passed since Livingston Stone had issued his first plea for a salmon refuge. Apparently, society was not ready yet.

—**Joseph Cone**

Notes

1. A. T. Pruter, "Commercial Fisheries of the Columbia River and Adjacent Ocean Waters," *Fishery Industrial Research* 3 (1966): 17-68, cited in Anthony Netboy, *The Columbia River Salmon and Steelhead Trout: Their Fight for Survival* (Seattle: Univ. of Washington Press, 1980), 22.
2. *Who Was Who in America,* vol. 1 (Chicago: A. N. Marquis, 1943), 1193.
3. Stone, 150.
4. Stone, 155.
5. Stone, 158.
6. Diane Zoslowsky and the Wilderness Society, *These American Lands* (New York: Holt, 1906), 255.
7. Lawrence W. Rakestraw, *A History of the United States Forest Service in Alaska* (Anchorage: Alaska Historical Commission, 1981), 10.
8. Joel W. Hedgpeth, "Livingston Stone and Fish Culture in California," *California Fish and Game* 27, no. 3 (1941): 141.
9. Bruce Brown, *Mountain in the Clouds* (New York: Simon and Schuster, 1982), 36.
10. In the 1930s, Afognak became part of the Chugach National Forest, and after Alaska was made a state in 1959, the salmon of the island became the responsibility of the Alaska Department of Fish and Game (ADFG). Then, as part of the Alaska Lands Act of 1980, much of the island ownership reverted to Native people. As of 1994, a private company, the Kodiak Regional Aquaculture Association, was managing a salmon hatchery on the island.

   According to Kevin Brennan, a biologist with the ADFG (letter to author, 1 July 1994), the state agency has "regularly been able to achieve escapement goals for most systems." However, "some areas [runs] are of concern," according to Brennan. "There are also numerous projects underway to supplement the wild stock production of Afognak, including stocking of lakes, fertilization of lakes to boost production, and of course the production of sockeye, pink, chum, and coho salmon at the Kitoi Bay Hatchery."
11. Ross L. Leffler, "The Program of the U.S. Fish and Wildlife Service for the Anadromous Fishes of the Columbia River," *Oregon State Game Commission Bulletin* (October 1959): 6.
12. U.S. Department of Agriculture, U.S. Department of the Interior, U.S. Department of Commerce, Environmental Protection Agency, *Forest Ecosystem Management: An Ecological, Economic, and Social Assessment. Report of the Forest Ecosystem Management Assessment Team* (1993), V-46.

VI. Conclusion

RIVER OF CHANGE:
SALMON, TIME, AND CRISIS
ON THE COLUMBIA RIVER

William L. Lang

"Political crises are moral crises." [Octavio Paz, 1970]

 THE SALMON CRISIS in the Pacific Northwest has generated an image of the unthinkable—a Columbia River without salmon. As long as human memory, salmon have been the quintessential symbol of life and fecundity in the Columbia River Basin, where thousands of miles of streams have provided anadromous salmon spawning beds for millions of years. The fish annually ran upstream millions strong after a multi-year transit in ocean waters as distant from the Columbia River as the Aleutian Islands. But just over a century ago the number of returning salmon began declining until some of the remaining wild species dropped to a nearly unsustainable number. The government's listing of three salmon runs under the terms of the Endangered Species Act in 1991-92 as either "threatened" or "endangered" publicly confirmed what specialists had known for years: Columbia River Basin salmon species could become extinct. By 1994, the three Snake River salmon runs had been listed as "endangered" and the federal government had halted commercial fishing for two species on the Columbia. In 1995, a U.S. federal court issued an order curtailing ocean salmon fishing in Alaskan waters. The salmon crisis had come to the region's doorstep with suddenness and manifest finality.[1]

These events have produced alarm among Pacific Northwest residents, a sense than an end of sorts is imminent, that something important is in danger, and that things have gone terribly wrong. That is the character of crisis. The word crisis itself communicates immediacy, inescapable reality, a demand for attention. Crises cannot be ignored, and avoiding them suggests a physical impossibility akin to obviating time or dematerializing place. The consequences

---

Previous page: Salmon fishing for sport became a popular pastime early; fresh-caught salmon also supplemented the diets of many Northwest families. 1910 photo.

are just too immense. In the salmon crisis the focus is on how little time remains to alter conditions and what consequences will occur to a territory equal to the size of some European nations. The enormity of those consequences—the loss of salmon in the Columbia-Snake river system—is a disturbance of place that is profoundly distressing and culturally disorienting. We measure time chronogeographically, by making connections between place, observed events, human activities, and natural processes. We understand our places through "repetitive tradition" in human affairs, and we define places as geographies that "denote stability and continuity." In the chronogeography of the Columbia River Basin, the salmon crisis portends a climactic disturbance of relationships and a disassembling of futures, making today unpredictable and tomorrow unacceptable. The character of place, in short, is in crisis now, because a relationship between geography and activities—a relationship as old as human memory—may soon be eclipsed. Time and place have been fractured.[2]

Yet the paradox in all crises, the salmon crisis included, is that they do not explode into reality with the suddenness we perceive. They have gestations and to understand them we must delve into their biographies. The Pacific Northwest salmon crisis has a long and disturbingly consistent biography. Some of the earliest warnings of declining salmon runs, for example, came in the 1880s, a scant two decades after commercial fishing had begun on the lower Columbia. "Nature does not provide against such greed," Frances Fuller Victor alarmingly wrote, "and it is doubtful if art can do it . . . . there is a prospect that the salmon, like the buffalo, may become extinct." But the extended history of this crisis is embedded in the longer history of the river and its people, a history that stretches into the recesses of geologic time.[3]

Salmon grew up in freshwater and adapted to an extended maturity in saltwater about the time the Columbia River settled into its modern course. The river had been born in the throes of violent volcanic wrenchings of the land, the work of plate tectonics and vulcanism. Originally exiting the continent far south of its current mouth, the Columbia flowed from Canadian glaciers south and west to an emerging and westward-expanding continental edge. Some ten to fifteen million years ago, massive lava flows pushed the river into a huge western bend in north central Washington, where it ran along the edge of major faults in a southeastern direction to present-day Wallula Gap. There it pivoted hard west and ran to the tidewater through a 2,000- to 3,000-foot-deep gorge that had been formed by complex faulting, uplifts, and erosion. The Columbia's course had been drawn on the landscape by catastrophes, not subtle corrosive forces, and the final catastrophes in the chain were a series of colossal floods that sluiced ten times the volume of all rivers on earth across central Washington, creating channeled scablands and crashing down the river's gullet, widening and steepening its gorges. In the gorge area, tilted geological anticlines and synclines and numerous land-slides created the river that humans have known for the last twelve thousand years.[4]

The river's catastrophic geological history begat a peculiar salmon geography. The world of Columbia River salmon is shaped like a double-ended funnel, with the basin's fan-shaped drainage on one end and the ocean feeding grounds on the other. Connecting the two funnels are tributary streams and the main stem, where geologic forces created impediments to the salmon's return to its spawning grounds. Those impediments at the Cascades, The Dalles, Celilo Falls, Priest Rapids, and Kettle Falls on the main stem, at Willamette Falls on the Willamette, at falls and rapids on the Deschutes, the White Salmon, Klickitat, Yakima, Spokane and other salmon streams brought native people to the river to glean its riches. For more than ten thousand years, these were profoundly economic places, but they were also cultural places that aboriginal people named for the fish they caught and the trade they conducted there. Those names identified fishing spots, family-claimed locations, the birth places of specific fish, and locales where Coyote had released trapped salmon for use by people. It is a geography that merges people with salmon and does not draw any line between the spiritual and the material.[5]

The symbiotic history of the river, which merges salmon and people, underscores the inseparability of geological, biological, and cultural dimensions on the Columbia. From the oldest archaeological evidence, it is clear that the earliest people here lived in a world dominated by water and focused on fish. The "People of the Salmon," as anthropologist Richard Daugherty has called them, lived along the main stem and tributary streams throughout much of the Columbia River Basin. Although Chinookan speakers on the lower river, mid-Columbia Sahaptins, and upper river Salish spoke languages as distinct as French and Chinese, they shared a larger relationship with the river that shortened and narrowed cultural distances. Coyote stories about salmon, for example, are part of oral tradition all along the river. Each one is different, as Jarold Ramsey has explained, but each "eloquently implies a climate, a landscape, a set of ecological conditions that the Indians have been coming to terms of existence with since the beginning."[6]

Coming to terms with the Columbia was a much swifter process for Euro-Americans. From their first discovery of the river in 1792 by American mariner Robert Gray, whites looked at the river in a much more limited way than did the indigenous population. Euro-Americans reduced all that they saw and experienced into components of their two great engines of historical change: imperialistic acquisition and capitalistic enterprise. The imperial thrust pushed Indian nations away from the river and onto restricted reserves, while the economic impulse led to investment in commercial salmon fishing and the development of steamboat transportation. For the invading groups, including the Oregon Trail emigrants, the Columbia River Valley was an empty and underused landscape, one that should come under the political domination of empire and the economic domination of capitalist development.

This domination cut off Indians from many of their historic relationships with the Columbia, even though some continued to take fish at Celilo, Kettle Falls, and other prime locations. Columbia River Indians suffered a fundamental altering of their river world. The changes delineated a deep and indelible alteration in a millennia of relationships between human communities and the river. In effect, this first salmon crisis on the Columbia was a cultural crisis that affected two populations. The Indians, who had long taken great numbers of salmon, no longer constituted the important fishing population. They were replaced by industrial fishers and canners, the spectacular growth in whose numbers during the 1860s and 1870s made them the important force on the river. Yet both populations suffered a sharp decline in salmon catch: the Indians because they had been decimated by new pathogens and pressured into abandoning their river, and, soon, the whites because they had overfished the river and faced much diminished harvests. For the Indians, there was no recourse. For the whites, however, there was science and investment in the region's first salmon hatcheries in 1877.[7]

These were the first currents flowing toward today's salmon crisis. During the century beginning in 1870, the economic changes wrought by the invading whites affected the river and its environment more profoundly than even removal and relocation had affected Columbia River Indian tribes. In essence, the new occupiers and users of the Columbia laid claim to the river itself and introduced new ways of valuing it, principally by defining it as a capitalistic causeway and an unfettered creator of wealth. Evidence for this new viewpoint appeared early on, when engineers began "improving" the river by building a jetty at its mouth, digging boat channels, and finally cutting canals around instream obstructions. New relationships were created on the river, first by making the river a place of work and making its people workers, and then by altering the connections between places. Working the river meant moving goods on steamboats during the nineteenth century and towboats during the twentieth. It has meant the development of industrial fishing and the production of kilowatts.[8]

The relationships of place were rearranged. The historic fishing grounds on the Columbia did not disappear, but the fishing places multiplied. In the estuary, where gillnetters and horse seiners took millions of fish, and upriver, where the ubiquitous and gluttonous fish wheels effortlessly scooped salmon out of their migratory channels, industrial salmon fishers made the Columbia a massive gleaning place. By extending and exponentially increasing the salmon harvest, including the building of dozens of canneries along the lower river, the new fishing culture both increased salmon wealth and spread its influence well beyond the Columbia. Landings of chinook salmon, for example, escalated from 4.1 million pounds in 1870 to more than 30 million pounds in 1920, while the canneries packed a high of 579,000 cases in 1885 and consistently more than 300,000 a year from 1880 to 1920. While this steep increase in salmon harvest was enriching fishing communities along the lower river, salmon runs at Celilo, Kettle Falls, and other traditional native fishing sites were steadily declining. The richness of salmon fishing no longer resided at the traditional sites; the whole river glistened with silver-sided wealth. The change in the river's salmon geography was profound. Through its salmon, a portion of the river's wealth flowed away from local places toward a generalized national and even international marketplace. The gravitational pull of the market exerted great force on the Columbia, transforming it from many places into one place.[9]

Even more profoundly, the new economics on the Columbia changed the relative economic distance between places. As environmental ethicist Colin Duncan has explained, the commodification of nature and its wealth in the modern era has effectively homogenized space by making economies unidimensional, by evaluating all investments on the same scale. On the Columbia, this means that income realized from transporting goods in boats and from hauling out salmon are equal. The details, operations, relationships, and consequences of these distinctive activities are irrelevant. This calculus makes all places on the river potentially equivalent. It rationalizes the river's world and marginalizes locality. In such a world, power shifts from the periphery to a powerful and controlling center and the specifics of place are both diminished and devalued. Even within the place-specific fishing world on the Columbia—where the gillnetter's favorite "drifts" on the lower river and the fish wheel placement in a shoreline channel make the difference between success and failure—all fishing places were reduced to pounds of salmon delivered to market. Fish taken at Kettle Falls, at the Seufert's No. 5 fish wheel near The Dalles, and at the Gut Drift near Skamokawa were equated only by species and weight. Where they were caught made no difference.[10]

Nowhere on the river were these changes more graphically realized than on the middle Columbia, the stretch between Bonneville and the mouth of the Snake River. Historically this portion of the Columbia had been the focus of the most site-specific activity on the entire main stem. Nineteenth-century entrepreneurs recognized this stretch of the river as a natural sea-level causeway, one they could capitalize. The Oregon Steam Navigation Company, Portland's transportation combine, did just that by dominating river transit through control of steamboats and river portages at the Cascades and The Dalles. The funneling of natural resource products from the interior downriver to Portland quickly made that city the preeminent economic place in the region and reallocated power in the Columbia River Basin. The effect was to alter economic space by connecting the lower river first with the distant gold-producing areas in Idaho and Montana and later with the wheat-producing regions on the Columbia Plateau in eastern Oregon and Washington. The river became a conduit for the flow of capital throughout the region.[11]

By the early twentieth century, however, fortune had begun to turn on Portland, putting it in unfavorable competition with wheat marketers in Puget Sound and the Great Lakes. The river's place and its power suddenly seemed fickle, even perfidious. The Columbia needed an improvement on nature, Portland capitalists argued, to make river transportation more efficient. Wheat shippers and other freighters advocated what they called an "open river," a Columbia free of rapids and other impediments to smooth transit from the interior to the coast. The Columbia needed improvement to guarantee its commercial future, the agents of change harped, because it was not malleable enough to meet the demands of a capricious market. The first call for government-funded engineering had come as early as 1846, two years before Oregon became a territory. By the mid-1860s, the Oregon Steam Navigation Company's John C. Ainsworth had argued strenuously that the U.S. Army Corps of Engineers should blast away the rapids and large obstructions on the river above Celilo. By the late 1870s, Portland's business community had secured congressional approval for a canal and lock at the Cascades, which the engineers completed in 1896. In 1915, a second canal—a 9-mile, 8-foot-deep ditch with three locks—circumvented the narrow chutes at The Dalles and the sharp drop at Celilo. The improvers had achieved their goal: an "open

The Celilo Canal, built in 1915 and shown in this 1920s photo, was eclipsed by rail and highway as a means of moving goods downriver. But this second Columbia canal firmly established the practice of engineering the river to benefit upriver interests.

river" from tidewater through the Gorge to the upper stretches of the middle Columbia.[12]

The canalization projects promised great economic rewards, but the reality fell far short of the ambitions. The efficiencies inherent in water transport were not enough to compete against the powerful railroad combines that were determined to control natural resource transportation. Nonetheless, these alterations to the Columbia presaged larger, more ambitious projects, ones that promised even larger returns. By the mid-1920s, communities along the middle Columbia placed most of their hopes on the successful cultivation of cash crops that they could send downriver to Portland and into the world market. In the Umatilla River region, a sandy and semiarid landscape bounded by the John Day drainage on the west and the Snake River on the east, irrigated agriculture had drawn increased settlement since 1907. For a decade, irrigated acreage expanded along the Columbia, but the post-World War I depression stalled growth, and irrigation seemed to stagnate. Even before the Great Depression struck, irrigators had called for a dam project at Umatilla Rapids to create a large reservoir to spread water on 120,000 acres of arid lands.[13]

The Umatilla Rapids Dam project took root in local desires and a proprietary view of the Columbia and its water. The river, the promoters of the dam reasoned, flowed through their region as a "wasted" resource. Impounding the Columbia at the Umatilla Rapids would provide enough stored water to satisfy irrigation needs for the foreseeable future, while it would also eliminate the largest navigation hazard between Celilo Falls and the mouth of the Snake River. Their argument reflected the needs of a local economy that was dominantly agricultural in a region that had the highest percentage of acreage under private ownership in the Columbia River Basin. Their viewpoint was local, self-interested, and focused on attaching the river's wealth to their specific place. Unlike the fate of salmon fishing, which had everywhere reduced the importance of places to components of a larger enterprise, the focus of the Umatilla Rapids Association—the local advocacy organization—was the preservation of a local economy that had sputtered and threatened to collapse. With membership in Pendleton, Walla Walla, and Hermiston, the association developed elaborate plans for damming the Columbia and Snake rivers, arguing in 1928 that the project

> is one that proposes the securing of every form of service from the Columbia River for the benefit of the people along its shores . . . reclamation, power, navigation, and an interstate bridge are links in a program of national defense and will serve . . . [as a] contribution to the stability of the Nation.[14]

By the late 1920s, localities along the Columbia had begun to develop plans for using the river to enhance their economies. Far upriver, irrigation advocates in the Big Bend country in Washington had proposed a huge dam at the Grand Coulee as the most effective way to stimulate settlement and agricultural development on the Columbia River Plateau. In Walla Walla, Yakima, and Wenatchee, local groups reached similar conclusions: if they wanted to prosper, they had to tap the Columbia's wealth and to gain control of the water that flowed by their doorsteps. Umatilla Dam proponents used an early survey of dam sites on the Columbia and Snake rivers conducted by the Bureau of Reclamation in 1922 as proof that building a dam would convert "practically all this land [along the Columbia], under existing climatic conditions . . . into general farming land, raising fodders, grains, fruit, legumes, roots or berries in remunerative quality and quantity." The need was genuine, they argued, and no time should be wasted in beginning the project.[15]

But Congress had shown little enthusiasm for projects like the Umatilla Rapids Dam. The U.S. Army Corps of Engineers, the Bureau of Reclamation's chief governmental adversary and competitor, had long viewed multipurpose dams with suspicion and skepticism, believing them to be extravagant and inefficient. The Corps supported dams as navigation projects, seeing them as supportive of national defense and efficient expenditures of public monies. Nonetheless, regional and local advocates of water projects had pressured the Corps, and by 1927 the agency had agreed to survey the nation's navigable rivers with multipurpose dams in mind. The "308 Reports"—the results of the surveys named for the authorizing legislation—specified the locations, purposes, and efficiencies of dams on America's rivers, including the Columbia.[16]

Completed in March 1932, the Corps' survey of the Columbia River identified potential locations for ten dams on the main stem, including Bonneville, Grand Coulee (which would be started the following year), and a site at Umatilla Rapids. The middle Columbia agricultural promoters had kept pace with the increasing interest in Columbia River water projects during the late 1920s, and when the report on their stretch of the river emphasized that irrigation was "not an economical proposition at this time" but improved navigation was, they switched strategies. They argued that improved navigation was the best use of Columbia River water, that building a dam at Umatilla Rapids would inundate the rapids and create a slack-water transportation corridor up the Columbia and Snake rivers all the way to Lewiston. Those on the middle Columbia would gain the irrigation water they wanted and the potential for becoming an agricultural depot on a revitalized commercial waterway.[17]

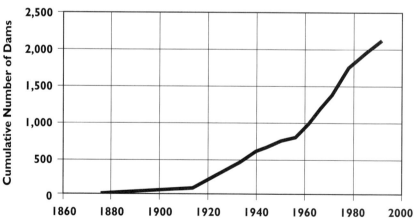

The number of federal and nonfederal dams in the Pacific Northwest (Idaho, Oregon, Washington, and northern California) has increased explosively since 1860. Source: State water resource agencies.

The boosters of the middle Columbia did not know it at the time, but they had taken a long step toward the ultimate negation of their object—control of local resource development. Like other local interest groups along the Columbia during the early years of the New Deal, they found themselves drawn into a competition for federally funded water projects. The same rivalry took place far up the Columbia, where a decade-long competition over opposing schemes to use Columbia Basin water on the arid plateau lands in central Washington had pitted developers in Wenatchee and Spokane against each other. The story of that struggle, which Paul Pitzer masterfully relates in *Grand Coulee*, is in part a tale of the loss of local control. After failing to secure state or private sponsorship, local promoters struck a bargain for Grand Coulee in 1933, which brought both a $60 million federal investment and the directive force of regional and national agendas. By 1939, when the recently created Bonneville Power Administration approved a regionwide rate for electricity generated at Grand Coulee and Bonneville dams, the local men knew they had bartered away their future. As one of them commented later,

> We are fighting the plundering of our region; hauling away our power, our minerals, our produce and our men . . . Grand Coulee Dam, which we fathered, has become a Frankenstein—its power is building industries elsewhere and they are draining our manpower to run those industries.[18]

Meanwhile, on the middle Columbia during the early 1930s, the Umatilla Dam promoters intensified their pursuit of federal support by joining with other groups in the Tri-State Development League. The league advocated a string of five dams, beginning with Umatilla Rapids and stair-stepping up the lower Snake, transforming the two rivers into a linked series of pools, perfect for enhanced river transportation. Each agricultural community, so the league argued, had potential as a local depot and commercial center. The league failed to win support from the Roosevelt administration, but its more aggressive stepchild, the Inland Empire Waterways Association, carried on the fight and played a major role in the approval of the Umatilla Dam—renamed McNary Dam—and four dams on the Snake River between 1947 and 1975.[19]

It took the irrigationists on the Umatilla more than two decades to get their dam on the Columbia and another two decades to create the engineered river system that has made Lewiston, Idaho, a major port. During those years, the Corps filled in the potential that their engineers had suggested in the "308 Reports" by converting many separate economic places into one, integrated place. What happened to Umatilla and Grand Coulee supporters also happened to the promoters of other dams in the Columbia River Basin. The whole basin became a vast interdependent and regulated system, changing the economic geography in new ways and emphasizing the loss of local control over place.[20]

Throughout the post-World War II period of increasing manipulations of the river—which included the creation of an electrical power grid system in the Pacific Northwest, the sustenance of aluminum reduction plants, and the dramatic expansion of an irrigation empire on the Columbia Plateau—the seminal goal continued to be the rationalization of the river itself. By the late 1970s, the United States had negotiated a treaty with Canada for the joint development of the upper Columbia, which outlined a systematic and cooperative development. In the language of the treaty, it was "designed to provide optimum benefits to each country . . . in order of the most favorable benefit-cost ratio." The construction of huge storage dams on the river in British Columbia made it possible to manage the Columbia's flow on practically an hourly basis by releasing specified volumes of water from each reservoir to maximize hydroelectric generation and provide sufficient water for navigation, irrigation, industry, and recreation.[21]

The river and its wealth had been transmogrified into a benefit-cost equation, where the evaluation of utility and efficiency fundamentally rearranged historical relationships. Salmon simply could not compete against hydroelectricity or irrigation. When the high dam was built at Grand Coulee, obviating a fish ladder, or the lower Snake was turned into what historian Keith Petersen has called the "Channel of Death," there was slight consideration of the effect on native salmon. The pursuit of hydroelectric power and irrigated agriculture had marginalized salmon. The historic fisheries at Celilo and Kettle Falls became submerged under kilowatt-producing impoundments and, worse, the chain of dams killed salmon smolts on their downriver journey, thereby steadily eroding anadromous fish culture throughout the Columbia River Basin. At each decision point, from the first choices made at Grand Coulee and Bonneville during the Great Depression, engineers and scientists knew the likely effect of their actions on salmon. One of the earliest evaluations of how dams would affect spawning fish in the Columbia dates to 1888. The dam builders answered objections with two responses: fish were not as valuable as the wealth created by dams, and besides science had determined how to save the salmon.[22]

On the Columbia at midcentury, the science of saving the endangered salmon was just another form of engineering, another manipulation of the river. Knowing much less about the life cycle of the great voyaging salmon than they wished, scientists invested in fish hatcheries and instream mitigations ranging from installation of fish screens on turbines and irrigation diversions to barging smolts around Snake and Columbia dams. The more they learned the more it became obvious that the Columbia had become more and more inhospitable to native fish, that hatchery fish would dominate, that the historic river of fish had nearly vanished. The questions of what should be done, when it should be done, and how it should be done divided scientists as cleanly and adversarily as the issue divided fishing and industrial groups.[23]

When the fate of the salmon entered the world of science, it also entered the world of politics. As the numbers of salmon steadily declined, especially during the 1960s and 1970s, the effects coursed all along the Columbia-Snake main stem, affecting communities even more than the scramble for dams had during the 1930s. Each constituent group argued for its portion and use of the river, dividing the unified and engineered river into a contending geography. But unlike the earlier salmon cartography, which specified the culturally and economically rich fishing places, this salmon crisis map was a set of competing overlays, each one arguing for its vision of the river. Recognition of the political logjam on the Columbia was manifest in 1980, when Congress passed the Pacific Northwest Electric Power Planning and Conservation Act. Born of this legislation, the Northwest Power Planning Council in Portland has carried the burden of managing a broad-ranging attempt to solve the salmon crisis and avoid political disaster.[24]

Mitigating the salmon decline became the province of scientists and the managers of the dams, principally the Corps of Engineers. Meanwhile, the blame for the salmon's decline flowed downriver, infecting community after community, pitting economic interests against one another, and setting fishing communities at odds. Timber operators far up the tributary drainages, irrigators on the Columbia benchlands, pulp mill operators, towboat companies, and even municipalities became accused salmon executioners. Commercial fishing interests on the lower river tried to blame sports fishers, and both charged Indians—who had won the right to half of the Columbia's catch in the 1970s—with taking too many fish. Recognition of the salmon crisis became a recognition that the Columbia had changed. The river suddenly looked like a patchwork of competing places rather than the rationalized and unified system that managers and users had steadily constructed since the 1930s.

In many respects, though, the rationalized and engineered Columbia is mythical. The manipulation of the "water budget," which sets the proscribed releases of water from each reservoir, represents a veneer of control and management, this age's assurance of predictability. But the river itself is deeper and stronger. In the "virtual river," historian Richard White's name for the post-modern stage of the Columbia's development, the future is embedded in computer models that try to predict the salmon's fate in the hands of one mitigation scheme or another—drawdowns to sweep smolts to the sea or barging fish around the dams. But it is all too easy to focus solely on recent events, the critical, modern decisions that changed the river from a salmon stream to an industrial corridor. There is a longer, biological view that suggests a deeper past and a different river. It is a chronogeographical perspective that extends back to the geological origins of the Columbia River and the even longer history of organic life. Darwinian scientist Richard Dawkins has coined the term "digital river" to describe that progression, an endless chain of genetic connections—a river of digital DNA codes—that link all living things together. Rapids or obstructions in that digital river are part and parcel of evolutionary change, as Dawkins explains, but the changes on the Columbia and the obstructions on this river are not so much evolutionary in character as they are economic, cultural, and political.[25]

The salmon crisis on the Columbia is understood primarily as a human crisis, not an evolutionary departure point. It is visibly political, and its primary actors explain what is wrong or not wrong, publicly argue over what should or should not be done, and manipulate conditions. But as Octavio Paz has reminded us: "Political crises are moral crises." Seen from this perspective, the crisis lives as much in our human responses and our history as it does in the material changes on the Columbia. The spectre of the river without salmon, the clarion of this crisis, cannot be described easily in the language of science and politics. Those descriptions and explanations, in the end, fail to communicate the distress we feel. Only the poet's imagery seems adequate to penetrate the meaning of this crisis for our people in our time. A stanza in Columbia River Indian poet Elizabeth Woody's verse speaks to this alteration to time, place, and community:

> Dislocated from one another, we are now flooded,
> resting in place.
> We suffocate in the backwater of decadence
> and fractious contempt.
> Purity of the ancient is the language without tongues.
> The river elegantly marks swirls on its surface,
> a spiral that tells of a place
> that remains undisturbed.[26]

Notes

1. Anthony Netboy, *The Columbia River Salmon and Steelhead Trout: Their Fight for Survival* (Seattle: University of Washington Press, 1980), 39-41; "U.S. Proposes Listing a Salmon as Endangered," *New York Times,* 3 April, 1991; "U.S. Agency Gives Sockeye Salmon Endangered Status," *Wall Street Journal,* 15 November, 1991; "Salmon Issue Poses a Stiffer Challenge Than the Spotted Owl," *Christian Science Monitor,* 20 October, 1993; "Ruling Stokes Salmon Conflict," *The Oregonian,* 9 September, 1995; Environmental Defense Fund, *Water for Salmon: An Economic Analysis of Salmon Recovery alternatives in the Lower Snake and Columbia Rivers* (New York: Environmental Defense Fund, 1995), 3-5; National Marine Fisheries Service, News Release, August 17, 1994.

2. Don Parkes and Nigel Thrift, *Times, Spaces, and Places: A Chronogeographic Perspective* (New York: John Wiley, 1980), 10-34; Edward Relph, *Rational Landscapes and Humanistic Geography* (London: Croom and Helm, 1981), 173-74; Yi-fu Tuan, *Space and Place* (Minneapolis: University of Minnesota Press, 1977), 27-28.

3. H. H. Bancroft, *The Works,* vol. 30, *History of Oregon, 1848-1888* (San Francisco: H. H. Bancroft, 1888), 758.

4. John Eliot Allen, *The Magnificent Gateway* (Portland: Timber Press, 1979), 32-39; John Eliot Allen et al., *Cataclysms on the Columbia* (Portland: Timber Press, 1986), 131-51; Richard B. Waitt, Jr., "Case for Periodic, Colossal Jokulhaups from Pleistocene Glacial Lake Missoula," *Geological Society of America Bulletin* 96 (October 1985): 1271-86. Waitt argues that the famous Lake Missoula floods numbered more than forty and that each carried ten times the flow of all rivers on the globe down the Columbia at 50 miles per hour.

5. Eugene Hunn, *Nch'i-Wana, "The Big River": Mid-Columbia Indians and Their Land* (Seattle: University of Washington Press, 1990), 149-54.

6. Richard Daugherty, "The People of the Salmon," in *America in 1492: The World of the Indian Peoples Before the Arrival of Columbus,* ed. Alvin M. Josephy, Jr. (New York: Alfred A. Knopf, 1992), 49-84; Jarold Ramsey, *Coyote Was Going There: Indian Literature of the Oregon Country* (Seattle: University of Washington Press, 1977), xx.

7. For a brilliant discussion of the relationships between imperialism, racism, and economic development in the region, see D. W. Meinig, *The Shaping of America: A Geographical Perspective on 500 Years of History, Continental America, 1800-1867* (New Haven: Yale University Press, 1993), 170-88. One Indian response to the changes during the 1850s was the rise of the prophet Smohalla, whose village was not coincidentally located at one of the last salmon gathering locations on the upper Columbia: Priests Rapids. See Clifford Trafzer and Margery Ann Beach Sharkey, "Smoholla, the Washani, and Religion as a Factor in Northwestern Indian History," *American Indian Quarterly* 9 (Summer 1985), and Robert H. Ruby and John A. Brown, *Dreamer-Prophets of the Columbia Plateau: Smohalla and Skolaskin* (Norman: University of Oklahoma Press, 1989), 22-25. On the first hatcheries, see P.A. Larkin, "Management of Pacific Salmon of North America, in *A Century of Fisheries in North America,* ed. Norman G. Benson (Washington: American Fisheries Society, 1970).

8. Richard White, in *The Organic Machine* (New York: Hill and Wang, 1995), 5-8, suggests measuring the river itself as a working element in nature by remarking on its power, the energy it contains, and the work it performs.

9. Statistics from A. T. Pruter, "Commercial Fisheries of the Columbia River and Adjacent Ocean Waters, *Fishery Industrial Research* (Washington, D.C.: U.S. Bureau of Fisheries) as quoted in Netboy, *Columbia River Salmon*, 22-23; White, *Organic Machine*, 40-45.

10. Colin A. M. Duncan, "On Identifying a Sound Environmental Ethic in History: Prolegomena to Any Future Environmental History," *Environmental History Review* (Summer 1981): 9-29. On the gillnetter's definitions of "place" in fishing, see Irene Martin, *Legacy and Testament: The Story of Columbia River Gillnetters* (Pullman: Washington State University Press, 1994), 83-99.

11. D. W. Meinig, *The Great Columbia Plain: A Historical Geography, 1805-1910* (Seattle: University of Washington Press, 1968) 352-54, 402; Randall V. Mills, *Stern-Wheelers Up Columbia: A Century of Steamboating in the Oregon Country* (1947; reprint, Lincoln: University of Nebraska Press, 1977), 39-50.

12. Memorial of the Legislature of the Oregon Provisional Government, 30th Cong., 1st sess., 1847, S. Doc 3 (Serial 511), 1; John C. Ainsworth to Brevet Lt. Col. R. S. Williamson, July 20, 1867, Report of Secretary of War, 40th Cong., 2nd sess., 1867 (Serial 1325), 509-11; Sen John H. Mitchell, Testimony, Cascades Canal, Sen Rep. 251, 44th Con. 1st sess, 1876, S. Rep. 251 (Serial 1667), 3-4; A. A. Humphreys to W. W. Belknap, December 20, 1871, Improvement of the Columbia River, 42nd Cong., 2nd sess., 1871 (Serial 1478), 2; Mills, *Stern-Wheelers*, 148-50. On the Celilo Canal and its vaunted promise, see Marshall Dana, "The Celilo Canal—Its Origins—Its Building and Meaning," *Oregon Historical Quarterly* 16 (June 1915): 120-31. For the larger context of early engineering on the Columbia, see William F. Willingham, *Army Corps of Engineers and the Development of Oregon: A History of the Portland District, U.S. Army Corps of Engineers* (Washington, D.C.: GPO, 1983).

13. [Hermiston Commercial Club] Memorial to the Department of the Interior . . . West Unit of the Umatilla Irrigation Project, 1911, Oregon Historical Society Archives [OHS], Portland; Resolutions, Umatilla Irrigation League, August 23, 1918, Box 1, Elmer Dodd Papers, OHS [Dodd Papers]; J. A. Krug, *The Columbia: A Comprehensive Report on the Development of the Water Resources of the Columbia River Basin* (Washington, D.C.: Bureau of Reclamation, 1947), 274-75.

14. George C. Baer, Testimony, January 10, 1928, Committee on Irrigation and Reclamation, 70th Cong., 1st sess., 1928, 9; Krug, *The Columbia*, 259-60.

15. E.G. Hopson, "Report on Five Mile Dam Project," August 1922, p. 3, Box 1, Dodd Papers; E. R. Crocker Report (1924), Committee on Irrigation and Reclamation, 68th Cong., 1st sess., 1924, 5-7.

16. For background on U.S. Army Corps of Engineers and dam building, see Todd Shallat, *Structures in the Stream: Water, Science, and the Rise of the U.S. Army Corps of Engineers* (Austin: University of Texas Press, 1994). For

the Corps on the Columbia, see Willingham, *Army Corps of Engineers and the Development of Oregon,* and on the Snake River, Keith Petersen, *River of Life, Channel of Death: Fish and Dams on the Lower Snake* (Lewiston, Idaho: Confluence Press, 1995), 71-79.

17. Maj. General Lytle Brown, Report on the Columbia River, H. Doc. 398, 69th Cong., 1st sess., March 29, 1932, 4-5; Bonneville Power Administration, First Annual Report of the Bonneville Administrator, Committee on Rivers and Harbors, January 4, 1939 (Washington, D.C.: GPO, 1939), 1-2; Gus Norwood, *Columbia River Power For the People: A History of Policies of the Bonneville Power Administration* (Washington, D.C.: GPO, 1981), 43-45; Paul Pitzer, *Grand Coulee: Harnessing a Dream* (Pullman: Washington State University Press, 1994), 43-46, 224.

18. Kirby Billingsly, as quoted in Pitzer, *Grand Coulee,* 238.

19. On the IEWA, see Petersen, *River of Life, Channel of Death,* 73-97. The dams and their completion dates are McNary, 1954; Ice Harbor, 1961; Lower Monumental, 1969; Little Goose, 1970; and Lower Granite, 1975.

20. For discussion of the changing geographies of power in the Columbia River Basin after World War II, see Edward L. Ullman, "Rivers as Regional Bonds: The Columbia-Snake Example," *The Geographical Review* 41 (1951): 210-25.

21. John V. Krutilla, *The Columbia River Treaty: The Economics of an International River Basin Development* (Baltimore: the Johns Hopkins University Press, 1967), 60.

22. Lisa Mighetto and Wesley Ebel, *Saving the Salmon: A History of the U.S. Army Corps of Engineer's Role in the Protection of Anadromous fish on the Columbia and Snake Rivers* (Draft Report, No. DACW68-91-0025, February 17, 1994), 85-86; Pitzer, *Grand Coulee,* 223-27; White, *Organic Machine,* 89-90.

23. For representative discussion of the political-scientific conflicts, see Keith W. Muckleston, "Salmon vs. Hydropower: Striking a Balance in the Pacific Northwest," *Environment* 32 (Jan./Feb., 1990): 10-36; Northwest Public Power Association, "The Columbia River: Conflict Between Man and Nature," *Northwest Public Power Association Bulletin* (Jan. 1985): 8-10; White, *Organic Machine,* 100-105.

24. Mighetto and Edel, *Saving the Salmon,* 85-100; Kris Wermstedt et al., "Evaluating Alternatives for Increasing Fish Stocks in the Columbia River Basin," *Resources* (fall 1992).

25. White, *Organic Machine,* 106; Richard Dawkins, *River Out of Eden: A Darwinian View of Life* (New York: Basic Books, 1995), esp. chap. 1.

26. From "Waterways Endeavor to Translate Silence from Currents," in Elizabeth Woody, *The Luminaries of the Humble* (Tucson, University of Arizona Press, 1994), 98.

Biographical Notes

BILL M. BAKKE is an advocate for the protection and conservation management of native, wild fish in the Northwest. He is the founder of the Native Fish Society.

MICHAEL C. BLUMM is a professor at Northwestern School of Law, where he directs the law school's Northwest Water Law and Policy Project. From 1979 to 1990 he edited the *Anadromous Fish Law Memo*. He has published numerous articles on salmon law and policy and is preparing a book on the subject, tentatively entitled *Sacrificing the Salmon*.

F. LORRAINE BODI, co-director of the Northwest office of American Rivers, was previously counsel to the National Marine Fisheries Service and the Environmental Protection Agency. She has worked on salmon habitat, instream flows, and watershed restoration issues for almost two decades.

JOSEPH CONE is a science writer and assistant director for communications of Oregon Sea Grant. His book *A Common Fate: Endangered Salmon and the People of the Pacific Northwest* was published by Henry Holt in 1995.

DOUGLAS W. DOMPIER is senior tribal policy analyst for the Columbia River Inter-Tribal Fish Commission, with whom he has been associated since 1979. Before that time he was a fisheries biologist with the National Marine Fisheries Service.

STANLEY V. GREGORY, a salmon ecologist, is a professor of fisheries at Oregon State University, leader of OSU's nationally recognized "stream team," and a member of the research team conducting studies at the H. J. Andrews Experimental Forest in the Oregon Cascades.

ROBERT KENTTA is the cultural resources protection specialist with the Confederated Tribes of Siletz Indians of Oregon and a Siletz tribal member. He has an associate of fine arts degree from the Institute of American Indian Arts in Santa Fe, New Mexico.

WILLIAM L. LANG, director of the Center for Columbia River History, also teaches history at Portland State University. He has published widely on Columbia River history and is editor of *Centennial West: Essays on the Northern Tier States*.

JAMES A. LICHATOWICH, a salmon biologist, independent consultant, and writer, was chief of fish research for the Oregon Department of Fish and Wildlife from 1983 to 1988. He was a co-author of "Pacific Salmon at the Crossroads," published by the American Fisheries Society in 1991. He is writing a book on salmon biology and politics for Island Press.

SANDY RIDLINGTON is managing editor of Oregon Sea Grant.

WILLIAM G. ROBBINS, a professor of history and associate dean of the College of Liberal Arts at Oregon State University, specializes in the history of the American West. He has written numerous books and articles, including *Colony and Empire: the Capitalist Transformation of the American West*.

COURTLAND L. SMITH, a professor of anthropology at Oregon State University, has brought a social scientist's perspective to Northwest salmon issues in publications spanning two decades. He is the author of *Salmon Fishers of the Columbia*.

Glossary

The number in parentheses following each definition in this glossary refers to the source in the bibliography at the end of the glossary. Most of the terms were taken, or adapted, from the glossaries of public documents. Where there is no number, the definition was supplied by the editors.

acre-foot Unit of volume measurement used to describe a quantity of water stored in a reservoir. One acre-foot of water covers one acre to a depth of one foot or 325, 850 gallons. (1)

anadromous Describes fish that are born in fresh water, migrate to the sea, and return to fresh water to spawn. Examples are salmon, sturgeon, shad, smelt, and steelhead. (4)

anticline An arch of stratified rock in which the layers bend downward in opposite directions from the crest. (6)

artificial production or artificial propagation Spawning, incubating, hatching, or rearing fish in a hatchery or other facility constructed for fish production. (2)

bole The trunk of a tree. (6)

broodstock A group of adult or maturing fish, usually representing a certain population, that are used to generate a subsequent generation. (4)

cryopreservation The long-term preservation of fish gametes (eggs and sperm) by freezing. (2)

dip nets A harvest method in which a long-handled net is used to sweep salmon from a river or stream. It is a method of capture commonly used by Native Americans. (4)

drawdown The release of water from a reservoir for power generation, flood control, irrigation, or other water management activity. (2)

emergence The act of fish leaving their incubation environment in the gravel to forage for food. (2)

enhancement Management activities, including rehabilitation and suplementation, that increase fish production beyond existing levels. (5)

escapement The number of salmon and steelhead that return to a specified point of measurement after all natural mortality and harvest have occurred. Spawning escapement consists of those fish that survive to spawn. (5)

evolutionarily significant unit A population or group of populations that is considered distinct (and hence a "species") for purposes of conservation under the Endangered Species Act. To qualify as an ESU, a population must (1) be reproductively isolated from other conspecific populations and (2) represent an important component in the evolutionary legacy of the biological species. (4)

fingerling A young fish from the time of the disappearance of the yolk sac to the end of the first year of growth. It ranges in size from approximately 2 to 3 inches. (2)

fish ladder A system for facilitating passage of upstream migrating fish over a natural or artificial barrier. A fish ladder usually consists of a series of resting pools separated by low obstructions easily passable for fish. (1)

fishway A general term for fish passage facilities at dams or falls. (4)

fish wheel A salmon harvesting mechanism (no longer permitted by fisheries regulation) in which salmon are directed into the path of a large rotating wheel with net compartments that scoop the fish out of the water. (4)

fixed gear Fishing gear that is stationary, e.g. traps and fish wheels.

flows The rate at which water passes a given point in a stream or river, usually expressed in cubic-feet per second (cfs). (2)

freshet A great rise or overflowing of a stream caused by heavy rains or melted snow. (6)

fry The stage in the life of a fish from the hatching of the egg through the absorption of the yolk sac until it is about 1 inch long. (2)

gillnetting A harvest method in which fish are trapped in a net stretched across their migration path. The net may either be set from a drifting boat (drift gill net) or from a fixed position (set gill net). The fish become entangled by their gill plates or jaws and can neither back out nor move forward. (4)

hatchery fish A group of interbreeding fish that are artificially propagated in a hatchery setting and for which the breeding history or ancestors may or may not be known. (4)

horse seining See **seine.**

impoundment A body of water formed behind a dam. (2)

intertie A transmission line or system of lines permitting a flow of energy between major power systems. The Northwest has an intertie connection with California. (2)

juvenile Fish from one year of age until sexual maturity. (2)

mainstem The main channel of the river in a river basin, as opposed to the streams and smaller rivers that feed into it. In the fish and wildlife program, mainstem refers to the Columbia and Snake rivers. (2)

maximum sustainable yield An often used goal for fisheries management. It represents an equilibrium point determined by stock productivity, natural mortality, and exploitation rate, and is an estimate of the maximum average harvest of a given stock or group of stocks that can be sustained indefinitely. (4)

mitigation Efforts to alleviate the impacts of hydropower development to the Columbia Basin's salmon and steelhead runs. (1)

natural fish Naturally reproducing stocks of fish that have been at one time supplemented with hatchery fish. (8)

old growth For forest communities, a stage of growth that exists from approximately age 200 until when stand replacement occurs and secondary succession begins again. (3)

population A group of fish spawning in a particular area at a particular time that do not interbreed to any substantial degree with any other group spawning in a different area or in the same area at a different time. (5)

pound net A fish trap consisting of a netting arranged into a directing wing and an enclosure with a narrow entrance. (6)

puller The fisher who pulls in the net on a commercial fishing vessel.

purse seine A commercial fishing system in which a school of fish are encircled by a vertically hanging net and then are trapped by closing the bottom of the net (pursing). (4)

rearing The juvenile life stage of anadromous fish spent in freshwater rivers, lakes, and streams before they migrate to the ocean. (2)

rebuilding Planting hatchery products to augment natural runs of salmon and steelhead; often used synonymously with supplementation. (8)

redd A spawning nest made in the gravel bed of a river by salmon or steelhead. (4)

reprogramming The development of a new plan for the time and location of the release of hatchery-produced fish into rivers and streams, especially in the upper river areas. (2)

restoration Planting hatchery products or improving habitat to reestablish extirpated runs or runs that are critically low in numbers. (8)

run A population of fish of the same species consisting of one or more stocks migrating at a distinct time. (1, 2)

seine A large net with sinkers on one edge and floats on the other that hangs vertically in the water and is used to enclose fish when its ends are pulled together or are drawn ashore. (6) **Horse seining** is the use of horses to draw the net toward shore.

set net See **gill net**.

slack water The period at the turn of the tide when there is little or no horizontal motion of tidal water—called also slack tide. (6) On the Columbia River, the reservoirs are often described as slack water (tideless) pools.

slash Branches and other residue left on a forest floor after the cutting of timber. (9)

smolt A juvenile salmon or steelhead migrating to the ocean and undergoing physiological changes (smoltification) to adapt from a freshwater to a saltwater environment. (1)

snag Any standing dead, partially dead, or defective tree at least 10 inches in diameter at breast height and at least 6 feet tall. (3)

snagging To clear (as a river) of snags. (6)

spill Water released through a dam's spillway rather than through its turbines. (1)

spillway The channel or passageway around or over a dam through which excess water is released or "spilled" past the dam without going through the turbines. A spillway is a safety valve for a dam and, as such, must be capable of discharging major floods without damaging the dam, while maintaining the reservoir level below some predetermined maximum level. (2)

sternwheeler A steamboat driven by a single paddle wheel at the stern. (6)

stock A population of fish spawning in a particular stream during a particular season. They generally do not interbreed with fish spawning in a different stream or at a different time. (2)

supplementation The practice of releasing hatchery-reared fry or fingerlings into a stream environment to "supplement" or add to existing fish production in the stream; the use of artificial propagation of fish to increase natural fish production while maintaining the long-term fitness of the target population, and while keeping the ecological and genetic impacts on nontarget populations within acceptable limits. (1)

syncline A trough of stratified rock in which the beds dip toward each other from either side. (6)

take Under the federal Endangered Species Act (as of 1995), "take" means to harass, harm, pursue, hunt, shoot, would, kill, trap, capture, or collect an animal, or to attempt to engage in any such conduct. (3)

troll A commercial harvest method for chinook and coho salmon, usually occurring in the open ocean, that captures individual fish on lures or baited hooks which are slowly pulled through the water. (4)

water budget A program intended to increase the survival of downstream migrating juvenile fish by releasing water stored in reservoirs to increase Columbia and Snake River flows during the spring and summer migration period. (4)

watershed The area that drains into a stream or river. (2)

wild stock Fish that have maintained successful natural reproduction and are known to have had little or no supplementation from hatcheries in past generations. (7)

yarding The moving of logs from the stump to a central concentration area or landing. (3)

Sources

1. Columbia Basin Fish and Wildlife Authority, *Integrated System Plan for Salmon and Steelhead Production in the Columbia River Basin,* June 1991.
2. *Glossary,* Columbia River Basin Fish and Wildlife Program, December 1994.
3. Forest Ecosystem Management Assessment Team, *Forest Ecosystem Management: An Ecological, Economic, and Social Assessment,* July 1993.
4. National Marine Fisheries Service, *Proposed Recovery Plan for Snake River Salmon,* March 1995.
5. Oregon Department of Fish and Wildlife
6. *Merriam Webster's Collegiate Dictionary,* 10th ed. (Springfield, Mass., 1993).
7. Kapuscinski, A. R. *Genetic Analysis of Policies and Guidelines for Salmon and Steelhead Hatchery Production in the Columbia River Basin.* Report Prepared for the Northwest Power Planning Council. January 9, 1991
8. Miller, William H., et al., *Analysis of Salmon and Steelhead Supplementation* (Portland, Ore.: Bonneville Power Administration, 1990).
9. *The American Heritage Dictionary of the English Language* (Boston: Houghton Mifflin, 1981).

Acknowledgments

Text

Selection by Willis H. Rich from "Local Populations and Migration in Relation to the Conservation of Pacific Salmon in the Western States and Alaska," in *The Migration and Conservation of Salmon,* publication no. 8, American Association for the Advancement of Science (Lancaster, Pennsylvania, Science Press, 1939), 45-47. Reprinted by permission of the American Association for the Advancement of Science. Selection by Willis H. Rich from "The Future Of The Columbia River Salmon Fisheries," *Stanford Ichthyological Bulletin* 2(2) (1940), 37, 46. Reprinted by permission of Stanford University. Selection by Leo L. Laythe from "The Fishery Development Program in the Lower Columbia River." *Transactions of the American Fisheries Society* 78, no. 48 (1948), 50-51, 53. Reprinted by permission of the American Fisheries Society. Selection by Gary K. Meffe from "Techno-Arrogance and Halfway Technologies, Salmon Hatcheries on the Pacific Coast of North America," *Conservation Biology* 6, no. 3 (1992), 351-52. Reprinted by permission of Blackwell Science, Inc. and of the author. Selection by Miller Freeman from the Fiftieth Anniversary Number, *Pacific Fisherman* August 1952, 12, 11, 27, 29, 39, 51, 58, 69, 77. Reprinted by permission of *National Fisherman. (Pacific Fisherman* is now part of *National Fisherman.)* Selection by Richard L. Neuberger from "The Great Salmon Mystery," *Saturday Evening Post,* 13 Sept. 1941, 20-21, 44. Reprinted by permission of Maureen Neuberger. Selection by Willa Nehlsen, Jack E. Williams, and James A. Lichatowich from "Pacific Salmon at the Crossroads, Stocks at Risk from California, Oregon, Idaho, and Washington," *Fisheries* 16, no. 2 (1991), 4-5, 7-8. Reprinted by permission of the American Fisheries Society. Selection by Elizabeth Woody from "Waterways Endeavor to Translate Silence from Currents," in Elizabeth Woody, *The Luminaries of the Humble* (Tucson, University of Arizona Press, 1994), 98. Reprinted by permission of University of Arizona Press and the author.

Illustrations

Cover photograph, Courtesy of the Columbia River Maritime Museum, Astoria, Oregon; page 1, Angelus Collection, P6, Special Collections, University of Oregon Library; page 7, copyright Photo Research Group, Portland, Oregon; photographs courtesy Oregon Historical Society on page 10, negative #Gi7189; page 26, negative #4349; page 97, negative #6025; page 97, negative #92882; page 130, negative #CN005261; page 141, negative #12387; page 173, negative #92427; page 177, negative #29562; page 184, negative #Gi7492; page 185, negative #CN000828; page 208, negative #44181; page 11, Washington Department of Fish and Wildlife; page 15, courtesy Portland General Electric Co.; pages 18, 58, courtesy StreamNet, funded by the Bonneville Power Administration; pages 25, 60, 325, courtesy Courtland Smith; page 27, reproduced with permission of *California Fish and Game;* page 33, the Stanford University Archives; page 70, reprinted from William L. Finley, *Game and Fish Protection and Propagation in Oregon, 1911-1912,* Boyer Printing Co., Portland, Oregon, 1912; pages 85, 136, Oregon Department of Fish and Wildlife; page 87, courtesy U.S. Bureau of Reclamation; page 107, National Marine Fisheries Service; pages 118, 146, 318, Oregon Sea Grant; pages 157, 196, 221, 347, Douglas County (Oregon) Museum of History and Natural History; page 155, courtesy James Sedell redrawn by Tom Weeks; page 165, courtesy Portland General Electric Company; pages 174, 191, 202, Columbia River Inter-Tribal Fish Commission; page 189, Lee Moorhouse Collection, M2396, Special Collections, University of Oregon Library; page 204, Northwest Power Planning Council; page 206, Oregon Department of Transportation; pages 212, 267, courtesy Pacific States Marine Fisheries Commission and StreamNet, funded by BPA; page 229, California Department of Fish and Game; page 239, courtesy Lynn Ketchum; page 249, courtesy National Academy of Sciences. Reprinted with permission; page 291, © The Wilderness Society. Reprinted with permission; page 319, Lewiston Morning Tribune; page 354, photograph by B. C. Markham, late 1920s. Copyright Photo Research Group, Portland, Oregon; page 356, courtesy National Academy of Sciences. Reprinted with permission; line art at start of each commentary by Yasui Osawa/Upstream Productions, from *Northwest Energy News,* March/April 1985.

Index